The House of CLIFFORD

FROM BEFORE THE CONQUEST

Hugh Clifford

Phillimore

1987

Published by
PHILLIMORE & CO. LTD.
Shopwyke Hall, Chichester, Sussex

ISBN 0 85033 634 1

Printed and bound in Great Britain by
BIDDLES LTD.
Guildford, Surrey

Contents

Part One: Fitzpons and the Clifford Barons of Clifford Castle

Part Two: The Lords Clifford, Earls of Cumberland

Part Three: The Lords Clifford of Chudleigh

Part Four: The Cliffords of Tixall, Staffordshire, and Flaxbourne, New Zealand

Part Five: Other Branches of the Cliffords

List of Illustrations

ix

Lord Clifford wishes to thank the following for permission to reproduce illustrations: David Clifford, no. 1; Major Peter Hamilton, M.B.E., no. 5; the Royal Commission on Historical Monuments (England), nos. 6 and 7; Hugh Fattorini, nos. 8, 14, 16 and 18; the Courtauld Institute of Art, nos. 17 (Devonshire Collection, Chatsworth, reproduced by permission of the Chatsworth Settlement Trustees), 19, 20, 21, 24, 25, 28, 29, 30, 31, 32, 33, 34, 40, 41, 42, 44, 45, 51 and 52; Sir Simon and Lady Benton Jones, no. 38; Frank Rodgers, no. 43; Robert Holmes, no. 48; Hugo Clifford Holmes, nos. 49 and 50.

Introduction

This egg has taken a long time in the hatching.

It started in 1969 when my uncle, the late Sir Bede Clifford, telephoned me and asked if I knew what he had been doing. I replied that his daughter Anne, Lady Norwich, had told me that he had started on a family history. That, he said, was what he was telephoning me about. I'd got to finish it! I protested that he had already a couple of books to his credit, including his memoirs *Proconsul,* and that it was just the thing he was cut out to do. He replied that he was dying of cancer. I buried him in the family vault, and a fortnight later received a package of notes he had made.

He had only got as far as the Wars of the Roses. So with the help of the family tree – issued by the College of Arms in 1672 – and with the help of Arthur Clifford's *Collectanea Cliffordiana* (1817) plus George Oliver's *Cliffordiana* (1828) I set to work. I also made extensive use of the House of Lords Library and of the muniment room at Ugbrooke.

After three years I gave my MS to Lord Longford. He returned it saying his 'young men' said it was not the sort of thing his firm did. However, they put me on to Denham Publications – a Mr. Paulin – who said he would publish it. His sub-editor who had promised to complete it in six months had done less than a third in five years. This was understandable as she went and got married. Then Denham Publications sold up.

By this time I had been getting more and more worried about the accuracy of my source material. In my ignorance I had overlooked the so-called 'experts' who seemed to delight in proving each other wrong. This applied particularly to the family tree by the College of Arms in 1672. I had received several letters from the late R. Garrett telling me how the tree published in *Proconsul* was wrong, and producing an alternative theory concerning the origins of Sir Lewis Clifford, the Lollard. I myself found one mistake relating to that gentleman, namely, that his wife was the daughter of Lord Mowbray and not Lord De la Warr, of whom she was the widow. The last straw was when one of these 'busybodies' (to use Winston Churchill's term) said that I would make myself the laughing stock of his fellow experts if I published the work as it stood. So I withdrew the MS from the people who had taken over Denham Publications and handed it over to the late Sir Iain Moncreiffe.

Several years earlier he had taken me and my wife, when staying with my cousin, to his place. Iain told my wife that she was married into one of the most interesting families in the history of these islands, and that he would love to write something on the Cliffords sometime. So I packed the documents up and sent them to Scotland by kindness of the aforementioned cousin.

In the course of the following years Iain gradually went through the papers – adding to them, collecting new material and correcting my original MS, so when he died in March 1985 there was not much more work to do. After Sir Iain's death, Noel Currer-Briggs took on the editorial role, and prepared the MS for press.

While all this was progressing, two other experts came on the scene. The first was Hugh Peskett, who produced several papers, the chief of which proved that the late R. Garrett's theory was wrong. The other was R. N. Clifford of Hereford, who contacted me several years ago. I put him in touch with Sir Iain and they discussed together their findings. R. N. Clifford has written the chapters in Part Five 'The Other Cliffords'; he also founded the Clifford Association.

I have made very few alterations to Sir Iain's text. The first concerns the prefix 'de'. When Walter Fitz-Pons became the *de facto* baron of Clifford he and his immediate descendants, as was then the custom, were known as de Clifford. But even his daughter, the Fair Rosamund (*c.* 1137-75), refers to herself as Rosamund Clifford, and Shakespeare in *Henry VI* refers to Lord Clifford. Sir John Lloyd, in his *History of Wales* (vol. II, p. 469 *et seq.*) does not use the 'de' when referring to persons living as early as the 12th century. The present title of Lord de Clifford must therefore be explained. It arose like this: in 1770 a descendant of the daughter of Lady Anne Clifford, herself daughter of the 3rd Earl of Cumberland, succeeded in getting the Clifford Barony (of the first creation) out of abeyance. In 1777 she and her husband added the 'de' to differentiate between them and the then Lord Clifford of Chudleigh. (See Williamson's life of Lady Anne Clifford and her father George Clifford, 3rd Earl of Cumberland.) The family name of the Lords de Clifford is Russell.

A second alteration I have made to Sir Iain's text is the spelling of Boscombe (Wiltshire), which is now Borscombe.

Of my original work, I have taken out my chapters on Sir Henry Clifford V.C. and his son Sir Hugh Clifford and substituted a text by Pat Grout Ph.D. who is working on a biography of the V.C. The chapter on Sir Hugh Clifford is by his grandson, Hugo Clifford Holmes. The chapter on the Cliffords of Stow-on-the-Wold is by David Clifford of Paignton.

As a young man in the early 1930s I sat at the feet of Sir Arthur Bryant when he, among others, was staying at Ugbrooke. We discussed the papers we were finding to do with the Secret Treaty of Dover and other matters connected with the Cabal administration in the reign of Charles II. In 1971 I gave a dinner in the House of Lords for the descendants of the Cabal to celebrate its tercentenary: Sir Arthur Bryant was the chief speaker. I kept in touch with him over the years and he showed interest in the production of this book. He said he would like to write the Foreword, but he died only a few months before Sir Iain Moncreiffe.

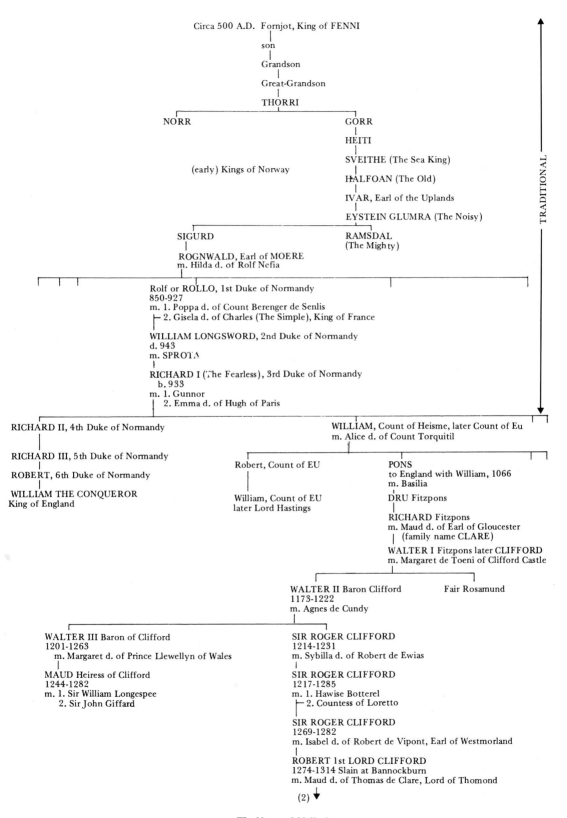

Circa 500 A.D. Fornjot, King of FENNI
|
son
|
Grandson
|
Great-Grandson
|
THORRI

NORR ———————————————— GORR
|
HEITI
|
SVEITHE (The Sea King)
|
(early) Kings of Norway   HALFOAN (The Old)
|
IVAR, Earl of the Uplands
|
EYSTEIN GLUMRA (The Noisy)

SIGURD ——————————— RAMSDAL
| (The Mighty)
ROGNWALD, Earl of MOERE
m. Hilda d. of Rolf Nefia

Rolf or ROLLO, 1st Duke of Normandy
850-927
m. 1. Poppa d. of Count Berenger de Senlis
   2. Gisela d. of Charles (The Simple), King of France

WILLIAM LONGSWORD, 2nd Duke of Normandy
d. 943
m. SPROTA
|
RICHARD I (The Fearless), 3rd Duke of Normandy
b. 933
m. 1. Gunnor
   2. Emma d. of Hugh of Paris

RICHARD II, 4th Duke of Normandy   WILLIAM, Count of Heisme, later Count of Eu
| m. Alice d. of Count Torquitil
RICHARD III, 5th Duke of Normandy
| Robert, Count of EU   PONS
ROBERT, 6th Duke of Normandy   to England with William, 1066
| m. Basilia
WILLIAM THE CONQUEROR   William, Count of EU   DRU Fitzpons
King of England   later Lord Hastings |
                                                         RICHARD Fitzpons
                                                         m. Maud d. of Earl of Gloucester
                                                           (family name CLARE)

                                                         WALTER I Fitzpons later CLIFFORD
                                                         m. Margaret de Toeni of Clifford Castle

                        WALTER II Baron Clifford   Fair Rosamund
                        1173-1222
                        m. Agnes de Cundy

WALTER III Baron of Clifford   SIR ROGER CLIFFORD
1201-1263   1214-1231
   m. Margaret d. of Prince Llewellyn of Wales   m. Sybilla d. of Robert de Ewias
MAUD Heiress of Clifford   SIR ROGER CLIFFORD
1244-1282   1217-1285
m. 1. Sir William Longespee   m. 1. Hawise Botterel
   2. Sir John Giffard   2. Countess of Loretto

                                    SIR ROGER CLIFFORD
                                    1269-1282
                                    m. Isabel d. of Robert de Vipont, Earl of Westmorland

                                    ROBERT 1st LORD CLIFFORD
                                    1274-1314 Slain at Bannockburn
                                    m. Maud d. of Thomas de Clare, Lord of Thomond

                                    (2) ▼

TRADITIONAL

The House of Clifford

ROGER 2nd Lord Clifford
1299-1326

ROBERT 3rd Lord Clifford
1305-1344
m. Isabel d. of 2nd Lord Berkeley

IDIONE
m. 2nd Lord Percy
(Grandmother to 1st Earl of
Northumberland)

ROBERT 4th Lord Clifford
1329-1345
m. Euphonia d. of 2nd Lord Nevill

ROGER 5th Lord Clifford
1333-1389
m. Lady Maude de Beauchamp d. of
3rd Earl of Warwick

Sir Thomas Clifford
(Lord of Thomond)

THOMAS 6th Lord Clifford
1363-1391
m. Elizabeth d. of 5th Lord de Ros

Sir William Clifford

SIR LEWIS CLIFFORD K.G.
1357-1404
m. Eleanor d. of Lord John Mowbray

JOHN 7th Lord Clifford K.G.
1388-1422
m. Elizabeth Percy d. of 'Harry Hotspur'

WILLIAM Clifford
1380-1438
m. Elizabeth d. of Sir Arnold Savage

THOMAS 8th Lord Clifford
1414-1455 (Killed at Battle of St Albans)
m. Joan d. of 7th Lord Dacre

JOHN Clifford
1438-1461
m. Florentia St Leger

JOHN 9th Lord Clifford
1435-1461 (Killed at Battle of
Ferrybridge)
m. Margaret d. of Lord Vescy

Sir Roger
Clifford

Sir Robert
Clifford

THOMAS Clifford
(M.P. of Borscombe & Kingsteignton)
1462-1520
m. Thomasina Thorpe

HENRY 10th Lord Clifford
('The Shepherd Lord')
1454-1523
m. (1) Anne d. of Sir John St John of Bletso

WILLIAM Clifford
1490-1533

HENRY Clifford, 1st Earl of Cumberland K.G.
1493-1592
m. (1) Lady Margot Talbot d. of Earl of Shrewsbury
m. (2) Lady Margaret Percy d. of 3rd Earl of
Northumberland

Sir Ingram Thomas
Clifford

HENRY Clifford of Borscombe
1515-1577
m. (1) Elizabeth Hungerford

HENRY 2nd Earl of Cumberland K.G.
1517-1570
m. (1) Lady Eleanor Brandon (K. Henry VIII's niece)
m. (2) Anne d. of Lord Dacre of Gilleshand

Ingram.

ANTHONY Clifford of Borscombe &
Kingsteignton
1541-1580
m. Anne Courtenay d. of Sir Piers
Courtenay of Powderham & Ugbrooke

GEORGE 3rd Earl of Cumberland K.G.
1558-1605
m. Lady Margaret Russell d. of
Lord Bedford

FRANCIS 4th Earl of Cumberland
1559-1641
m. Lady Abergavenny

James C. of
Kingsteignton

Rev. Dr. THOMAS Clifford
of Ugbrooke
1572-1634
m. Amy Steplehill

2 sons died
in childhood

Lady Anne Clifford
1590-1676
Countess of Dorset,
Pembroke and
Montgomery

HENRY 5th (and last) Earl of Cumberland
1592-1643
m. Lady Francis Cecil d. of Robert Cecil,
1st Earl of Salisbury

Mary C.
m. Col.
Bamfylde

EARLS OF
POLTIMORE

Col. HUGH Clifford
of Ugbrooke
1603-1639
m. Mary d. of Sir George
Chudleigh of Ashton

2 daughters

3 sons and 1 daughter
who died in infancy

Elizabeth
m. Richard
Boyle 2nd
Earl of Cork
created Baron
C. of
Lanesborough

END OF THE FIRST LINE OF CLIFFORD PEERS

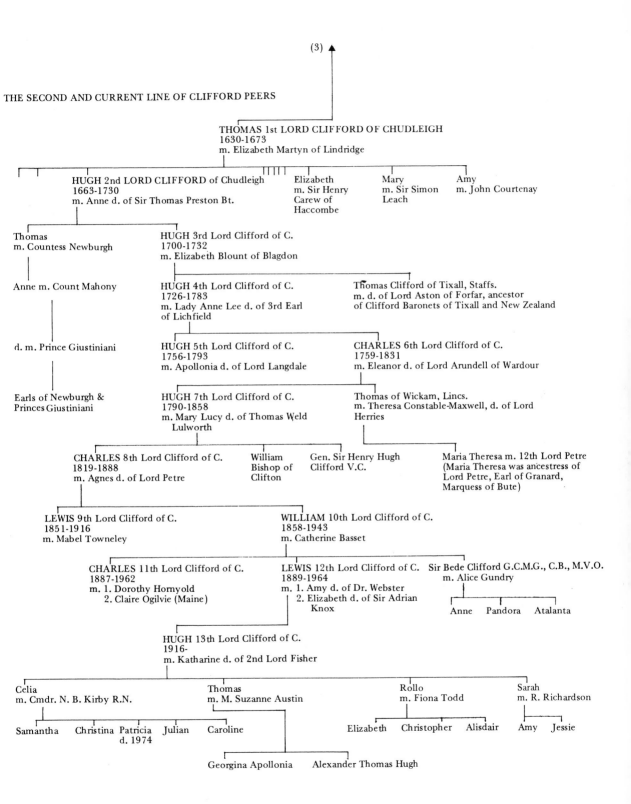

THE SECOND AND CURRENT LINE OF CLIFFORD PEERS

THOMAS 1st LORD CLIFFORD OF CHUDLEIGH
1630-1673
m. Elizabeth Martyn of Lindridge

HUGH 2nd LORD CLIFFORD of Chudleigh
1663-1730
m. Anne d. of Sir Thomas Preston Bt.

Elizabeth
m. Sir Henry
Carew of
Haccombe

Mary
m. Sir Simon
Leach

Amy
m. John Courtenay

Thomas
m. Countess Newburgh

HUGH 3rd Lord Clifford of C.
1700-1732
m. Elizabeth Blount of Blagdon

Anne m. Count Mahony

HUGH 4th Lord Clifford of C.
1726-1783
m. Lady Anne Lee d. of 3rd Earl
of Lichfield

Thomas Clifford of Tixall, Staffs.
m. d. of Lord Aston of Forfar, ancestor
of Clifford Baronets of Tixall and New Zealand

d. m. Prince Giustiniani

HUGH 5th Lord Clifford of C.
1756-1793
m. Apollonia d. of Lord Langdale

CHARLES 6th Lord Clifford of C.
1759-1831
m. Eleanor d. of Lord Arundell of Wardour

Earls of Newburgh &
Princes Giustiniani

HUGH 7th Lord Clifford of C.
1790-1858
m. Mary Lucy d. of Thomas Weld
Lulworth

Thomas of Wickam, Lincs.
m. Theresa Constable-Maxwell, d. of Lord
Herries

CHARLES 8th Lord Clifford of C.
1819-1888
m. Agnes d. of Lord Petre

William
Bishop of
Clifton

Gen. Sir Henry Hugh
Clifford V.C.

Maria Theresa m. 12th Lord Petre
(Maria Theresa was ancestress of
Lord Petre, Earl of Granard,
Marquess of Bute)

LEWIS 9th Lord Clifford of C.
1851-1916
m. Mabel Towneley

WILLIAM 10th Lord Clifford of C.
1858-1943
m. Catherine Basset

CHARLES 11th Lord Clifford of C.
1887-1962
m. 1. Dorothy Hornyold
2. Claire Ogilvie (Maine)

LEWIS 12th Lord Clifford of C.
1889-1964
m. 1. Amy d. of Dr. Webster
2. Elizabeth d. of Sir Adrian
Knox

Sir Bede Clifford G.C.M.G., C.B., M.V.O.
m. Alice Gundry

Anne   Pandora   Atalanta

HUGH 13th Lord Clifford of C.
1916-
m. Katharine d. of 2nd Lord Fisher

Celia
m. Cmdr. N. B. Kirby R.N.

Thomas
m. M. Suzanne Austin

Rollo
m. Fiona Todd

Sarah
m. R. Richardson

Samantha   Christina Patricia   Julian   Caroline
d. 1974

Elizabeth   Christopher   Alisdair

Amy   Jessie

Georgina Apollonia   Alexander Thomas Hugh

PART ONE

FITZPONS AND THE CLIFFORD BARONS OF CLIFFORD CASTLE

Chapter One

Generation I – Pons, Norman Baron (1066)

Pons, the forefather of the historic house of Clifford, flits briefly across the stage at one of the tensest moments of world history.

The scene is Normandy in 1066. The death of the last Anglo-Saxon king, Edward the Confessor, without immediate heirs, had left the crown of England the prey to several claimants. Harald Hardrada, King of Norway, had assembled an army and battle fleet to seize the English crown as the successor of Canute and captured Orkney, threatening the north of England. Simultaneously the Anglo-Saxon defence forces were watching the Channel against the threat from William of Normandy. The English themselves had chosen Harold Godwinson, a member of a powerful branch of the old Wessex family, to be their new king, despite the fact that Harold, while a captive of the Normans, had sworn an oath – admittedly under duress – to support the claims of William 'the Bastard', Duke of Normandy. Meanwhile Duke William was also assembling a fleet and an army, determined to put his fate to the touch, to gain or lose it all. At this critical juncture, William sought divine sanction from the Pope for his proposed invasion of England. Although this met with the violent opposition of many of the cardinals on the ground that the Church should not sanction slaughter, the duke's cause was supported by Archbishop Hildebrand, better known to history as the redoubtable Pope Gregory VIII. Acting on his advice, the Pope sent William his blessing, a ring, a relic of St Peter and a consecrated banner, thus giving the expedition the character of a crusade.

At about this time William learnt that the land of Steyning in Sussex had been given to the Church of the Holy Trinity at Fécamp in Normandy by Edward the Confessor, but that it was being unlawfully withheld by King Harold. This was the *casus belli*.

Accordingly, William issued a charter before setting sail with his invasion force. It is the first of his forthcoming reign, and, had he failed in his enterprise, it would have added to the ridicule his failure would have occasioned.[1] This optimistic document reads as follows: 'Grant by Duke William to the Church of the Holy Trinity at Fécamp of the land of Steyning in the county of Sussex, the duke gives seisin to the Church by the token of a knife before he went to England. The grant to take effect if God should give him victory in England'. The grant is witnessed by Aymeri the vicomte, Richard fitz Gilbert, and Pons.

The other two witnesses who were in attendance on the future Conqueror that day with Pons were both Norman barons of great distinction. Aymeri, Vicomte de Thouars, one of only 20 names[2] to have come down to us of those who were certainly with William at the battle of Hastings, fought soon after the granting of the charter.

3

Richard FitzGilbert was a son of the Comte de Brionne, of an illegitimate branch of the ducal House of Normandy. Richard founded the House of Clare[3] which was given large estates after the Norman conquest in Wales. A century later, his great-grandson 'Strongbow' was to lead an Anglo-Norman invasion of Ireland.

According to a family tradition traceable, however, only as far back as Tudor times, Pons himself also belonged to an illegitimate branch of the ducal House, namely to that of the counts of Eu.[4] Like that of his fellow witness, Richard FitzGilbert, Pons' descendants were to have a large share of the Norman conquests in Wales.

We do not know whether, soon after attending William at the granting of the charter to the church of Fécamp, Pons called up his men, donned his hauberk, or shirt of mail, and conical steel helmet with its characterstic nose-guard, and embarked with his charger and followers with his duke for England.[5] If he were that same Pons who witnessed another charter (this time to the abbey of Fécamp),[6] granted by the Conqueror's grandfather, Duke Richard the Good in 1025, then he may have been too old for campaigning, in which case he was probably represented by his sons in the invasion of England. Consequently we cannot be sure whether all the 23 manors in six different English counties held directly of King William after Pons' death by his two sons, and recorded in the Domesday Survey 20 years after the Conquest, were originally bestowed in 1066 by William on Pons himself. But Pons was certainly a king's baron as tenant-in-chief under William of the manor of Eaton (later Eaton Hastings) in Berkshire, where he, in turn, had granted three hides of land 'for his soul's sake' to Westminster Abbey. By 1086 this manor had been inherited by one of his sons.

It seems clear that Pons and his family were on close terms with the 'princely' Norman baron, Ralf III de Toeni,[7] Seigneur de Conches, Porte Oriflamme, or Banner-Bearer of the Norman dukes. The historian Horace Round writes of Ralf: 'Grandson of a Count of Barcelona, stepson of a Count of Evreux, son-in-law of Simon de Montfort, brother-in-law of the Earl of Hereford, and father-in-law of a king of Jerusalem, Ralf was no ordinary baron'. One of Pons' sons, perhaps originally Pons himself, was among the favoured Norman barons who were to hold land within Ralf's privileged *castellaria* around Clifford Castle in Herefordshire. The connection between the two families could, of course, have arisen in Normandy, either directly or through Ralf de Toeni's brother-in-law, William FitzOsbern, later created first Earl of Hereford and Viceroy of England, as it could have been he who originally enfeoffed Pons' family in the neighbourhood of Clifford Castle when he founded it. Moreover, one of Pons' sons held Charlton in Berkshire of Ralf de Toeni, but the Domesday Survey comments: 'This land is of Earl Roger's holding', which means that it had originally been held of William FitzOsbern but forfeited by his son, Roger. However, it should be noted that in the Domesday Survey seven hides at Swell in Gloucestershire were also held by Pons' family under Ralf III de Toeni, while another member of Pons' family held three Worcestershire manors under the same Ralf de Toeni.

In this context, and in view of the much later family tradition that Pons was a scion of the House of Eu, it may possibly be significant that the remaining three hides of land at Swell were held of the king by William d'Eu.

The name of Pons' wife does not appear in surviving records, but is given in old genealogies as Basilia.[8] Pons had at least three sons:

1. DRU fitz Pons for whom see Chapter Two ('Fitz' is no more than the Norman-French word for 'son'; in modern French 'fils'.)

2. PONS fitz Pons (or Ponson), whose existence was inferred by Horace Round[9] to account for the chronological gap between the Pons of 1066 and his eventual heir, Richard, called 'son of Ponson' in a Welsh chronicle. This Richard was too young for the Domesday Survey, and is first known to have been active half a century after the Battle of Hastings. The second Pons (if there were two) must have been dead before 1086, leaving three sons:

i. RICHARD fitz Pons (or son of Ponson), Lord of Cantref Bychan, for whom see Chapter Three.

ii. SIMON fitz Pons, who witnessed a charter of his brother, Richard, in about 1127, and gave the tithe of his demesne land at Swell to Tewkesbury Abbey. His son, PONS fitz Simon, held eight knight's fees of the old feoffment under the Honour of Gloucester in 1166 during the reign of Henry II, and was the father of Nicholas Ponz, who, in 1194-5, gave 300 marks of benevolence towards the ransom of Richard Coeur-de-Lion from his imprisonment by the Duke of Austria, and indirectly of the Emperor Henry VI, to be paid in instalments. This Nicholas Ponz (or Poyntz) later sided with the barons against King John at the time of Magna Carta, and was the ancestor in the male line of the families of Poyntz of Curry Malet and Poyntz of Iron Acton,[10] their name being merely a form of Pons or Ponz. These included the lords Poyntz, summoned to Parliament as Barons from 1295 to 1376; Stephen Poyntz,[11] whose daughter Georgiana, Countess Spencer, was the mother of the celebrated Georgiana, Duchess of Devonshire and ancestress of Lady Diana Spencer, now Princess of Wales; and Colonel William Stephen Poyntz, whose two sons were drowned in 1815, it was believed as a result of the 'Curse of Cowdray' that haunted former church land.[12] The male line of the Poyntz family still exists (see Burke's *Landed Gentry*).

iii. OSBERN (or OSBERT) fitz Pons, who also witnessed his brother Richard's charter in about 1127, before which date he had given Longney-on-Severn in Gloucestershire to Malvern Priory. Here he styled himself 'Osbernus Pontium' instead of 'filius Pontii', which may perhaps be taken as further evidence that his father was a second Pons, and the name was becoming fixed as a surname, e.g. Ponson.[13] In 1130 he was pardoned Danegeld, which obsolete tax was still in force, on his lands in Worcestershire and Buckinghamshire. He had two sons, WILLIAM, and RALPH, a monk.

3. WALTER fitz Pons succeeded his father, the original Pons, as baronial tenant-in-chief of William the Conqueror in the manor of Eaton, Berkshire. He was also tenant-in-chief of the Crown of three estates in Oxfordshire – Aizleforde (probably Yelford), Westwell and Allbury – and (with his elder brother Dru) at Leach in Gloucestershire, where his share was ten hides, now called Southrop. He held 12 more hides at Leach under the Archbishop of York as well as three Worcestershire manors in 1086 under Ralf de Toeni. He was doubtless also the Walter who held lands neighbouring those of Dru as under-tenant at Stoke and in Peritone Hundred, Buckinghamshire. Walter fitz Pons was probably the ancestor of the later family which took the name of Hastings of Eaton Hastings.[14]

Chapter Two

Generation II – Dru Fitzpons (fl. 1086-1095)

Twenty years after his decisive victory at Hastings, when most of the lands of the Anglo-Saxon nobility had been redistributed among his own followers, William the Conqueror caused a complete survey to be made of what they held. 'The king wanted to know what he had, and who held it ... The survey was unmatched in Europe for many centuries, the product of a sophisticated and experienced English administration, fully exploited by the Conqueror's commanding energy ... and because it was the final authoritative register of rightful possession the natives called it Domesday Book, by analogy with the Day of Judgement.'[1]

Two of Pons' sons, Dru and Walter Fitzpons, are included in this 1086 survey. (The name Dru or Dreux, common at this period in France, appears in Latin texts as Drogo.) Of the 23 manors held directly 'in chief' of the king by the two brothers, Dru held seventeen. Moreover, in Gloucestershire returns the lands of Dru Fitzpons[2] are entered immediately before those of Walter Fitzpons, which makes it clear that Dru was the elder brother. Since Walter was succeeded by his own descendants, whereas Dru was succeeded by Richard son of the pre-deceasing Pons Ponson, it would appear that the second Pons must have been dead before Domesday, and that he was the middle brother. The family estates held directly of the king were scattered through six counties – Herefordshire, Gloucestershire, Wiltshire, Worcestershire, Oxfordshire and Berkshire – and they held other lands as under-tenants in Buckinghamshire as well.

Domesday Book was compiled by the existing Anglo-Saxon civil service for tax purposes rather than as a Norman assessment of military strength. The Great Survey, therefore, deals with manorial estates rather than Norman knights' fees. The object of a knight's fee or *fief de hauberc* was to mount a cavalier in fairly heavy armour (a hauberk was a shirt of mail), which had only become possible some centuries before with the introduction of the stirrup from Central Asia. Such an armoured knight was the equivalent of a modern military tank in armoured warfare: a body of armoured knights was like a highly mobile armoured division, as William proved when he conquered England so rapidly. It is impossible to be precise, but in early Normandy[3] it took about five hundred acres of good land to maintain such a *fief de hauberc*. In principle the Norman baronies dating from the time of Duke Robert the Devil (1028-1035) were made up of five knights' fees each, and an Honour was made up of ten knights' fees,[4] but the system soon became overlaid by the movement of fees through inheritance and alienation, so that some barons held more or less than the original number of fees. Consequently at this stage a royal baron was simply a tenant-in-chief of the Crown.

As a king's baron, Dru Fitzpons was responsible for raising a certain number of armed and mounted knights for the sovereign in time of war. But Domesday Book was compiled to supply the king with essentially different information. From it we learn that Dru held 17 manors directly from the king, two in Gloucestershire, eight in Herefordshire, four in Worcestershire, and three in Wiltshire. There were six mills on these estates; the land was assessed for tax purposes at 52 hides and three and a half virgates;[5] and the working population on his land consisted of 40 villagers, 47 cottagers, 36 slaves (or serfs), one radman (rider), two burgesses, one priest and one smith. At Frampton in Gloucestershire, which appears to have been his chief residence, he had a wood one league long by three furlongs wide. But it is impossible from this information to guess the actual acreage he owned. At that date the population of England was roughly one person per thirty acres (as opposed to 0.77 acres in 1971), but Domesday Book only includes the actual working population, omitting children and the aged. Wasteland, pasture, meadow or woodland were not normally taxed as hidage, and although the hide (theoretically the arable land that could support one family) is sometimes reckoned at 120 acres, in some counties where the land was poorer it was reckoned at as much as 240 acres. So all we can really say is that Dru Fitzpons held several thousand acres from the king, as well as several thousand more on other manors of which he was a sub-tenant: e.g. at Lower Swell, where he held of his friend Ralf III de Toeni.

The following are Dru Fitzpons' manors held directly of the king in 1086:

GLOUCESTERSHIRE
Frampton: 10 hides, 9 ploughs, 10 villagers (villeins), 8 cottagers, 9 serfs, 1 mill, 1 wood 1 league long by 3 quarantens broad.

Eastleach: 10 hides, 13 ploughs, 15 villeins, 4 cottagers, 9 serfs, 1 mill.

HEREFORDSHIRE
Hampton: 1 hide, 2 ploughs, 1 cottager, 1 mill, which Stephen holds of Dru Fitzpons.

Hamnish: (in Kimbolton): 1 hide, 3 ploughs, 2 cottagers, 4 serfs. (Walter holds it of Dru Fitzpons; Ernesi held it of Edward the Confessor.)

Rochford: 1 hide and 1 virgate, 3 ploughs, 4 cottagers, 6 serfs.

Dorstone: 7 hides.

Burcstanestune (Burrington): 3 hides.

Ruuenore: (in the Golden Valley) 1 hide, 7 ploughs, 7 villeins, 2 smallholders, 4 serfs, 1 mill, 1 priest, 1 smith.

Hanleys (End): 1 hide and 1½ virgates, 3 ploughs, 4 small holders, 1 serf and a burgess rendering 4d. (Aethelhelm holds it of Dru Fitzpons.)

Mathon: ½ hide which pays tax, 1 plough. (Aethelhelm holds it of Dru Fitzpons.)

WORCESTERSHIRE
Hollin: 1 hide which pays tax, 1 plough, wasteland.

Stildon: ½ hide which pays tax, land for 2 ploughs, waste.

Glasshampton: 1 hide which pays tax, 1 villein, 3 smallholders with 1 plough, 1 mill.

Martley: 1 virgate which pays tax. 1 rider who pays 6s. a year.

WILTSHIRE
Seagry: Tax for 5 hides, 4 ploughs (2 in lordship), 5 villeins, 6 smallholders, 5 cottagers with 1 plough, 2 mills, meadow, 30 acres in Malmesbury, 1 house which pays 9d.

Easton: Tax for 5 hides, land for 3 ploughs, of which 4 hides are in lordship; 2 ploughs there, 2 serfs, 1 villein, 4 smallholders, 2 cottagers, meadow of 10 acres,

woodland 2 furlongs long and 2 furlongs wide, which Gilbert holds of Dru
Fitzpons.

Alderton: 3 hides, 3 ploughs, 2 smallholders, 1 serf. From part of a mill 22d., meadow
of 15 acres. (Hugh holds of Dru Fitzpons.)

Dru Fitzpons, of course, also held at least six other manors *en vavasseur* as a
sub-tenant, and probably some more in Oxfordshire, Buckinghamshire and
Berkshire, where a Walter (probably his brother) often appears holding lands nearby.
For instance, Dru Fitzpons held ten hides in Aston, Gloucestershire of the Church
of Worcester. But his most interesting sub-tenancies were those which he held of Ralf
de Toeni. In Berkshire, Dru held Charlton of Ralf in 1086, although his family may
originally have been enfeoffed there by Ralf's brother-in-law William FitzOsbern,
Earl of Hereford, Viceroy of England, for Domesday Book notes that Charlton had
been forfeited (in 1075) by the viceroy's son, Roger. In Gloucestershire, as we have
seen, Dru held Lower Swell of Ralf de Toeni, its pre-conquest owner having been one
Ernesi,[6] who also held Frampton, the chief place of Dru's own Honour. Dru also held
the Herefordshire manors of Ford, Broadfield (in Bodenham) and Sarnesfield of Ralf
de Toeni. On these Herefordshire estates Dru kept in hand on the demesne land two
ploughs, two villeins, five cottagers, three serfs, two bondswomen, three ox-men and
a fishery which rendered 600 eels.

All the above brings Pons' family to Clifford Castle, from which they were
eventually to take their name. We have already mentioned that Ralf III de Toeni's
brother-in-law was a second cousin of the Conqueror and his right-hand man,
William Fitzosbern, Lord of Breteuil, Hereditary Steward of Normandy, who later
became Earl of Hereford and was left behind to rule England in William's place when
the Conqueror returned to Normandy in 1067. Earl William was a man of immense
energy and a brilliant organiser. His earldom was invested with a quasi-palatine
character to give him a free hand on the Welsh border. Using forced labour he set
out to build a line of strong castles, which he achieved between 1067 and 1070, when
he returned to Normandy. There he was killed in 1071 in an attempt to come to the
aid of the widowed Countess of Flanders.

Earl William FitzOsbern's meteoric career has been summarised thus:[7]
Notwithstanding the difficulties of what might be called the aftermath of Hastings,
he had achieved great things as Earl of Hereford. His dashing leadership drew
around him a great number of adventurous knights, whom he lavishly rewarded out
of the royal coffers, not altogether to the satisfaction of the careful king. With their
aid he protected the earldom from the ravages of the Welsh by building strong
castles along the border at Wigmore, Clifford,[8] Eywas Harold,[9] Monmouth and
Chepstow, each becoming the centre of a Norman settlement. In the case of Wigmore
and of Clifford he is known to have provided for the economic needs of the castle by
establishing beneath its shadow a chartered borough, to which he no doubt granted
those liberal 'customs of Breteuil' already conceded to the Norman burgesses of
Hereford.

After the forfeiture of William FitzOsbern's son, Earl Roger, for rebellion in 1075,
Clifford Castle and other of his lands were given by the king to Ralf III de Toeni, who
was its lord at the time of the Domesday Survey. This means that we do not know

for certain whether the great men selected to be tenants around Clifford Castle were originally chosen by Earl William or by Ralf de Toeni.

Lynn Nelson, in his *The Normans in South Wales*[10] writes: 'Just to the south of Elsedune Hundred lies the valley of the Wye which descends here from the highlands of Brecknockshire and passes into the heart of Herefordshire. This was a prime invasion route and it was guarded by the great castle of Clifford, constructed by William Fitzosbern ... Clifford was virtually a sovereign realm ... it belonged to no Hundred, nor did it pay any customary dues. All the tenants of the area held directly from Ralf de Toeni. These tenants numbered four, named by Domesday Book as Gilbert, Roger, Herbert and Drew. It is not difficult to identify Gilbert FitzTurold, Roger de Lacy, and Drew (Dru) Fitzpons, three of the greatest landholders in the shire. Between the three of them, excluding Herbert, they held nine ploughs in demesne and had established the nucleus of a borough which at the time claimed sixteen burgesses'.

Ralf III de Toeni had already fixed the *caput* (or chief place) of his extensive Honour in England at Flamstead in Hertfordshire, and since none of his great fief was charged with any military service owing to the very exceptional privileges conferred on him by the Conqueror, it was not attached to any county for shrievalty purposes. It seems probable, however, that he chose Flamstead originally because Clifford Castle was not made over to him until after his nephew Earl Roger's revolt in 1075; and he may have accepted it from King William to protect his late brother-in-law's former tenants there, since they were of baronial rank and presumably well known to him.

Lynn Nelson goes on to say that Ralf appears to have taken little interest in Clifford, for he had farmed the whole castle to Gilbert, the Sheriff of Herefordshire, for an annual rent of sixty shillings. The credit for improving Clifford and for guarding this important approach to Herefordshire must remain with the small group of barons who held of him.[11] Among these, of course, was Dru Fitzpons, so the family who were to make the name of Clifford so famous already had a lodging within its environs from at least 1086 and very possibly from the time Clifford Castle was first built in 1067.

Horace Round summed up the position at Clifford in 1086 as follows: 'Just as the lord of Monmouth gripped the passage of the Wye at the point where it left the county, so the lord of Clifford commanded the important point where it entered the county from Wales. High upon its red sandstone steep, Clifford Castle had a natural strength that rendered needless the moated mound associated, especially in this county, with the stronghold of Norman lords. But another of their features it possessed: about it lay a "castlery" (Castellaria), of which the extent should be observed. The lord's demesne was of three ploughlands; the holdings of his knightly tenants contained no fewer than twenty-three among them. And these holdings forcibly illustrate my theory of the class of men who held around a baron's castle. For Roger, the first holder, was none other than Roger de Laci, the greatest man in the shire; Drogo, the third was Dru Fitzpons, founder of the famous house of Clifford and a Herefordshire tenant-in-chief ... Herbert, the fourth holder, was probably a tenant of Ralf in Worcestershire so named, who also held of him at Eaton in this county, while Gilbert, the second holder was clearly Gilbert the Sheriff ... Ralf de

Tosny (Toeni), Lord of the fief, was no ordinary baron. Born of a princely house ... he was Banner Bearer of the Normans.'[12]

Dru Fitzpons was alive as late as 1095, when he was unjustly obliged by William Rufus to pay £10 'relief', a tax improperly levied by that king on the tenants of the See of Worcester on the death of Bishop Wulfstan (18 January 1095). In his criticism of William Rufus and his rapacious and unpopular minister, Ranulf Flambard, Dr. Round[13] remarks on what formed so bitter a grievance at that time: 'Ranulf Flambard saw no other difference between an ecclesiastical and a lay fief than the superior facilities which they first gave for extortion'. The estate on which Dru Fitzpons was forced to pay up unjustly was, of course, the ten hides he held at Aston (Glos.) of the See of Worcester. This is the last we hear of him alive.

A few more details are worth recording. From the Rev. Jonathan Williams' *History of Radnorshire* we learn that Sir Ralph de Baskerville of Aberedw had married a daughter of Dru Fitzpons. A violent dispute respecting property arose between father and son-in-law when the former unjustly dispossessed the latter. A challenge ensued and they fought at a place near Hereford where Dru was slain, and to mark the spot a white cross was erected. This cross stood for many years and is said to have been torn down by one Garnons in Queen Elizabeth's time. Sir Ralph de Baskerville purchased a pardon from the Pope for the killing of his father-in-law, and it would appear that, by way of restitution, the Cliffords took over certain lands in fee in the Baskerville manor of Bredwardine as they held them in the 1180s.

The date of this is not known, but must have taken place before 1127 as after that date we find Richard, Dru's nephew and the son of his younger brother, Ponson, taking over Clifford.

Chapter Three

Generation III – Richard Fitzpons, Lord of Cantref Bychan (1088-1129)

When William FitzOsbern's son, Earl Roger, forfeited his estates for rebellion in 1075, William the Conqueror appointed no palatine Earl of Hereford to replace him. The castle of Clifford was placed in the hands of Earl Roger's maternal uncle, Ralf de Toeni, whose great estates and interests elsewhere in the country ensured that he became to some extent an absentee landlord. The local baronial families were restrained for a while, as it were on a leash, and the pressure of the Norman Conquest on South Wales was likewise abated.

At that time Wales was partitioned among a number of native kings and princes, whose dynasties could all be traced back to Kings Coel and Cunedda in the sixth century (about a hundred years after the Romans left Britain). The largest kingdom or principality in the south, threatened by the Normans from Herefordshire and Gloucestershire, was Deheubarth, ruled by the descendants of the famous Kings Rhodri Mawr and Hywel Dda. In 1081 the powerful Rhys ap Tewdwr, King of Deheubarth, overthrew his internal Welsh enemies at the battle of Mynydd Carn and firmly established himself on the throne of South Wales. In the same year, 1081, William the Conqueror paid his only visit to Wales, which he penetrated as far as St Davids. The Welsh and the English accounts of this expedition differ; according to the monks of St Davids, the king's journey was a pilgrimage, undertaken out of respect for the saint. According to the English, it was made at the head of an armed force and resulted in the 'freeing' of many hundred men. There can be little doubt that the latter is more probable, devout as William undoubtedly was, and that his real motive was to impress the local chieftains with a due sense of his power and to relieve the small bands of Normans which were shut up in isolated castles out of reach of the border. But he did not omit to pay his respects to the shrine of the great Dewi, and it is more than likely that he met there the new ruler of Deheubarth and concluded a peace with him, which lasted William's lifetime.[1]

From this time onward, William discouraged the border barons from disturbing the stability of the frontier. But meanwhile, sometime between 1086 and 1088,[2] Bernard de Neufmarché came into possession of a compact group of estates lying athwart the Wye. From here the comparatively broad valley of the Wye and the remains of an old Roman military road led directly into the heart of the independent Welsh kingdom of Brycheiniog (Brecknock). On the death of the Conqueror in September 1087, however, the border barons began to organise that rebellion against his son, William Rufus, which finally erupted during Lent 1088. The rebels enlisted the help of virtually all the border families, including the newly arrived Bernard, but by summer the rebellion had been put down. The king's vengeance against the border nobles appears to have been strangely mild, and in Bernard's case no punishment was meted out at all. On the contrary, almost immediately after the collapse of the rebellion he invaded the Welsh buffer states lying west of the frontier, and by the autumn of 1088 had advanced as far as Glasbury.

Later events show that although the king abandoned the buffer states, he continued to honour at least the letter of the royal agreement with Rhys ap Tewdwr, King of Deheubarth. When Bernard reached Glasbury in the autumn of 1088, he was probably helped by Richard Fitzpons[3] and his advance continued during the next two years. Talgarth was reached early and a castle, Bronllys,[4] built at the confluence of the Dulais and Llyfni rivers. He then moved south along the Llyfni river extending his control into the valley of the Usk. Moving up the latter, he reached the area where Brecon now stands in about 1091. Brecon was the strategic key to Brycheiniog.

Richard Fitzpons was given this new castle of Bronllys by Bernard de Neufmarché to hold under the new Honour of Brecon, and the castle continued to be held by Richard's Clifford descendants until Clifford itself passed out of the family a couple of centuries later. Situated on the banks of the Llyfni about eight miles from Brecon, Bronllys stands isolated from all other buildings commanding wide views of the vale of Talgarth and the Black Mountains. From here Richard Fitzpons was to control the district of Cantref Selyff.

The early Norman invaders of Wales usually occupied and colonised as agriculturalists the arable lands up to about the six hundred foot contour line along the rivers, while the native Welsh held on to the pastoral high ground in the mountains. In the moorland regions the Norman lords displaced the native Welsh rulers and collected the dues and tributes which hitherto had been rendered to them. For another two years Bernard de Neufmarché continued to extend his control over the countryside around the strategic fortress he had established at Brecon, until 1093, goaded beyond endurance, Rhys ap Tewder came to the assistance of the king of Brycheiniog, and both were slain in battle against the Normans.

BRWYNLLYS or BRUNLES CASTLE is situated on the Lheveny, a small River which enters itself into the Wye, and stands within sight of the Road from the Hay to Br When this Castle was built is uncertain, but here it was about the Reign of K. Henry II that Mahel the Son of Bernard Newmarch L. of Brecon by Nesta a Princess of C met with the just Punishment of his Enormities. As He was plundering the Lands & Possessions of David Fitzgerald B. of S. Davies, He was entertain'd by Walter Clifford Castle for one Night, In which Night the Castle took fire, & Mahel was slain by a Stone that fell down upon his Head . The present Proprietor is D. Morgan

1. 'The North View of Brwynllys Castle, in the County of Brecknock.'

2. Llandovery Castle, built by Richard Fitzpons: the first Clifford castle in Wales.

The conquered kingdom of Brycheiniog was divided into three princely cantrefs. To guard the western frontier of Brecknockshire, Bernard established Richard Fitzpons in Cantreff Selyff, on the far western border of the lordship. From this base Richard continued on his own to extend Norman power westward. He moved across the border and by 1115 was in control of Llandovery and the surrounding Cantref Bychan. He made this conquest with the express permission of Henry I, and the area was long held in fief by the Clifford family. Richard's achievement offers some indication that the process which led to the creation of the marcher lordships was to some degree self generating.

Richard Fitzpons was now the Marcher Lord of Cantref Bychan; but he was more than that, for he had become what was in effect, though not in name, a Welsh *tywysog*, or prince. Cantref Bychan was a vast area comprising the whole of what was to become east Carmarthenshire, that wide district between the eastern bank of the Towy and Brecknockshire. Here on the river Towy he built another castle of his own at Llandovery, where he held his *lyss* or court.[5]

In England, which had been a single kingdom before the Conquest, the Norman landowners simply took over the position of the Anglo-Saxon thegns whom they had displaced. But in Wales, they took over the position of the dynasts whom they now also displaced. In Welsh law, when referring to the institution known by the various names of *arglwydd* (lord) or *tywysog* (prince), or *brenin* (king) the three terms – lord, prince and king – were synonymous, and the position of the 'lord' was fully royal within his *commote* or *cantref*. In other words they had the right to make war, which many modern books erroneously describe as private war, but for the medieval men of Wales and the March there was nothing 'private' about it – it was recognised as a right of the 'lord', and was called simply 'war' – *guerra*. The result was that, unlike the barons of England, the Marcher lords had the right 'by the custom of the March' to make personal war and to build castles without royal sanction. Their territorial lordships were 'regalities' exempt from appeal to the royal courts, and the Court of the Marcher lord administered all justice, civil and criminal, high and low, and administered it, not in the name of the king, but in the name of the Marcher lord, who also received all the profits and had the power of pardon. It was to this exclusiveness of the jurisdiction of the Marcher lords that English lawyers referred in their aphorism that 'in the Welsh March the king's writ does not run'.[6] Such, then, was the almost regal position of Richard Fitzpons as Marcher Lord of Cantref Bychan.

Soon after Richard had built Llandovery castle, it came under attack from Gruffydd ap Rhys, son of the late King Rhys ap Tewdwr. Richard was away at the time, but had committed the custody of his castle to his seneschal, a local Welsh chieftain named Maredudd ap Rhydderch ap Caradog, of the dynastic house of Gwynllwg, who remained loyal to his new Norman lord. At Llandovery, Richard founded a cell (later broken up about 1185 as a result of the scandalous misconduct of the monks), which he gave, along with its church, to Malvern Priory. Here again, like his younger brother, Osbern, he styled himself 'Ricardus Pontium'[7] which implies once more that he was the son of a second, successive Pons, and that a family surname on the lines of Ponson was being evolved; indeed, his other brother Simon's descendants eventually assumed the surname Ponz or Poyntz. Richard Fitzpons is last mentioned as Lord of Cantref Bychan in 1128, and he probably died about that time.[8]

A number of interesting charters relating to Richard and his immediate family have been edited and published by Horace Round.[9] The third of these is of special interest as it was granted about 1127 by 'R. Puncii filius' (Richard Fitzpons) at Clifford, in the house of Master Hugh: *apud Cliffordia in hospicio Hugonis Magistri*. Round suggests that Hugh was the family lawyer. The Fitzpons family, whom we know to have held land in the environs of Clifford Castle since the time of the Conqueror, are here shown in actual residence there. Richard's then son and heir, Simon (who died young), was away in Wales at the time and sanctions the document from Ystrad.

The first of the charters edited by Round is of double interest. By it Henry I provided in 1121 for the succession to Bernard de Neufmarché's conquests, including the former Welsh kingdom of Brycheiniog, now the Honour of Brecon, in which Richard Fitzpons had played so prominent a part. Bernard (a great-great-grandson of Duke Richard the Good of Normandy) was nearing his end, dying some time in 1125. His wife, Agnes, was the daughter of the Marcher lord Osbern FitzRichard (founder of Richard's Castle) by the Welsh princess, Nest, daughter of

3. & 4.   Clifford Castle, Hay-on-Wye.

King Gruffydd ap Llewelyn (by his Mercian wife, granddaughter of Godgifu, Countess of Mercia, the celebrated 'Lady Godiva'). But Bernard de Neufmarché's wife Agnes had a lover, whom her son, Mahel, caught coming out of her room and whom he beat and wounded. In revenge, Agnes went to King Henry and swore that Mahel was not the son of her husband Bernard,and therefore not the rightful heir to his great inheritance, but that her daughter, Sybil, alone was legitimate. Accordingly the royal charter was issued in 1121 whereby Sybil, as daughter and heiress of Bernard de Neufmarché, with all the vast possessions of both her parents, was given in marriage to Miles of Gloucester, who thus became successor to the great conquests in which Richard Fitzpons had had so prominent a command. Moreover, Miles was Richard's brother-in-law, and in the body of the charter the boundaries of Brecon are mentioned as extending up to those of Richard Fitzpons in Cantref Bychan.

For the second and third charters demonstrate that Richard Fitzpons' wife, Maud of Gloucester, was the daughter (by his wife Bertha, possibly de Ballon) of Walter, hereditary Sheriff (*Vicomte*) of Gloucester, Constable to King Henry I, son of Roger de Pitres, Sheriff of Gloucester under the Conqueror. Maud's father was a cousin of the famous conquistador Brian Fitz Count, lord of Abergavenny, ruler of upper Gwent in Wales, natural son of Alan Fergant, reigning Count of Brittany.

Richard's brother-in-law, Miles of Gloucester, played a very prominent part in the troubles between King Stephen and the Empress Maud at the outbreak of which (with Pain FitzJohn), he ruled the whole Welsh border from the Severn to the sea. As one of the great magnates of the west of England, Miles attended King Stephen, who did him great honour, but acted as the Empress Maud's Constable on her arrival in 1139, and accompanied her flight to Gloucester, where, on 25 July 1141, he was created Earl of Hereford.[10] 'With singular unanimity hostile chroniclers testify to his devotion to her cause. He even boasted that she had lived at his expense throughout her stay in England.'[11] But on Christmas Eve, 1143, Earl Miles was accidentally killed by an arrow shot by a companion while out hunting together in the Forest of Dean.

By his wife, Maud, Richard Fitzpons had at least three sons and a daughter:

1. Sir SIMON FitzRichard, who appears both as son and heir and as a Knight in his father's charter granted at Clifford in *c.* 1127, when he himself was away at Ystrad. He is said to have founded the Cluniac Clifford Priory,[12] presumably on the family holding within the *castellaria*, as the castle itself did not yet belong to the family. Sir Simon appears to have died without issue.

2. ROGER Fitz Richard, who witnessed a charter of his father's *c.* 1129.[13]

3. WALTER Fitz Richard, afterwards de Clifford, baron of Clifford, for whom see Chapter Four.

1. BERTHA, who married Elias II Giffard of Brimpsfield, Gloucestershire, receiving from her father the manor of Ullingswick[14] in Herefordshire for her marriage portion. Ullingswick is of especial interest to students of the legends of King Arthur and the Holy Grail, for its principal sub-tenant was a family named Map, of which Master Walter Map (*c.* 1140-*c.* 1210) is the most famous. Among his works was the Great Vulgate Cycle of Arthurian legends. Bertha left issue and her great-grandson John (1st Lord Giffard) abducted and married Maud Clifford, heiress of the Barony of Clifford and widow of Sir William Longespee (see Chapter Eight below).

Chapter Four

Generation IV – Walter Clifford, Baron of Clifford (1127-1187)

Through the early death of his two elder brothers, Sir Simon and Roger FitzRichard, Walter FitzRichard (as he was then still called – later to become the first Clifford) became unexpectedly lord of the whole of what is now east Dyfed the former Welsh principality of Cantref Bychan, with all the powers of regality that that entailed for a Marcher lord in the Cambro-Norman world. Everywhere the Normans went they were quick to adopt the local customs.

We have already mentioned that the king's writ did not run in the Marcher lordships, and that each was like a petty kingdom, possessing its own parliament and system of justice. The Marcher lords recognised that they were feudal nobles, of course, but they held their land by right of their and their fathers' conquests. They were tenants *in capite*, each holding directly from the king. They occupied a special status, however, for their holdings did not form part of the realm of England, and within them they enjoyed an almost complete immunity from royal interference.[1] They appointed their own sheriffs, possessed their own chanceries and their personal great seals. They had jurisdiction over all cases, with the exception of high treason, and they established their own courts to try offences, execute sentences and amerce fines. They owned the right to many royal prerogatives such as salvage, treasure trove, plunder and fishing. They could establish forests and forest laws, declare and wage war, establish boroughs, and grant extensive charters of liberties. They were, indeed, the embodiment of sovereignty within their own lordship.

The Norman policy of castle building provided a refuge for men as well as a place for the safekeeping of treasure and chattels. In any case other than surprise attacks all moveable wealth could be placed within the castle. In order to obtain any appreciable amount of plunder, the Welsh would have to carry at least the outer works of the castle. Since they lacked the organisation and technology for effective siege operations, this was anything but an easy task. And in Wales Walter Clifford held with a strong arm the castles of Llandovery and Bronllys. (Contemporary charters and documents refer to Walter as de Clifford in accordance with the custom of the time. However, the name Clifford became an hereditary surname rather earlier than in most families, and we shall henceforce omit the 'de' in this work. See also Introduction for further comment on this point.)

Some idea of the Arthurian manner in which Walter lived as lord of Cantref Bychan may be gathered from Dr. Mary Williams' *Life in Wales in Medieval Times*.[2] 'Once past the Porter at the gate', she writes, 'the tiled floor of the hall of the lord's castle where notable strangers were received was strewn with green rushes. Upon these, in the middle of the room, a carpet of satin or velvet was placed. This was considered the most honourable place in the hall and consequently here sat the principal people of the household. In the centre, the lord reclined on cushions or sat on a chair with a red cushion beneath him and a pillow under each elbow. It appears that the chair was a Norman introduction, and that the native Welsh kings and princes had preferred to recline on cushions alone.'

As for the lord's hall, 'every nail was painted with bright colours, not a single panel but had sundry images in gold portrayed upon it ... The table in such a room, set with benches for a banquet, was of silver, inlaid with gold, upon it was spread a cloth of yellow linen. When it was time to eat, a horn was sounded, that all might wash before sitting down to table.

'The nine superior officers of the lord's household included the Master of the Household, the Steward, the Chief Huntsman, and the Page of the Chamber. The inferior officers included the Bard, the Physician, the Chief Porter and the Watchman and the Footholder. Each different district within the lordship was run by a special officer called the *maer*. The Chief of Song was by this time the same person as the chaired Bard, and a magnificent harp was the most important feature of the Great Hall. There was hunting by day and chess by night ...'.

Walter FitzRichard was already a great Welsh Marcher lord when he first appears as 'Walter de Cliffort' in a charter by which he exchanged the manor of Eastleach for that of Glasbury with Gloucester Abbey, afterwards confirmed in 1138 by King Stephen.[3] This is the first appearance of what was to become one of England's great medieval surnames. Walter chose the surname Clifford when he acquired in addition the great castle and barony of Clifford as the dowry of his wife, Margaret de Toeni, daughter of Ralf IV, Seigneur de Conches (1102-26),[4] son of the Ralf III de Toeni mentioned in previous chapters. Walter himself was seneschal to Margaret's brother, Roger III de Toeni, Seigneur de Conches,[5] a position of considerable further power.

Margaret's ancestry was equally distinguished on both sides of her family. Her paternal grandfather's princely descent is described in Chapter One, and her mother, Alice, was a sister of Queen Maud, consort of the King of Scotland. Alice was the younger daughter and co-heiress of the Anglo-Danish martyr, Waltheof, Earl of Northumberland, Northampton and Huntingdon by his wife, Judith, daughter of Lambert, Count of Lens by Adelaide, sister of the Conqueror.

Walter took over the Barony of Clifford at a very difficult time for the great Welsh revolt of 1136-7 against the Norman feudatories of King Stephen took them entirely by surprise. The Welsh dynasts had been accustomed for centuries to re-arrange their dynastic appanages by force, if necessary, on the death of a strong ruler. Such a moment occurred when Henry I died abroad on 1 December 1135. As Sir John Lloyd puts it:[7] 'the great revolution in Welsh affairs which now took place was long remembered by the foreign settlers as a turning point in the history of their adopted country. The day of Henry's death was for them as fateful as was for another aristocracy in a later age the capture of the Bastille ... It was immediately after the coronation of Stephen that the first outburst took place ...' The Welsh leader was Prince Gruffydd ap Rhys, the son of King Rhys ap Tewdwr, so much of whose territory Walter's father, Richard, had helped to conquer.

At that time the greatest Norman baron in Wales was Richard FitzGilbert de Clare, lord of Cardigan, and grandson of that Richard FitzGilbert who had witnessed, with Pons and the Vicomte de Thouars, the future Conqueror's grant to Fécamp in 1066. Richard was with King Stephen in the early part of 1136, but quarrelled with him and returned to Wales. On reaching Abergavenny in mid-April he was warned by Brian FitzCount, the ruler of upper Gwent and a cousin of Walter Clifford's mother, of the dangerous state of the country. Brian offered to escort Richard but the offer was refused, and Richard rode on unarmed, such was the confidence with which he regarded the situation. He had not gone far before his party was ambushed and he was killed. The Welsh insurgents then made for his castle at Cardigan and laid siege to it, but failed to take it against the strong defence put up by Richard's widow, a sister of the Earl of Chester.

King Stephen ordered Miles of Gloucester, Walter Clifford's uncle, to go to the rescue of the besieged lady and bring her back to England, but though this commission was duly accomplished, no further measures were taken. Richard FitzGilbert's brother reached Brecon, where news that the insurgents had blocked all the roads across the mountains with felled trees persuaded him that no further action was possible, so he returned to England. Robert FitzHarold of Ewyas, whose daughter, Sybil, later married Walter Clifford's grandson, Sir Roger Clifford of Tenbury, was sent to another part of Wales, but was equally unsuccessful in putting down the rebellion. Such information as has survived suggests that the revolt extended to almost every part of Wales, with the result that the Clifford family lost their authority in the region of Llandovery.[8] This appears to have been the restoration under the Prince of South Wales of the original dynastic house of Cantref following the humiliation of a period of Norman rule, and it was many years before Walter Clifford recovered his extensive lordship of Cantref Bychan.

It is not known which side Walter Clifford supported in the bitter struggle between King Stephen and the Empress Maud, but most of his family were ranged with the other Marcher lords on the side of the Empress, especially his uncle, Miles of Gloucester, and his cousin Brian Fitz Count, lord of Abergavenny and Upper Gwent. Moreover, his powerful brother-in-law, Roger III de Toeni, was a strong supporter of Geoffrey Plantagenet, the Empress's husband, against King Stephen. The only possible reason for thinking that Walter might have supported the king is based on the heraldic device adopted by the family about this time,[9] and this seems hardly reason enough to suppose anything of the sort.

Whichever side Walter took there remains, however, one other interesting possibility. This was a period of anarchy during which a number of semi-independent barons issued their own coins. For example, Henri de Neubourg, heir to the Marcher lordship of Gower, struck his own coinage at Swansea.[10] So it is not impossible that Walter Clifford as a Marcher lord may have done likewise, though none of his coins have so far been found. When the period of anarchy ended and Henry II, son of Geoffrey Plantagenet and the Empress Maud, was firmly seated on the English throne, the situation changed radically. First, the king's mistress was Walter Clifford's daughter, the Fair Rosamund; second, the new king broke all Welsh resistance in 1157, only Rhys ap Gruffydd holding out against him, though even he was compelled to make his peace with Henry II in the end. Early in 1158 Rhys ap Gruffydd found that the day of reckoning with the English king was no longer to be put off. The restoration of the royal authority meant the re-establishment of the barons in the lordships from which they had been ejected during the revolt. This, of course, included the Clares in Cardigan and the Cliffords in Cantref Bychan and

Llandovery. The new order of things was not readily acceptable by the Welsh, and the southern prince himself reopened hostilities against Clifford and Earl Roger. But when Henry II came west in force for a second Welsh expedition, Rhys again made a complete submission. In 1162, however, Rhys once again raised the banner of revolt and attacked Llandovery Castle. For some years the government had recognised the insecurity of this stronghold and had disbursed large sums of money for its defence, as though it were one of the buttresses of the realm, and more was involved in its maintenance than the private purse of Walter Clifford could afford. Nevertheless, it fell, and the name no longer appears in royal records. Rhys had temporarily disposed of the Clares in Cardigan and of the Cliffords in Cantref Bychan.[11] In 1171 Henry II, on his way to Ireland, received the South Welsh prince Rhys, who did homage to him at Pembroke, and for the rest of his life Rhys held a position of unquestioned supremacy in South Wales.[12]

Walter Clifford still retained an interest in Wales, however, as he continued to hold Bronllys Castle and Cantref Selyff of his cousin the Earl of Hereford, who was also Marcher lord of Brecon. In 1175 his cousin, Mahel, Earl of Hereford, came to stay with Walter Clifford at Bronllys. Geraldus Cambrensis tells us that 'Mahel was remarkable for his inhumanity, and had persecuted the Bishop of St David's to such an extent that the unfortunate prelate dared not enter Brecknock. But retribution overtook the tyrant, for when he was being hospitably entertained by Walter, the house was accidentally burnt down, and he received a mortal blow on his head from a stone falling from the principal tower, upon which he instantly despatched messengers to recall the bishop, exclaiming in a loud voice: "O my father and high priest, your Saint has taken most cruel vengeance on me, not waiting the conversion of a sinner, but hastening his death and overthrow". Thus he ended his tyranny and his life together'.[13]

Walter Clifford's life was obviously much affected by his daughter, the Fair Rosamund, being King Henry II's mistress, and this position became more delicate after Queen Eleanor herself was imprisoned by her husband and Rosamund Clifford openly recognised as his true love. Walter Clifford was given Corfham Manor, one of the finest Crown estates in Shropshire, by the king 'for love of Rosamund'. This included Culmington, Priors Ditton and the Clee. But the king in the full flush of love went further and gave the Cliffords rights in the Forest of Clee which ordinarily belonged to the Royal Forests, and these rights were still enforced by the Clifford family in the following century.[15] However, after Rosamund's death, the king was not so tolerant of his nobles encroaching on his own game rights. In 1176 Walter Clifford and his son-in-law, Osbern FitzHugh, were each fined six marks by the king personally for forest trespass in Worcestershire.[16]

The vicar of Cannington (the Rev. A. R. Moss) told the present Lord Clifford in 1965 that the Priory of Cannington was one of Walter Clifford's foundations (it is now once more in the possession of the Cliffords), and that when the Welsh rising became too great for safety, Walter was wont to send his wife and unmarried daughter, Rosamund, to this Somerset nunnery. Certainly Walter was a great benefactor of the church, giving lands to the monasteries of Haughmond, Dore and Godstow.[17] He was still living in 1187, when he paid scutage for Galway (scutage was the tax on a shield – *scutum* – to be carried into battle on your behalf instead of the royal retainer so armed whom you were required to supply) on one of his many knights' fees: in this case for an estate in Wiltshire. Eyton, the historian of Shropshire, says that Walter died about 1190 at a great age.

By his wife, Margaret de Toeni, Walter had several children including three sons and three daughters:

1. WALTER, Baron of Clifford, for whom see Chapter Six.

2. RICHARD, ancestor of the Cliffords of Frampton, for whom see Part Five. He appears to have caused his elder brother considerable trouble in the reign of Richard I, and through the king's favour, over a claim to Corfham. But at Michaelmas 1200, soon after King John's accession, Richard Clifford renounced all claim for himself and his heirs to Corfham, Culmington and the Haye of Ernestre with the forest of Clee. In return Walter, his brother, gave him the manor of Frampton for one knight's fee.[18]

3. WILLIAM, who appears as a witness to a transaction concerning the soul of his famous sister, King Henry II's mistress. The Rev. R. W. Eyton writes: 'The fair Rosamund Clifford died about 1175 or 1176 and was buried at Godstow, a place ostensibly dedicated to the holiness of female chastity! There are two charters to Godstow Nunnery, which, passing as they did within two years of Rosamund's death, next claim our attention. Walter de Clifford, for his soul's health and for the souls of his wife, Margaret, and their daughter, Rosamund, gave to the nuns aforesaid his mill at Frampton with a meadow near thereunto. Also he gave them his salt-pit in Wich. This he did with the consent of the King (Henry II) and of his heirs. Walter de Clifford junior, calling himself son and heir of the grantor, conceded the gift in a distinct clause of the charter. There were witnesses of the whole, Osbern FitzHugh, Hugh de Say, Richard de Clifford, William his brother, Richard de Karesi and William Charbunell'.

1. AMICE, who married the Marcher baron, Osbern FitzHugh, lord of Richard's Castle and baron of Burford. He died about 1185 without legitimate issue. In 1168 his barony was assumed to consist of 23 knights' fees for tax. Eyton gives his pedigree in his *Antiquities of Shropshire*.[19] Osbern was lord of Tenbury in Worcestershire, where his father-in-law, Walter Clifford, was his tenant. He was also a benefactor of Haughmond Abbey to whom he gave a cup of gold worth four marks.

2. LUCY, who married firstly Hugh de Say, Marcher lord of Richard's Castle and baron of Burford in succession to his brother, Osbern FitzHugh, who had married her elder sister Amice. Before his death, Osbern, with his brother's consent, gave Matilda, the daughter of John Poher, the *vill* called Hugelmeston or Cotheridge Parva and other lands, on condition that if she should have an heir, either by the grantor or by any espoused husband, she and her heirs should hold the vill hereditarily. Hugh de Say attested the deed and apparently after his brother's death confirmed it, receiving from the lady a golden ring with a turquoise in the Hall at Burford. After her first husband's death, leaving her with two Say sons, Lucy managed to get back from the canons of Haughmond the golden cup her late brother-in-law Osbern had given them in exchange for some land to which her elder son Hugh de Say consented. Lucy Clifford married secondly Bartholomew de Mortimer, the bearer of another famous Marcher name.[20]

3. JOAN, known to history and to her family as Rosamund, the beautiful and celebrated mistress of Henry II, for whom see Chapter Five.

5. Fair Rosamund Clifford.

Chapter Five

Generation V – Fair Rosamund Clifford (c. 1137-76)

Rosamund Clifford's association with King Henry II was kept secret for many years, but it was openly acknowledged by him when he imprisoned his Queen, Eleanor of Aquitaine, for inciting her sons to rebel against their father in 1173. Henry had two illegitimate sons – William Longsword (or Longespée), who became Earl of Salisbury, and Geoffrey Plantagenet, who became Archbishop of York. Much controversy surrounds the identity of their mother, for Rosamund was not the king's only mistress, though there are many who believe that she was. Those who dispute Rosamund's claim base their case on the disparity in the ages of all concerned, but there is other evidence as well which cannot be ignored. Unfortunately, the records date neither the birth of Rosamund nor that of her father, Walter, or her reputed sons, William and Geoffrey. Even if they did, the habit of kings of having more than one mistress at a time would not be sure proof of these men's maternity. It is, however, known that Rosamund's grandfather married in 1113, and assuming that he was then in his twenties, Walter might have been born around 1115. If Walter also married at about twenty, Rosamund could have been born either side of 1135. There is some evidence, which will be set out in a moment, to suggest that this date is fairly close to the mark. Some authorities state that Geoffrey Plantagenet was born as early as 1152, though it is recorded that he entered the Church and was elected Bishop of Lincoln in 1182 'when he was 23 years old', which suggests his date of birth as 1159. He was appointed Archbishop of York in 1190 and received papal consent to his consecration in the same year.

Some genealogies claim that William was the elder brother, but available evidence[1] favours Geoffrey as the elder, placing William's birth at 1160 or later – a date more readily reconciled with subsequent events in his career. If, however, they had different mothers, then nothing can be deduced from this. William Longsword received from Richard I[2] the hand of Ela, daughter and heiress of the Earl of Salisbury, together with the title of that earldom, in 1198. The same authority states that he took part in the siege of Damietta in 1219 and in the Welsh wars of 1224. Had he been born before 1152, this would mean that he married at about forty-eight and was campaigning into his seventies: in both cases this would have been highly unusual for the times. It seems more likely, therefore, that William was not born before 1160, when Rosamund, if she were his mother, would have been in her twenties and a few years younger than the king.

It must be said, however, that the identity of William Longsword's mother is far from certain. He refers to her in two documents as 'Comitissa Ida, mater mea', and while the word 'mater' is usually taken to mean mother, it was sometimes used loosely to mean 'mother-in-law'. Ida has been identified with Ida, Countess of Boulogne, another of Henry II's mistresses. As for Geoffrey, Walter Map,[3] whose knowledge of court life and gossip was intimate, says that his mother's name was Ykenai or Hikenai, and it is a fact that William later laid claim to the estates of a Sir Roger de Akeney, a name close enough to Ykenai to be significant, though the place itself has so far defied identification, unless it is an antique form of Hackney. There is certainly no evidence for Rosamund's being associated with anyone of this name, so the mystery remains.

There is no record of how Henry met Rosamund, but once again circumstantial evidence suggests that it was through Master Walter Map or his father and namesake, Walter Map the elder. Rosamund and Walter junior were almost exact contemporaries, both being born between 1135 and 1140. Rosamund's aunt, Bertha (see Chapter Three), had received the Manor of Ullingswick, young Walter Map's birthplace, as part of her dowry, so it is not inconceivable that Walter and Rosamund knew each other from childhood. Master Walter was presented at Court in 1162, where his father, Walter senior, had been for many years a member of the royal household. There is thus a strong possibility that it was through the Maps that Rosamund was brought to the king's notice.

All the early authorities seem to agree that she spent much of her youth in the nunnery at Godstow, near Oxford, where Master Walter spent part of his youth as a student (in later years he was appointed Archdeacon of Oxford). Godstow had been generously endowed by Rosamund's father, Walter Clifford, by herself and by the king. It is recorded that the nuns held her in high esteem as 'she wrote a very neat hand ... was skilled in the fine arts ... an excellent needlewoman'. 'At Bildwas Abbey in Shropshire there was kept a cope of this lady's exquisite needlework about the skirts whereof were these words "Rosamund Clifford propriis manibus me fecit" – Rosamund Clifford made me with her own hands.'

Henry probably visited her frequently at the nunnery, which no doubt caused the nuns some embarrassment, and Henry's misgivings about the arrangement caused him to make 'for her at Woodstock a house of wonderful working so that no man or woman might come to her but such as were right secret with him touching the matter'.[4] This house was concealed within a most intricate labyrinth, but when Henry was called away suddenly to France, Queen Eleanor is said to have penetrated it with the aid of a silken thread and, confronting Rosamund, offered her the choice of poison or the dagger. Rather than have her beautiful body hacked about by the amateur swordsmanship of Eleanor, Rosamund took poison. Even Hearne's credulity seems to have faltered here, because he naively observes that 'the story about Rosamund being poisoned was to prevent and deter others from committing the same fault ... and would frighten other young ladies from engaging in the same course of life'.[5]

Rosamund died in 1176 or 1177. Her body was first placed in a marble tomb which stood before the high altar of the priory church of Godstow 'with very fine lights burning around it'. On it were inscribed the words 'Tumba Rosamundae'. According to Stow, however, in 1191, 'Hugh, Bishop of Lincoln came ... to the abbey of nuns called Godstow between Oxford and Woodstock, and when he entered the church to pray, he saw the tomb in the middle of the quire covered with a pall of silk and set about with lights of wax. And demanding whose tomb it was, he was answered that it was the tomb of Rosamund that was sometime lemman to Henry II, King of

England, who for love of her had done so much good to that church. Then, quoth the bishop, take her out of this place and bury her without the church'. The nuns, who reverenced her memory and believed she had died a true penitent removed her tomb to the Chapter House, where it appears to have remained until the dissolution of the monasteries in Henry VIII's reign.

By some accounts when Henry II acknowledged Rosamund after the imprisonment of the Queen in 1173, he established her in a house in London. Maitland in his *History of London* writes: 'Upon Paul's wharf hill within a great gate and next to Doctors Commons were many fair tenements, which, in the leases made by the Dean and Chapter went by the name of "Camera Dianae", that is Diana's Chamber; so denominated from a spacious building which in the time of Henry II stood where they were. In this camera, or arched and vaulted structure full of intricate ways and windings, this Henry kept, or was supposed to have kept, that jewel of his heart "Fair Rosamund": she whom at Woodstock he called Rosa Mundi, and here by the name of Diana, and hence had this house that title'.

Fair Rosamund's story has inspired writers and poets throughout subsequent generations. Addison wrote an opera about her and the fairest of our roses has been named after her. Vernon wrote a beautiful Latin poem about her of which the following is a translation of the final stanza, beginning 'Hic ego marmoreo jaceo Rosamunda ... ':

> Here in this marble tomb enclosed I lie,
> Fair Rosamund whose name will never die.
> With ardent passion by a King beloved,
> Alive, in pleasure and in pomp I moved.
> But of my former state here all you see,
> A heap of dust alone remains of me.

Winston Churchill wrote: ' ... generations have enjoyed the romantic tragedy of Queen Eleanor penetrating the protected maze at Woodstock by the clue of the silken thread and offering her hapless supplanter the hard choice between the dagger and the poisoned cup. Tiresome investigators have undermined this excellent tale, but it certainly should find its place in any history worthy of its name'. (*A History of the English Speaking People*, vol. 1, p. 160).

A history book jingle – given to the present Lord Clifford by the late Lord Amory has it:

> Queen Eleanor reckoned
> That Harry the Second
> Should have shunned
> Fair Rosamund
> Therein they differed
> About Miss Clifford.

Chapter Six

Generation V – Walter Clifford, Baron of Clifford (1173-1221)

The esteem in which Walter Clifford II was held by King John is proved by numerous entries in the Court Rolls of that reign. We find him sometimes in personal attendance at Court, sometimes as *Custos* or Keeper of the royal castles of Hereford and those on the Welsh border. He held the shrievalty of Herefordshire in 1199 and again for another period beginning early in 1205 and lasting until May 1208. His conduct in this office, however, seems to have been rapacious, but a fine of 1,000 marks prevented any troublesome enquiries and secured the king's goodwill.

A document of 1207 distinguishes Walter Clifford II from his son of the same name by calling him *Vetus*, or the elder. It is indeed probable that he was at that time sixty years old and more. The Rev. R. W. Eyton[1] suggests that there is some reason for thinking that Walter Clifford I was intermittently or continuously imbecile during the last few years of his life, though he may have been incapacited for some other reason.

Walter Clifford II married Agnes de Condet (or Cundy), Lady of Cavenby (or Caenby) and Glentham, a great heiress who materially increased the importance of the House of Clifford. She brought him Wickham and other manors in Kent, also estates in Oxfordshire, Essex, Lincolnshire and Nottinghamshire. She also inherited from her father, Roger de Condet, eight knights' fees under the Bishops of Lincoln, and Roger's office of Seneschal to these prelates descended to the Cliffords.

It has been recently suggested[2] that Roger de Condet was the son of Alice, daughter of Ranulf le Meschin, Earl of Chester and Vicomte of Bayeux, and the widow of Richard FitzGilbert de Clare, who had been so romantically rescued from Cardigan Castle by Walter Clifford II's great-uncle, Miles of Gloucester. Certainly Alice was a woman of considerable importance. She held Thorngate Castle outside the walls of Lincoln, Wickhambreux in Kent, Grimston in Nottinghamshire, South Carlton, Thurlby, Eagle and Skellingthorpe in Lincolnshire. She was undoubtedly connected with the Clares, as she confirmed a gift by Richard FitzGilbert's brother, Baldwin, to Bardney Abbey.

In 1151 an important charter of King Stephen states that 'For the love the king bore to the said Earl Ranulf [of Chester] he has returned to Adelidis de Condia [Alice de Condet] all her land, as she fined, namely Thorngate Castle when that castle has been demolished, and the king has restored to her all her other lands'.

Walter Clifford II's wife, Agnes, had evidently inherited Cavenby and Glentham through the marriage of an ancestor (perhaps Robert de Condet's father) to a Chesney heiress. She may have been Adelidis, daughter of William de Chesney, whose father, Osbert de Chesney, founded the church of St Nicholas at Cavenby before the Conquest, so Agnes de Condet's Chesney forefathers appear to have been originally high-born Anglo-Saxons.

In 1201 Walter Clifford paid a fine of 15 marks that he should not be compelled to cross the sea in the king's service, as tenant-in-chief of five knights' fees held of the king, the fine being registered in Nottinghamshire. Again in March 1208 a fine was tendered singly by Agnes de Condet, Walter Clifford's wife. She offered the king a palfrey that she might hold all her life her manor of Wickham in Kent. It was unusual for a wife thus fining in her husband's lifetime, and a patent, dated 10 October 1216, again presents Agnes Clifford in a somewhat mysteriously independent position. It certifies that her chaplain, Walter, in journeying anywhere through her husband, Walter Clifford Senior's manors is under royal letters of safe conduct, without any limitation as to time.

The Latin will of Dame Agnes de Condet, wife of Walter Clifford II, still exists, and at the time it was made he was both alive and capable. Dame Agnes leaves her body for burial, together with 100 solidates of land, to the Prior and Convent of the Holy Trinity, i.e. the cathedral monastery at Canterbury. She makes other religious bequests: to the Augustine Monastery at Canterbury, to St Gregory's church, to the church of the Holy Sepulchre, to Wenlock Priory and 40 shillings to the church of St Ethelbert (now Hereford Cathedral) towards the building of the later Ladye Chapel. She also makes a bequest to three maidens on their marriage with the obligation of observing three anniversaries for her soul. After many bequests to servants, she leaves 20 marks to her daughter, Basilia; 5 marks to Dame Cecilia; a gold ring to her mother (also called Basilia); gold rings to her sons Walter, Roger, Simon and Giles, and the same to her daughters. To fulfil this her testament she certifies that her lord, Walter Clifford, has conceded the issues of the manor of Cavenby arising in the year after her death. Among her executors she appoints her lord, Walter Clifford, the Lord Bishop of Hereford, and the Prior of the Cathedral Church of Canterbury.

From 1208 Walter Clifford was referred to in official documents as the 'elder' and his son and heir, Walter III, as the 'younger', and, although there seems no doubt of Walter II's continued loyalty to King John, it is difficult to resist the Rev. R. W. Eyton's belief that most references after this year to a Walter Clifford acting energetically are more likely to be to the son rather than the father. Nevertheless, Walter II must have been engaged in family and public affairs in the Welsh March, and especially in the rebuilding and strengthening of Clifford Castle. When the family inherited it in the 12th century, at the time of Walter I's marriage, it was almost certainly built of wood. George Marshall[3] tells us that Clifford was a most important strongpoint and one of the first sites to be fortified by the Normans. It is of the usual motte and bailey type, the motte being formed as at Ewyas Harold by severing a jutting tongue of high ground overlooking the river from the main body by a deep cutting. By the end of the 12th century it was at least partly fortified in stone, either by Walter I or Walter II.

This type of fortified residence consisted of a lofty mound of earth with steep sides surrounded by a fosse, or deep ditch, filled, if possible, by water, to which was attached an enclosed area known as the bailey, also surrounded by a ditch and embankment. Both motte and bailey varied in size according to the importance of the holder and the number of retainers he kept and the quantity of stock he had to accommodate. The motte was protected by a palisade of wood with a wooden tower, which in the case of Clifford was soon replaced by a stone one, in the centre of which were the lord's living quarters. This tower was approached by a wooden bridge across the fosse and the summit of the mount was reached by a ladder, both of which could be removed wholly or in part if need arose. The bailey on its inner rim would have had a strong fence and inside sheds for the retainers, horses, cattle and sheep and other domestic livestock.

Apart from building a stone tower at Clifford, Walter II had witnessed great military changes. Besides the fully armoured knights who formed the heavy cavalry, he had seen the introduction of the light cavalry consisting of the knights' mounted retainers, who wore lighter armour and used a special saddle enabling them to mount and dismount more quickly. Then there were the archers, most of whom were recruited from among the native Welsh. The bow had long been the national weapon of the men of South Wales and the arrows of the Welshmen could penetrate three-inch oak slabs and could inflict mortal wounds through the armour of the heavy cavalrymen. The Norman Marcher lords were quick to adapt this peculiarly effective weapon for their own purposes.[4]

Walter's life did not exclusively consist of frontier warfare, for the Cliffords not only enjoyed the chase on their Welsh estates but kept up their royal forestry rights in Shropshire, which Henry II had conferred on them for love of Fair Rosamund. Tournaments likewise played an important part in their lives. These required special, expensive armour, such as the hauberk, or coat of steel mesh which reached to the knee and had sleeves ending in iron gauntlets. Attached to this, and forming one piece with the hauberk, was a cap of chain-mail which was drawn over the head below the helm. Feet and legs were clad in iron hose and the knees and elbows were specially protected by iron plates. Over the harness many knights wore a long sleeveless garment of silk on which their special heraldic device was embroidered, and the sword was girt above this garment. The shield was of wood strengthened by metal bands. It was usually kite-shaped and was held in the left hand close to the body, the spear being carried in the right so that the horse was guided by the knees, not by the reins.[5]

This period saw the dawn of heraldry as we know it today, and there is little doubt that Walter I was the first Clifford to bear the original coat-of-arms − whether on shield, surcoat or banner − of Chequy Or and Azure, a bendlet gules, and that it was with Walter II that it became hereditary. Three important groups of 12th-century families − connected by blood and marriage − took related arms about this time. The first group is based on differenced versions of the *quarterly or and gules* that Dr. Round[6] shows were focused around Geoffrey de Mandeville, Earl of Essex, who was killed in 1144. The second group is based on differenced versions of *or with chevrons gules* of the Clare earls of Hereford and Pembroke. The Cliffords belong to the third group based on differenced versions of the *chequy or and azure*, probably borne originally by Ralph, Count of Vermandois, who died in 1151, grandson of King Henri I of France.[7] The gold-and-blue chequy coat came to England with Count Ralph's sister, Isabel, mother by her first husband of Waleran de Beaumont, Count of Meulan and Earl of Worcester (died 1166) and Robert de Beaumont, Earl of Leicester, who was given the earldom of Hereford by King Stephen in 1139. Isabel's Beaumont descendants bore checkers gold and red by way of difference, while her descendants by her second husband, William de Warenne, Earl of Surrey (died 1138) bore them gold and blue.[8]

That the Cliffords belonged to this 'checkered' group there can be no doubt, but the connection is hard to unravel. Robert de Beaumont, it is true, was married to the heiress of the William FitzOsbern, Earl of Hereford, who first built Clifford Castle more than seventy years before. He and his twin brother[9] had been hereditary enemies of Roger de Toeni, Walter Clifford I's brother-in-law, though Roger had made peace with the twins before the end of 1138. Aside from these tenuous connections, there seems to be no obvious relationship between Walter Clifford and the twins or their Warenne stepfather, nor with their cousins, the Earls of Warwick, who also belonged to the 'checkered' group. Walter I's mother, Maud of Gloucester, was a distant cousin of the Duke of Brittany, whose descendant, Alice, Duchess of Brittany in her own right, sealed in 1214 with checkers and a canton ermine.[10] But if the coat was first assumed by Walter II (which seems unlikely as the Frampton line of his brother Richard, with whom he was on bad terms, also bore it duly differenced) then it may be significant, in view of Walter II's wife being the senior heiress of the Chesneys, that in the reign of Henry II John, Henry and Robert Chesney bore chequy or and azure, a fess gules fretty ermine,[11] which, but for the fretty ermine, is identical with the coat of the then Sir Richard Clifford of Tenbury. It is also worth noting that in 1086 a Ralf de Chesney was an under-tenant of William de Warenne in Sussex and Norfolk.[12] However, the precise reason for the Cliffords deciding at the dawn of heraldry to join the Vermandois/Warenne group with gold and blue checkered coats remains for the present a mystery.

In any case there is no doubt that the Clifford arms date from the very beginning of heraldry. The line of Walter II bore the gold and blue checkers with a red bend or bendlet. The line of his second son, Richard of Frampton, differenced these arms by placing three golden lions passant on the red bend, and what was to become the most important Clifford line, that of Walter II's younger son, Sir Roger of Tenbury, differenced the arms by changing the red bend to a red fess.

Walter II died at a considerable age shortly before 23 January 1221, when the Sheriffs of Wiltshire and Shropshire were ordered to give his lands to Walter Clifford junior, his son and heir. By his wife, Agnes de Condet, Walter II had several children, five sons and at least two daughters:

1. WALTER III, baron of Clifford, for whom see Chapter Seven.
2. Sir ROGER, for whom see Part Two, Chapter Nine. He was the ancestor of the Lords Clifford, Earls of Cumberland and of the Lords Clifford of Chudleigh.
3. RICHARD, still living in 1245.
4. SIMON, Prior of Craswall in Herefordshire before 1231.
5. Sir GILES, for whom see Part Five, Chapter Fifty-Eight. He was the ancestor of the knightly branch of the Cliffords in Devon during the 13th and 14th centuries.
1. BASILIA, mentioned in her mother's will.
2. CECILIA, mentioned in her mother's will.

Chapter Seven

Generation VI – Walter Clifford, Baron of Clifford (1187-1263)

Walter III, who succeeded to the castle and feudal barony of Clifford in 1221, was born in 1187 and appears as a witness to important documents from about 1201. From 1207 onwards, when he is styled Walter de Clifford *juvenis* or junior, he played an increasing part in national affairs, and it is not always possible to distinguish him from his ageing father, Walter II, who retired from being Sheriff of Hereford in the summer of the following year, when Walter III was sent from Winchester on 23 May 1208 by King John to notify his father tactfully that a successor in the Shrievalty had been appointed.

Indeed, Walter III was clearly on good terms with and a strong supporter of King John, from whom some of his fellow barons were soon to wrest Magna Carta. This may perhaps have been the consequence of the unjust installation by Richard Coeur de Lion of Walter's own uncle, Richard Clifford, in Corfham Castle, that had caused so much trouble during Walter III's boyhood. Thus, in February 1210 King John sent personal letters from the Tower of London to Walter III, who in the following year accompanied the king in person to Ireland.

When the baronial crisis came, four great Marcher lords – Walter de Lacy, John of Monmouth, Hugh de Mortimer and Walter Clifford – ranged themselves on the side of the king and of royal authority ... at the head of a force assembled at Gloucester for the king's defence towards the end of April 1215.[1] The first three barons were the lords of Ludlow, Monmouth and Wigmore[2] respectively, but, due to Walter II's probable incapacity or senility, it is possible that the fourth was Walter III rather than his father who led the Clifford forces to the royalist rendezvous. The same doubt arises in May 1216 when Walter Clifford was commissioned to treat with Reginald de Braose concerning the latter's appointment as Keeper of Beauchamp's Castle at Elmley. Certainly Walter III was in high favour with the king when the crisis came to a head early in 1215; but the mobilisation of the Marcher lords in April came too late, for on 15 June 1215 King John was forced to seal Magna Carta at Runnymede. Nevertheless, the king showed his gratitude to his loyal supporters, and in particular to Walter Clifford. On 14 August 1215, during his father's lifetime, Walter III was himself appointed Sheriff of Herefordshire. The sheriff, or *vicomte*, was the royal representative in each county, and possessed far more power than his comparatively modern successor the lord lieutenant. On 18 November 1215 Walter III was made *custos* (royal guardian) of the lands of the See of Hereford, made vacant and temporarily in the hands of the Crown by the death of Bishop Giles de Braose (whose mother had been starved to death by King John at Windsor due to her opposition to the king concerning the lordship of Brecon). On 25 February 1216 Walter Clifford was told to hand over the lands of the See, and in August following Walter de Lacy was appointed his successor in the Shrievalty. That this was no sign of the king's displeasure is shown by a writ of 19 August 1216 whereby the king gave

Dimmoc (or Dymock in Gloucestershire) to Walter III to maintain him in the royal service. The memory of this transaction remains in the continued existence of the hamlet of Clifford's Mesne about two miles from Dymock.

Following the king's death during the autumn of 1216[3] the Dymock estate had been temporarily seized back by the Crown as a royal demesne, but it was restored to Walter on 28 October 1217 by Henry III. The king, however, was but a boy, and the effective power in the land lay with the veteran William Marshal, Earl of Pembroke, as Regent (from whom the descent of Roger, 1st Lord Clifford, afterwards Marshal of England, was to be so proudly set out in the rhyming Roll of the Siege of Caerlaverock in 1300). The insurgent barons had invited Louis, heir to the throne of France, to come to England, but after King John's death most Englishmen rallied to the boy king, Henry III, and by 1217 the French prince had been sent packing.

After his father's death, Walter III had various tax problems. That Clifford itself was a barony there was no doubt,[4] but it had always held a special status 'by courtesy of England' since the time of the Conqueror. As early as 1164, the greater barons like Clifford had received personal summonses to the *Curia Regis*, or King's Court, while ordinary barons and freeholders received a general summons through the local sheriffs, and this distinction was recognised in Magna Carta. But by 1221 the position of baronies in general had become an inland revenue problem: on a baron's death, the heir had to pay a flat tax of £100 relief. This was worth it to the heir if he held more than twenty knights' fees directly from the Crown, as by the end of the 12th century it had become the practice to pay £5 relief on each knight's fee. But if he held less than twenty knights' fees immediately under the Crown (as opposed, for instance, to the various knights' fees in the Clifford holdings under the Honour of Brecknock or the Bishopric of Lincoln), then it paid the new baron to claim his lands were *not* a barony.

Accordingly, on 22 January 1221, Walter Clifford's tax on succeeding to his paternal barony was fixed at £100 relief, the standard payment for a baron, and, indeed, as late as 1240 the authorities were calling his Shropshire tenure of Corfham Castle a barony. But leaving independent Clifford Castle aside because it was held 'by courtesy of England', Walter III claimed that for revenue purposes he did not hold a taxable barony. When he was duly charged the baronial £100 relief, therefore, he petitioned the Crown against this, and an inquisition found that he held of the king in chief by knight's fee and not as a baron. His relief was reduced to £6 13s. 4d. But although by the final relief of 1225 Walter Clifford was excused the baronial relief, the estates of the family were called a barony in the 13th century Book of Fees.[5]

The new Baron of Clifford was already an experienced soldier. The Regent Earl of Pembroke had died and the country was now ruled by the Justiciar, Hubert du Bourg, or de Burgh, afterwards Earl of Kent, who in 1221 demanded that royal castles which had been seized by the barons, and some of which were in the hands of foreigners, should be restored to the Crown. Meanwhile, William Count of Aumale left Court and began a revolt by making war on his neighbours from his castle at Biham in Lincolnshire, plundering the countryside and torturing prisoners. Accordingly, Walter Clifford was present in arms with the 13-year-old king and the papal legate during their six-day siege of Biham Castle, which was captured on 8 February.[6]

In 1224 Henry III wrote in a letter to the Pope on the state of his realm: 'Be pleased to write to Walter and Roger de Clifford firmly enjoining them to promote our affairs with their accustomed diligence and always to stand by us manfully; and be pleased to commend them for laudable proofs of diligence and fidelity already shown'.[7] The brothers continued loyal, and on 25 April 1228 the elder brother, Walter, was appointed Keeper of the royal castles of Cardigan and Carmarthen.[8]

As baron of Clifford, Walter III seems to have done much to convert his own castles at Clifford and Bronllys from largely wooden into completely stone strongholds. Although the killing of the Earl of Hereford by a falling stone, already mentioned above, during the fire at Bronllys in 1175 may imply that at least part of the tower there was already built of stone, its present circular stone donjon tower seems to date from Walter III's time. J. R. Knight[9] is of the opinion that the round keep, which had been introduced by Hubert de Burgh and William Marshal, Earl of Pembroke, and which they had borrowed from France, must be Walter III's work. Entry is at first-floor level, above the battered base. The tower was originally lower, but heightened in the early 14th century. A detailed account of the Clifford castle at Bronllys is given in *Archaeologia Cambrensis*, 3rd Series, no. xxx (April 1862) and need not be repeated here. The writer of this article ascribes the circular tower at Bronllys to the influence of the Crusades, in which it is not improbable that a Clifford may have taken part.

About the same time, Walter Clifford (or maybe his elderly father) appears to have rebuilt Clifford castle in stone. D. J. C. King[9] maintains that no radical change was made to the castle's arrangements until the 13th century. The motte was given stone defences of a highly effective and very expensive nature, a cluster of stout round towers joined by very short curtain walls. Two towers placed very close together, form a gatehouse giving access from the large enclosure on the east. The general form of the plan is hexagonal, but on the north side one of the six towers has been dropped out, and the castle's hall stands here instead. The great hall itself, measuring 36 feet by 17, appears to have been two storeys high.[10]

Castles and warfare featured large in Walter Clifford's life: in 1229 we find him, with two of his knights, on the royal muster roll for Henry III's projected expedition to join the Duke of Brittany in an attempt to recover the English king's former possessions in Normandy. This army assembled at Portsmouth at Michaelmas, but the king, on the point of embarking, found that he had not enough ships and fell into a great and characteristically Angevin rage with the unfortunate Justiciar, Hubert de Burgh. Nevertheless, Henry carried out his campaign the following year with singular lack of success.

This year, Walter III had a violent row with the Prior of Wenlock over the special rights he had in the Forest of Clee which had been given to his grandfather by Henry II for the love of the Fair Rosamund. The Clifford foresters had been wont to levy a certain impost called *doverett* on all lands within the jurisdiction of Clee Forest. Part of the manor of Prior's Ditton, which belonged to the Priory of Wenlock, lay within the forest jurisdiction, but Prior Joybert had come to an agreement with Walter II to relieve the prior's tenants of this liability. Walter III would have none of this, and Prior Imbert sued him in 1230 to observe the convention made by his father. Clifford not only failed to appear in Court, but before the adjourned case could be heard, attacked the prior's men with a force of his own, including the beadle of Corfham.

After much litigation a new convention was agreed by which the prior conceded that Clifford should maintain the same forest rights in the woods of Ditton and Stoke as he maintained in the woods pertaining to the Forest of Clee. The prior was to keep in tillage all lands in the enclosures of Ditton and Stoke which were under tillage at the date of this Fine, also to assart 40 acres more in Pakemore, but he was not to build any house or houses on the assarted land. Clifford conceded that the prior and his successors should quit the customs first alluded to in the Fine (e.g. that the prior or his men at Ditton and Stoke were not to keep any dogs not *expeditated* – i.e. maimed of a paw to prevent them hunting – nor to have pasture for their goats within the woods), and should have certain common pastures and easements. The prior should moreover have his own foresters in his demesne woods at Ditton and Stoke, provided they swore fealty to Clifford concerning the good care to be taken of his venison. These men should be dealt with in Clifford's own court in cases of malfeasance.[11]

Walter's first wife, Isabel, died without issue, and in July 1232 another great Marcher baron, John de Braose, lord of Bramber and Gower, died, and before 2 November that same year Walter[12] Clifford married secondly his widow, Margaret, daughter of Llywelyn the Great, Prince of Wales. This wise prince, then the most important descendant in the direct male line of the ancient British fifth-century king, Coel Hen (Old King Cole), was one of the most remarkable of Welsh dynasts. By repressing dissensions and enforcing obedience among the Welsh chieftains, and later by allying himself with the English barons against his suzerain, Llywelyn, during a reign of 44 years, was enabled to give a considerable amount of peace and prosperity to his country, which he persistently sought to rule as an independent sovereign, although acknowledging a personal vassalage to the king of England.[13] Meanwhile, Walter III, while as yet childless, had kept control of the succession within his own family; and on 16 December 1231 he had paid a fine of £100 in order to have the custody and right of choosing the marriage of the heirs of his deceased brother, Roger Clifford (ancestor of the Earls of Cumberland and of the present lords Clifford of Chudleigh).

Less than two years later, a conflict arose in Wales and elsewhere between the Marcher lords and Henry III, whose foreign favourites they much disliked. For example, the king had once made over 19 out of the 35 sheriffdoms in England to the nephew of his Poitevin chancellor, Pierre des Roches, Bishop of Winchester. In the summer of 1233 the crisis came to a head, and in August, Henry, abandoning a scheme for an expedition to Ireland, established himself in the West Country with the intention of bringing the recalcitrant barons to heel. After taking measures against Walter Clifford, the king laid siege to the castle of Usk. His failure to take it, however, led to a brief peace, which lasted until the following October.[14]

Walter III had sided with the rebel barons led by Richard, the Earl Marshal, who ordered the arrest of the rebellious barons and gave their lands to the Poitevins. Walter's manor of Corfham was seized and similar writs were sent to the sheriffs of Kent, Oxfordshire and Lincolnshire to seize the Clifford lands in those counties. Walter's treason was short-lived, however. A Patent dated 1 September 1233 gives safe conduct through the king's land to Richard Fitz Simon and others of Clifford's men who were in garrison at Clifford Castle. A second Patent gives Walter a safe conduct himself to come to the king to treat for peace. On 17 March 1234 Clifford Castle was restored to Walter by the king.

In spite of this treasonable behaviour, Walter Clifford continued to lead a somewhat litigious life. In 1238 he quarrelled with the Prior of Little Malvern and again in 1243 and 1244. At the same time, he made generous gifts to Haughmond Abbey, Abbey Dore and Salop Abbey, though he continued peppery about his rights in Forest Law. In October 1253 he sued William Mauduit, William Fitz John and Hugh de Dudmaston for taking a boar in his forest of Corfham and won his case.

By now Walter III was getting on in years, and had an only daughter by his wife, the Welsh princess. The succession to his powerful position was therefore of some importance to the king, who by a Patent of April 1244 intimated that a contract of marriage should be made between Walter's daughter and heiress, Maud Clifford, and one of the sons of Sir William Longsword (Longespée), the eldest son and heir of the Earl of Salisbury, for the outcome of which see the next chapter.

The lord of Clifford remained cantankerous about King Henry III, whom he clearly did not like as much as he had his father, King John, and once again, in January 1250, he appeared in a rebellious mood,[15] when he was accused of violent and disgraceful treatment of a King's Messenger, whom he had compelled to swallow, seal and all, the royal epistle of which he was the bearer. Clifford, submitting to the king's sentence, hardly escaped forfeiture and death. He lost his franchises and was fined 1,000 marks, and was banished to his estates. He continued to have legal difficulties, especially after the temporary loss of his franchises at Corfham, and was engaged in a law-suit with John de Braose when his appeal stood for hearing before the king himself in Michaelmas Term 1260, but was adjourned because John de Braose failed to appear. The eventual outcome was a Patent of 6 May 1262, by which Corfham Castle was restored to Walter 'seeing that the said Walter had recovered seisin thereof against John de Breus' (Braose).

Walter III Clifford, last baron Clifford in the male line, died in December 1263. By his second wife, Margaret, daughter of Llywelyn, Prince of Wales, he had an only daughter, Maud, for whom see Chapter Eight. She carried Clifford Castle and the other estates to her own descendants and their heirs.

A touching sequel to this account of Walter III's energetic life is that in 1230 he had, for now unknown reasons, enfeoffed Walter de Lacy's daughter Catherine in a small estate at Burley, a part of his lands of Culmington attached to the Manor of Corfham. Some thirty years later, between 1257 and 1262, she granted the whole holding, which she held of Sir Walter Clifford in the Manor of Corfham, to the Church of the Holy Cross at Aconbury, and to the Prioress and Nuns there serving God: to maintain a chaplain at Aconbury to celebrate daily mass for the health of the said Walter Clifford and Margaret, his wife, and Dame Maud de Longespée, their daughter, and Margaret Longespée, her daughter. Catherine de Lacy's sister, Maud de Lacy, had married Geoffrey de Joinville, Seigneur de Vaucouleurs, Mery-sur-Seine, Soudron and Etrelles, brother of Jean de Joinville, the friend and biographer of St Louis.[16] He was one of the 'foreigners' befriended by Henry III. By Maud de Lacy Geoffrey de Vaucouleurs had nine children, the eldest of whom, Pierre, inherited the Lacy estates in Wales, Herefordshire and Shropshire, and the youngest of whom, Catherine, became in time Prioress of Aconbury. This French connection is significant in the light of later marriage ties of the Cliffords which will be discussed in Part Two, Chapter Ten.

The heart of Margaret, the widow of Walter III, was buried in Aconbury Church near Hereford, where her tomb bears the arms of Clifford with the Dragon of Wales.

Chapter Eight

Generation VII – Maud, Heiress of Clifford (c. 1240-82)

Maud Clifford, the only daughter and heiress of Walter III, Baron of Clifford, was from her birth a great match. By a Patent of 30 April 1244, referred to in the previous chapter, Henry III signified to her father, while she was still an infant, that a contract of marriage should be made between Maud and one of the sons of Sir William Longespée, the eldest son and heir of the Earl of Salisbury, who, as we have already seen, was an illegitimate son of Henry II, perhaps, but not probably, by the Fair Rosamund Clifford.

The Damsel of Clifford was still very young then, so the marriage was not consummated until about ten years later, by which time the bridegroom's father himself had fallen in battle on Crusade, fighting heroically against the Saracens at Mansourah on the Nile, before he could succeed to the earldom of Salisbury. Maud's own husband, the second Sir William Longespée, died before he, too, could succeed to the earldom in 1257 from injuries received at a tournament at Blyth in Nottinghamshire in June 1256.

The king designed Maud as a wife for Geoffrey de Lusignan[1] (the king's near relation of a branch of the family who were kings of Cyprus and Jerusalem, and who claimed descent from the water-sprite, Melusine), but she was kidnapped instead and forcibly married by Sir John Giffard of Brimpsfield, afterwards – when parliamentary peerages were first evolved – 1st Lord Giffard. The Giffards were a proud and ancient house, whose head had been a cousin of the Conqueror, and had brought 30 longships full of retainers with him to the battle of Hastings nearly two centuries before. Maud Longespée notified the king that John Giffard had abducted her from her manor of Canford in Dorset and taken her against her will to his castle at Brimpsfield and detained her there. Giffard appeared before the king and professed himself ready to prove that he had not abducted the lady against her will, and offered a fine of 300 marks for the marriage already contracted, as it was said, between them, provided she made no further complaint against him. On 10 March 1270-1 the king ordained that if she were not content, the fine in question would be void and Giffard should stand trial a month from Easter. As Maud was too unwell to appear before the king, commissioners were sent to inquire into the truth of the matter and to report back to the king.[2] By Giffard, Maud had three, perhaps four, daughters.[3] By her first husband, Sir William Longespée, she had one daughter, who was the principal heiress. She died in December 1282.

MARGARET Longespée, *de jure* Countess of Salisbury in her own right, inherited the Salisbury and Clifford estates and married Henry de Lacy, Earl of Lincoln, in 1256.

Meanwhile, the male line of the House of Clifford was continued by the descendants of Maud's uncle, Sir Roger Clifford, for whom see Parts Two and Three below.

If Maud Clifford and her father Walter III had never lived, the present lords Clifford of Chudleigh could never have been born, for Eleanor Giffard, one of Maud Clifford's three daughters by her vigorously rapist second husband, the 1st Lord Giffard, married Fulk, 1st Lord Strange of Blackmere according to the new parliamentary peerage that was being evolved out of the old nobility. The heiress of her line carried the Strange of Blackmere barony to the lords Talbot, of whom the celebrated John Talbot, 1st Earl of Shrewsbury, K.G., was Joan of Arc's great adversary at the end of the Hundred Years War, and who was slain at the battle of Castillon in 1453, after having been victorious in 40 pitched battles. His descendant Gilbert Talbot, 7th Earl of Shrewsbury, K.G. had a daughter, Alathea, who married Thomas Howard, Earl of Arundel, whose eventual heiress – thus also a co-heiress of the original barons of Clifford – married the 9th Lord Petre, whose grandson, the 11th Lord Petre, was the father of Agnes Petre, wife of Charles Hugh, 8th Lord Clifford of Chudleigh, and thus through her all the subsequent lords Clifford also descend from the last feudal baron of Clifford Castle itself.

PART TWO

THE LORDS CLIFFORD, EARLS OF CUMBERLAND

Chapter Nine

Generation VI – Roger Clifford, Marcher Lord (1214-31)

Sir Roger Clifford, second son of Walter II, baron of Clifford, is of particular genealogical significance. As his elder brother, Walter III, the last baron of Clifford, left no male heir, it was through Roger that the male line continued, and from him the subsequent historic peerage branches of the Cliffords descended.

Sir Roger's mother and father, anxious to find a suitable bride for their son, stayed their hand until Sybilla, the daughter of their neighbour, Robert de Ewyas, became available. Sybilla was already the widow of Robert de Tregos before she married William de Newmarch, who conveniently died without issue in 1211. Having set their sights on Sybilla they did everything in their power to bring about this marriage.

In September 1213 the king granted Roger the service of five knights from the Honour of Kington in Herefordshire; possibly a temporary gift arising from the king's action against William de Braose. In 1214 Roger's father paid King John the vast sum of £1,000 for the hand and estates of his neighbour, Sybilla, who was her father's sole heiress of a considerable Herefordshire barony on the Welsh March, and before 13 February 1217 she was married to Sir Roger Clifford. As she had already had a son, Robert II de Tregos, Sir Roger only acquired control of her substantial Marcher baronial estates during her lifetime, but they comprised no less than 19 knights' fees.[1]

Sir Roger inherited from his father manors in Herefordshire and Worcestershire, including Tenbury, and during his lifetime the control over his wife's properties made him as important, if not more so, than his elder brother, Walter. The lady whom Sir Roger had married was herself extremely well connected, for she was the only daughter of Robert II de Ewyas, baron of Ewyas Harold. He was the son of Robert de Ewyas, son of Harold de Sudeley, to whom William Rufus gave the barony of Ewyas, which became known as Ewyas Harold after him. The castlery of Ewyas Harold was the oldest Norman settlement in the district of the Black Mountain and Golden Valley in Herefordshire. The motte and bailey were constructed about 1046 by Harold de Sudeley's father, Earl Ralph the Timid, and the tower re-erected by Earl William FitzOsbern.[2]

Sybilla's lineage is of exceptional interest. She came from a Frankish family of the highest rank which had held an earldom in Anglo-Saxon England before the Conquest. Count Ralph the Timid was Earl of Worcestershire and Herefordshire and also of Oxfordshire.[3] He died on 21 December 1057. He was the son of Dru, Count of Amiens and the Vexin by his wife, Godgifu (who married secondly Eustace II, Count of Boulogne), sister of King Edward the Confessor and daughter of King Aethelred the Unready. Count Dru, Earl Ralph's father, was the son of Walter II the White, Count de Valois, Amiens and the Vexin, son of Walter I, Count of Amiens and probably also of Valois and the Vexin (who died between 992 and 998). He descended in all probability through the Nibelungen counts of the Vexin in the direct male line from Count Childrebrand (died 752), paternal uncle of the Emperor Charlemagne.[4]

The armorial rolls of the reign of Henry III show that Sir Roger Clifford was the first to assume the red fess instead of the red bend over the gold-and-blue chequers on the original Clifford coat of arms by way of difference from the arms of his father and elder brother, the last barons of Clifford. This is the coat still borne by his descendants, the lords Clifford of Chudleigh, today.

In 1218 Sir Roger was summoned by the Regent to muster at Stamford in the royal army, which proceeded to besiege and capture Newark Castle from Robert de Gaugy. His elder brother, Walter junior, also turned up, and their aged father sent two knights, but they were not required to bring their whole military force with them. Later, Roger was to fight for Henry III in France and on the Welsh border. As mentioned earlier, King Henry III wrote to the Pope in 1224 asking him to write to Walter and Roger Clifford, firmly enjoining them to promote his affairs with diligence and always to stand by him. Two years later, in 1226, Sir Roger appears among the baronial tenants-in-chief of the Crown.[5]

In 1228 Henry III granted the castle and lordship of Montgomery to the powerful Justiciar of England, Hubert de Burgh, who promptly caused a Welsh crisis by giving orders for preparations to invade Wales by clearing the forest which protected that part of the border. This made war with Prince Llywelyn inevitable. The leading men of the March, the Earls of Gloucester and Pembroke, William de Braose, Roger Clifford and others, had been summoned to Montgomery, but the English had little zeal for the enterprise which they saw as a means of making the Justiciar even richer than he was already, so everything went badly for the king, and in October there was a humiliating retreat before Llywelyn's forces. This showed the Welsh prince that he had little to fear henceforth from the English.[6]

The following year Henry III collected an army at Portsmouth intending to cross to Brittany to join its duke in an invasion of France, but, as already mentioned, the expedition had to be put off for lack of transports. Sir Roger Clifford had been summoned but had failed to turn up, and his name appears on the muster roll as a defaulter. However, he was given a letter of protection to come in April 1230 and duly sailed to France with the king in May.[7]

Sir Roger's default may have been due to ill-health, for, although he was a witness in about 1230 to his brother Walter's gift of Burley at Culmington in the manor of Corfham to Catherine de Lacy, he was dead by 16 December 1231, when his brother bought from the king the right to the custody and marriage of his heirs, thus keeping control of their future in the family.[8] His tomb effigy at Abbey Dore can still be seen.

By his wife, Sybilla de Ewyas, who died in 1236, Sir Roger had two sons who survived him:

1. Sir ROGER, Marcher Lord and Crusader, for whom see Chapter Ten.
2. Sir HUGH, witness with his elder brother, to their uncle Walter Clifford's confirmation charter of Catherine de Lacy's grant of Burley to the church of Aconbury between 1257 and 1262.[9]

Chapter Ten

Generation VII – Roger Clifford, Marcher Lord and Crusader (1221-85)

Roger Clifford succeeded his father, the first Sir Roger, as lord of the manors of Tenbury and Bruges, and also to his other estates, in 1231, when his uncle, Walter, last baron of Clifford, paid King Henry III in a fine of £100 for his custody and marriage, i.e. the decision whom he should marry in due course, for young Roger was still a minor at his father's death. The great estates of his mother, Sybilla de Ewyas, passed at her death shortly before 1 July 1236 to his elder half-brother, Robert de Tregos. Ewyas Harold in Herefordshire naturally descended to her son by her first marriage, as did Lydiard in Wiltshire which later became the present-day Lydiard Tregos. Robert de Tregos' son John was summoned to Parliament as Lord Tregos from 1299.[1]

Roger Clifford's mother Sybilla, as a wealthy widow once again, does not seem to have followed in the footsteps of her own grandmother and namesake, widow of Robert I, baron of Ewyas Harold, of whose last illness Geraldus Cambrensis[2] tells us: 'The monks of Dore, knowing that she was rich, and would leave much money ... visited her assiduously, and never ceased from their solicitations until they made her a monk with tonsure and cowl complete'. The widowed Dame Sybilla Clifford, on the other hand, appears to have overspent, as in 1242 young Roger Clifford's elder half-brother, Robert de Tregos, owed money to Ursell ben Hamon, a Jewish moneylender in Hereford, because of their mother's extravagances. Indeed, Robert also owed money to King Henry III, who in 1254 was personally to act as a surety for him to borrow 100 marks in Bordeaux, but eventually orders were given for a balance to be struck between Robert's debts to the king and the debts which the king owed him. Meanwhile, Roger Clifford came of age in 1242, when he in turn was summoned to pay his father's debts.

Shortly before his death, Roger Clifford's father had obtained for him in 1230 a grant from the king of the marriage of John de Botterel's widow, Hawise or Avice, daughter and co-heiress of James de Neufmarché, baron of North Cadbury in Somerset who owned vast Welsh estates as well, but (perhaps because of his father's death so soon afterwards) the marriage did not take place, and Hawise married secondly instead Nicholas de Molis. The name of Roger's first wife, the mother of his son (also called Roger), has therefore not been ascertained at present.[3]

Roger Clifford was high in favour at Court as a young man. In 1246 he was granted £30 a year until the king could find lands of that value for him. In 1250 Sir Roger was one of the knights who accompanied Richard de Clare, Earl of Gloucester, on a pilgrimage to the shrine of St James at Compostella in Spain, when they were entertained on the way by the Pope himself at Lyons. In 1255 Roger was lord of Mapledurham in Oxfordshire; and the next year the king gave him special hunting privileges in the royal forests. Later, he was granted a further 50 marks a year until the king could find wards or escheats for him, and by March 1259 he was one of a group of young men who supported Prince Edward, whom he accompanied to France the following year.[4]

Indeed, Roger Clifford was to make his mark on English history, being the second of the more than two dozen Cliffords whose lives are thought worthy of record in the *Dictionary of National Biography*. This tells us of Roger that 'in 1259 he was among the suite of Henry III in France during the negotiations for the treaty of peace which was concluded in that year with Louis IX. Three years later suspicions of his loyalty were aroused by a letter which, as representing the Marcher barons, he sent to the king urging upon him the observance of the provisions of Oxford, and he was forbidden to joust or appear in arms, particularly during the king's absence overseas, without royal licence. The effect of this injunction was, however, neutralised by a commission issued almost simultaneously, and doubtless at the instance of de Montfort, by which he was placed in command of the royal castles of Ludgershall and Marlborough'.

At this time Henry III's policies were very unpopular, and, at the 'Mad Parliament' held at Oxford in 1258, the barons had framed the celebrated Provisions of Oxford referred to above, limiting his powers. Their leader was the king's own brother-in-law, Simon de Montfort, Earl of Leicester, whom Roger Clifford supported at this stage. However, three years later the king obtained a papal bull absolving him from his oath to observe the Provisions.

In 1263, the landing of Simon de Montfort at the end of April, after a short absence abroad, marks the beginning of the Civil War. Simon now placed himself at the head of the party of reform and organised it for war. The Welsh March was still the stronghold of the baronial interest, and it was here that the struggle broke out. About the end of June an attack was made on the bishop of Hereford, who had been persuaded to return to his diocese, by a coalition which included Roger Clifford, John FitzAlan (Lord of Arundel), Humphrey de Bohun (eldest son of the Earl of Hereford), the young Earl Gilbert of Gloucester and Hamo Lestrange (son of the lord of Knokin). Bishop Peter and his Savoyard canons were captured in their cathedral and shut up in the castle of Eardisley. The allies next took possession of Gloucester, Worcester and Bridgnorth until they had made themselves supreme in the West.[5] Eardisley Castle, which had belonged to Walter de Baskerville, a stronghold on the Welsh border, was one of the many properties which were transferred to Roger Clifford after Baskerville was attainted following the battle of Evesham. Although Baskerville was pardoned in 1274 his lands were to be retained by Roger Clifford till the latter died, so Eardisley, .Orcop and several other Baskerville properties remained in Roger's hands between 1265 and 1285.[6] For the sacrilege of imprisoning the bishop, Clifford and Baskerville, with Earl Simon himself and others, were excommunicated by Boniface, Archbishop of Canterbury. Roger later abandoned the baronial cause and reverted to the king, leaving Baskerville to take the consequences.

That same year Sir Macy de Bescile, a Frenchman, was made sheriff and constable of Gloucester by the king, which so offended the barons that they prevailed on Sir Roger Clifford to march on Gloucester, where he laid siege to the castle and burnt the bridge across the Severn. He entered the town, took the Frenchman prisoner and captured the castle.[7] Roger's principal companion-in-arms in ravaging the Welsh

Marches and taking Hereford and Bristol was Roger de Leyburn, a powerful baron who had temporarily broken with Prince Edward and was also on the barons' side.[8]

In December 1263, Roger's uncle Walter, the last lord of Clifford, died, and at his uncle's prompting Roger at once broke with the baronial cause and became a leading royalist. He held Hereford Castle for the king in November and December 1263, playing a prominent part in the siege of Nottingham and taking prisoner Simon de Montfort the younger at the capture of that city, which the earl's son had defended with great gallantry. Earl Simon's alliance with their enemy, Prince Llywelyn of Wales, had driven the Marcher lords to the king's side. Henry now rewarded Roger Clifford with lands in Monmouth and by appointing him to succeed the deposed Macy de Bescile as Sheriff of Gloucester and governor of Gloucester Castle, of which he had of course taken possession by force the previous year.[9]

Roger Clifford and his friend Roger de Leyburn both fought for Henry III at the battle of Lewes on 14 May 1264, being taken prisoner together with the king himself and his eldest son, Prince Edward, by the victorious Earl Simon. The two Marcher lords were released and allowed to return home, as were other lords Marcher who had escaped from the battlefield, on giving hostages that they would come to Parliament when summoned to stand trial by their peers. But they did not attend de Montfort's 'Parliament' at Midsummer 1264. Ironically, had Roger attended, the subsequent peerage barony of Clifford might have been retrospectively accorded precedence, thus becoming the parliamentary premier barony of England. Instead, Roger Mortimer, James of Audley, Roger Clifford, Roger Leyburn, Hamo Lestrange and the knights of Turberville, with many others from the Welsh Marches who had escaped from the battlefield of Lewes, having assembled their forces, stirred up war in the Marches and tried to resist the barons. Therefore, Simon de Montfort made an alliance with Prince Llywelyn of Wales and advanced on them with a large army,[10] reducing them to nominal submission. Roger Clifford, Roger de Leyburn and Roger Mortimer were banished for a year to Ireland, where they each had estates, but they did not go,[11] as they now had the tacit support of the Earl of Gloucester, who had quarrelled with de Montfort, whom he feared was becoming over-mighty.

During 1264 and 1265, while Henry III was a captive, Roger Clifford was associated with Roger de Mortimer and Hamo Lestrange in those fabricated patents which de Montfort devised for the purpose of getting rid of the Marcher lords.[12] However, Roger Clifford and Roger de Leyburn pretended to come to terms with de Montfort's government, and in December 1264 were permitted to meet the king at Pershore and to visit the prince at Kenilworth. After taking up arms again, Clifford and Leyburn obtained a safe-conduct and were allowed to have an historic interview with the captive Prince Edward at Hereford Castle in May 1265. They had contrived a plan with Roger de Mortimer for the prince's escape, and were thus able secretly to brief Edward, who was furnished with a specially swift horse ostensibly as a present. The prince's young chamberlain, Sir Thomas de Clare (whose daughter was long afterwards to marry Roger's grandson, Lord Clifford) had been knighted by Simon de Montfort personally before the battle of Lewes, but as he was the brother of the Earl of Gloucester was himself now becoming disillusioned with Simon's regime and joined the plot, keeping Prince Edward in touch with the Marcher lords. As a result, on 28 May the prince made his escape. While outside the castle confines for recreation he rode the horses of several of his keepers one after another as though to try their speed, and, when he had tired them out, mounted his own fresh, swift steed and galloped away with Thomas de Clare, another household knight and four squires towards Wigmore, where Roger de Mortimer and Roger Clifford rode out to meet him with a strong force and banners flying, and drove off his pursuers.[13]

The prince's escape was a signal for the royalist leaders to bestir themselves. On 25 July, Roger Clifford ejected its Welsh mistress from the manor of Culmington and took possession of it himself. Ten days later he fought under Prince Edward at Evesham, and 14 days after that the liberated king gave him custody of all the forests south of the Trent.[14] The Welsh mistress of Culmington was, of course, his aunt, Margaret, the widow of Walter III and the aunt of his enemy Llywelyn ap Gruffyd, Prince of Wales, who had been left dowered there less than two years before.[15]

The lords Marcher were the principal generals under Prince Edward at the battle of Evesham, and the divisions they commanded ensured his sweeping victory. Simon de Montfort's army was completely defeated and he himself slain. His head and testicles were sent as a grisly trophy to Mortimer's wife at Wigmore. One of the few barons in Montfort's army to survive the battle was John FitzJohn, who was wounded but taken prisoner through the intervention of Roger Clifford. His forfeited estates were temporarily granted to Gloucester and Clifford, who seem to have been his friends, for they were soon restored to him. John FitzJohn's sister, Isabel, was the widow of Robert de Vipont, Lord of Westmorland, who had died less than two months before the battle, leaving two enormously rich daughters as his co-heiresses, wards of the Crown. The king accordingly rewarded Clifford and Leyburn by granting them the wardship and marriage of the two Vipont girls for their sons. Sadly, this soon led to a quarrel between the two old friends about their sons' respective share of the vast Vipont estates.

Besides also making him Justice of the Royal Forests south of the Trent, the grateful King Henry III further rewarded Roger Clifford with extensive estates in Warwickshire and Leicestershire; released him from a debt he owed the king of £399 17s. 0d.; granted him (January 1266) the manor of Birmingham, nucleus site of the present city of Birmingham, and in 1269 appointed him one of the itinerant justices for Rutland, Surrey (where he had a residence near Guildford), Hampshire, Dorset, Somerset and Gloucester.

Roger also held on to Culmington by a series of legal manoeuvres, and when the Welsh princess, Margaret Clifford, tried to sue him for its recovery, he had himself impleaded for the manor by one Walter of Wanford, who nominally entered into possession on 24 June 1270 but promptly made it over to Clifford's son, young Roger, two days later. She complained to the king in person, and an inquest was held at Ludlow on 11 October 1272, but it is not clear whether she ever recovered the manor. However, after their deaths the manors passed anyway by Walter Clifford's deed of 1254 to her late husband's heirs.

Meanwhile Roger Clifford had taken the Cross, and gone on crusade with Prince Edward. He was blessed by the papal legate, Cardinal Ottoboni, and set out for the East with the prince and his force of about a thousand men-at-arms in the summer of 1270. It was a small army for the purpose, but unfortunately, though many of the other English nobles had agreed to accompany them, one by one most of them made their excuses and left. Among those who kept to their oaths and came, however, was Gloucester's brother, Thomas de Clare, and Roger de Leyburn came with them as far as Paris. The prince was accompanied by his wife, Eleanor of Castile.

The crusaders intended to join St Louis, the King of France, at Tunis, but when they reached Africa, they found the saintly king was already dead and his demoralised army was preparing to return to France. Disillusioned at the lack of enthusiasm among their allies, the English crusaders sailed from Africa, wintered in Sicily, went on to Cyprus, and then landed at Acre in the Holy Land on 9 May 1271. As Chesterton put it of another historic English Catholic family, 'the Clifford's pennon saw Palestine'.

At this time the crusader kingdom of Jerusalem had been reduced to the narrow coastal plain from Acre to Sidon, together with access for Christians to Nazareth by the pilgrim road. At Acre, which was now besieged by the Moslems, Prince Edward was joined by Hugh de Lusignan, King of Jerusalem and Cyprus, and by Prince Bohemond of Antioch. Prince Edward was in his early thirties, an able, vigorous and cold-blooded man who had already shown his gifts as a statesman in dealing with his father's rebels. His brother Edmund of Lancaster, one time candidate for the Sicilian throne, followed him with reinforcements a few months later. Edward was horrified by the state of affairs in Outremer. He knew that his own army was small, but he hoped to unite the Christians of the East into a formidable body and then to use the help of the Mongols to attack the Moslems. Failing to get much support, he could only undertake limited expeditions against the Saracens.

A month after relieving Acre, Prince Edward and his Christian warriors took Nazareth, slew all they found there, and routed a force that tried to cut off their return. At midsummer they won another victory at Haifa, and advanced as far as Castle Pilgrim. The prince then led the English and Frankish crusaders across Mount Carmel to raid the Saracens in the Plain of Sharon. But his troops were too few for him even to attempt to storm the little Mameluke fortress of Qaqun which guarded the road across the hills.[16] Nevertheless, it gave Sir Roger Clifford and his fellow crusaders opportunities to strike some blows against the infidel.

After a year of desultory campaigning, Prince Edward realised that he could achieve no more, and felt obliged to make a truce with the Sultan Baibars, 'the greatest enemy to Christendom since Saladin'. This did not save him from a murderous attempt by a member of the secret sect of Assassins, who gave their name to political slaying, when he was seriously wounded with a poisoned dagger and lingered near death, making his last testament. All this time, Sir Roger was one of the little group of nobles with the prince, and indeed was so much esteemed by him that he was one of the executors of Prince Edward's will, made at Acre in 1272.[17] That autumn he accompanied the prince when the crusaders embarked again on their homeward journey.

In Sicily, on their unhurried way back, the crusaders learnt of the death of Henry III. Thus both Roger Clifford and Thomas de Clare were among the few men of consequence in daily contact with King Edward I at the time of his accession, and able to do homage at once.[18] They had many adventures in Italy and France, taking the best part of a year on the journey, and pacifying turbulent Gascony on their way. In 1273, Sir Roger was a witness to the marriage contract by which King Edward agreed to marry his eldest daughter to the eldest son of King Pedro of Aragon.[19] At about this time Roger Clifford himself married in France, as his second wife, a mysterious lady variously described as the Countess of Loretto, Lorette or Lauretania, whom he is said to have married at Saint-Georges near the castle of Beaufort.[20] There are two possible theories concerning this lady's identity. She may have been the Dame de Lorette-sur-Loire, though there is nothing to identify her as such beyond the fact that the marriage took place at St Georges-du-Bois, near Beaufort-en-Vallée (Maine-et-Loire) not far from Angers. A more probable candidate is a member of the noble family of Milly-en-Gatinois. Perenelle de Milly, Countess of Loretto in Italy in the early 14th century, was the daughter of Geoffrey de Milly, Seneschal of the Kingdom of Naples during the last couple of decades of the 13th century. The family had been prominent in Outremer and with the Templars from the 12th century, and was closely related by blood and marriage to the families of Joinville and Dampierre. It will be remembered that Geoffrey de Joinville, Comte de Vaucouleurs, had married the Cliffords' neighbour Maud de Lacy, and their daughter, Jeanne de Joinville was the wife of Roger Mortimer, while two of her sisters were nuns at Aconbury. Guy de Dampierre, Count of Flanders, Marquis of Namur, had taken part in the crusade to Tunis in 1270, and was present at the deathbed of St Louis. He had 19 children by his two wives, and his third son, Philip de Dampierre, was created Count of Chieti in the kingdom of Naples. It is probable that Roger Clifford's wife was a member of one of these families, and that his marriage would have strengthened the already existing bonds between the Cliffords and these powerful French nobles. As to the place of marriage, Sir Iain Moncreiffe suggests St-Georges-de-Reneins (Rhone) not far from Villefranche-sur-Saône, where Edward I and a thousand picked men fought a strange melé with the Count of Chalons, in response to the count's challenge received while the crusaders had passed through Italy.[21] This would certainly be closer to the Milly, Joinville and Dampierre estates than Saint Georges-du-Bois.

At last they arrived home, where Roger Clifford was at once sent with William de Beauchamp into Wales in 1274 to examine the state of the border and to exact reparations for breaches of the peace. But in 1275 Clifford was sent back as ambassador to France, to explain to King Philip III le Hardi why King Edward was unwilling to act as arbitrator in a dispute between the Duke of Burgundy and the Count of Nivernais.[22] However, he was home again in time to take part in the preparations the following year for war on the Welsh March, where Prince Llywelyn was causing trouble. Edward I's ships had intercepted and captured the late Earl Simon de Montfort's daughter on her way to marry the Welsh prince and to revive the cause of disaffected barons.

In August 1277 the invasion of Wales began. King Edward marched against Llywelyn in the north, while the Earls of Lincoln and Hereford and Edmund of Lancaster led other armies in the south. Roger de Mortimer, Roger Clifford and other Marcher lords also attacked South Wales. Llywelyn was utterly defeated; he was forced to throw himself on Edward's mercy and agreed to the Treaty of Conway.

Accordingly, Roger Clifford was appointed sole Justiciar of Wales in 1279 with a jurisdiction extending for the first time over the whole of the principality.[23] It was Edward's intention to bring all Wales under English law, and Clifford set about this task with the utmost severity, arousing bitter anger among the native Welsh. What followed in 1282 is related by the chronicler in *Flores Historiarum*.

At the dead of night on Palm Sunday, Llywelyn, Prince of Wales, and David, his brother, surrounded the castles of Rhuddlan and Flint with a large army, and destroyed such other castles of the king as they could effect an entrance into, and having wounded, taken prisoner, and loaded with chains, that noble and illustrious knight, the Lord Roger Clifford, after having first slain all his friends, they sent him across, suddenly and unexpectedly, to the mountain of Snowdon, slaying all they met with, young and old, women and children, in their beds, and devastating afterwards with plunder and conflagration the greater part of the Marches. The king, hearing of this, but scarcely believing it ... and having assembled an army, he reduced all Wales ... under his authority. ... The head of Prince Llywelyn was cut off and carried to London, where it was placed on a stake and crowned with ivy, and erected for a long time on the top of the Tower of London.[24]

The leader of Roger Clifford's actual assailants in this general uprising was Prince Llywelyn's brother, David, who was afterwards hanged, drawn and quartered. Clifford had been asleep at Hawarden Castle in Flint on the eve of Palm Sunday when the castle was surprised and he was dragged off as a fettered captive to Snowdon, but only after being wounded very severely, in the end mortally, after a desperate struggle. So it was that this dramatic assault on King Edward's old friend and justiciar, Roger Clifford, was the occasion for the final conquest of Wales.

The wounded warrior justiciar was duly liberated from his imprisonment on Snowdon, but sadly his son and heir, Sir Roger Clifford the younger, had been killed in action during the campaign, and the old Marcher lord died of his wounds in or about 1285. His estate being in debt to the Crown, execution was ordered on his personal goods in 1286, the jewels of his widow, the Countess, being especially exempted by the writ. Before his death, he had made over to the City of London certain property which he held in the Jewry.[25]

By his first wife, Roger Clifford had a son:

Sir ROGER, the younger, for whom see the next chapter. Roger Clifford's second wife, the mysterious Countess of Loretto, survived him. Soon after their marriage, while still in France, at La Rochelle on the morrow of St Valentine's Day 1274 Roger Clifford and the Countess had sold to Queen Eleanor his manor of Ratouthe in Ireland for £500 sterling. Throughout their marriage and in widowhood, continuing marks of the royal favour to her are recorded. In 1278, there was an order to cause the Countess de Lorett, wife of Roger Clifford to have 12 oaks for timber by the king's gift; in 1279 an order was given for her to have ten oak trunks for fuel; in 1293 the countess, as a widow, was given protection for two years on going beyond the seas; in 1295, protection was renewed for the widowed countess staying beyond the seas; and in 1296, the Treasurer and barons of the Exchequer were ordered to cause to be restored to her her lands, goods and chattels, if they were taken into the king's hands solely because she was an alien, as she had gone to parts beyond the seas under the king's protection.[26] The countess died in 1301, and was buried in Worcester Cathedral.[27] It is possible that by the countess Roger had a son, who fought at the battle of Falkirk in 1298 and who is also buried at Worcester near the Countess. The evidence is purely circumstantial, but it is strongly suggestive that this young man died in his twenties before his mother.[28]

6. (*left*) The keep of Appleby Castle, Cumbria, from the south-east.

7. (*below*) Brough Castle, Cumbria: the south front and Clifford's Tower.

Chapter Eleven

Generation VIII – Sir Roger Clifford (1248-82)

After playing so prominent a part in the escape of Prince Edward and the victory of Evesham, young Roger Clifford's father, the Marcher lord, had, as we have seen, been rewarded by King Henry III with a grant for his son of the land and hand of Isabel, elder daughter and senior co-heiress of Robert de Vipont, Lord of Westmorland, and in 1269 young Roger duly married her. She was then aged about fifteen.[1]

Isabel's father, a great northern baron who had died on 7 June 1264,[2] had left vast estates, including the Honour of Appleby and Brough, with the castles of Appleby, Brough, Brougham and Pendragon, also the hereditary sheriffdom of Westmorland, as well as manors in other counties. The Norman surname Vipont, or Vieux Pont, means 'Old Bridge', and was rendered in charter Latin as 'de Veteri Ponte'. Their extensive baronial position in Westmorland had been given by King John to Robert's grandfather, Robert I de Vipont in 1202-3, after he distinguished himself in John's great victory at Mirebeau in France, where that king's unfortunate nephew, Arthur of Brittany, was captured.[3] Robert I was succeeded in 1228 by his son John de Vipont, who died in 1241, leaving his own son Robert II as Lord of Westmorland.[4] As the Viponts were the greatest baronial family in their part of the north, on the Vipont arms of gules, six annulets or were based those of some of the local knightly families connected with them, in particular the Musgraves, now baronets (Azure six annulets or) and the Lowthers, now Earls of Lonsdale (Or six annulets sable).

Roger Clifford's wife, Isabel de Vipont, was even further endowed. Her mother, Isabel, was daughter of John FitzGeoffrey, Justiciar of Ireland (1245-56), son of Geoffrey FitzPiers, Earl of Essex, Justiciar of England (1198-1213). Her brothers, John FitzJohn (who was one of the barons wounded and captured at Evesham, when his lands were confiscated and given to the Earl of Gloucester and young Roger Clifford's father) and Richard, 1st Lord FitzJohn (who bore quarterly or and gules, a bordure vair), both died childless, the co-heirs to their very substantial estates in 1297 being their four sisters. By this time young Roger Clifford and his wife, Isabel, were both dead, and so the FitzJohn heirs were Isabel's aunt, Maud, Countess of Warwick, her son Robert, now Lord Clifford, her sister, Idoine, widow of the Marcher lord Roger de Leyburn, her first cousin, Richard, Earl of Ulster, and her aunt, Joan, widow of Theobald, hereditary Butler of Ireland, which gives some idea of the Clifford family connections at this time. On the death, childless, of Isabel de Vipont's younger sister, Idoine, in 1333, the rest of the Vipont lands and Idoine's share of the FitzJohn inheritance also passed to the Cliffords.[5]

Roger Clifford was appointed temporary Justice of the Royal Forests south of the Trent from 1270 in place of his father who had gone on crusade.[6] In 1282, after his father, the Justiciar of Wales, had been unexpectedly wounded and taken prisoner by the Welsh, Roger took part in King Edward I's campaign and final conquest of Wales.

Sir Roger Clifford was one of the 16 knights in armour drowned with their followers in an ill-advised encounter with the Welsh on St Leonard's day, 6 November 1282. During August and September, at a place called Moel y Donn near Bangor, by the king's orders, Luke de Tany, former Seneschal of Gascony, had built a pontoon bridge across the Menai Straits to the mainland of Wales from Anglesey, the idea being that when Edward advanced to the Conway from the east, Tany and his troops should cross from Anglesey by the bridge and take the Welsh in the rear. 'At the beginning of November, Archbishop Peckham, an exceedingly well-meaning but tactless and arrogant cleric, was trying to arrange a peace. A truce had been declared, but during the peace negotiations Tany treacherously crossed his bridge to attack the Welsh, and met with the defeat which he richly deserved.'[7]

The fatal encounter in which Sir Roger met his death is described in *Flores Historiarum*:

> Some of the nobles of the king's army, passing over this bridge for the sake of taking exercise, were set upon, and being alarmed by the numbers and shouts of the Welsh who came against them, endeavoured unsuccessfully to effect their return to the island of Anglesey from which they had come, but were miserably drowned in the water. The Welsh ascribed this victory not to English misfortune but to a miracle.[8]

Sir Roger Clifford's inquisition post mortem[9] records that nine and three-quarters knights' fees were held directly of the king but notes that they were of the inheritance of his wife, Isabel, yet to be divided between her and her sister. His widow survived him, dying aged 37 in 1291, when she was buried at Shap Abbey in Westmorland.

By his wife Isabel, Sir Roger left a son:

ROBERT, 1st Lord Clifford, for whom see next chapter.

Chapter Twelve

Generation IX – Robert, 1st Lord Clifford (1274-1314)

Robert, first Lord Clifford, but the eighth baron since the Conquest, was born about Easter 1274. This stern warrior and able governor was one of the most distinguished members of the Clifford race. According to the *Dictionary of National Biography*, 'Clifford was one of the greatest barons of the age ... one of Edward I's most vigorous soldiers and administrators'.

While still in his teens, he succeeded his grandfather as head of the baronial house of Clifford, and his mother as hereditary sheriff of Westmorland and lord of half of the Honour of Appleby and the other Vipont estates in the north, and also her share of the barony of Old Warden in Bedfordshire.[1] He had control of this great inheritance in May 1295, and two years later he succeeded to yet more lands as a co-heir of his great-uncle Richard, Lord FitzJohn. In 1308 he was to cede the barony of Staveley (granted to him by the king) in Derbyshire to his childless aunt Idoine de Vipont's husband, John de Cromwell (Lord Cromwell) for life, in return for her share of Appleby, thus securing the whole of that Honour for himself.[2] His castles, therefore, included Appleby, Brough-under-Stainmoor, Brougham and Pendragon, and in 1310 he was also to be granted by Edward II the fine Yorkshire castle of Skipton, thereafter the principal family residence, together with the whole Honour of Skipton-in-Craven.[3] He was thus one of the most powerful lords in the north, which became the main Clifford sphere of influence for the next three and a half centuries.

At the age of 19, Robert Clifford was already in the employ of his grandfather's old friend King Edward I, according to Sir Robert Hale, and from 1297 to 1307-8 he was Justice in Eyre North of the Trent, being also Justice South of the Trent in 1307 and 1308. But his main activity was as a soldier from an early age, and he was accustomed from his youth to don his armour for war and tournament.

In 1296, aged 22 but already displaying his banner as a banneret, he led a levy of 14 lances – himself, two knights and 11 troopers with, of course, their followers – at the battle of Dunbar and onwards in the army of Edward I, when the King of England overthrew King John de Balliol and conquered Scotland. But the following year many Scots rose in arms in different parts of the country, among them the future king Robert the Bruce, son of the lord of Annandale, the Douglas lord of Douglasdale, the Steward of Scotland – and, above all, Sir Andrew of Murray and Sir William Wallace who proclaimed themselves leaders of the army of Scotland in Balliol's name and promptly defeated the English forces under John de Warenne, Earl of Surrey at the battle of Stirling Bridge.

Meanwhile, Surrey's grandson, Henry Percy, had been ordered to invade Scotland with Robert Clifford. Together, Clifford and Percy had 'quickly recruited levies from the English border counties and moved with great dispatch through Annandale and Nithsdale to reach Ayr by the end of June. The Scots, chiefly foot soldiers and much weaker than the English troops, were at Irvine a few miles north.[4] As soon as Percy and Clifford's cavalry came in sight, the Scots of the south-west asked for terms, and there followed the capitulation of Irvine. On 12 July 1297, Clifford was appointed Governor of Carlisle and captain of the Cumberland fortresses, while in the autumn he was also made Captain and Guardian of the Scottish Marches and of the county of Cumberland.

None of this affected Wallace who, after his victory at Stirling Bridge, occupied the town of Berwick and crossed the border, ravaging Cumberland and Northumberland. Clifford and Percy drove him back and immediately before Christmas 1297 Clifford made a brilliant raid into Scotland with 100 mounted men-at-arms and 20,000 foot. After burning ten townships, the English withdrew.[5]

Next year, King Edward I returned from campaigning in Flanders and almost immediately set out for Scotland, placing himself at the head of a powerful army. He was attended by Robert Clifford with 35 lances including himself and eight knights, namely Sir Simon Clifford (probably his young uncle and contemporary), John de Cromwell, Robert de Haustede, Richard de Kirkbridge, Roger de Kirkpatrick, Thomas de Torturald (Torthorwald), Thomas de Hellebek and Robert l'Engleys. Of these Robert Clifford himself rode a fine charger worth £30 and Sir Simon Clifford an iron grey valued at £20. (This compares with a value of £8 for most of the other knights' horses.) On 22 July 1298, they took part under King Edward I in his decisive victory over Wallace and the Scottish schiltroms – four massed hedgehog phalanxes of spearmen, shot down by Edward's archers – at the battle of Falkirk. (Robert Clifford's chequey arms with the red fess appeared afterwards on the commemorative Falkirk Roll.) Clifford was rewarded with the governorship of Nottingham Castle.

In September, the king held a council at Carlisle, where he granted the estates of forfeited Scottish nobles to his own lords. In satisfaction of a claim on the Exchequer for £500 a year, Clifford received wide lands in Douglasdale with the castle of Douglas, which was to be known as the siege perilous – the seat of danger as at King Arthur's Court in the legend – because Clifford's captain and garrison were in such constant peril from its disinherited lord, the Black Douglas. More than one border ballad tells of the vengeance taken by the 'good Lord James of Douglas' on the men of his rival and foe 'the Clifford'.

In December 1299 Clifford was summoned to Parliament as a Baron, by a royal writ dated at Berwick. By his attendance at this Parliament, and by sitting in it, he was retrospectively held by peerage lawyers centuries later to have become a peer. The still existing peerage barony of de Clifford, held by his descendant in the female line, the present Lord de Clifford, is given precedence of 1299 from this chance happening. His friend and companion-in-arms Henry Percy was summoned at the same time, and thus also became retrospectively the first Lord Percy. What these two great lords, whose forefathers had been noble time out of mind (Percy's had been dukes of Brabant) and who had both been peers since childhood, would have made of this is hard to say. Since they still habitually spoke Norman-French among themselves, and the style 'Sire' or 'Sieur' could equally be translated 'sir' or 'lord', it was not for another two generations that any distinction was made between the form of address Sir Robert Clifford and Lord Clifford. On the other hand, it is generally recognised that this reign saw the dawn of parliamentary peerages in England, and the Cliffords were among the barons summoned to Parliament during these early beginnings of the system which is now so different from the system which existed in France up to the Revolution out of which it had originally grown.

Lord Clifford's valour is celebrated in the contemporary Norman-French verses known as the 'Roll of Arms of the Princes, Barons and Knights who attended King Edward to the siege of Caerlaverock in 1300'.[6] This Maxwell castle was held in vain by the Scots, and the poet describes the coats of arms of the English besiegers, among them those of Robert, Lord Clifford.

> *Le roi son bon seigneur connoie* – The king his good lord knows
> *Sa banier mout honouree,* – His much honoured banner
> *De or e de asur eschequere,* – Chequered with gold and azure,
> *O une fesse vermellette.* – with a vermilion fess.
> *Si je estoise une pucellete,* – If I were a young maiden,
> *Je li donroie quer e cors,* – I would give him my heart and body,
> *Tant est de li bons li recors.* – So good is his fame.

The poet describes Clifford's ancestry accurately, mentioning his grandmother, Isabel de Bigod, daughter of Hugh le Bigod, Earl of Norfolk by his wife, Maud, eldest daughter of William Marshal, Earl of Pembroke and hereditary Marshal of England, who was reputed to have slain a unicorn while on crusade. In 1300 the then Marshal, the Earl of Norfolk, was childless and, if his brother John le Bigod was also without issue, Lord Clifford may well have been potential co-heir to the Marshalcy at the time the verses were composed. The poet goes on to tell us of an assault repulsed by the garrison, which forced the besiegers to retire and in which one of Clifford's knights, Sir Richard de Kirkbridge, was wounded, but how in the end the royal banner, the banners of St Edmund, St George and St Edward and those of the Constable, the Earl of Hereford, the acting Marshal (Lord Segrave) and of Lord Clifford were hoisted on the battlements, and how the captured castle was given into Clifford's custody.

In February 1301 Clifford was among the barons at Lincoln who signed a letter to Pope Boniface VIII denying the claim that Scotland was a fief of the papacy. His seal bears the Clifford shield of chequy with a fess, within delicate tracery incorporating the six Vipont annulets which later powder Clifford historic standards.[7]

In February 1304, while Edward I wintered at Dunfermline, Segrave, Clifford and Latimer were sent on a commando raid into Lothian, where they routed Wallace and Fraser a few miles from Peebles. They were supported by Robert the Bruce, Earl of Carrick, then temporarily at peace with Edward I, but they failed to capture Wallace and Fraser, though they did prevent them from breaking out north of the Forth in any strength.[8]

Meanwhile, Clifford had been acting from time to time as 'custos' for the Bishop of Durham, and on 11 December 1305 it was in this role that he was deputed to inquire into the question of the forfeiture of King John Balliol's manors of Gaynesford and Barnard Castle in County Durham. Robert the Bruce's sudden coronation as King of Scots in March 1306 roused Edward I's extreme anger and led to further lucrative forfeitures, so that by October 1306 Clifford was enfeoffed in

Bruce's forfeited manor of Hart and Hartlepool, a grant which in later times embroiled the Cliffords with the bishops of Durham, who claimed that these estates, being situated within their county palatine, should revert to them on the treason of the original holder.[9] In other words, the bishops claimed, in virtue of their palatine powers, that Bruce's lands in County Durham were theirs and not King Edward's to grant to anyone else, a claim both Clifford and the Crown ignored. Clifford was also given by King Edward I the estate of Skelton in Cumberland, forfeited by the gallant Sir Christopher de Seton who had been executed that year.

In January 1307, Clifford was summoned to Edward I's last parliament, which met at Carlisle in March. Things were stirring again in Scotland, where King Robert the Bruce had landed in his own earldom of Carrick, and the English, under Aymer de Valence, Earl of Pembroke, were intent on holding Ayr and Turnbery in order to keep open communication between these castles and the east, and to tempt Bruce into an engagement on favourable ground. Edward, though a dying man, was alert and impatient to hear news of success, but Bruce eluded the English and slowly won the initiative.[10] Douglas took his own castle in Douglasdale, killing Clifford's English garrison and throwing them down a well – an exploit celebrated by the Scots as the 'Douglas Larder'.[11] Douglas Castle was, however, immediately recovered and re-garrisoned for Lord Clifford.

Then, on 7 July 1307, the vigorous old King Edward I – Hammer of the Scots, Conqueror of Wales, with whom Clifford's grandfather had been on crusade to the Holy Land – died at Burgh-by-Sands in Cumberland on the edge of the new Clifford country. Lord Clifford was present at the king's death-bed, when the dying monarch called upon him, the Earl of Lincoln, the Earl of Warwick and the Earl of Pembroke to be good to his son and exhorted them not to allow Piers Gaveston to re-enter the kingdom to lead his son astray, thus appointing them counsellors to the new king. Notwithstanding the old king's wish, Edward II's first act was to recall his friend Gaveston from exile in France, and to make him Earl of Cornwall and Regent of England during his own absences abroad, and to marry him to Lady Margaret de Clare, a cousin of Lord Clifford's wife, Maud de Clare, all to the considerable dismay of the barons.

All the same Clifford seems to have been in the young king's favour,[12] for Edward II appointed him Marshal of England in September 1307, an office he held for several months, doubtless as a special compliment to his military prowess and to his descent from the former Regent, William the Marshal, Earl of Pembroke. Clifford's cousin Roger le Bigod, Earl of Norfolk and hereditary Marshal of England, had died that year shortly before Edward I, whom he had made his heir in both that earldom and marshalcy. But the late king had asked his son to confer both on Thomas of Brotherton, his youngest son, and the new king's half-brother, who was accordingly created Earl of Norfolk and Marshal of England five years later at the age of eleven. He became the ancestor in the female line of the Howard dukes of Norfolk, the present Earls Marshal of England. In 1307, Edward II also appointed Lord Clifford to be Justiciar of England South of the Trent.

The Scottish war of independence continued, and in the autumn the Black Douglas recovered Douglasdale and, in accordance with Bruce's firm policy, razed his own castle of Douglas to the ground. It was the third time he had retaken it from

Clifford's unfortunate garrisons.[13] In 1308, Clifford was again made Warden of the Scottish Marches in charge of the troubled border country, and on 20 August he was also appointed joint Captain and chief Guardian of all Scotland in company with the Earl of Angus.[14]

However, other events drew Clifford's attention southwards. At the turn of the year 1307-8 he had been invited to Edward II's coronation and reappointed Governor of Nottingham Castle. Early in 1308 he entered into a league with Antony Bek, Bishop of Durham, to preserve the king's rights.[15] This year, he also jousted at the first great Dunstable tournament;[16] and before November he became lord of the barony of Staveley in Derbyshire by a grant from the grateful king. Clifford in turn granted these lands to Lord Cromwell for life, as the husband of his aunt Idoine, as has already been mentioned. This consolidated his holdings in the north, which were taken in hand in exchange.[17]

In March 1310 Edward II granted Clifford the castle of Skipton for life, a grant which was later made hereditary in exchange for his claims in the Vale of Monmouth. The strategic importance of Skipton at the head of Airedale permitted it to dominate the easy line of communication across the Pennines at this point. It explains why the Cliffords made it their principal residence for several hundred years, for it gave them easy access to their northern lands in Cumbria as well as to the south and east. The castle has been occupied by Clifford's descendants, albeit in the female line, until recent times.

8.   Skipton Castle, Yorkshire, showing the massive main gate and adjoining gatehouse.

The north had already reclaimed Clifford's attention. In the autumn of 1309 he had been despatched against the Scots and was later re-appointed Guardian of all Scotland. During 1310 he continued to campaign north of the border and in the spring of 1311 he was made governor of the lowlands and a commissioner of array for Westmorland and Cumberland. At the same time affairs in the south began to demand his attention as the situation between Edward II and his lords began to worsen over the king's affair with Gaveston, whose power and insolence increased with his hold over Edward's affections. The baronial party formed itself into the lords ordainers, and Clifford's name appears in a list among those ordainers. That he had as yet hardly thrown himself wholeheartedly into opposition is shown by his declaration of 17 March 1310 that the king's concessions should not be construed as a precedent, while a special clause in the ordainers' ordinances on 28 October 1311, by which the royal grants to Clifford were exempt from the general restoration of Crown lands decreed by the baronial opposition after the renewed exile of Gaveston, seems to show that at that time he was not viewed with mistrust by the barons.[18] In October he had also received a mandate to deliver Skipton Castle to the king's Escheator beyond Trent in accordance with the ordinances of the prelates and barons appointed for the ordering of the realm, but by December the same year he had a re-grant of the castle with the assent of the barons.[18]

The following year found Clifford in a very difficult position. On the one hand he remained loyal to Edward II, yet he found himself obliged to honour his promise to King Edward I, concerning Gaveston, and when it came to the crunch, Clifford stood by the dead king. In 1312, on the rumour of Gaveston's return, Clifford was assigned to guard the northern counties against any possible alliance between the favourite and Robert Bruce.[19] In May 1312 Clifford, together with the Earl of Lancaster and other barons, entered Newcastle, which was the base from which they besieged Gaveston who had taken refuge in Scarborough Castle and who soon surrendered, only to be put to death without trial by the victorious barons.

After Gaveston's death, Edward II was indignant but powerless to do anything. Clifford was appointed by the baronial party to attempt a reconciliation with the king. This resulted in a treaty of peace made before the Pope's envoys, who had come to act as arbitrators by which the earls and barons came before the king on their knees to humble themselves and swear that what they did was not evilly intended against him, begging foregiveness and to be restored to favour. Second, whatever they took from Gaveston was to be surrendered to the king; third that in the next parliament security would be given that no one should be called to account for Gaveston's death; fourth, that when matters were reconciled, they would do their best to see that the king had enough aid for the war in Scotland; fifth, that everyone should have liberty to pass and repass, and to transact his affairs without let or hindrance. The treaty was signed shortly before Christmas 1312 and the following February the king declared from Windsor that he had received from Robert Clifford the jewels, horses etc. which had belonged to Gaveston, and ultimately (in October 1313) the Earls of Lancaster, Hereford and Warwick were granted a royal pardon for their share in Gaveston's murder.[20]

During Lent 1314 news came that the garrison of Stirling Castle was being threatened, and Clifford was urgently requested by the king to muster his men at

Berwick by the middle of April.[21] Accordingly, he was appointed governor of Norham Castle and, with his personal levy of northern knights, he set out for what was to be the decisive battle of the war. On the eve of Bannockburn, Robert Clifford commanded the several hundred picked horsemen sent to by-pass if possible the New Park and to force a way through to Stirling to relieve the English garrison there. He was accompanied by his old companion-in-arms Henry, Lord Beaumont and two or three bannerets with perhaps two of the ten cavalry brigades of Edward II's army. This powerful force moved in close formation across open country, confident that the Scots would not attack, for the disposition of Bruce's forces showed that the very idea that the English cavalry might advance in this way had never occurred to them. At the last moment, however, King Robert's nephew, the Earl of Moray, made a gallant attempt to intercept Clifford's force. The situation was not quite hopeless; Clifford had still to advance across ground near enough for the Scottish infantry to reach him, and it was Moray's aim to confront the English with an impenetrable hedge of spearpoints wherever they attacked. Clifford had no archers, so the Scots were able to inflict heavy casualties and to break the impetus of the English attack. This hard fight between Moray and Clifford was the crux of the whole battle.[22] It was late in the day before Clifford and Beaumont regained the main body of the English army. The next morning, 24 June 1314, the battle of Bannockburn was over in a few more hard-fought hours, and Edward II was completely defeated by Bruce. Thousands perished, among them nearly forty English barons and knights, the veteran lord, Robert Clifford and his wife's cousin, Gilbert de Clare, Earl of Gloucester among them. Gloucester, whom Bruce mourned as a cousin, and over whose corpse he mounted a night's vigil, was sent to King Edward at Berwick along with the body of Clifford. *He* was probably buried near his mother at Shap Abbey, although there is some suggestion that he might have been buried at Bolton Abbey in Craven.

Robert, 1st Lord Clifford married Maud de Clare, younger daughter and eventual co-heiress of Thomas de Clare, Lord of Thomond[23] by his wife, Julian, daughter and co-heiress of Sir Maurice FitzMaurice, Justiciar of Ireland of the great Geraldine house, barons of Offaly and earls of Kildare. It was Thomas de Clare who gave his name to County Clare which eventually passed to the Cliffords. The vast Clare inheritance eventually passed through an heiress to the royal family later in the 14th century, giving its name to the royal dukedom of Clarence and to Clarenceux King of Arms. In this way Gloucester also became a royal dukedom. By Maud de Clare, Robert Clifford had at least two sons[24] and a daughter:

    1. ROGER, 2nd Lord Clifford, for whom see Chapter Thirteen.
    2. ROBERT, 3rd Lord Clifford, for whom see Chapter Fourteen.
    1. IDOINE, who married Henry de Percy, 2nd Lord Percy (d. 23 February 1351/2) of Alnwick, by whom she was grandmother of the 1st Earl of Northumberland.

As the first Lord Clifford's executrix, Maud de Clare had her late husband's will proved on 18 September 1314. A year later, on about 11 November 1315, she was abducted and carried off while on a journey and forcibly remarried, without the king's permission, by Sir Robert de Welles, 2nd Lord Welles, who died without issue in 1320.

Chapter Thirteen

Generation X – Roger, 2nd Lord Clifford (1299-1326)

Roger, second Lord Clifford, hereditary Sheriff of Westmorland, was born 21 January 1299 old style, 2 February 1300 new style, and was 14 when he succeeded to the barony, castles and estates on his father's death on the field of Bannockburn. During his minority the custody of his castles at Skipton and elsewhere was granted to his uncle, Bartholomew de Badlesmere, the husband of his mother's sister, Margaret de Clare. Badlesmere, however, soon joined that group of nobles who were increasingly opposed to Edward II's new boyfriend Hugh, Lord de Despencer. Thus it is not surprising that in November 1317 a group of local notabilities were appointed by the king to prevent Skipton Castle falling into the hands of 'evilly disposed' persons.[1] In March 1320 Clifford went in the train of Lord Badlesmere on the king's service overseas.[2] In November 1319 and again in May 1321 Roger Clifford was summoned to Parliament as a baron, thus becoming accustomed while still in his teens to being consulted about national affairs.

At the age of 21, Roger Clifford and his uncle were numbered among those barons who were opposed to Despencer, and who entered the Welsh Marches to occupy Despencer's castles there. They proceeded to despoil them of their contents and put in their own supporters to hold them on their behalf. They also seized the king's castles thereabouts, and compelled the king to hold a parliament in the course of which Hugh Despencer was banished. In October 1321, during the absence of her husband, Margaret de Clare, Lady de Badlesmere, refused the queen admittance to Leeds Castle in Kent, six of the queen's retainers being killed when she tried to force an entry. This had the effect of rallying six earls to the king's side, they feeling that Lady Badlesmere had gone too far, and soon the castle was taken, after which Badlesmere sought the support of the Earl of Lancaster and the Marcher lords as well as of Roger himself. With the Mortimers and other rebellious barons, Clifford attacked and burnt Bridgnorth early in 1322,[3] while Lancaster held an assembly of his supporters at Doncaster, where he issued the 'Doncaster Petition' against the Despencers who had now returned from exile. But the Mortimers were soon forced to surrender, and Clifford fled north to join Lancaster. The Earls of Hereford and Lancaster, together with Clifford, then laid siege to Tickhill Castle, which they failed to capture, so they fell back on Pontefract, where they held a council at which some of the barons urged Lancaster to go to Dunstanburgh in Northumberland. But Lancaster refused, lest it might be thought he were going to make an alliance with the Scots, so he said he would remain at Pontefract.[4] This enraged the young, impetuous Roger Clifford, who drew his dagger and threatened Lancaster, who gave way and the rebels set out for the north. On 22 March 1322 they were intercepted by Edward II's northern forces at Boroughbridge, where the Earl of Hereford was killed and Roger Clifford severely wounded in the head. Hereford's men deserted and fled together with many of the Earl of Lancaster's and of Lord Clifford. When morning came the Earl of Lancaster and lords Clifford and Mowbray and their followers surrendered to the royal commander, Sir Andrew de Harclay, and were taken captive to York. Lancaster was eventually beheaded, and Badlesmere hanged at Canterbury. Roger Clifford was condemned to death at York together with Lord Mowbray, who was hanged on 23 March 1322. It is usually said that Clifford too was duly hanged, but by reason of his grievous wounds he was reprieved, and he survived until the beginning of 1327. There is no record of a pardon, but this account is borne out by the fact that the writ for inquest *post mortem* was not issued until 12 February 1326-7. Clifford's estates were, however, forfeited, including his London house at Clifford's Inn.[7] Skipton Castle, his principal seat, had held out against the royal forces, but was now garrisoned for the king and placed in the charge of Sir William Grammary. The castle had been looted after its lord's capture and the king ordered that it be searched and all Clifford's charters inspected, but in the confusion it is possible that some of the family records were lost or dispersed at that time.[8]

According to the Chronicle of Lanercost, Roger, 2nd Lord Clifford was married to a daughter of Humphrey de Bohun, Earl of Hereford and Essex, Constable of England, King Edward II's rebellious brother-in-law who was slain at Borough-bridge. This marriage is not recorded elsewhere, and Roger Clifford may have been only affianced to her, the marriage being cancelled or annulled after the rebellion. On the other hand, it may well have been to the earl's daughter Lady Eleanor de Bohun, who did not marry James Butler, afterwards 1st Earl of Ormonde, until 1327; her sister Margaret, on the other hand, had already been betrothed to Hugh de Courtenay, afterwards Earl of Devon, whom she married in 1325. Their mother Elizabeth was a daughter of Edward I and the widow of John, Count of Holland. Whatever the facts of the case, Roger Clifford's heart was elsewhere. He left some natural children by his mistress Julian of the Bower, for whom he built a little house near Whinfield which he called Julian's Bower after her.[9] It was still used as a Clifford shooting lodge in Whinfell Forest in Westmorland three centuries later, and we are told that masses were said in Kendal church for the soul of Julian de Clifford until the Reformation.[10]

Chapter Fourteen

Generation X – Robert, 3rd Lord Clifford (1305-44)

Robert, 3rd Lord Clifford was born on 5 November 1305. It was fortunate for the family that his elder brother died just at the beginning of Edward III's reign, when Edward II had been deposed and murdered by the Queen's lover, Roger Mortimer, Earl of March, head of the great Welsh Marcher house which had always been allies of the Cliffords. Consequently no difficulties were made about the succession to the peerage and the restoration of Roger's forfeited estates, and in August 1327 Robert Clifford had seisin of his mother's and brother's lands, being summoned to parliament as a baron.

By reason of his mother's large inheritance in Ireland as co-heiress of her nephew, Thomas de Clare, Lord of Thomond, Robert Clifford was also summoned by Edward III to attend him on a visit to enquire into the grievances of the Irish. But Robert Clifford's main concern was with the repair of his castles, building an additional tower at Skipton Castle, and in dealing with the Scots, who had caused the Clifford territories so much damage.

He himself fought in the new Scottish wars, having an interest to attempt the recovery of Douglasdale. After Robert the Bruce's death, his infant son David Bruce had succeeded as King of Scots. The 'disinherited' lords, both English barons with claims to Scottish estates and Scottish nobles who had lost everything through remaining loyal to the Balliol cause, could get no help from young King Edward III, who had only just seized power in England. So under the leadership of the late King John de Balliol's son, Edward, and of the veteran Henry de Beaumont, now Earl of Buchan (the 1st Lord Clifford's colleague at Bannockburn), they raised 500 men-at-arms and 1,500 archers and landed in Scotland. Here they defeated the forces of the Regent, Mar, at the battle of Dupplin in 1332, and proclaimed Edward de Balliol King of Scots. After a reign of only 11 weeks he was driven out again, but the following year Edward III of England came north in person to support Edward de Balliol, and inflicted another crushing defeat on David Bruce's supporters at Halidon Hill. But by 1334 the Balliol cause was lost, and thereafter the desultory warfare between the Scots and English was fought again on straightforwardly national lines.

In 1333 King Edward de Balliol was entertained by Lord Clifford at Brougham Castle when a famous stag hunt was held in his honour. The tale is told of how the hart, giving its last desperate leap over a wall in Whinfell Forest, cleared it and fell dead, while the hound, Hercules, failed to leap the wall and fell dead on the other side. The old rhyme ran: 'Hercules killed Hart a-grees; Hart a-grees killed Hercules.' The stag's antlers were nailed to a tree close by and gradually the horns became embedded in the growing wood. The Hart's Horn Tree was still standing, very decayed, in 1658 when Lady Anne Clifford recorded that 'in the year 1648, one of those hornes was broken downe by some of the Army' and that the other horn now had been broken off too 'by some few mischievous people secretly in the night'.[1]

Robert, 3rd Lord Clifford married at Berkeley Castle in June 1328 Isabel Berkeley, daughter of Maurice, 2nd Lord Berkeley, Justiciar of South Wales and Seneschal of Aquitaine, by his wife Eve de la Zouche, sister of William, 1st Lord Zouche of Haryngworth. The Berkeleys were then almost the only pre-Conquest Anglo-Saxon family in the peerage, descending in the direct male line from Eadnoth the Staller, a high officer of King Edward the Confessor's royal household. They had held their castle and feudal barony of Berkeley since the 12th century, and like the Cliffords had recently become Lords of Parliament at the dawn of that institution. Only 14 months before the marriage, Lady Clifford's brother, Thomas, 3rd Lord Berkeley had received the deposed King Edward II as his prisoner at Berkeley Castle, but had taken no part in the unfortunate king's horrendous murder there when a red hot poker was thrust up his anus to leave no mark upon his body and as a grisly allusion to Gaveston and Despencer.

Robert Clifford was Warden of the West Marches against Scotland, but died aged 38 on 20 May 1344. By his wife, Isabel he had three sons:

1. ROBERT, 4th Lord Clifford, for whom see Chapter Fifteen.

2. ROGER, 5th Lord Clifford, for whom see Chapter Sixteen.

3. Sir THOMAS Clifford, Lord of Thomond (i.e. North Munster), the Clifford inheritance from the de Clares in Ireland. He appears to have been given this territory without royal licence by his brother Roger, for whom he acted in Ireland, and who also granted him for life his castle of Cony in Ireland and lands near Cockermouth in Cumberland. In March 1383, as Thomas Clifford, knight, the elder, he was appointed for life to the lucrative office of Escheator for Ireland and Clerk of the Market of the King's Household there, on condition that he made his residence there in person, but by July he was already allowed to appoint a deputy, being occupied in England on business. In 1388 his brother Roger obtained a licence for him to execute these offices by deputy from May to Michaelmas as he was too infirm to execute them in person.[2] Next year, Sir Thomas and his wife Joan were officially pardoned for entering without royal licence upon lands in Ireland originally settled on Roger Clifford. In 1389 he was also Mayor of Limerick. It is not clear, however, whether he was ever able to re-establish himself in such of the Clare castles as Bunratty and Quin, although the lands in Thomond which Sir Thomas held against the O'Brien dynasts through his Clare ancestry eventually gave their name to County Clare, which ironically in turn was to give its name to an O'Brien earldom centuries later.

Sir Thomas Clifford, lord of Thomond, died in 1393. His arms were evidently those of Lord Clifford within a bordure azure. It seems equally evident that his wife, Joan, was an heiress of the family of Eaglesfield of Eaglesfield near Cockermouth in Cumberland, which bore a coat of arms Or, three eagles displayed gules. They had at least three sons:[3]

i. Sir THOMAS, the younger.

ii. ROBERT, Sheriff of Kent in 1399-1400 and again in 1414, through the influence of his brother Bishop Richard Clifford, of whose will he was executor in 1421. A sketch of his effigy in armour by the 17th-century antiquarian Dodsworth is in the Bodleian Library (MS Dodsworth, vol. 71, pp. 51-2). This shows him wearing his Eaglesfield eagles on his vambraces, and surrounded by eight shields: three display the arms of Lord Clifford within a bordure, one of these having the fess plain, the other two having the fess charged with a mitre (for Bishop Richard Clifford) and a cross paty respectively. He appears to be standing on a wingless wyvern.

iii. RICHARD, Bishop of London, whose career is given in the *Dictionary of National Biography*, as he was one of the most eminent churchmen of his time – 'a close intimate of King Richard II and by repute his chosen boon-companion at table'.[4] He was educated at Queen's College, Oxford, which had been founded in 1340-1 by Robert of Eaglesfield (perhaps his uncle), whose arms of argent three eagles gules are still those of the college. The 12 scholars at which were to be chosen by preference from the counties of Westmorland and Cumberland. In 1385 he was

Canon of the Chapel Royal in the Palace of Westminster, where he made himself so obnoxious to the king's opponents in 1388 he was imprisoned by them in Rochester Castle. But he was soon released and from 1390 to 1398 he was Keeper of the Great Wardrobe. Clifford had the honour to be the first clerical executor nominated in King Richard II's will. In November 1397, the king appointed him Lord Privy Seal, and the usurper, Henry IV, continued him in that office until 1401.[5] But when he was promoted by papal provision in 1401 to be Bishop of Bath and Wells, the new king refused him the temporalities of that see, so he was transferred to Worcester instead. In 1402 he helped to conduct King Henry IV's daughter Blanche to Cologne for her marriage to Louis, afterwards Elector Palatine of the Rhine, son of Rupert, King of the Romans.

Bishop Clifford was present during Sir John Oldcastle's trial for heresy in 1413, and two years later he assisted the Archbishop of Canterbury when John Clayton, the London Lollard, was handed over to the civil power. He was also present at the Council of Westminster when King Henry V determined on war with France, leading to the Agincourt campaign.[6] But the most important act of his life was when he was one of the English envoys to the Council of Constance, where he received some instructions personally from Henry V in the king's own handwriting. For here at Constance, Bishop Clifford not only took a very prominent part, but was even proposed for the papacy himself – he would not only have been the first Clifford to be Pope, but also the only other Englishman. However, it was he who at the conclave of 11 November 1417 voted for Cardinal Colonna, who became Pope as Martin V.[7] his being the deciding vote.

This Council ended the contest between the two rival popes and ended the schism and many heresies, including that of Wycliffe in England. During the Council Bishop Clifford preached a Latin sermon before the future Emperor Sigismund, the enemy-to-be of the Hussites, and on Sunday, 31 January 1417, before leaving Constance, Clifford entertained the future Emperor, the Duke of Bavaria and the Hohenzollern Burgave of Nuremberg. After his return, the bishop made substantial gifts of money to institutions such as Balliol College library at Oxford. He died on 20 August 1421, and was buried under the marble stone where formerly stood the shrine of St Erkenwald in St Paul's Cathedral.

Robert, 3rd Lord Clifford's widow, Isabel de Berkeley, is noted for having made over to students of law for a small rent the then London residence of the Clifford family (acquired in 1310 by the first Lord Clifford) still known as Clifford's Inn. The students formed themselves into the Society of Clifford's Inn, and finally purchased it outright in 1618. In 1902 the Society was dissolved and the property sold, but the interest of the fund is devoted to the legal education of future barristers and solicitors. Astonishingly, in 1934 the Hall was bought for the Henry Ford Foundation in America, carefully dismantled brick by brick and transported across the Atlantic to be re-erected in the United States. The Clifford arms still appear above the gateway to this curious abode of lawyers of former days.[8]

Shortly before 9 June 1345, the widowed Lady Clifford married Sir Thomas de Musgrave, Sheriff of York, both being pardoned on payment of a fine of £200 for marrying without the king's licence. He was summoned to Parliament as a Baron from 1350 to 1374; she died on 25 July 1362.

Robert Clifford had a daughter Isabella, who married in 1361 Sir John de Eure, Constable of Dover Castle, of Wintringham St Peter, Lincolnshire.

Chapter Fifteen

Generation XI – Robert, 4th Lord Clifford (1329-45)

There is not a great deal to say about Robert, 4th Lord Clifford, who was not yet sixteen when his father died in 1344. His wardship was granted to his father-in-law Lord Nevill, whose daughter, Eupheme de Nevill, he had married in April 1343. She was the daughter of Ralph, 2nd Lord Nevill by his wife Alice d'Audley, sister of Hugh, Earl of Gloucester, and it was a great match between these two northern houses.

Robert's short life saw the opening of England's attempt to conquer France in the Hundred Years War , in which he took part himself, since great nobles were accustomed to command in their teens, so perhaps this would be the place to say something of the elaborate armour they wore, for it constituted a substantial part of their expenditure. Plate armour was being developed to such an extent that those who could afford to have it tailor-made were covered from head to foot like lobsters in their jointed carapaces for both war and tournament. If properly fitted, with the weight carefully distributed over the body, it was lighter than might at first glance appear, yet even so, to wear it effectively it was necessary to undergo rigorous training to keep fit. Like the modern commando, the noble trainee was expected to do somersaults fully armed except for his bascinet, or helmet, jump fully armed on to the back of his horse and to exercise in full armour to get accustomed to it and to strengthen his arms. One exercise required him to leap from the ground to the shoulders of a man on horseback, using only one hand to grasp the man's sleeve. He had to practise climbing ladders wearing armour and using only his arms, or when climbing without his armour to do so using one arm only. This training was only part of a newly evolving system of military tactics which made the English army almost the most invincible in Europe for a century. The essence was to dismount the men-at-arms; to take up a strong defensive position; to dispose the archers thrown forward on the wings under natural cover if it could be found, or support them with the infantry if natural cover failed. The enemy was encouraged to attack; the infantry would halt the attack and the archers would then break it.

But young Lord Clifford's training availed him little. He was killed on campaign in France before November 1345 within less than 18 months of succeeding to the peerage and several months before the great English victory of Crécy. He left no issue and was succeeded by his brother. His widow married secondly, early in 1347, Reynold Lucy, son of Thomas, 2nd Lord Lucy; and thirdly Sir Walter de Heselarton. She died in October 1393.

Chapter Sixteen

Generation XI – Roger, 5th Lord Clifford (1333-89)

Roger, 5th Lord Clifford was born on 10 July 1333, and had livery of his lands in 1354, being summoned to Parliament as a Baron from 1357 to 1388, where he frequently acted as a trier of petitions. This administrator and able soldier began his military career when hardly more than twelve years old, being armed at the time of Jacob van Artevaldt's death in 1345. He also took part in the successful sea fight against the Spaniards off Winchelsea in 1350, where the English tactics at sea were similar to those on land, archers with the invincible longbow on their flanking ships.

Young Lord Clifford married Lady Maud de Beauchamp, daughter of Thomas, 3rd Earl of Warwick, a founder Knight of the Garter, one of the chief commanders at Crécy and afterwards a crusader, by his wife Lady Catherine de Mortimer, the daughter of the infamous Roger Mortimer, Earl of March, the murderer of Edward II who was himself hanged by Edward III. Accordingly, when rebuilding much of Brougham Castle, Roger placed there a carving of the arms of Clifford impaling Beauchamp: Gules a fess between six cross-crosslets Or. He also constructed a pool of water on the west side of the castle and a canal from the river Lowther to the river Eamont. It had an island in its centre and formed part of the pleasure grounds attached to the castle. He called it 'Maud's Pool' after his wife, and a small piece of water near Brougham still bears that name.[1]

Lord Clifford's chief services, however, were in guarding the Scottish border. He was defending it as early as 1354, and was one of a commission to correct truce-breakers and decide border disputes in 1367. Two years later he signed the truce with Scotland shortly before the death of King David Bruce and the accession of the first Stewart king of Scots, and was one of the Wardens of the West Marches the next year. In 1372 he was a Commissioner of Array against the Scots, and again appointed to correct truce-breakers and decide border disputes. The greatest of these was in 1374 when Lord Clifford was chosen as one of the commission to settle the dispute between Henry, Lord Percy and William, Earl of Douglas over the possession of Jedworth (Jedburgh) Forest. In 1377 he was made Sheriff of Cumberland and Governor of Carlisle, and was re-appointed to these offices on the accession of Richard II. He was Warden of both the East and West Marches five times from 1380 to 1385.

Roger is the first peer of the line who was undoubtedly styled Lord Clifford in the modern sense of a Peer of Parliament as opposed to an immemorially noble baronial lord by feudal tenure. In August 1385 he accompanied King Richard II on his campaign in Scotland, bringing with him 60 men-at-arms and 40 archers.It was on this occasion that Lord Scrope of Bolton, the Chancellor of England, fell out with a Cheshire knight called Sir Robert Grosvenor (forefather of the present Dukes of Westminster) over their coats of arms, which were both Azure a bend Or. The resulting lawsuit lasted for five years. Henry Bolingbroke (afterwards King Henry IV), Chaucer and two Cliffords were among the distinguished witnesses who gave evidence for Scrope, who won. The Scropes still wear a blue family tie with golden diagonal stripes (bends Or), while the first Duke of Westminster called his Derby winner Bend Or, which led to the second Duke's nickname 'Bendor'. The two Cliffords were Roger, Lord Clifford and Sir Lewis Clifford, K.G. (ancestor of the Lords Clifford of Chudleigh). It is a further instance of the modern peerage style that while Sir Lewis is called 'Mons. Lowes de Clyfford', Roger is simply styled 'Mons. de Clifford', i.e. milord de Clifford.

In May 1388 Roger Clifford accompanied Richard Fitzalan, Earl of Arundel, Admiral of the Fleet, on the victorious naval expedition against the combined fleets of France and Castile that took a hundred ships all laden with wine, and the port of Brest in Brittany. In October, back at home in his northern castles, Roger was ordered for the last time to prepare measures to secure the defence of the Scottish border. He died on 13 July 1389 and was probably buried at Shap.

9. Brougham Castle.

Over the years he had improved and embellished his castles and estates. In particular he had obtained the charter to hold the Kirkby Stephen market and permission to enclose a park of some five hundred acres, together with Calder Woods, at Skipton, and had much restored Brougham.

By his wife, Maud de Beauchamp, he had two sons and three daughters:

1. THOMAS, 6th Lord Clifford, for whom see Chapter Seventeen.

2. Sir WILLIAM, Governor of Berwick in 1403-4, who married Anne Bardolf, the elder daughter and co-heiress of Thomas, 5th Lord Bardolf. They had a daughter, Alice Clifford, mentioned in his will of 25 March 1418, signed at the castle of Frannsak (presumably Fronsac, near Libourne in Aquitaine) when he was Constable of Bordeaux. He died in 1419.

1. PHILIPPA, first wife of William, 5th Lord Ferrers of Groby (died 1445) by whom she left issue. His arms, impaling Clifford, appear on the vaulting of Canterbury Cathedral.

2. MARGARET, married Sir John Melton.

3. CATHERINE, married Ralph de Greystock, 5th Lord de Greystock or Greystoke (a title to be immortalised in modern fiction as that of Tarzan of the Apes), who was captured while commanding an expedition against the Scots, but ransomed for 3,000 marks. He died in 1417.

Chapter Seventeen

Generation XII – Thomas, 6th Lord Clifford (c. 1363-91)

Thomas, 6th Lord Clifford, and like his predecessors hereditary Sheriff of Westmorland, was 26 years old when he succeeded to the peerage on his father's death in 1389. He was brought up at the height of the age of chivalry and was deeply imbued with its ideals. Before his succession, as young Sir Thomas Clifford, he had been made Governor of Carlisle for life in 1384, had become a Knight of the King's Chamber in Richard II's personal household in 1385, Warden of the East Marches in 1386 and was evidently in high favour at Court. On 25 June 1386, the king allowed Northampton Herald to carry a challenge to France from 'Thomas de Clifford, chivalier l'eisne FitzRogeri, Sire de Clifford' to a French knight called Bursigande, the eldest son of 'le Sire de Bursigande'. Sir Thomas accordingly crossed the Channel for this tournament the following May. Again, in January 1387, the king had licensed 'our very dear and loyal knight, Sir Thomas Clifford, to perform all manner of feats of arms' on the Scottish border, as well on foot as on horseback, until Easter. In 1388 Thomas was appointed Richard II's Master of the Horse.[1]

Clifford's chivalric disposition, while it endeared him to the king, seems to have provoked the jealousy of the barons, who engineered his banishment from Court in 1388, with the proviso that he appear before the next parliament.[2] Yet on his father's death the following year, he had livery of all his lands, and at about the same time was appointed a commissioner of the peace on the Scottish Marches. He was summoned to parliament as a baron from 1389 to 1391, and his name occurs in the list of Privy Councillors for 1390.

After his succession his love of jousting did not cease. It was a period of peace with both Scotland and France, a brief interlude in the Hundred Years War, and Lord Clifford and two other English knights challenged some French knights to a tournament on the marches between Boulogne and Calais, and on 20 June 1390 he obtained a safe-conduct from Richard II for William Douglas, Lord of Nithsdale to pass through England with 40 knights in a wager of battle with him over certain lands in dispute between them.

Thomas's next adventure took him on crusade with the Teutonic Knights against the pagan Lithuanians of eastern Prussia. He travelled with the king's uncle, Thomas, Duke of Gloucester, and met out there his old adversary Douglas of Nithsdale, whom he is rumoured to have killed in a quarrel at Danzig, though there is reason for supposing Douglas in fact survived him for some months.[3] Perhaps he only inflicted a mortal wound. However, on 18 August 1391, Thomas Clifford was himself slain in battle against the Lithuanians in East Prussia.

Thomas Clifford married Elizabeth de Ros, daughter of Thomas, 5th Lord de Ros, by his wife Beatrice de Stafford, daughter of Ralph, 1st Earl of Stafford, K.G., Lord Lieutenant of Aquitaine (one of the victors of Crécy). Elizabeth Lady Clifford died in March 1424 and was buried in Bondgate Church, Appleby. They had a son and a daughter:

1. JOHN, 7th Lord Clifford, K.G., for whom see Chapter Eighteen.

1. MAUD, who married firstly, before 24 July 1406, John Nevill, 6th Lord Latymer. They were divorced *causa frigiditatis ujusdem Johannis Nevill*, after which Maud married secondly, after 1411, the widower Richard Plantagenet, Earl of Cambridge (brother of Edward, Duke of York, who was killed at Agincourt), who was a grandson of both King Edward III of England and King Pedro the Cruel of Castile. Her new husband's late wife, Anne Mortimer, had been the rightful eventual heiress to the throne as opposed to the usurping House of Lancaster. Accordingly, before leaving for the Agincourt campaign, King Henry V safeguarded himself by having Maud's husband beheaded for high treason in August 1415. However, Cambridge's son by his first wife, Richard, became Duke of York, Regent of France and Protector of England (and also the father of Kings Edward IV and Richard III), and was to kill Maud's nephew Thomas, 8th Lord Clifford in the opening battle of the Wars of the Roses. In 1445-6 Maud induced this nephew to give to the Carmelite Friars at Appleby timber for the repair of their house, to be taken out of Whinfell Forest. In her will, she left Thomas, who she styles *Dominus de Clifford et de Westmorland*, a bed, and to her godson, John Clifford, she left 12 silver dishes. She left her grand-niece, Beatrice Waterton, a gold cross and also mentions her god-daughter Maud and her cousin Alice, Countess of Salisbury. In a codicil she left her niece Joan, Lady Clifford her golden collar.[4] Maud Clifford, Countess of Cambridge died on 16 October 1446, having lived mainly at Conisborough Castle where her royal husband had been born.

Chapter Eighteen

Generation XIII – John, 7th Lord Clifford, K.G. (c. 1388-1422)

John Clifford was barely three years old when his father was killed in Prussia and he succeeded as 7th Lord Clifford and hereditary Sheriff of Westmorland. He was old enough to be summoned to parliament as a baron from 1411 onward, and he attended the coronation of Henry V in 1413. A soldier like all his line, he was with Henry V in France, took part in the siege of Harfleur and fought at Agincourt in 1415, where the French were routed by the English longbowmen in the traditional way. He also took part in the siege of Cherbourg and received its surrender. In 1416 he was retained by the king for service in the north with 200 men-at-arms and 400 archers.[1] Two years later Henry V again secured his services, requiring him to raise a force for the king's campaign to recapture Normandy for the English Crown.

Like his father, John Clifford was fond of jousting, and was badly wounded in the great tournament of Carlisle between six English and six Scottish knights, organised by Ralph Nevill, 1st Earl of Westmorland. On 3 May 1421 he was elected a Knight of the Garter: the second Clifford to attain that honour. Returning to campaign in France, he was killed in action 13 March 1421-2 at the siege of Meaux, where Henry V caught dysentery and also died the following August. Lord Clifford's body was brought home to be buried in Bolton Abbey, of which the family had been patrons since they acquired the Honour of Skipton. Recent research has shown that some pieces of once blue-grey marble tombstone lying in the north aisle near the vestry come from his grave and still show the inset for part of Lord Clifford's Garter insignia.

John, 7th Lord Clifford married in May 1404 Elizabeth Percy, daughter of the famous Harry Hotspur, Lord Percy, K.G. by his wife Elizabeth Mortimer, the daughter of Edmund, 3rd Earl of March by his wife Princess Philippa of Clarence, daughter and heiress of Lionel, Duke of Clarence, the second surviving son of King Edward III. Lady Clifford's father, Harry Hotspur, was, of course, with his opponent the Earl of Douglas, one of the heroes of the Ballad of Chevy Chase, that *chevauchée*, or cavalry raid *par excellence* that ended in the moonlight fight at Otterburn. The dead Douglas won the fight, and the ransomed Hotspur lived on to be slain at Shrewsbury in rebellion against the usurper King Henry IV.

By his wife, Elizabeth Percy, John Clifford had two sons and a daughter:

1. THOMAS, 8th Lord Clifford, for whom see Chapter Nineteen.
2. HENRY, who died without issue, but who had married a cousin, Anne Percy.[2]
1. MARY, who married Sir Philip Wentworth of Nettlested, and was ancestress of the Wentworth earls of Stafford. She was buried in Friars Minors at Ipswich.

As a widow, Elizabeth Percy, Lady Clifford married secondly, in 1426, Ralph Nevill, 2nd Earl of Westmorland, and had further issue by him, who died 3 November 1484 aged about eighty. This strong-minded and powerful lady had first contracted to marry the earl on 7 May 1426, had then obtained from the Regency a licence to marry whom she would, on 20 July, and finally a papal dispensation after marriage on 28 November 1426. Her grandsons (by both husbands) Lord Clifford and Lord Nevill were both to be killed at Towton in 1460. She herself died on 26 October 1437 and was buried in Staindrop church.

Chapter Nineteen

Generation XIV – Thomas, 8th Lord Clifford (1414-55)

Like his father, Thomas, 8th Lord Clifford was only a child (of seven) when his father was killed (in France in 1422), and he was for much of his youth under the guardianship and influence of his grandmother and mother, Elizabeth Percy, who became Countess of Westmorland four years later. Elizabeth was a determined matchmaker, and she contracted with Lord Dacre in 1424 for the payment of 1,100 marks if her son Thomas (then ten years old) should marry his daughter, Joan Dacre, and in the event of her death, his younger daughter, Margaret Dacre. If Thomas should die before reaching marriageable age, his younger brother Henry should inherit the right to marry one of the Dacre girls. Meanwhile, Thomas's grandmother, Elizabeth de Ros, paid the king £200 in 1423 for the right to decide his marriage. In the event, after his grandmother's death in March 1424, Thomas Clifford duly married Joan Dacre.

Thomas Clifford's duties in the north began early and continued all his life. In 1434-5 he was joined in commission with his uncle the Earl of Northumberland to array the northern counties against the Scots, who were then threatening to retake Berwick; in 1449 he was a conservator of the truce between England and Scotland; and as late as 1450-1, with the Bishop of Durham, he was one of the ambassadors from King Henry VI to James III, King of Scots. From 1436 onwards he was regularly summoned to parliament as a baron.

By 1435 he had joined the retinue of the Duke of Bedford, Regent of France, and was playing his part in the Hundred Years War. In 1437 he laid siege to Pontoise, just outside Paris, and, taking advantage of a snow storm, dressed his soldiers in white, and thus camouflaged scaled the ramparts, surprised the garrison and captured the fortress. Two years later, Thomas was still holding Pontoise against the French king. In 1452 and again in 1454 he was called upon to muster men and ships from the northern counties for the relief of Calais, as the English war effort in France weakened rapidly. The French had developed artillery as a counter to the hitherto invincible English longbow, which in the end proved decisive. Furthermore, the days when the retainers of great nobles fought as private armies on 'hire' to the Crown were coming to an end. Mercenary soldiers wearing the livery or uniform of their lord, such as the Clifford Wyvern, and who were maintained by them had produced a situation not unlike the over-mighty trades unions of the present day, who enjoyed privileges placing them above the law. Internecine feuds between baronial retainers became intolerable to the people of England and to the Crown, and while the energies of these obstreperous men could be diverted into battles against the French, they were tolerable, but when, as at the onset of the Wars of the Roses, they were fought out in England, the country suffered grievously.

The retainers of great nobles at first fought private wars with each other, as between Clifford's cousins the Percies and Nevills. Then these groups began to amalgamate and forge alliances to form larger unions, until at last, when Henry VI went temporarily mad (perhaps from porphyria, that scourge of the English royal family down to the time of George III), it became a struggle for the Regency between those magnates with retainers who supported the *status quo* under the Lancastrian Duke of Somerset and those who supported the Duke of York, who (through the Duke of Clarence) was the legitimate heir to the throne. Later, from the badges retrospectively used to describe the two factions – the Red Rose of Lancaster and the White Rose of York – the struggle became known as the Wars of the Roses. From the very start, the Wyvern badge of Clifford was deeply committed to the Lancastrian cause.

The last battle of the Hundred Years War was fought at Castillon on the Dordogne, when the new French artillery defeated John Talbot, 1st Earl of Shrewsbury, who was killed with a battle-axe, in July 1453 (see Chapter Eight above for the Earl's connection with the Clifford family). Less than two years later, on 22 May 1455, the first battle of the Wars of the Roses was fought at St Albans. Lord Clifford, commanding the vanguard of the greatly outnumbered Lancastrian forces loyal to the king, barricaded the streets. He was already heavily engaged with the Duke of York's men when Richard Nevill, Earl of Warwick, with another force, attacked him from the rear. The Lancastrians were overwhelmed and Clifford, his uncle Northumberland and the Duke of Somerset were slain and their bodies left naked in the street, and the king was captured. Shakespeare describes how Thomas Clifford's son found his father's body and swore a lifelong vendetta against the House of York:

> Even this sight
> My heart is turned to stone: and while tis mine
> It shall be stony. York not our old men spares;
> No more will I their babes: ...
> Meet I an infant of the House of York,
> Into as many gobbets will I cut it
> As mild Media young Aboyrtus did:
> In cruelty will I seek out my fame:
> Come thou new ruin of old Clifford's house.

This oath is intended by Shakespeare to prepare his audience for the subsequent scene at the battle of Wakefield in which John Clifford is supposed to have encountered York's son, the young Earl of Rutland, and his tutor who pleads 'Ah, Clifford, murder not this innocent child'. This is a fantastic piece of poetic licence: it is unlikely that a child and his tutor would be found sauntering around a field of battle, and furthermore Rutland, born in 1443, was already 17 years old.

Thomas Clifford was only 40 when he was killed at St Albans, and it is an indication of the precariousness of life that his son, John, should complain that 'York not our old men spares'. The Wars of the Roses took a frightful toll of the English nobility, many being killed while still in their teens.

Thomas Clifford's wife, Joan, was the daughter of Thomas, 7th Lord Dacre of the North by his wife Philippa Nevill, daughter of Ralph, 1st Earl of Westmorland, K.G. They had four sons and six daughters:

1. JOHN, 9th Lord Clifford, for whom see Chapter Twenty.

2. Sir ROGER, knight, who was implicated in his cousin the Duke of Buckingham's rising against Richard III in 1483 and executed in 1485. Sir Roger Clifford was caught outside Southampton, probably while trying to find a ship to take him abroad to safety, and brought back to London for trial and execution. Fabyan, perhaps an eye-witness, tells us that as he was being dragged on the customary hurdle to Tower Hill through the City, the priest attending him untied his bonds, and, when they passed the church of St Martin-le-Grand, his servants tried to pull him into the sanctuary. But the Sheriff's officers threw themselves on him and held him down till he could be secured again.[1]

The ill-fated Sir Roger married Joan Courtenay, daughter of the Lancastrian leader Hugh, 4th Earl of Devon by his wife Lady Margaret Beaufort, sister of Queen Joan Beaufort of Scotland and grand-daughter of John of Gaunt, Duke of Lancaster, and titular King of Castile. Two of Lady Joan's brothers, the 5th Earl of Devon and Hugh Courtenay, had been beheaded as Lancastrians, while her third brother, the 6th Earl, was killed commanding the Lancastrian rearguard for Queen Margaret at Tewkesbury in 1471. After Sir Roger was beheaded, his widow married secondly Sir William Knyvett. By Lady Joan, Sir Roger had two daughters and a son, CHARLES Clifford, who in 1513 was captain of H.M. ship *La Baptiste* of Calais of 20 tons, with a crew of 101 men. She is listed in the same naval flotilla as the famous *Mary Rose*. Captain Charles Clifford married Anne, daughter of Sir William Knyvett of Bokenham in Norfolk, and in turn had a daughter and two sons, EDWARD Clifford (who married Margaret Layton and left a daughter DOROTHY) and WILLIAM Clifford (who was included in Lord Cumberland's entail of 1555 but died without issue).

3. Sir ROBERT, of Brackenborough in Lincolnshire and Aspenden in Hertfordshire, for whom see below.

4. THOMAS, the Scrivener, who may have died without issue, but *Boyd's Inhabitants of London* suggests he might have had sons John, Richard, Edward and William, and a daughter Idonea.

1. ELIZABETH, who was contracted at the age of six to marry Robert Plumpton,[2] who died, eventually married his brother, William, who was killed at Towton. She then married in 1466 Sir Richard Hamerton of Hamerton. By William Plumpton she had a daughter who married John Radcliffe.

2. ANNE, married first Sir Richard Tempest of Bracewell as his second wife, and second Sir William Conyers of Marske.[3]

3. MAUD, married first Sir John Harington of Aldingham in Lancashire, son of Sir Thomas Harington of Homby and Brierly, killed at the battle of Wakefield in 1460; second, Sir Edmund Dudley; and third, Richard Wentworth of West Bretton, Yorkshire.[4]

4. JOAN, married Sir Simon Musgrave of Harcla Castle, Westmorland.

5. MARGARET, married Robert Carr, who was in the service of the Earl of Warwick in 1467 at Catton.[5]

6. BEATRICE, married Robert Waterton and died without issue in 1480-1. Waterton, however, left an illegitimate son, Thomas.[6]

Sir ROBERT Clifford Brackenborough and Aspenden fought a duel in 1478 with John Cheyne (afterwards Master of the Horse) at a tournament to celebrate the marriage of the Duke of Gloucester to Anne Nevill, daughter of Warwick 'The Kingmaker'. Although Cheyne appeared on a horse arrayed in 'a footcloth of goldsmith's work', they fought on foot and the contest became overheated, but Cheyne showed such chivalrous restraint that the heralds awarded him a special prize. In 1496, Sir Robert Clifford was deeply involved in the business of Perkin Warbeck, but was later pardoned by Henry VII. Perkin Warbeck was the Yorkist pretender who so closely resembled King Edward IV that he may have been his natural son. He claimed to be the younger of the little princes murdered in the Tower, and was accepted as such by the King of Scots, who even gave him his cousin in marriage. But the attempted rising failed and Warbeck was eventually executed.

By his wife, daughter of William Barlee, or Berkeley, of Aspenden (widow of Sir Ralph Jocelyn, K.B., twice Lord Mayor of London, who died in 1478), Sir Robert Clifford left an only son:

i. Sir THOMAS Clifford of Brackenborough and Aspenden, who was living in 1555 but dead by 1558. He married Ellen, daughter of John Ewerby of Ewerby (widow of William Cutler), who died in 1668. By her he had two sons and two daughters:

A. THOMAS Clifford, born before 1528, married Elizabeth daughter of Sir William Skipwith, by whom he had two sons and four daughters:

a. HENRY Clifford, who married first, Jane Manby by whom he had no issue; and second, Elizabeth Thimelby of Irnham, Lincolnshire, by whom he had four sons and five daughters. After his death on a voyage to Spain in the service of his cousin, George, 3rd Earl of Cumberland, his wife became a nun and died in the convent of Louvain in 1642. Henry Clifford and his family still held Brackenborough and Fotherby at the beginning of the 17th century according to Henry's IPM held at Grantham in 1601, at which date his eldest son, George, was aged fifteen. Henry died at Portarica (Puerto Rico) in the West Indies in the service of the Queen. For details of the issue of Henry Clifford see below.

b. FRANCIS, died by 1592, probably without issue.

a. GARTRED, married George Metham 1579.

b. BARBARA, living in 1558 but dead by 1572.

c. THOMASINE, living 1592.

d. ELEANOR/ELLEN married William Yarborough, died 1616.

HENRY Clifford and Elizabeth Thimelby had, as stated above, three sons and six daughters:

aa. GEORGE Clifford, for whom see below.

bb. THOMAS, died young without issue between 1585 and 1589.

cc. WILLIAM, born in 1594, died 1670, was a priest and was educated at Douay, of whom more below.

dd. ROBERT, born posthumously at Fotherby 1597, died without issue 1599.

aa. JUDITH, born 1585, died 1586 at Fotherby.

bb. JANE, died 1585 at Fotherby without issue.

cc. MAUDLYNE, born 1587, married Thomas Blythe in 1623.

dd. MARY, living in 1639 having married ... Hammond.

ee. JANE, born 1591, died 1594.

GEORGE Clifford was born in 1585 and died in 1639. By his lengthy will dated 15 April 1639 it appears that he had an only daughter, Ursula by his first wife, Ursula Digby of Laffenham. His second wife, Mary Daniell, who died in 1653, was a recusant. On her death her estate passed to her step-daughter, Ursula Clifford, who was recorded in 1687 as a recusant also, where her name is coupled with that of a John Clifford, both of Lincoln. With the death in infancy of Thomas and Robert, the sole heir to this branch of the Clifford family was William, a priest. Some authorities believe that this William was a pretender to the earldom of Cumberland, but it has not been possible to find evidence to support this. On the contrary, a copy of a letter he wrote to Lady Anne Clifford, dated 24 December 1664,[7] tends to demolish the theory. William writes:

Madam,

Though the divine Providence hath disposed me to end my days in another course than many wellwishers coude have desired, yet since Beatitude is to be sought in Eternity I cannot but conceive all temporary enjoyments which are only lent us for so uncertaine a tyme to be but of little value, amongst which may be reckoned those vaine hopes of immortalizing our names by a numerous posterity, since from so many auncestors of yore noble family which have shined in their severall generations for above six hundred yeres, I am the only survivor of my sex. This relation, Madam, has emboldned me to hope that the testimonie of my humble respects and wishes of truest happinesse might not be ungrateful to your Honor in acknowledgement of your gracious favours to my nearest kindred, my brother whilst he lived, and since to his only daughter my neece Clifford. For all which both nature and duty doe justly oblige me ever to remayne

Madam

Your Honors most humble servant
W. Clifford.

B. GEORGE Clifford, died without issue.

THOMAS and GEORGE Clifford are mentioned in the 2nd Earl of Cumberland's entail of 1555, but only Thomas, as we have seen, had male issue, and though the writer of the letter quoted above was one of these, it is quite clear that no thought of claiming the earldom occurred to members of the Brackenborough branch. According to the Hothfield MS, George held the appointment of 'Greenwax' in London and is said to have died without issue. This, however, is debatable, since there exists the will of a George Clifford of Hanney dated 10 October 1557, proved in January 1586 showing issue and possible connections with this George who is said to have died without issue.

A. LUCY married John Thorney of Lincolnshire.

B. ELIZABETH married John Barnard. Both had issue.

Chapter Twenty

Generation XV – John, 9th Lord Clifford (1435-61)

John, 9th Lord Clifford, hereditary Sheriff of Westmorland, was born and baptised at Conisborough Castle, the home of his godmother and great-aunt, Maud Clifford, Countess of Cambridge, on 8 April 1435. When he was just 20 his father was killed by the Yorkists while he was commanding Henry VI's vanguard in the opening battle of the Wars of the Roses, and the whole of the rest of his life was devoted to avenging his father's death. Known as 'Black-faced' or 'Bloody' Clifford, his inexorable hatred of Yorkists earned him the nickname of 'the Butcher' as well.

The black-visaged Lord Clifford made his first forceful appearance in February 1458 when he arrived with a large force outside the walls of London near Temple Bar accompanied by his cousin, the new Earl of Northumberland, and his kinsman, the new Duke of Somerset, clamouring for compensation for the deaths of their fathers at St Albans. The almost powerless King Henry VI and his Council intervened and successfully ordered the Duke of York and the Earls of Salisbury and Warwick to establish masses for the souls of the slain noblemen and to pay their representatives a 'notable sum of money'.

Meanwhile, ever since the Duke of York had made himself Protector of England after his victory at St Albans, Henry VI's vigorous queen, Margaret of Anjou, had been planning to restore the Lancastrian cause. In 1459 she made an unsuccessful attempt at Blore Heath, but the Yorkist force deserted wholesale soon afterwards and its leaders went into exile. Lord Clifford promptly took the oath of fealty

10. John, 9th Lord Clifford: known as Black-faced Clifford, he was killed at the Battle of Towton in 1461.

to Henry VI at the Parliament of Coventry in November, and was appointed Governor of Penrith Castle, Commissary-General of the Scottish Marches, and a conservator of the truce with Scotland by the revived Lancastrian government.

But in 1460 the Duke of York and his Nevill relations returned from exile, defeating the Lancastrians at Northampton, and capturing the king himself. York now appeared in London to lay claim to the throne (it must be remembered that he was the stepson of Maud Clifford, Countess of Cambridge, whose husband's first wife had been the heiress of the true Clarence line). Meanwhile Queen Margaret and

77

Lord Clifford were gathering fresh levies in the north. York marched north to meet them, but was caught with an inferior force, defeated and killed at the battle of Wakefield on 31 December 1460. Clifford, the principal Red Rose commander, was knighted on the battlefield: he was still only twenty-five.

At Wakefield, where for the slaughter of so many men he earned the nickname of 'Butcher', black-faced Clifford certainly took the opportunity to avenge with acts of bitter cruelty his beloved father's death at the hands of the White Rose five years earlier. According to Shakespeare, Clifford and Northumberland captured the Duke of York and were about to slay him when Queen Margaret intervened, saying,

> Brave warriors, Clifford and Northumberland
> Come make him stand upon this molehill here

whereupon they put a paper cap on his head and mocked him for his pretensions to the throne. York deplored the death of his uncles and his son in the battle and, sobbing, exclaimed,

> These tears are my sweet Rutland's obsequies
> And every drop cries vengeance for his death
> 'Gainst thee fell Clifford, and thee, false Frenchwoman.

This imaginary interchange of abuse came to an end when York is stabbed, first by Clifford and then by the Queen who ordered

> Off with this head and set it on York gates
> So York may overlook the town of York.

York's death caused consternation in the Yorkist camp where the Duke's son bewails,

> Sweet Duke of York! Our prop to lean upon
> Now thou art gone, we have no staff, no stay!
> O Clifford! Boisterous Clifford! Thou hast slain
> The flower of Europe for his chivalry.

According to Holinshed, Lord Clifford cut the head off the Duke of York's corpse and presented it, bedecked with a paper crown to Queen Margaret. This grisly relic was placed thus over the gates of York in mocking derision of the duke's hopes of a kingdom. In dealing with the Clifford family, York's sons, King Edward IV and Richard III were never to forget this. Moreover, Clifford is reported to have killed York's youngest son, Edmund, Earl of Rutland, whom he caught on the bridge at Wakefield and stabbed to death in cold blood after he had surrendered, despite the boy's pleas for mercy. 'Bloody' Clifford is reported to have shouted above the din of battle, 'By God's blood, thy father slew mine, so will I do to thee'.

History confirms Shakespeare's estimate of York's character. He conquered Ireland and yet retained the goodwill of the Irish, which nobody has done before or since. In marked contrast to the conduct of others in similar circumstances, he not only spared the life of his rival, King Henry VI, but actually permitted him to continue on the throne for life. Henry himself recognised York's merits and clemency and deplored the exposure of his head on the walls of York. The Duke of York was succeeded by his son, Edward, Earl of March, then 19 years old. He assumed command of the Yorkist forces and defeated a detachment of Lancastrians at Mortimer's Cross in 1461. The captured nobles were promptly beheaded, among them Owen Tudor who had married Catherine, widow of Henry V, whose grandson later became Henry VII.

The command of the Lancastrians in 1461 after their victory at the second battle of St Albans, in which both took part, was shared by Clifford and Northumberland. Edward had himself crowned at Westminster as King Edward IV, and at once rallied his armies and marched north against the Lancastrians. On arrival at Pontefract an advance guard was sent under Lord FitzWalter and Warwick's brother to seize the crossing of the river Aire at Ferrybridge. It was a vital point, and Clifford led a force to recapture it, which he did successfully. Finding it impossible to dislodge Clifford from his position, Edward outflanked him by crossing the river a few miles upstream at Castleford, and surrounded him with a force superior in strength. Clifford fought with desperate courage and so exhausted himself that he had to loosen the gorget

11. Clifford's Tower, York, from the south.

of his armour, and while so exposed was shot through the throat with an arrow and fell dead. With him fell the Lancastrian cause. Having disposed of Clifford's advance guard, the Yorkists marched against the Lancastrians' main army, drawn up between Towton and Saxton, and after a particularly bloody battle the Lancastrians were defeated. The victory was followed by attainders and forfeitures of estates surpassing all previous severities. Later King Edward showed clemency to many nobles killed at Towton, including Sir Ralph Percy. But no such mercy was shown to the House of Clifford, and all their vast domains and castles remained forfeit for more than a quarter of a century before they were restored by Henry VIII.

The body of 'Black-faced' John, 9th Lord Clifford was buried in a pit with some fellow soldiers killed on the battlefield. He had married Margaret Bromflete, daughter and heiress of Henry, Lord Vescy by his wife Eleanor, daughter of William 5th Lord FitzHugh. They had two sons and two daughters:

> 1. HENRY, 10th Lord Clifford, for whom see Chapter Twenty-One.
> 2. RICHARD, allegedly sent abroad as a child by his mother for safety after the Yorkist victory at Towton in 1461. He is also alleged to have died in exile when young and without issue, but more recent research shows that he was certainly alive in 1490, aged 34. In that year 'Dame Margaret Clifford, daughter and heir of Henry Bromflete, Kt, late Lord Vescy of the one part and Richard Clifford, her son of the other part demised lands which he holds for the payment of a rose at the Nativity of St John the Baptist. The land to revert to him on her death'.[1] This appears in a Deed dated 4 February 1490/1 and further references to Richard appear for a few more years thereafter up to the date of his possible death in 1502 or soon afterwards. It is not known whether he married and had issue.[2]
> 1. ELIZABETH married Sir Robert Aske of Aughton. Their son, Robert Aske, was the leader of the Pilgrimage of Grace, who took for a banner the Five Wounds of Christ, and demanded that the monasteries be restored, but he was disarmed by guile and executed in 1537.
> 2. MARJORIE, contracted to marry Martin Attsea (del See) in 1492/3, whose marriage settlement was agreed by her brother Richard in that year.[3]

Lord Clifford was posthumously attainted on 4 November 1461, whereby his peerage was forfeited and all his estates confiscated. His Lordship of Westmorland was given to Richard, Duke of Gloucester (afterwards King Richard III), while his Honour of Skipton was granted to the opportunist Sir William Stanley (brother of Lord Stanley, the future 1st Earl of Derby).

His widow, Margaret Bromflete, married secondly Sir Lancelot Threlkeld of Threlkeld in Cumberland, and died on 12 April 1493. She was buried at Londesborough in Yorkshire, where her monumental brass was to be seen until it recently went missing.

Chapter Twenty-One

Generation XVI – Henry, 10th Lord Clifford 'The Shepherd Lord' (c. 1454-1523)

Henry, 10th Lord Clifford, although scarcely seven years old, was in great peril at his father's death, since King Edward IV sought vengeance for his brother Rutland's slaying by 'Butcher' Clifford. The Yorkists were just as determined to eliminate leading Lancastrians as the Cliffords had been to eliminate Yorkists. Henry's widowed mother therefore entrusted the boy to the care of a woman who had been a nursery-maid at Skipton Castle but was now married to a shepherd living near Londesborough, her family's estate in Yorkshire.

Soon after the battle of Towton the Yorkists examined Lady Clifford about her sons. She said that she had sent them to the Low Countries to be educated in safety, and surprisingly she was believed, because she could prove that she had taken them to an English port for embarkation to Europe. In fact, only Richard, her younger son, had left the country, while she had smuggled Henry back to the shepherd's lonely farm in Yorkshire. Here Henry lived from the age of seven to 14 without fully realising his secret importance. In order to maintain the secret, and to ensure his safety, he was brought up without education as a member of the shepherd's family. Lady Clifford, meanwhile, had moved to her father's house at Londesborough, from where she could occasionally visit her son and generally keep an eye on him, but after Lord Vescy's death in 1468 reports reached Edward IV that the young Lord Clifford was alive and possibly in England. Perhaps as a bait a general pardon for him was issued on 16 March 1471/2, but his mother, now married to Sir Lancelot Threlkeld, had him and his shepherd foster-parents moved to an even more remote farm near the Scottish border across which he could escape in the event of further searches being made for him.

When at last the Red Rose triumphed over the White at the battle of Bosworth in 1485 and Henry VII became king, a richly dressed cavalcade of loyal knights and gentlemen rode out of the remote farm, sought out the startled shepherd and, dismounting, did homage to him as their liege lord of Clifford, hereditary Sheriff of Westmorland. Thus the shepherd lord came out of hiding and found himself restored to royal favour and once more the vast family estates became his responsibility. In one sense it was like the happy ending to a fairy tale, but although he was now over thirty years old, his lack of education had been such that he could not even sign his name. It speaks much for his sturdy character that in spite of this handicap he became an able administrator, and the simple, country life he had learnt to love encouraged him to take special interest in the repair and upkeep of his castles, the management of his lands and the welfare of his tenants.

His marvellous mother had lived long enough to see her wise precautions vindicated and her son's restoration to the peerage, the shrievalty and the fine castles of Skipton, Brough, Brougham, Appleby and Pendragon. Henry VII knighted him at once, and he was summoned to parliament as a baron in September 1485, his attainder being reversed on 9 November after parliament had duly assembled. That September he was also appointed a Yorkshire commissioner of array against the Scots and receiver of Crown lands. The following May he was made Steward of Middleton and employed to receive the remaining Yorkist rebels to allegiance. In February 1491, he laid claim to the Durham manors of Hart and Hartlepool, and three years later paid a rare visit to London to attend the ceremonies at which the Duke of York (later King Henry VIII) was made a Knight of the Bath.

His famous descendant, Lady Anne Clifford, Countess of Dorset, Pembroke and Montgomery, wrote of him as 'a plain man, who lived for the part a country life, and came seldom to court or London, except when called to Parliament', for the shepherd lord preferred to live in semi-retirement at Barden Tower, which he had built for himself in upper Wharfedale near Bolton Abbey. As a shepherd lad he had lain out many a night with his sheep watching the stars and pondering. So here at Barden he built his tower to be an observatory where, with the help of the neighbouring canons of Bolton, he could study the heavenly bodies. In spite of his lack of education – indeed, perhaps, because of it – he was a man of studious bent with a special interest in astronomy, astrology and chemistry. This feature of his life, and the romantic story of his early years, form the basis of one of Wordsworth's poems, 'Song of the Feast of Brougham Castle', and of what is perhaps the finest passage in the 'White Doe of Rylstone'. Thus in two generations, the Clifford lords are immortalised for war by Shakespeare and for peace by Wordsworth.

> But not in wars did he delight,
> *This* Clifford wished for worthier might;
> Nor in broad pomp, or courtly state;
> Him his own thoughts did elevate, –
> Most happy in the shy recess
> Of Barden's lowly quietness.
> And choice of studious friends had he
> Of Bolton's dear fraternity;
> Who, standing on this old church tower,
> In many a calm propitious hour,
> Perused with him, the starry sky;
> Or, in their cells, with him did pry
> For other lore – by keen desire
> Urged to close toil with chemic fire;
> In quest belike of transmutations
> Rich as the mine's most bright creations.
> But they and their good works are fled,
> And all is now disquieted –
> And peace is none, for living or dead!

In the former poem Wordsworth wrote:

> – Now another day is come,
> Fitter hope, and nobler doom;
> He hath thrown aside his crook
> And hath buried deep his book;
> Armour rusting in his halls
> On the blood of Clifford calls;
> 'Quell the Scot', exclaims the Lance –
> Bear me to the heart of France ...

But in vain. This Clifford's heart was softened by his life on the fells tending his sheep:

> Love had he found in huts where poor men lie;
> His daily teachers had been woods and rills,
> The silence that is in the starry sky,
> The sleep that is among the lonely hills.
> In him the savage virtue of the Race,
> Revenge, and all ferocious thoughts were dead:
> Nor did he change; but kept in lofty place
> The wisdom which adversity had bred.

Henry Clifford remained in rural retirement until he was nearly sixty years old, when he roused himself to be one of the principal commanders against the Scots at Flodden Field. When all other martial enterprise failed to appeal no Clifford could resist a border fight: it was in the blood. As the Ballad of Flodden Field has it:

> From Penyghent to Pendle kill
> From Linton to Lond Addingham
> And all the Craven Cotes did till
> They with the lusty Clifford came.

Lord Clifford first assisted the Earl of Surrey, the royal commander-in-chief, at the relief of Norham Castle and then fought at Flodden itself on 9 September 1513 with Surrey's central vanguard against the division commanded by the Earl of Crawford, who was killed as was the King of Scots himself. Old Clifford captured three pieces of artillery from King James IV's famous ordnance, 'the Seven Sisters', to adorn his castle at Skipton. It is probable that the Clifford standard at Flodden had the Cross of St George in the hoist, then the red wyvern with the motto *Desormais* in the fly and a powdering of golden Vipont annulets.

Clifford continued to act as a Commissioner of Array for the defence of the three Yorkshire Ridings, Cumberland and Westmorland. In 1522, he lent Henry VIII 1,000 marks for the king's French campaign – almost the largest sum on the list. But he was too old and infirm in September 1522 for military service so his eldest son, Sir Henry Clifford, had to lead the Clifford force against the Scots for him.

The Shepherd Lord died the following year, on 23 April 1523, leaving instructions for his burial at Shap Abbey in Westmorland or Bolton Abbey in Craven.

The Shepherd Lord was nearly forty when he married, some time before 1493, Anne, daughter of Sir John St John of Bletso, K.B., by his wife Anne, daughter of Sir Thomas Bradshaugh, of Haigh in Lancashire. The St Johns (afterwards Lords St John of Bletso from 1558 and Viscounts Bolingbroke) are an ancient Anglo-Norman baronial family, descended in the direct male line from Hugh de Port, Baron of Basing, a powerful Norman nobleman at the time of the Conquest. Anne St John, Lady Clifford, was herself a first cousin of King Henry VII, their mutual grandmother being Margaret Beauchamp (sister and heiress of Lord Beauchamp of Bletso), whose first husband had been Sir Oliver St John and whose second husband had been John Beaufort, Duke of Somerset, K.G. In bestowing his own cousin's hand on the Shepherd Lord, King Henry VII was thus honouring him for his years of tribulation in the cause of the Red Rose.

By Anne St John, the Shepherd Lord had at least two sons and five daughters:

1. HENRY, 1st Earl of Cumberland, K.G. for whom see Chapter Twenty-Two.
2. Sir THOMAS Clifford, Governor of Berwick, who held the manor of Burnside in Westmorland and died in 1544. He is buried in Westminster Abbey in spite of his will of 10 December 1543 modestly directing that his body be buried in the parish church wherein he should happen to die. Sir Thomas Clifford married Lucy Browne, daughter of Sir Anthony Browne, Standard-Bearer of England, by his wife Lucy Nevill, daughter and co-heiress of John, Marquess of Montagu (brother of Warwick the Kingmaker). After Sir Thomas's death, his widow held the

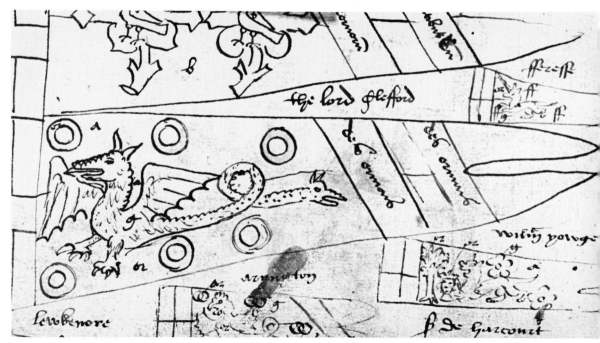

12.   The Shepherd Lord Clifford's standard. The top half was argent (white) and the bottom half or (gold or yellow)
The motto 'Des ormais' appears twice on transverse bands.

manor or late priory of Sandwall in Staffordshire, and died in November 1557, being buried in Shenley Church in Hertfordshire. By her Sir Thomas left a daughter, ELIZABETH Clifford, who married John Fitzwilliam of Kingsley, Hampshire. One of Elizabeth's grand-daughters was Frances Eure, the wife of Robert Lambton of Lambton. Her grandson was Sir Ralph Blakiston, Bt., of Gibside from whom descended Claude Bowes-Lyon, 13th Earl of Strathmore and Kinghorne, the grandfather of Queen Elizabeth the Queen Mother.

1. MABEL, married William FitzWilliam, Earl of Southampton, K.G., Admiral of England, who died at Newcastle in 1543 upon his march into Scotland leading the van of the English army, but, so highly was he esteemed, that to do honour to his memory, his standard was borne in the forward throughout the ensuing campaign. Mabel Clifford, Countess of Southampton, was buried at Farnham on 1 September, 1550.

2. ELIZABETH, married first Sir Ralph Bowes of Streatlam, who died in 1516. One of her great-great-great-great-grand-daughters was Mary Eleanor Bowes, who marred John Lyon, 9th Earl of Strathmore, who took the additional surname of Bowes since Mary Eleanor was the last of her line. John and Mary Eleanor Bowes-Lyon were two of the great-great-great-grandparents of Queen Elizabeth the Queen Mother. In this way the Shepherd Lord is twice over a direct ancestor of the present Queen and her children and grandchildren. Elizabeth married second, William Tongue.

3. ELEANOR married first Sir Ninian Markenfield, and second (by papal dispensation, 18 May 1526) as his third wife, Sir John Constable of Burton Constable, who died in 1537. She died in 1540.

4. ANNE married Robert Clifton of Clifton, Nottinghamshire, who died in 1517/8 leaving issue by her.

5. DOROTHY who married Sir Hugh Lowther of Lowther in Westmorland, by whom she was ancestress of the Lowther earls of Lonsdale.

The Shepherd Lord's second wife, Florence, was a lady of singular virtue and industry, and with the help of her ladies made many tapestries in the Arras style, which were still hanging at Skipton in Charles I's time, but were lost or destroyed during the Civil War. As a widow, Florence Pudsey, Lady Clifford remarried Lord Richard Grey, younger son of Thomas, 1st Marquess of Dorset, K.G. Her new husband's grand-niece was the unfortunate Queen, Jane Grey, beheaded in 1553/4 after a reign of less than ten days.

Lady Anne Clifford tells us in her diary that the Shepherd Lord had 'many base children'.[1]

Chapter Twenty-Two

Generation XVIII – Henry Clifford, 1st Earl of Cumberland, K.G. (1493-1542)

Henry Clifford, 11th Lord Clifford, 1st Earl of Cumberland, Knight of the Garter, hereditary Sheriff of Westmorland, was born in 1493. He is said to have been brought up with the future King Henry VIII. On 23 June 1509 he was made a Knight of the Bath by the ancient ceremony of bathing to wash away sins after a chapel vigil in the White Tower at the Tower of London, in preparation for the coronation of the monarch. Thereafter he was known as Sir Harry Clifford until his father's death in 1523.

As a young man, Sir Harry appears to have sown his wild oats, and to have caused his father much worry. A letter from the wise old Shepherd Lord to a Privy Councillor complains of the ungodly and ungoodly disposition of his son, Henry, in such 'wise as it was abominable to hear it'. The old man goes on to accuse his son of open robbery and violence 'in such wise as some whole towns are fain to keep to the churches both day and night, and dare not come to their own houses', as well as of apparelling himself and his horse in cloth of gold and goldsmith's work, 'more like a duke than a poor baron's son as he is'.[1] Lord Clifford also expressed the wish that his son would cease associating with 'certain ill-disposed persons as well young gents as others'. Perhaps this is why, although young Sir Harry was one of the gentlemen of Yorkshire originally chosen to be present at the Field of the Cloth of Gold, the magnificent occasion at which Henry VIII and Francis I met in France, his name was struck off the list.

By 1522, however, Sir Harry Clifford was not only Sheriff of Yorkshire, but took command of the Clifford forces in the campaign against Scotland that year, his father being too ill to ride with them in person. A contemporary sketch of his red wyvern badge from his battle standard on this occasion survives in the College of Arms MS. 1.2.

The following year the fiery Sir Harry succeeded his father as 11th Lord Clifford, and continued to be active in border warfare until 1526.

Meanwhile, on 18 June 1525, Harry was created Earl of Cumberland by his old friend King Henry VIII. The occasion was one of great public rejoicing over the capture of the King of France by the Emperor Charles V (Henry VIII's brother-in-law) at the battle of Pavia, where the last Yorkist claimant, Richard de la Pole, Duke of Suffolk, was among the slain. In celebration, King Henry made his own natural son Duke of Richmond, and created one Marquess (Exeter), three Earls (Rutland, Cumberland and Lincoln) and two Viscounts (FitzWalter and Rochford). Of these, the only creations to survive today are Rutland and Lincoln in the persons of the Dukes of Rutland and Newcastle.

The new Earl of Cumberland was also appointed Lord Warden of the West Marches, and Governor of Carlisle Castle, a post he relinquished to William, Lord Dacre in 1528 after a bitter quarrel. Both noblemen had been bidden to attend the Council of the North in November 1528, after the Earl of Northumberland had vainly striven to make a final award. In 1533 the earl had a similar dispute with the young Duke of Richmond over his right to hold a sheriff's tourn at Kendal. In May and June 1534 he was engaged in the inquiry into Lord Dacre's treason, and on 27 October was once more ruling the borders quietly. In 1534 he was re-appointed to govern Carlisle Castle for life, and he afterwards became Lord President of the Council of the North.

Meanwhile, Lord Cumberland stuck by his old friend the king in the religious and political troubles of the reign that saw the separation of the Church in England from Rome. In July 1530 he signed the letter to Pope Clement VII in which the king sought papal sanction for his divorce from Catherine of Aragon. In 1534 he was sent to search Bishop Tunstall's house at Bishop Auckland for a copy of that prelate's treatise *De Differentia Regiae et Ecclesiasticae Potestatis*, and the following year he was given charge of the Privy Seal 'because none of the king's council would receive it'. In April 1535 he was one of the Middlesex commissioners of Oyer and Terminer for the trials of the Prior of the Charterhouse, Bishop Fisher of Rochester and Sir Thomas More himself.

During the Pilgrimage of Grace, the northern Catholic rising which was led by Cumberland's cousin, Robert Aske, the Cliffords were one of the three great families of the north to remain loyal to the Crown. 'The earl had hard work to hold his castle of Skipton (October 1536), weakened as it was by wholesale desertion, against the rebels' siege. Froude tells us the romantic story that his eldest son's wife, Lady Eleanor Clifford (King Henry VIII's niece) and her infant children were rescued from danger at Bolton Abbey and carried safely to Skipton through the very heart of the besieging host by the chivalrous courage of Robert Aske's brother, Christopher.'[2]

As a reward for his loyalty, Cumberland was granted the newly dissolved abbey of Bolton for the sum of £2,400 1s. 1d. together with its Skipton possessions and nine manors in Yorkshire.[3] In 1537 he was installed as Knight of the Garter. He died on 22 April 1542 and was buried on 2 May at Skipton.

Henry Clifford, 1st Earl of Cumberland married first, Margaret Talbot, daughter of George, 4th Earl of Shrewsbury, K.G. by his wife Anne, daughter of William, 1st Lord Hastings, K.G. However, Margaret Talbot died childless soon after their marriage which took place when she was still a child. He married second, Margaret Percy, daughter of Henry Algernon, 5th Earl of Northumberland, K.G. by his wife Catherine, daughter and eventual co-heiress of Edmund, Duke of Somerset, Regent of France. Margaret Percy brought the Cliffords as a dowry the whole Percy fee in the Bolton district, thus making them lords of almost all Craven. She died on 25 November 1540. By her Henry Clifford had two sons and four daughters:

1. HENRY, 2nd Earl of Cumberland, for whom see Chapter Twenty-Three.
2. Sir INGRAM, of Cowthorpe, High Sheriff of Yorkshire in 1554. By his first wife, Anne, daughter and heiress of John Ratcliffe of Cowthorpe, Sir Ingram had two daughters; the younger died in infancy, but the elder, ELEANOR, married first in 1567, Robert, the son and heir of William Plumpton, Esquire, and second, in 1572, Michael Porter, but was dead by 1577. Sir Ingram's second wife, Ursula Maddyson, was executrix of his will, made in 1577 and proved in

1579, by which time his issue was extinct. He left most of his property, including his hawks, to his nephew George, 3rd Earl of Cumberland, and much of the rest to his other nephew, Francis Clifford (afterwards 4th Earl).

1. CATHERINE, 'beautiful and pious', who married first, John, 8th Lord Scrope of Bolton, who was implicated in the Pilgrimage of Grace. She married secondly, Sir Richard Cholmley of Whitby, Yorkshire, and died in 1598 and is buried at Whitby. Through her marriage to Lord Scrope, Catherine Clifford was ancestress of the present Lords Clifford of Chudleigh (see Part Three, Chapter Thirty-Four).

2. MAUD, married John, Lord Conyers of Hornby Castle and had issue three daughters.

3. ELIZABETH, married in 1533, Sir Christopher Metcalfe of Nappa.

4. JANE, married Sir John Huddlestone of Millom, Cumberland.

In his will, dated 2 April 1542, the first Earl of Cumberland also left to his bastard son, Thomas Clifford, the sum of £40.[4] This illegitimate son was totally accepted and served his father well as Deputy Captain of Carlisle in 1537. He settled at Nesfield, some few miles from Skipton, and was also engaged as a Steward of his father's estates. Although married he does not appear to have had any children for, by his will dated 20 March 1569, he bequeathed most of his estate to his wife. He styled himself Esquire and held land at Silsden and Nesfield. It will be seen in the following chapter that he was included in the 2nd earl's entail of 1555, when the latter was fearful that he might die without a male heir. The 2nd earl was, of course, his half-brother.

Chapter Twenty-Three

Generation XVIII – Henry Clifford, 2nd Earl of Cumberland, K.B. (c. 1517-70)

When Henry Clifford, 12th Lord Clifford and 2nd Earl of Cumberland, succeeded his father in 1542 he was 25 years old, until which time he held the courtesy title of Lord Clifford. As such he was made a Knight of the Bath in 1533 on the vigil of Queen Anne Boleyn's coronation. In the same year he was contracted to make one of the grandest marriages in the realm to the Lady Eleanor Brandon, daughter of Charles, Duke of Suffolk by his Tudor wife Mary, Dowager Queen of France, sister of King Henry VIII himself. In order to pay for the necessary magnificence of this royal marriage, which took place in the summer of 1537 at her father's house in London, and at which Henry VIII was present, the Cliffords had to sell their manor of Tenbury in Worcestershire, the oldest part of their inheritance, which they had held since the 12th century, and which was their last remaining estate in the west.

By this marriage, Henry Clifford had two sons who both died in infancy (perhaps of the royal malady, porphyria) and a daughter, Margaret, who thus became politically important, for in his will King Henry VIII entailed the crown for default of issue of his son Prince Edward (Edward VI) and of his daughters Mary and Elizabeth to the Lady Frances, daughter of his sister the French Queen, and for default of issue by Frances, to the Lady Eleanor and her issue, namely Margaret Clifford. Five years after Henry had succeeded to the earldom, his wife Eleanor died and was buried in Skipton on 27 November 1574. The earl was heartbroken and 'on learning he was a widower he swooned and lay as one dead'. He was laid out and covered with a hearse-cloth ready for burial and did not revive until his startled attendants, supposing him to be actually dead, were making arrangements to embalm his body. He made a slow recovery after having been fed on human milk for over a month, and lived to be a strong man in later life.[1] After the shock of his wife's death, the earl retired to the country and only visited Court three times – at Queen Mary's coronation, on the occasion of his daughter's wedding, and again soon after Queen Elizabeth's accession.

In 1553, on the death of Edward VI, the Duke of Northumberland supported Lady Jane Grey in her unwilling claim to the throne, having married her to his son, Lord Guildford Dudley. Furthermore, he also betrothed his brother, Sir Andrew Dudley, to little Margaret Clifford, aware, no doubt, of the terms of the late King Henry's will. However, on Mary Tudor's accession, the Earl of Cumberland declared his allegiance to her, and took possession of his daughter's treasures in the queen's name. He went to London, handed over the Garter jewel and the other treasures to the queen and, on payment of £500, was allowed to keep the rest of the forfeited property of Sir Andrew Dudley, who had been duly executed for treason when his brother, Northumberland and Jane Grey were beheaded. Cumberland was bearer of the Third Sword at Queen Mary's coronation, and from 1553 and 1559 was Lord

ÆTATIS
M·D·

13. Portrait of Margaret Clifford, Lady Strange, by Hans Eworth. The arms depicted are those of the marriage of Lady Eleanor Brandon to Henry Clifford, 2nd Earl of Cumberland (1537).

Lieutenant of Westmorland, being also appointed in 1557 to be High Steward of the estates of the Duchy of Lancaster: all marks of the queen's favour.

On Queen Elizabeth's accession Cumberland faced further difficulties on account of his religion. In July 1561 and again in February 1562 he and his new father-in-law, Lord Dacre, were accused of protecting the popish priests in the north. Seven years later he supported the claims of Mary, Queen of Scots to the English throne but he did not take part in the Catholic Rising of the Northern Earls that led to the execution of Thomas, 7th Earl of Northumberland and to the ruin of the Nevill earls of Westmorland. Maybe his non-adherence was due to his health, for he died at Brougham Castle on 2 January 1569-70 and was buried at Skipton. His skeleton was exposed in 1803 and is described by Whitaker in his history of Craven as that 'of a very tall and slender man ... Something of the face might still be distinguished, and a long prominent nose was very conspicuous'. According to his grand-daughter, the Lady Anne Clifford, he was studious 'of all manner of learning and much given to alchemy'.

By his first wife, Lady Eleanor Brandon, he had two sons and a daughter:

1. HENRY, died in infancy and buried at Skipton.
2. CHARLES, died in infancy and buried at Skipton.
1. MARGARET, born at Brougham in 1540, died at Clerkenwell on 29 September 1596, buried in St Edmund's Chapel in Westminster Abbey. She married on 12 February 1554-5 Henry Stanley, Lord Strange, afterwards 4th Earl of Derby, who died on 25 September 1593, leaving issue by her. She married secondly, Sir Cuthbert Ratclyff. Lady Margaret Clifford, Countess of Derby, was looked upon by many as the legal heir to the English throne in 1557.[2]

The 2nd Earl of Cumberland married again in 1552 or 1553 Anne, daughter of William, Lord Dacre of Gillesland, by his wife Elizabeth Talbot, daughter of George, 4th Earl of Shrewsbury. By her he had two more sons and three more daughters:

3. GEORGE, 3rd Earl of Cumberland, for whom see Chapter Twenty-Four.
4. FRANCIS, 4th Earl of Cumberland, for whom see Chapter Twenty-Five.
2. FRANCES, born at Skipton 1555 and married in 1577 Philip, 3rd Lord Wharton, who died in 1625, leaving issue. She died in 1592 and was buried at Kirkby Stephen.
3. MARY, born at Skipton in 1556, died in infancy.
4. ELEANOR, born at Skipton in 1557, died in 1573 and was buried at Appleby.

In 1555, having then as yet no surviving son, and anxious that his vast estates should not pass through the female line but remain with male Cliffords, although descended from the Vipont heiress, Lord Cumberland made an entail settling them with remainders in the following order, failing male issue to himself: 1. Sir Ingram Clifford, his brother; 2. Thomas Clifford of Bolton, his natural brother; 3. Thomas Clifford of Aspenden, a cadet of the 8th Lord Clifford; 4. George Clifford, brother of the foregoing; 5. William Clifford of London, senior cadet of the 8th Lord Clifford; 6. Henry Clifford of Borscombe, ancestor of the Lords Clifford of Chudleigh.

The widowed Anne Dacre, Countess of Cumberland, died at Skipton and was buried there on 31 July 1581.

Like his father before him, Henry was not without his own illegitimate offspring, and it is safe to record the existence of at least two such children: Elizabeth, who later married Benjamin Lambert, and Joan who married Edward Birkbeck in 1553.[4] He may have had illegitimate sons, but no record of them survives with certainty. By his will of 1569 he left many of his manors to his younger son, including Londesborough, so as to cut out his heir. This had the effect that Lady Anne could not claim them or ever try to get them back. They included Wighton, Sutton, Bromflete, Malton and Londesborough. The last-named is important in that it continued in the Boyle line.

Chapter Twenty-Four

Generation XIX – George Clifford, 3rd Earl of Cumberland, K.G. (1558-1605)

George Clifford, 13th Lord Clifford and 3rd Earl of Cumberland, Knight of the Garter, hereditary Sheriff of Westmorland, was born on 8 August 1558 at Brougham Castle. He was a great mathematician and navigator, performing nine voyages as commander or captain, mostly to the West Indies; he captured the town of Faial in the Azores in 1589, and in his last voyage the fort of Puerto Rico. A full account of his life was published by the Cambridge University Press in 1920 – *George, third Earl of Cumberland: His Life and His Voyages*, by G. C. Williamson. Vita Sackville-West, in her introduction to his daughter's diary, which she edited and published in 1923,[1] writes of Earl George:

> The Elizabethan Lord Cumberland, with his personal beauty, his golden armour, his pointed ring, and the Queen's glove in his cap, was, like many of his less exalted contemporaries, little more than a buccaneer upon the maritime trade routes of France and Spain, 'these marine adventures being neither his profession nor yet urged by necessity thereunto, yet such was his lordship's natural inclination'. On eleven separate occasions his lordship's natural inclination prompted him to fit out a fleet (at his own expense) and to set sail for the River Plate, for Costa Rica, the Azores, the Canaries, or the coasts of Spain and Portugal, with the frank intention of plundering such towns as he could reduce and of taking captive such foreign merchantmen as he should encounter. He was wounded in battle, he nearly died of thirst, he was all but wrecked, but, undeterred, after each return to England he at once set about organising a fresh expedition, 'his spark of adventure further kindled and inflamed by former disasters'.

George Clifford succeeded to the earldom at the age of 11 at his father's death on 2 January 1569/70. With his vast estates, he was a great matrimonial prize, and it chanced that the very next day, even before either George or he knew of the late Lord Cumberland's actual death, that the Earl of Bedford wrote to Queen Elizabeth I[2] seeking the wardship of the young man, and informing her of a proposed marriage between him and one of his daughters. Thus Bedford achieved the lucrative post of wardship to young Cumberland, and later married him to his youngest daughter, Margaret Russell. Under Bedford's care George was educated first at Peterhouse, then at Trinity College, Cambridge, where he matriculated in May 1571. His tutors included John Whitgift, later Archbishop of Canterbury, and William Whitaker. His accounts are in the Masters' Book at Trinity College and make interesting reading of the expenses of a young nobleman at the time. His three years there cost £200, which was a considerable sum as he was not yet thirteen when he first became an undergraduate.[3]

George was good at mathematics and geography, and to further his study of the latter he transferred to Oxford, to which he eventually returned in 1592 to receive an Honorary M.A. His fairness of speech and ability to write poetry – as well became an Elizabethan – is mentioned by both John Dowland[4] and Anthony Holbourne.[5]

14. George Clifford, 3rd Earl of Cumberland, depicted in his specially-commissioned armour with Queen Elizabeth I's jewelled glove in his hat.

At the age of 18 Lord Cumberland was married in the presence of Queen Elizabeth at St Mary's Overy in Southwark on 24 June 1577 to Lady Margaret Russell. It was a double wedding, for George's sister, Frances, married Lord Wharton at the same time. It was a fairly happy marriage, and 28 years later Cumberland was writing to his wife as 'My sweet Meg'. She outlived him by ten years. However, their daughter, Lady Anne tells how her father fell in love with a 'lady of quality' whereby his affections from 'his well-deserving wife' were alienated, so perhaps this was but a passing fancy on the earl's part. Lady Anne also tells us of her father's great love of sport, especially of horse racing, tilting, bowling, shooting and hunting, which 'did contribute the more to the wasting of his estate'. His portrait by Nicholas Hilliard shows him in elaborately chased gold-inlaid armour specially made for tournaments by the royal armories at Greenwich. But the pursuit of sport and the writing of poetry soon gave way to the voyages for which he became famous. Indeed, his extravagances at Court made him short of cash, and in some quarters his desire to go to sea was hailed as a means of recouping his finances, and also with delight by those who were jealous of him who hoped he might not return.

Years later a beautiful manuscript account of his overseas adventures was prepared for Lady Anne when she was Countess of Dorset at Knole, probably by her secretary or a certain Richard Robinson, and this is the source of much that follows.

George Clifford's first voyage was intended for the South Seas, but only reached Brazil and was not a great success. His little fleet consisted of four ships, the *Red Dragon* of 260 tons, the barque *Clifford* were his; the *Roe* and the pinnace *Dorothy* belonged to Sir Walter Raleigh, who joined them at Plymouth. They set sail on 17 August 1586 but were driven back to Dartmouth by contrary winds; setting sail again on the 29th they eventually reached the Canaries. They continued to Sierra Leone where they captured 'a great foule monster' thought to be an 'allagata'. Thence they headed for the Straits of Magellan but on reaching the coast of Brazil they proceeded no farther. A Portuguese ship was taken off the River Plate in January, whose cargo of slaves they sold for 400 ducats each. They returned to England in September 1587 after a not very profitable expedition.

After this it was expected that Cumberland might go to help Drake, who had captured Santo Domingo in 1586, but nothing came of this project. Meanwhile he was one of the peers on the Commission that tried and sentenced Mary Queen of Scots in February 1587/8, being one of the four earls instructed to sign the deeds and attend her execution at Fotheringhay.

The preparations for his second voyage took some time, and he seems to have been disappointed that the queen did not at once help to finance it. He had gone to assist the beleagured forces in the Low Countries, but arrived too late to save Sluys, which the Duke of Parma had captured from Sir Roger Williams. He was back in England in time to command the *Elizabeth Bonaventure*, a royal ship of 600 tons, in action against the Spanish Armada in 1588, and after the decisive action off Gravelines on 29 July he personally carried the news to the queen in her camp at Tilbury, where the queen knighted him.[6] Three months later, George wrote to Sir Francis Walsingham from Plymouth reporting a rumour that the Duke of Medina-Sidonia, Commander-in-chief of the scattered Armada, had been driven ashore some twenty-three miles down the coast, but it proved to be false. Walsingham in his despatches to Burghley refers to George Cumberland's part in the defeat of the Armada and his bringing news of it. In the paylist of the fleet mobilised against the Armada, the *only* privately owned vessel was the Earl of Cumberland's *Samson*.[7]

The reports of Cumberland's gallantry so pleased the queen that she now lent him the *Golden Lion*, 500 tons, with a commission to attack the Spaniards. The cost of the other ships for his second voyage, as well as the equipment of the *Golden Lion*, he bore himself. He set sail on 14 October 1588, and soon captured the *Hare*, out of Dunkirk laden with merchandise for Spain, which he sent home. A storm drove him to Freshwater Bay and there the expedition ended. The following year the queen lent him the *Victory*, originally the *Great Christopher*, the sixth largest ship in the Royal Navy at 95 feet in length and 694 tons draft. An account of this voyage is to be found not only in Dr. Williamson's *Life* but also in Hakluyt's *Voyages*. The fleet consisted of four ships. The *Victory* with a crew of 400, the *Margaret*, the *Meg* and a small carvell set sail from Plymouth in June 1589. Three days later they met and captured three French ships of the League.[8] As the booty was mainly Newfoundland fish, it was distributed and two of the captured vessels were sent to England, while the third, with the French crews of the others, was sent back to France. On 13 July a battle took place off the Portuguese coast and cargoes worth some £4,500 were captured and divided among the four ships of Cumberland's fleet. Approaching the Azores they captured more ships transporting wine, cloth, silk and taffeta. From there Cumberland sailed to Flores for food and water and on to Terceira where more prizes were taken with the aid of other English ships that were in the vicinity, including one belonging to Sir Walter Raleigh. Next they attacked Faial, cutting out seven Spanish ships from under the guns of the castle, thus getting 'an unexpected victory, rather by valour than reason',[9] and the town quickly surrendered. The Governor, Don Diego Gomez, was given a safe conduct, and Cumberland behaved chivalrously with commendable restraint, ordering no looting by his men. Unhappily his orders were not obeyed in many districts of the city. The town was ransomed for 2,000 ducats – mostly paid in church plate – and the earl then gave a dinner on board his flagship for the principal inhabitants, though only four accepted his invitation.

Next he fell in with and captured one of the Spanish West India fleet, richly laden and valued at £100,000. They went then to Graciosa where, after initial resistance, they took on wine and victuals. From there they sailed on to take a prize from Brazil when, on the advice of Captain Lister, who had commanded the *Clifford* on Cumberland's first voyage, they rashly landed under the guns of the fort at St Mary's Isle, which cost them two dead and 16 wounded. Cumberland himself was wounded in the side, head and legs during the assault, but remained with his fleet. The rich West Indiaman was then sent back to England with the *Margaret*, because she was leaky, together with the wounded, under the command of Captain Lister. Two more vessels from Brazil were taken, richly laden, and then the main fleet set sail for home with its prizes. Foul weather hit them off the Scillies and they were forced to make for Ireland where, after great hardships in which men died daily from thirst – more than had been slain in the whole expedition – they eventually reached Bantry Bay. After revictualling, they set sail for England, only to learn on arrival that their richest prize, the West Indiaman, had been wrecked and Captain Lister drowned.

On his return to England, Cumberland heard that his eldest son, Francis, had died, and two years later he lost his younger son, Robert, leaving only his daughter Anne as heiress.

Lord Cumberland spent most of 1590 in London preparing for his next voyage and indulging in one of his favourite sports of tilting.[10] George Peele, the dramatist, writes in his *Polyhymnia*:

> Worthy Cumberland
> Thrice noble earle accoutred as became
> So great a warrior and so good a knight
> Encountered first, yclad in coat of steel
> And plumes and pendants all as white as swan
> And spear in rest right ready to perform
> What 'longed unto the honour of the place.

For his fourth voyage in 1591, the queen's ship which Cumberland commanded himself was the *Garland*, 600 tons, with a crew of 300, accompanied by the *Samson*, the *Golden Noble*, the *Allargata* and a pinnace, the *Discovery*. Captain (afterwards Sir William) Monson, who accompanied the fleet as his principal adviser, adds that there were also other ships of Lord Cumberland's and his friends.[11] The *Allagarta* was a former French ship taken on the previous voyage.

This voyage was less successful than its predecessor. A sugar ship which was captured leaked so much she had to be abandoned; another prize was lost in bad weather off Corunna; several Dutch ships laden with spices were taken and sent home under Monson, but were recaptured by the Spaniards and Monson was taken prisoner and sent to Lisbon, but eventually released. Cumberland was within earshot of the gunfire, but unable to help as he was becalmed.

It seems that the *Garland* was 'evil of sail', so Cumberland decided to return home, but not before he was able to warn Lord Thomas Howard,[12] commanding the English royal fleet, that the Spanish fleet was approaching the Azores in strength to surprise him. Howard heeded Cumberland's warning and drew off, but Sir Richard Grenville in command of the *Revenge*, was unwilling to abandon his sick who had been put ashore. The last fight of the *Revenge* has passed into English folklore.[13] Grenville, a cousin of Raleigh's, probably disobeyed his admiral and paid the price with the loss of his life and his ship. However, Cumberland's warning saved a far larger fleet to fight another day. So he returned somewhat out of pocket, but any privateering expedition which harried the Spaniards was in the national interest and the queen acknowledged this in a kindly letter she wrote him on 9 September 1591.[14] From Cumberland's letters to his wife we learn that he had difficulty in paying off his men, and when he returned to Skipton so many problems had built up that he took a long time getting away again. These problems explain wny Cumberland did not accompany his fifth voyage in person but merely paid for its cost. It was commanded by Captain Norton who engaged some Spanish galleons off Finisterre, and then went on to the Azores, where he fell in with part of Raleigh's fleet, commanded by Sir John Burgh,[15] which had originally been meant to capture Panama. The two fleets joined forces and were soon reinforced by Captain Thomson of Sir John Hawkins' fleet.

They captured the *Santa Croce*, which subsequently ran aground and caught fire, and the *Madre de Dios*, with a cargo of jewels, spices, quilts, carpets, ivory, ebony and china. It was taken after a furious fight and great carnage, and was the largest vessel that had yet been built. On arrival at Dartmouth, efforts to control looting were formidable but only partly successful, and though much was stolen, Sir Robert Cecil and Sir Walter Raleigh saved a lot for the queen and for the backers of the venture. Raleigh, Hawkins and Cumberland each got £36,000; the City of London, which had provided two ships for Raleigh's fleet, received £12,000, but there were many squabbles and complaints of unfair treatment, but the queen, who got all the pepper, made £80,000. To ensure that she got a good market price for it, all imports of pepper were banned for more than a year. Cumberland's expenses had amounted to £19,000, so he made a profit of £17,000.

On 23 April 1592, Lord Cumberland was made a Knight of the Garter, and in June his name was put forward for the post of Lord Warden of the West Marches and Captain of the City of Carlisle to which he was finally appointed in 1603. He also received another signal honour from the queen. Some four years earlier, when he was kneeling before her, she dropped her glove which he picked up, kissed, swore to keep always and to act for ever as her faithful champion against all comers. He mounted the precious glove with jewels in his hat, and it is wearing this hat that he is depicted in Nicholas Hilliard's miniature and in the 1588 portrait in the National Portrait Gallery. In 1592, then, after the resignation of Sir Henry Lee, who had held the position since 1588, George Cumberland was appointed Chief Champion of the Tiltyard to Queen Elizabeth by the name of the Knight of Pendragon Castle.[16]. On Coronation Day 1593 the earl as the Queen's Champion delivered a fine archaic address to Her Majesty at a masque at Windsor Castle, marked by such playful compliments as:

> When Windsor and Pendragon Castle do Kiss
> The Lion shall bring the Red Dragon to Bliss.

The financial success of the 1592 venture encouraged Cumberland to fit out another expedition. This time he determined to command it in person. He commissioned the *Golden Lion*, *Elizabeth Bonaventure*, the bark *Chalden*, *Pilgrim*, *Anthony* and *Discovery* and set out in June 1593. They soon captured two very rich French ships from St Malo, and later defeated 12 'hulks' which were left in Captain Monson's charge, while Cumberland sailed on for the Azores. There they got wind of 24 Spanish and Portuguese ships, but deciding they were too strong for them, discretion became the better part of valour and he sailed on. At this point Cumberland fell seriously ill, and believing that the only way to save his life was to get some cow's milk, the voyage was cut short and the fleet sailed for England. Notwithstanding the curtailment of the expedition, it was not unprofitable, the value of the ships and cargoes captured being estimated at seven million ducats.[17]

Early the following year, the queen sent Cumberland a command to attend the baptism in Scotland in February 1593/4 as her representative of King James VI's son and heir, Prince Henry, later Prince of Wales. But the earl had not yet fully recovered, and at the last moment he fell ill with a 'bloody flux' and the Earl of

Sussex was sent instead. In the meantime the seventh voyage was carrying on in Cumberland's absence. This was really an extension of the previous voyage undertaken by three ships which had been sent direct to the West Indies in June 1593. They attacked the pearl fisheries of Margareta and then sailed to the town where the pearls were stored, captured it and held it to ransom for 2,000 ducats. They went on to capture one or two Spanish ships and at Jamaica a couple of merchantmen laden with hides, all of which they sent back to England with the *Pilgrim*, which reached Plymouth in May 1594.

Meanwhile the *Anthony* fell in with seven Spanish ships in the Bay of Honduras and captured them. The Spaniards' brass ordnance was taken aboard, but their own iron cannon were thrown overboard. They set fire to the biggest Spanish ship, but took home one of 250 tons, arriving the day after the *Pilgrim*.

Lord Cumberland did not take part personally in the eighth voyage.[18] He sent three ships to Terceira in the Azores, where they caught up with the *Cinque Llagas*, then the richest ship afloat worth two million ducats. After a fierce fight the Spanish ship was set on fire and sank with the loss of nearly a thousand lives and all its cargo. Some of those who were saved were taken back to England as prisoners for Lord Cumberland and later ransomed.

In 1595 the earl sent out another squadron, which included a huge new ship of 900 tons, which he had built at Deptford and which the queen launched. She was called the *Malice Scourge*,[19] and, after making three voyages for Cumberland, later did good service for the East India Company. This time good food was laid on and the new ship plus the *Alcedo*, the *Anthony* and the *Olde Frigate* prepared to set sail. By using his own ships Cumberland could risk the fire hazard from boarding the enemy, a course of action forbidden by the queen for her own ships. His original plans seem to have been baulked by Hawkins and Drake who had captured one of the ships he was after, but Cumberland abandoned the operation and returned to Skipton; his captains were sent off independently though they achieved little success. Maybe Cumberland returned home on account of his health, for he is known to have been ill in 1595, though he had recovered enough by the end of the year to go hunting.[20] In October, one of his ships captured a fly-boat laden with corn, and in December Cumberland asked the queen for an extension of his commission to the following summer (1596). He intended to take command of his own fleet that year but the *Malice Scourge* was dismasted and forced to put back to port. In February he was still delayed by contrary winds.

Meanwhile, after much prevarication, Elizabeth authorised the expedition against Spain known as the singeing of the King of Spain's Beard. It is not known what part Cumberland played in the attack, or positively if he was actually there, but it seems probable, and three other Cliffords certainly were. They were Sir Conyers Clifford, who was Adjutant-General to the army, and Sir Alexander Clifford, who was a Vice-Admiral (see Chapter Sixty-One), and Thomas Clifford, later of Ugbrooke (see Chapter Thirty-Four).

In 1597 Cumberland was one of those who submitted plans for a further invasion of Spain, but nothing came of it. Instead he prepared for a tenth voyage, which turned out to be the least successful of them all, for the *Malice Scourge* was caught in a storm and again dismasted soon after leaving England, forcing the earl to return in one of the queen's ships. Later the same year an eleventh voyage was made in the *Ascension* with Lady Cumberland's cousin, Captain Francis Slingsby, in command.[21] Slingsby had the misfortune to run into a Spanish fleet of six ships, in which he lost heavily, and was lucky to get back to England at all. Later this year Cumberland was appointed Constable and Steward of Knaresborough Castle.

Cumberland's final and most successful voyage was launched in 1598. Four warships, one pinnace, one frigate and two barges belonged to him and the rest to various London merchants and others making up a fleet of 21 ships in all with 1,700 men aboard. The *Malice Scourge* was the flagship in which the earl embarked on 6 March 1598 at Portsmouth. Ten days later the fleet met and captured a Flemish ship after a three-hour fight, and soon after three more Flemish and one French ship. On 4 April they set sail for the Canaries, anchoring off Lanzarote on the 13th, where they stayed a week. From there they sailed to Tenerife and then on to Dominica and the Virgin Islands. At San Juan de Puerto Rico they lost 40 men killed and wounded trying to take the port, which they succeeded in doing the following day, and on 20 June the governor surrendered to the earl. The capture of San Juan was strategically important for it cut the Spanish lines of communication. All accounts agree on the earl's insistence on proper discipline among his men. A soldier who raped a Spanish woman was hanged in the market place, and a sailor who defaced a church was condemned to death but later reprieved. After taking as prizes several ships arriving at the port and evacuating 300 Spaniards, Cumberland returned with his fleet and booty to England landing at Blackwall on 1 October 1598. The profitability of this voyage is hard to assess, since accounts of it differ, but Cumberland appears to have decided that it should be his last, for he sold the *Malice Scourge* to the East India Company for £3,700 and the following year we find him engaged in preparations for home defence. There was a strong feeling in England that summer that the Spaniards might attack London, and Cumberland was appointed Lieutenant-General in London and Colonel of the London Trained Bands in command of the defence of the City and of the River Thames. The alarm, however, eventually subsided.

In 1600/1 Cumberland was still Lieutenant-General of the military force of the City when he was faced with the Earl of Essex's hare-brained scheme to seize the queen's person. His precautions were successful, and he later became a member of the Commission which tried and condemned Essex to death for high treason, and on 25 February was one of the six peers who witnessed Essex's execution.

During the closing years of the reign, Cumberland was often consulted by Queen Elizabeth, especially about raids on the Spanish Main. At the same time he tried, with limited success, to get some compensation from her for the great expenses he had incurred on her behalf, by which he had seriously impoverished his estate. In May 1600 he had obtained a licence to buy and sell cloth with the sole right to export white broad-cloths, but this led to conflict with the London Company of Clothworkers, and went very little way towards the reimbursement of the £100,000 he told Cecil his voyages had cost him.

In December 1600 the queen granted a charter to the East India Company of which Cumberland became the first governor, a post in which he showed his accustomed vigour. The company's first voyage in 1601 was sent out under his aegis.[22]

The following year Cumberland was put in charge of the arrangements to welcome Henry IV of France's special ambassador, the duc de Biron, and to escort him from London to meet the queen at Basing. As a reward for this he acquired the manorial rights over the Grafton Regis estate in Northamptonshire as High Steward of the Honour of Grafton and Ranger of Salcey Forest.

On the accession of James VI and I in March 1603, Cumberland was appointed a Privy Councillor. On the royal progress south, the earl claimed the right to bear the Sword of the City of York before the king and to stand next the throne.[23] When the king and queen reached Northamptonshire, they were entertained by Cumberland at Grafton, after which he accompanied them the rest of the way to London, where Lady Cumberland joined him for the coronation in July.

In February 1603/4 he obtained a grant from the Crown of Nichol Forest in Cumberland and of the manors of Arthuret, Lyddall and Radlington, together with sole fishing rights on the Esk. In August 1604 his appointment as Lord Warden of the Scottish Marches was revoked and he was made instead Lord Lieutenant of Westmorland and Northumberland and of the city of Newcastle-upon-Tyne,[24] posts he held with the Lord Lieutenancy of Cumberland till his death. On Twelfth Day 1605 he carried the Golden Rod before Prince Charles, afterwards King Charles I, when he was created Duke of York, and in August that year he entertained the king and queen again at Grafton for five days in August. This entertainment, at which his daughter, Lady Anne Clifford, was present as a child of 15, was, she remarks, 'a time of great sorrow to my saintlike mother' because the earl was living at Grafton 'by reason of some unhappy unkindness towards' Lady Cumberland.

During the last two years of his life he was still heavily in debt and was on uneasy terms with his wife, for, according to his daughter, he had 'fell to love a Lady of Quality', and the 'sweet Meg' of yesteryear took second place. This must have been going on for some time as she (whoever she was) died in the same year as Queen Elizabeth. The estrangement between husband and wife unhappily continued and their letters show no sign of affection but much worry about money.

Then he fell ill at Oxford. He was sent to London where his doctors gave him little time to live. He made his will and wrote a very gentle and kindly letter to 'sweet and dear Meg' asking her to treat his brother and daughter, 'sweet Nan', well. He begged her pardon for any wrong 'that ever in my life I did thee' and commended his requests to her wonted and undeserved kind wifely consideration. This letter brought the countess and their daughter to his deathbed, and he died on 30 October 1605, aged forty-seven. He is buried in Skipton church, where his daughter erected a magnificent tomb with his armorial achievements. His body, which was embalmed, was examined in 1808 by Dr. Whitaker, who found it quite perfect, so much so that the face could be seen to resemble the portraits.

The article about him in the *Dictionary of National Biography* sums up his character as follows:

He has often been spoken of as a sort of nautical Quixote, a title curiously unsuitable to the courtier, gambler and buccaneer, in all of which guises history presents him. His love of adventure was strong, and he staked his money on the success of his cruisers in much the same spirit that he did on the speed of his horses or the turn of his dice. And he spared his body no more than his purse. His courage was unimpeachable, and the temper which he showed in times of difficulty won him both credit and popularity.

But perhaps the finest memorial to him is Spenser's dedication to him of the *Faerie Queene*:

> Redoubted lord! in whose courageous mind
> The flower of chivalry now blooming fair
> Doth promise fruit, worthy the noble kind
> Which of their praises have left you the heir;
> To you, this humble present I prepare
> For love of virtue and of martial power,
> To which, though nobly you inclined are
> As goodly well you shewed in late essays,
> Yet brave examples of long passed days
> In which true honour you may fashioned see,
> To like desire of honour you may raise
> And fill your mind with magnanimity.
> Receive it, therefore, lord as it was meant
> For honour of your name and high descent.

15. Robert, Lord Clifford, who died at the age of five.

By his wife, Margaret Russell, daughter of Francis, 2nd Earl of Bedford, Cumberland had two sons who died in childhood and an only surviving daughter:

1. FRANCIS, Lord Clifford, born 1584, died 1589.
2. ROBERT, Lord Clifford, born at Northall in Hertfordshire 21 September 1585, died in 1591 and was buried with his maternal ancestors at Chenies in Buckinghamshire.
1. ANNE Clifford, Countess of Dorset, Pembroke and Montgomery, for whom see Chapter Twenty-Seven.

Margaret Russell, widowed Countess of Cumberland, was born on 7 and 8 July 1560 at Exeter. Her husband's long absences overseas gave her time to devote to good works such as the almshouses for poor women at Beamsley, near Skipton, which still bear her name. She was bookish, and is described as 'happier in the filial affections of her daughter than the conjugal tenderness of her husband'. Her resolute efforts to obtain for her daughter the family estates which had been settled on the late earl's brother and his heir, occupied much of the years that followed her husband's death and before her own. She died on 22 May 1616 in the chamber at Brougham Castle where her husband had been born. Her bowels are buried in the Nine Kirks in Westmorland and her body in Appleby church. Her daughter Anne was so fond of her that she erected a monument to her at the place near Brougham Castle where they last parted when Lady Anne was on her way home to Knole.

The earl's infatuation with 'a lady of quality' poses the question of her identity. It is suggested that she was Mrs. Douglas Sheffield, whom he contrived to draw as his Valentine at one of the festive occasions he was so fond of, and to whom he gave expensive presents.[25] Was she, perhaps, the mother of his two illegitimate children, a daughter, Frances, who later married Gervase Lascelles, and a son, George, who rose to the rank of Colonel in the Royalist forces and was buried in York Minster on 25 February 1642?[26]

16. Francis Clifford, 4th Earl of Cumberland.

Chapter Twenty-Five

Generation XIX – Francis Clifford,
4th Earl of Cumberland, K.B. (1559-1641)

Francis Clifford, 4th Earl of Cumberland, was born at Skipton Castle in 1559 and succeeded to the earldom on the death of his brother, George, in 1605. The third earl also left him the bulk of the entailed Clifford estates, for which he was sued by his niece, the Lady Anne. The third earl had died in the firm, though quite illogical belief that his brother's son would have no male issue, and that the estates he had left to Francis would come to his daughter in the end. So they did, but she had to wait and fight for them for nearly forty years, for George Clifford had died at the age of 47, whereas Francis lived to be nearly eighty-two. In spite of his longevity, Francis's was not a distinguished career. He was appointed Custos Rotulorum of Cumberland in 1606 and held the post till 1639; he was Lord Lieutenant of Cumberland from 1607 to 1641; and Lord Lieutenant of Northumberland, Westmorland and Newcastle-on-Tyne from 1611 to 1639.

In 1618 Francis entertained King James I at Brougham Castle. That year he was joined by Lord Sheffield, the Lord President of the North, in two commissions for suppressing all murders, felonies, robberies, riots etc. on the borders between England and Scotland, and three years later he was appointed to another commission with the Archbishop of York to correct and amend 'all errors, heresies, schisms, contempts which by any spiritual or ecclesiastical power might lawfully be reformed or redressed'.

He died in the same room at Skipton Castle in which he had been born on 21 January 1640/1, and was buried among his ancestors in the vault below the chancel of Skipton church, where a monument was erected to his memory.

Soon after March 1589 he married Grisold, Lady Abergavenny, widow of Edward Nevill, 7th Lord Abergavenny (known as 'Deaf' Nevill), and daughter of Thomas Hughes of Uxbridge in Middlesex, by his wife Elizabeth, daughter of Sir Griffith Dwnn. Grisold, Countess of Cumberland, died at Londesborough on 15 June 1613, and was buried there. By her the fourth earl had two sons and two daughters:

1. GEORGE, born and died in infancy at Uxbridge in 1590.

2. HENRY, 5th Earl of Cumberland, for whom see Chapter Twenty-Six.

1. MARGARET, married as his first wife, Sir Thomas Wentworth, afterwards 1st Earl of Stafford, K.G., Charles I's minister. She died without issue on 21 September 1622 and is buried in St Olave's church, York. Her husband was beheaded in 1644.

2. FRANCES, married on 7 September 1615 as his third wife, Sir Gervase Clifton, 1st Baronet of Clifton, K.B., M.P., and she died at Hodsock, Nottinghamshire on 22 November 1627, and was buried at Clifton. Sir Gervase was a distinguished Cavalier in the Civil War, was heavily fined by the Roundheads, and died on 28 June 1666, aged seventy-eight.

Chapter Twenty-Six

Generation XX – Henry Clifford, 5th and last Earl of Cumberland, K.B. (1592-1643)

17. Henry Clifford, 5th Earl of Cumberland, wearing armour made for the 3rd Earl. Portrait from the Flemish school, after Van Dyck.

Henry Clifford, 5th and last Earl of Cumberland, Hereditary Sheriff of Westmorland, was born at Londesborough on 28 February 1591/2. After his father's succession to the earldom in 1605, he was styled by courtesy, Lord Clifford, although in fact the medieval barony of Clifford had passed to his cousin Lady Anne, the third earl's daughter. He matriculated as an undergraduate at Christ Church, Oxford on 30 January 1607/8 as 'Baro de Skypton' and became a B.A. on 16 February 1608/9. The following year he was made a Knight of the Bath at the creation of the Prince of Wales. He then became M.P. for Westmorland in 1614, and again in 1621-2, and in 1619 a member of the Council of the North.

From 17 February 1627/8 to 20 February 1639/40 he was called to the House of Lords in his father's lifetime, as *Henrico Clifford, Chevalier*, i.e. Lord Clifford, under the erroneous assumption that the ancient barony of Clifford was vested in his father, largely because the Lady Anne had not claimed it for herself as was her right. He was accordingly placed in several Parliaments in the original precedency of 1299. This was held, a century later, to have created accidentally a new barony of Clifford with precedence from 1628, vested in his descendants.

Lord Clifford became joint Lord Lieutenant of Westmorland from 1636 to 1639, and sole Lord Lieutenant when he succeeded his father in 1641. The following July he was appointed Lord Lieutenant of Yorkshire as well.

Although he was not in any way an active or soldierly man, Henry Cumberland was a loyal Cavalier and supported King Charles I at the outbreak of the Civil War, and in 1642 became the Royalist commander-in-chief in Yorkshire and the north. But he was by this time a sick man, and he died of a fever at York on 11 December 1643 aged 51, and was buried at Skipton. With his death the earldom became extinct. His widow, who was born in 1593, died only two months after her husband, also at York, and was buried in York Minster. Lord Cumberland was the author of *Poetical Translations of some Psalms and the Song of Solomon* and his life is included in the *Dictionary of National Biography*.

Henry Cumberland had married Lady Frances Cecil, the only daughter of Robert Cecil, 1st Earl of Salisbury, Lord High Treasurer of England, the great Elizabethan and Jacobean statesman on 25 July 1610 at Kensington. By her Cumberland had three sons and a daughter who died in infancy, and a sole surviving daughter and heiress, ELIZABETH Clifford, born at Skipton on 18 September 1613. She was considered by Samuel Pepys to be an exceptionally talented woman. She married on 3 July 1634 at Skipton, Richard Boyle, Viscount Dungarvan, afterwards 2nd Earl of Cork in Ireland and 1st Earl of Burlington in England, who was created Baron Clifford of Lanesborough in 1644. He died in 1698. Elizabeth Clifford inherited her father's Barony of Clifford (accidentally created in 1628) but did not claim the title.

Her son, Charles Boyle, Viscount Dungarvan, was summoned to the House of Lords in 1689 in his father's lifetime as 2nd Lord Clifford of Lanesborough. He was the grandfather of Richard Boyle, Earl of Cork and Burlington, K.G., 4th Lord Clifford of Lanesborough, the celebrated connoisseur of Palladian architecture, who in 1737 successfully claimed the 1628 Barony of Clifford to provide a peerage to which his only surviving daughter could succeed. The Burlington Arcade links Cork Street to Clifford Street in London; all three names derive from this combination of titles. When the great Earl of Burlington died in December 1753 and the Barony of Clifford of Lanesborough became extinct, his daughter Lady Charlotte Elizabeth Boyle became Baroness Clifford in her own right. She married in 1748 William Cavendish, Marquess of Hartington, and died in 1754. After her death, the widower became the 4th Duke of Devonshire, and their son, William, 5th Duke of Devonshire was thus also the 7th Lord Clifford (from 1628), and his son, the 6th Duke, was thus also the 8th Lord Clifford. When the 6th Duke died in 1858, this Barony of Clifford fell into abeyance between his two sisters – Georgiana Dorothy, Dowager Countess of Carlisle and Henrietta Elizabeth, Dowager Countess Granville.

The 5th Duke of Devonshire and 7th Lord Clifford was the husband of the celebrated beauty, Georgiana, but had a natural son by Lady Elizabeth Foster, whom he married after Georgiana's death. This illegitimate son was given the surname of Clifford, much to the annoyance of the 6th Lord Clifford of Chudleigh (see Chapter Forty-One), and eventually became Admiral Sir Augustus Clifford, 1st Baronet (1788-1877), Gentleman Usher of the Black Rod.

Chapter Twenty-Seven

Generation XX – Lady Anne Clifford, Countess of Dorset, Pembroke and Montgomery (1590-1676)

18. The Great Picture of the Clifford Family, a triptych commissioned by Lady Anne Clifford in 1646. The left hand panel depicts her in 1605 when her father died and she expected to inherit the estates. The right hand panel (the only portion painted from life) shows her in 1646 when she finally came into her inheritance. The large central panel, a cop of an earlier picture by George Perfect Harding, portrays her parents and her brothers who both died young.

Lady Anne Clifford, the only surviving child and heiress of George, 3rd Earl of Cumberland and his wife, Lady Margaret Russell, was born on 30 January 1589/90 at Skipton Castle. She was a remarkable character, and in an age when women were merely their husbands' chattels, she remained steadfastly herself and her father's daughter. She defied King James, she defied Cromwell and she survived to see the restoration of King Charles II, leaving an indelible mark in the places and among the people who knew her. She was christened in Skipton church on 22 February with Lady Derby and Lady Warwick as godparents. Six weeks later she left Skipton with her parents and did not return for another 50 years. Her surviving brother died when she was 14 months old leaving her heiress to the vast Clifford estates. After her father died in 1605, and during her first marriage to the Earl of Dorset, she spent most of her time in litigation to regain these ancient lands which her father had left to his brother and nephew. It was only after her cousin, Henry, 5th and last Earl of Cumberland, died in 1643 that she finally got all the estates back. She found her castles and churches in ruins and spent the remainder of her life putting them to rights.

The history of most old families is spattered with a good deal of myth and nonsense. Due to Lady Anne's need to prove her claims to the Clifford estates, she undertook a great deal of genealogical research which she backed by uncontrovertible documentation. Thus she attached, quite rightly, much importance to the marriage of Roger Clifford son of the Crusader and Isabel de Vipont in 1269, which brought the Cliffords their northern lands. She mentions that Henry, the 10th baron (1455-1523), married Anne St John, a cousin of King Henry VII, and she tells how her father 'sold muche land and consumed his estate' in continual building of ships, voyages, horse racing, tilting, bowling matches and all such expensive sports. Notwithstanding that her father had left his brother and nephew all the estates and that she had to repair the neglect inflicted by his extravagances, she had a great affection and admiration for him.

Many have asked why the third earl left his estates as he did, and even his daughter says it was because he was determined that they should descend to his heirs male. He knew that his daughter could not succeed to the earldom and neither he nor, at first, Lady Anne thought the Barony of Clifford could go to her.

Owing to her father's absences abroad she was brought up by her mother and educated by a tutor, Samuel Daniel. Her books were of a serious nature, mostly religious, classical and the like including the works of Chaucer, Spenser and Philip Sidney. Her father would not have her taught any language other than English. At the age of 12 she was welcomed by Queen Elizabeth at Court, and, when the old queen died, Lady Anne was taken to see the lying-in-state and to hear the new king proclaimed. Her first visit to King James took place at Theobalds, where she noted that he 'used her mother very graciously'.

Her visits to great houses occupy much of her youthful diary. She went to Lady Blunt's at Ditten Hanger, to the Earl of Kent's at Wrest, to Rockingham Castle, Fawsley Park, Althorp and Grafton, where her father entertained the king and queen. She helped Sir Henry Wallop to entertain them at his house near Basingstoke, then went to stay with Sir Edmund Fettiplace at Swinbrook Manor in Oxfordshire. While the king was at Woodstock the Dowager Lady Cumberland broached the subject of Lady Anne's lands with him. Two years later, in July 1607, she went with her mother to Appleby Castle to set about the battle for her estates, which was to go on for so long, and the pleadings began the following April.

Along with the concern about her inheritance came the question of whom she should marry. One of her suitors was the king's favourite, Robert Carr, Earl of Somerset, but this came to nothing, and she married on 25 February 1609 Richard Sackville, then Lord Buckhurst, and two days later, on the death of his father, the Earl of Dorset.

Dorset was popular at Court and at first seems to have been fond of his wife, but he was not at all keen to support her claims to the Clifford land, and aimed to find a compromise. The Dowager Countess of Cumberland returned to Brougham after the wedding, and Dorset went abroad, so Anne went to Knole to await his return the following year. Her first child, a daughter, Margaret, was born on 2 July 1614.

The legal action was now in full swing, and everyone except Anne was set on a compromise. But she was obdurate, for she remained convinced that her father was wrong in breaking the entail. She went north to rejoin her mother, who gave her her full support, and together they set off to visit the estates. Dorset was furious and did all he could to hinder her, telling her she could not live at Knole and that her daughter should be taken away from her. He even demanded the return of her wedding ring. An added burden fell upon her with the illness and death of her mother in May 1616.

After her mother's death, those lands which had been the Dowager Countess's jointure now became, under the third earl's will, the property of the fourth earl. Dorset sent off letters in his wife's name asking that the jointure lands be held for him as his wife's representative. He also persuaded her to sign a deed conveying the lands to him should she die without heirs. This arrangement bought a temporary improvement in relations between them, but Dorset still continued to persuade her to come to a compromise agreement over the Craven estates. The fourth earl acted with great speed. On hearing of his sister-in-law's death he seized her jointure estates, apologising to the Lords in Council afterwards.

As soon as she had signed the deeds passing the Westmorland inheritance to Dorset failing heirs of her own body, Lady Anne went north to bury her mother, and to face further legal complications. A fight ensued between those who considered themselves her tenants and those her uncle's. Dorset agreed to come north and they went together from Appleby to Brougham. Then Henry, Lord Clifford turned up at Appleby and his attendants began fighting Lady Anne's. This led to an intervention by the Archbishop of Canterbury in June 1616, and a duel between Dorset and Henry Clifford was averted only by the king's intervention.

Everyone expected Lady Anne to sign some sort of compromise agreement as the king himself had consented to adjudicate, but when Dorset and his wife appeared before him she asked the king's pardon and said she would never part with the Westmorland estates as long as she lived. The king and Dorset tried to make her change her mind, but she was adamant, at which, she tells in her diary, the king 'grew in a great choffe'. Following her refusal she was sent down to Knole with her daughter, leaving Cumberland, Clifford and Dorset to come to an agreement without her.

At this point Dorset fell ill and joined her at Knole, but soon recovered and went to London from where further contradictory news soon reached her. Her personal money now became the subject of dispute, which made her life even more difficult, though she still refused to change her position over the Westmorland properties. In March 1617 the king announced his award. He decreed that Lady Anne should convey her lands to the Earl of Cumberland under various remainders and that Dorset should be paid £20,000. So the latter got their money and the former the land, but eventually, under the remainders, Lady Anne regained the whole amount. For the moment, though, she had lost Westmorland.

The summer of 1617 was taken up with lawsuits in the north between the tenantry and Cumberland and his son, which indirectly favoured Lady Anne. Dorset postponed action as long as he could and did not execute the deeds until July 1623, by which time he was a sick man. Three more children were born and died in infancy, which upset her, as she disliked her husband's heir, Sir Edward Sackville. Two of her daughters lived to grow up, Margaret and Isabella, and were her only comfort during the difficulties of her marriage. In March 1624 Dorset died, which made her situation even more difficult, since the new earl disliked her – it was mutual.

Her widowhood lasted six years spent in London, at Chenies and at her jointure house, Bollbroke, in Sussex, fending off attacks on her estates from her cousin, Henry, Lord Clifford, and her brother-in-law. In June 1630, she married her second reprobate husband, the Earl of Pembroke (later to become Earl of Pembroke and Montgomery), who had been a widower for two years, and whose first wife had borne him ten children. Anne bore him two more. As expected, the marriage was not much of a success. They lived together for four-and-a-half years only. In 1634 they parted and she lived separately, mainly in London at Baynard's Castle, near the site of the modern Blackfriars Bridge. In January 1640/1 her uncle Francis, 4th Earl of Cumberland died. This brought her nearer the estates, for his son Henry, the 5th and last earl, only survived his father by just under three years. As he had only one surviving daughter this meant that his estates would return to Lady Anne on his death.

In 1642 the Civil War in England broke out, tearing the country apart, and Lady Anne and her daughter, Isabella, hid themselves in Baynard's Castle for over six years, she being a strong adherent of the king, while her husband, Pembroke, supported Parliament. During this time, in 1647, Isabella married the Earl of Northampton and two years later Lady Anne made her final break with Pembroke and never saw him again, as he died a year later in January 1650. His epitaph, written by one of his royalist enemies runs:

For damning, stinking, swearing and cursing, all the inhabitants of Hell can hardly equal him.

It is something of a puzzle to understand why Lady Anne waited five years and more after her cousin's death before going to claim her estates in the north. In 1645 she appointed Henry Currer steward[1] of her Craven estates to collect her rents and care for her properties. He had been a captain in the royalist forces of the Earl of Newcastle, and had held Skipton Castle against the Parliamentary forces during part of the siege. But after a further Royalist uprising he had been ordered by the Cromwellian government to slight the castle, which meant pulling down its defences and disposing of its armaments. The west end was demolished almost to the ground, where a great breach had been made by a battery planted on a neighbouring ridge. Next, on parliament's orders, the whole of this part of the castle was unroofed, 44 tons of lead and massive quantities of timber being sold for a sum near £450. The upper parts of the walls were pulled down, in some places to about a third of their height, all of which explains why, when Lady Anne came to Skipton in July 1649, a

few months after the slighting, she only stayed in the town ten days before moving
on to Barden Tower, which was itself in only a slightly less dilapidated condition.
Not being a military building it had not suffered quite such a drastic fate as Skipton.
She returned to Skipton the following February and stayed almost a year, living in
the long gallery which had escaped destruction, holding courts, causing boundaries
to be ridden and making repairs. But the old castle lay in ruins until October 1655,
when she set about removing the rubbish which had lain there since the siege ended
in 1648. Over the modern entrance to the castle she had the following inscription
placed:[2]

> This Skipton Castle was repayred by the Lady Anne Clifford, Countess Dowager of Pembroke,
> Dorset and Montgomery, Baroness Clifford, Westmorland and Vescie, Lady of the Honour of
> Skipton in Craven, and Sheriffesse by inheritance of the Countye of Westmorland, in the years
> 1657 and 1658, after this maine part of itt had layne ruinous ever since December 1648, and
> January followinge, with itt was then pulled downe and demolished almost to the foundation by
> the command of the Parliament, then sitting at Westminster, because itt had bin a garrison in the
> then Civil Warres in England.
> Isaiah chap LVIII God's name be praised.

Notwithstanding his steadfast support of the Royalist cause, his obedience to the
orders of Parliament did not spare Henry Currer from being sued by Lady Anne in
the court of Chancery, where he was called upon to explain what he had done with
the rents he was supposed to collect for her and with the money he had received for
the lead, timber and guns which came from the castle when it was slighted.

But to return to 1650; in August that year Lady Anne went to Appleby, the 'most
auntient seat of mine inheritance' as she put it in her diary. From there she went on
to Brougham, Brough and Pendragon, the last two in a very poor state of repair. She
came back eventually to Appleby where she heard of her husband's death. She was
now 60 years old, but still full of energy and vigour. She was for some time short of
money, but settled her affairs with the Craven tenants through her action against
Henry Currer, and took similar action in 1653 and 1654 in Westmorland. Cromwell,
doubtless because Pembroke had supported the Parliamentary case, offered to help,
but she replied 'Does he imagine that I who refused to submit to King James will
submit to him?' When Cromwell heard she was repairing her castles he sent word
that if she did so he would destroy them again. 'Let him destroy them if he will', she
replied 'but he will surely find as he destroys them I will rebuild them'. Cromwell
is reported to have had a great respect for her as the only woman who dared to stand
up to him.

Only Skipton and Appleby were anywhere near fit to live in. She restored the tower
at Appleby and was there when General Harrison billetted his troops on her,
accusing her of being a Royalist, a charge she proudly refused to deny.

Litigation with her tenants continued. Many of them resented having to pay rents
for the Civil War years when she had been hiding in London.

Her diary contains much about her grandchildren, especially Nicholas, Earl of
Thanet, who came with his bride to visit her at Appleby in 1664. At the coronation
of Charles II she sent her page, Lancelot Machell, to represent her. She also
mentions in her diary the visit to England of the Duchess of Orleans to meet the king

at Dover. The king's chief minister at that time was none other than Sir Thomas Clifford (later Lord Clifford of Chudleigh), by this time the senior male descendant of the Cliffords of Skipton and Westmorland.

On 30 January 1676, she records the 86th anniversary of her birth, and the following day she kept as a fast for the martyrdom of Charles I. On 21 March she died, and practically every landowner in the north attended her funeral. Bishop Rainbow of Carlisle, preaching the sermon, described her as 'this great, wise woman, who while she lived was the Honour of her Sex and Age, fitter for an History than a Sermon ... the thrice illustrious Anne, Countess of Pembroke, Dorset and Montgomery stood immovable in her integrity of Manners, Vertue and Religion'.[3]

The estates were left to her surviving daughter, Lady Thanet, for life and then to her grandsons, John, Richard, Thomas and Sackville in that order and afterwards to Nicholas, Lord Thanet, who had inherited large estates in the south. Lady Thanet lived only two years and Nicholas seized the estates in defiance of his grandmother's will. However, he only survived her for three years, when he was succeeded by the brother (John) he had defrauded. The estates passed in turn to John, 4th Earl of Thanet until 1680, then to Richard, 5th Earl for four years, then to Thomas, 6th Earl, who married Lady Katherine Cavendish, daughter of the 2nd Duke of Newcastle. He claimed the ancient Barony of Clifford, and by asserting his grandmother's right to it, and then his brothers' and his own, he became known as the 18th Lord Clifford. The barony fell into abeyance between his daughters and was called out in 1734 by Margaret, Lady Lovell, afterwards Countess of Leicester. She died without issue and the title passed to her great nephew, thence to his son, who died without issue, then via another daughter, Catherine Southwell, who married Colonel George Coussmaker of Martinique. Their daughter, Sophia, born in 1791, became the 22nd Baroness, and married a John Russell. Since 1822 it has descended in the Russell family to the present 27th Baron de Clifford. The situation was confused by the 21st Baron, Edward Southwell, adding 'de' to Clifford in 1777. This was done to distinguish him from the Devonshire Cliffords.

PART THREE

THE LORDS CLIFFORD OF CHUDLEIGH

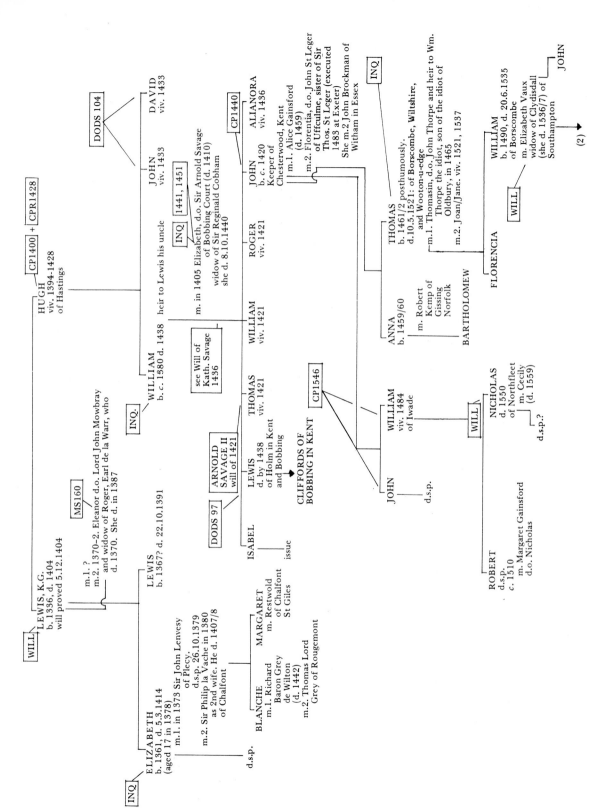

The descent of the Cliffords of Borscombe

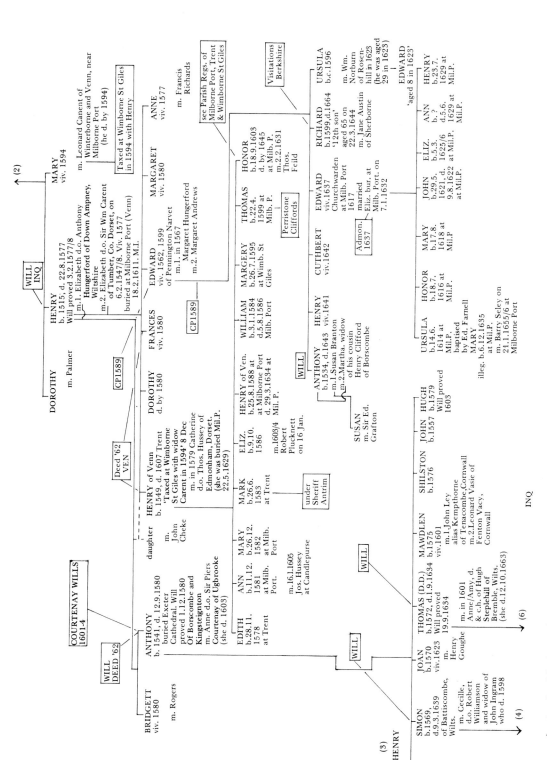

This is a genealogical family tree chart. The content, following the connected branches:

COURTENAY WILLS 16014

↑ (2)

HENRY b. 1515; d. 22.8.1577 Will proved 3.2.1577/8 m.1. Elizabeth d.o. Anthony Hungerford of Down Ampney, Wiltshire m.2. Elizabeth d.o. Sir Wm Carent of Tumber, Co. Dorset, on 6.2.1547/8. Viv. 1577 buried at Milborne Port (Venn) 18.2.1611. M.I.

WILL INQ

DOROTHY m. Palmer

MARY viv. 1594 m. Leonard Canent of Winterborne and Venn, near Milborne Port (he d. by 1594)

Taxed at Wimborne St Giles in 1594 with Henry

ANNE viv. 1577 m. Francis Richards

see Parish Regs. of Milborne Port, Trent & Wimborne St Giles

Visitations Berkshire

BRIDGETT viv. 1580 m. Rogers

ANTHONY b. 1541, d. 12.9.1580 buried Exeter Cathedral. Will proved 1.12.1580 Of Borscombe and Kingsteignton m. Anne d.o. Sir Piers Courtenay of Ugbrooke (she was d. 1603)

WILL DEED '62

daughter m. John Cheke

HENRY of Venn b. 1549, d. 1607 Trent 'Taxed at Wimborne St Giles with widow Carent in 1594' 8 Dec m. in 1579 Catherine d.o. Thos. Hussey of Edmonham, Dorset. (she was buried Mil.P. 22.5.1629)

Deed '62 VEN

FRANCES viv. 1580

DOROTHY d. by 1580

CP1589

MARGARET viv. 1580

EDWARD viv. 1562, 1599 of Pennington Narvet m.1. in 1567 Margaret Hungerford m.2. Margaret Andrews

CP1589

EDITH b. 28.11. 1578 at Trent

ANN b.11.12. 1581 at Milb. Port. m.16.1.1605 Jos. Hussey at Candlepurse

MARY b. 26.12. 1582 at Milb. Port

MARK b. 26.6. 1583 at Trent

under Sheriff Antrim

ELIZ. b. 9.10. 1586 m.1603/4 Robert Plucknett on 16 Jan.

HENRY of Ven. b. 25.8.1588 at Milborne Port d. 29.3.1634 at Mil. P.

WILLIAM b. 3.1.1584 d. 5.8.1586 Milb. Port

MARGERY b.26.7.1595 at Wimb. St Giles

THOMAS b. 22.4. 1599 at Milb. P.

HONOR b.18.9.1603 d. by 1645 at Milb. P. m.2.2.1631 Thos. Feild

Perristone Cliffords

EDWARD viv.1637 Churchwarden at Milb. Port 1617 married Eliz. bur. at Milb. Port on 7.1.1632

RICHARD b.1599,d.1664 '12th son' aged 65 on 22.3.1644 m.2.2.1631 Jane Austin of Sherborne

URSULA b.c.1596 m. Wm. Norburn of Rosenhill in 1623 (he was aged 29 in 1623)

EDWARD 'aged 8 in 1623'

SIMON b.1569, d.9.3.1639 of Battiscombe, Wilts. m. Cecille, d.o. Robert Williamson and widow of John Ingram who d. 1598

JOAN b.1570 viv.1623 m. Henry Goughe

THOMAS (D.D.) b.1572, d.19.1634 Will proved 19.9.1634 m. in 1601 Anne/Amy, d. & c.h. of Hugh Stephell of Bremble, Wilts. (she d.12.10.1663)

MAWDLEN b.1575 viv.1601 m.1.John Ley alias Kempthorne of Tenacombe,Cornwall m.2.Leonard Vasie of Fenton Vacy, Cornwall

SHILSTON b.1576

JOHN b.1557

HUGH b.1579 Will proved 1603

ANTHONY b.1534, d.1643 m.1.Susan Branton m.2.Martha, widow of his cousin Henry Clifford of Borscombe

WILL

HENRY viv.1641

SUSAN m. Sir Ed. Grafton

URSULA b.14.6. 1614 at Mil.P. baptised by Ed. Farnell MARY illeg. b.6.12.1635 at Mil.P. m. Barry Seley on 21.1.1655/6 at Milborne Port

HONOR b.18.7. 1616 at Mil.P.

MARY b.17.8. 1618 at Mil.P.

JOHN b.29.5. 1621, d. 9.8.1622 at Mil.P.

ELIZ. b.5.3. 1625/6 at Mil.P.

ANN b.? d.5.6. 1629 at Mil.P.

HENRY b.23.7. 1629 at Mil.P.

CUTHBERT viv.1642

Admon. 1637

WILL

WILL

INQ

(3)

(4)

(6)

HENRY

(continued on following pages)

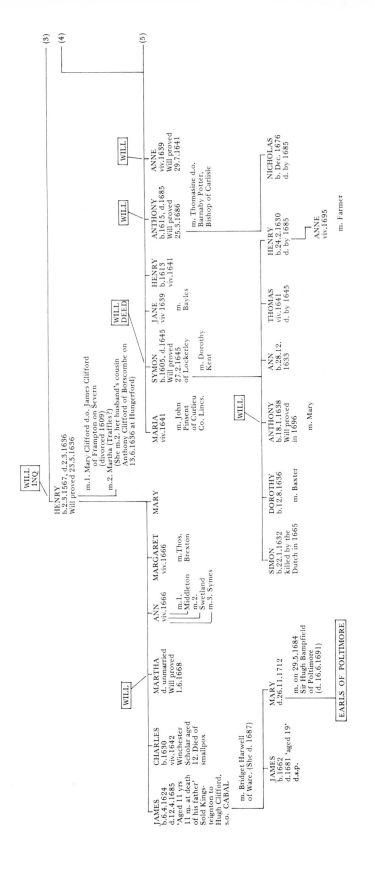

(3)

(4)

(5)

HENRY
b.2.3.1567, d.2.3.1636
Will proved 23.5.1636 [WILL] [INQ]

m.1. Mary Clifford d.o. James Clifford
of Frampton on Severn
(divorced 1609)
m.2. Martha (Traffles?)
(She m.2. her husband's cousin
Anthony Clifford of Borscombe on
13.6.1636 at Hungerford)

MARY

MARIA
viv.1641

m. John
Pinsent
of Curlieu
Co. Lincs.

SYMON
b.1605, d.1645
Will proved
27.2.1645
of Lockerley [WILL] [DEED]

m. Dorothy
Kent

JANE
viv 1639

m.
Bayles

HENRY
b.1613
viv.1641

ANTHONY
b.1615, d.1685
Will proved
25.3.1686 [WILL]

m. Thomasine d.o.
Barnaby Potter,
Bishop of Carlisle

ANNE
viv.1639
Will proved
29.7.1641 [WILL]

MARGARET
viv.1666

m.Thos.
Brexton

ANN
viv.1666

m.1.
Middleton
m.2.
Swetland
m.3. Symes

DOROTHY
b.12.8.1636

m. Baxter

ANN
b.28.12.
1633

ANTHONY
b.18.1.1638
Will proved
in 1696 [WILL]

m. Mary

THOMAS
viv.1641
d. by 1645

HENRY
b.24.2.1630
d. by 1685

ANNE
viv.1695

m. Farmer

NICHOLAS
b. Dec.1676
d. by 1685

MARTHA
d. unmarried
Will proved
1.6.1668 [WILL]

JAMES
b.6.4.1624
d.12.4.1685
'Aged 11 yrs
11 m. at death
of his father'
Sold Kings-
teignton to
Hugh Clifford,
s.o. CABAL

m. Bridget Harwell
of Ware. (She d. 1687)

CHARLES
b.1630
viv.1642
Winchester
Scholar aged
12. Died of
smallpox

SIMON
b.22.1.1632
killed by the
Dutch in 1665

MARY
d.26.11.1712

m. on 29.5.1684
Sir Hugh Bampfield
of Politmore
(d. 16.6.1691)

[EARLS OF POLITMORE]

JAMES
b.1662
d.1681 'aged 19'
d.s.p.

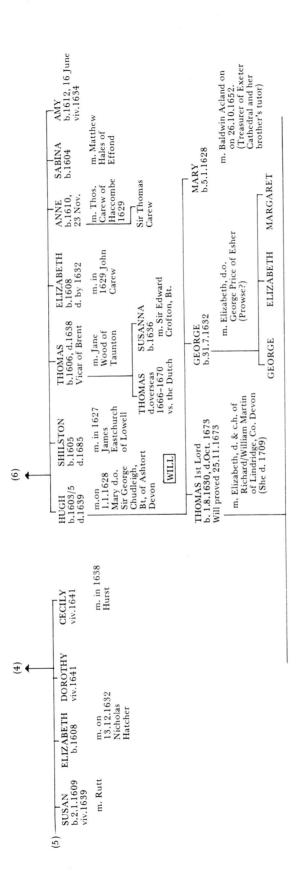

(6)

HUGH b.1603/5 d.1639
m.on 1.1.1628 Mary d.o. Sir George Chudleigh, Bt, of Ashtort Devon
[WILL]

SHILSTON b.1605 d.1685
m. in 1627 James Eastchurch of Lowell

THOMAS b.1606, d.1638 Vicar of Brent
m. Jane Wood of Taunton
THOMAS d.overseas 1666-1670 vs. the Dutch
SUSANNA b.1636 m. Sir Edward Crofton, Bt.

ELIZABETH b.1608 d. by 1632
m. in 1629 John Carew

ANNE b.1610, 23 Nov.
m. Thos. Carew of Haccombe 1629
Sir Thomas Carew

SABINA b.1604

AMY b.1612, 16 June viv.1634
m. Matthew Hales of Effond

THOMAS 1st Lord b.1.8.1630, d.Oct. 1673 Will proved 25.11.1673
m. Elizabeth, d. & c.h. of Richard/William Martin of Lindridge, Co. Devon (She d. 1709)

GEORGE b.31.7.1632
m. Elizabeth, d.o. George Price of Esher (Prowse?)
GEORGE   ELIZABETH   MARGARET

MARY b.5.1.1628
m. Baldwin Acland on 26.10.1652. (Treasurer of Exeter Cathedral and her brother's tutor)

(4)

(5)

SUSAN b.2.1.1609 viv.1639
m. Rutt

ELIZABETH b.1608
m. on 13.12.1632 Nicholas Hatcher

DOROTHY viv.1641

CECILY viv.1641
m. in 1638 Hurst

Sir Lewis Clifford, K.G., His Two Namesakes and William Clifford of Bobbing, Kent (1344 to 1438)

The identity of Sir Lewis Clifford, K.G. and his relationship to William Clifford of Bobbing, Kent, ancestor of the Lords Clifford of Chudleigh, has presented genealogists and historians with great problems. The pedigree drawn up by the College of Arms in 1672 shows him as the son of Roger, 5th Baron Clifford (1333-89) (see Chapter Sixteen), but this is quite impossible since he was clearly of the same generation as the fifth baron, being born about 1344. Sir Iain Moncreiffe believed that he was perhaps the posthumous son of Robert, 3rd Baron Clifford (1303-44), but the confusion is worse confounded by the suggestion of Hugh Peskett that there were probably two other Sir Lewis Cliffords who were his approximate contemporaries. One of them might have been a son or cousin of Robert, 1st Lord Clifford (1274-1314), and the third, who died before 14 August 1410, was probably a son of Sir Thomas Clifford, Lord of Thomond (see Chapter Fourteen), the third son of the 3rd Baron Clifford. We must now look at the claims and careers of these three Sir Lewis Cliffords and do our best to unravel the confusion which results from this duplication of names. Let us begin with the Knight of the Garter.

In 1360 or 1361, Lewis Clifford entered the household of the Duke of Cornwall, later Prince of Wales and Aquitaine, best known as the Black Prince. On 5 August 1364 he was granted £40 a year for life as the prince's esquire. As a member of the prince's household he would probably have taken part in the Rheims campaign of 1359-60 when Edward III set out to establish his claim to the throne of France by having himself crowned in the cathedral – a goal he was destined not to achieve. But the campaign ended in the signing of the treaty of Calais in October 1360 by which Edward III obtained sovereign rights in Aquitaine. Early in 1362 the prince was invested with the additional title of Prince of Aquitaine, and in June 1363 he and his newly wedded wife, accompanied by the Earl of Warwick and a large retinue, including Sir Lewis Clifford, set sail from Plymouth and landed at Bordeaux on the 29th.[1]

It is probable that Sir Lewis continued close to the Black Prince during the next seven years, during which the latter was ruling Aquitaine on his father's behalf, for he witnessed the prince's will in 1371.[2]

The following year he married, probably as his second wife, Eleanor, daughter of John Mowbray by his wife Joan, daughter of Henry of Lancaster, widow of Roger, 3rd Lord de la Warr.[3] The marriage was followed by an exchange of his wife's dowry for the castle and manor of Ewyas Harold with all its dependencies in Herefordshire,

Somerset, Shropshire, Wiltshire and Surrey[3] save the manors of Alington in Wiltshire and Albrighton in Shropshire.

Following the Black Prince's death in 1376 and the accession of his ten-year-old son to the throne as Richard II on the death of Edward III in 1377, Sir Lewis was made a Knight of the Garter and one of 26 Knights of the King's Chamber. The next year he served as joint commander with Sir William Beauchamp in John of Gaunt's expedition to Brittany, and about the same time the Black Prince's widow, Joan of Kent, gave him custody for life of Cardigan Castle. Between 1377 and 1381 and again in 1404, when they reverted to the Crown, he enjoyed the income from the Manor of Princes Risborough[5] in Buckinghamshire and of Mere in Wiltshire. He also had large investments in monastic lands and after 1379 in manors in Warwickshire and Leicestershire.

In 1382 Sir Lewis was sent with Lord Percy as an ambassador to France to negotiate the preliminaries which led to the treaty of Amiens. Eight years later he was one of the signatories of a royal letter of remonstrance to the Pope complaining about encroachments by the Holy See. This was the age of John Wycliffe and his Lollard followers, whose supporters, tacit or otherwise, included not only John of Gaunt but a number of other prominent men. Sir Lewis Clifford may well have been one of them as we shall see by and by. When in 1377 a Wycliffite mob rioted and threatened to attack the Palace of the Savoy then occupied by Joan, Princess of Wales, she sent Sir Lewis and two other knights to remonstrate with it. The ringleaders answered that they would obey for the honour of the Princess, and that they were ready 'with all reverence' to do what she required. This happy outcome may have been partly due to Sir Lewis's adherence to their cause.

From 1382 until her death in 1385, Sir Lewis was in constant attendance upon the Princess of Wales, the king's mother, and in the latter year he was an executor of her will. In 1386 one of the Sir Lewis Cliffords was appointed Governor of Carlisle, whereas Froissart tells us that a Sir Lewis Clifford was with John of Gaunt in Spain then. Since Carlisle was attacked in 1386 by a large army of Scots and French, it is hard to believe that the Garter Knight could have been in both places at once. Sir William Clifford, the son of Roger, 5th Lord Clifford, was Governor of Berwick at this time; thus the two most important border fortresses were in the care of members of the Clifford family.

In addition to his military exploits Sir Lewis was a cultivated man of considerable literacy. He was a friend of the French poet, Eustace Deschamps and of Geoffrey Chaucer. By the former he was called 'amoureux Cliffort', and the latter's poem 'Truth: Balade de Bon Consey' was dedicated to Clifford's son-in-law, Sir Philip La Vache. The dedication of Chaucer's *Treatise on the Astrolabe* to the 'litell Lowis' has caused some speculation. The name Lewis is unknown in Chaucer's family, and the theory that Clifford may have been godfather to Chaucer's son of that name cannot be substantiated. 'Litell Lowis' may, in fact, have been Clifford's own son, whose date of birth is unknown, but whose death took place on 22 October 1391.[7]

Of Lewis Clifford's family life next to nothing is known. He married between 1370 and 1372 Eleanor Mowbray. She brought him a considerable fortune, which she acquired in large part from the family of her first husband, Earl de la Warr. Of his children we know that he had a daughter, Elizabeth, who, since she was at least seventeen in 1379, may perhaps have been the issue of a previous marriage, or possibly illegitimate. Since she was married first in 1373 to Sir John Lenveysey, who died in October 1379 without issue, she must have been born before 1362. In February 1380, she married Sir Philip La Vache, who died in 1409. It is not known if she had any children by him. Of his son or sons we know only of one, Lewis, who predeceased his father. Whether he was the issue of the first or second wife is unknown. He died on 22 October 1391. If he were the son of the second wife, Eleanor, he would have been about twenty years old when he died, but somewhat older if he were the son of the first wife. There is an account of a certain Lewis Clifford taking part in a jousting match against the French which lasted four days in 1390, and it is unlikely that this was the Garter Knight, who would have been near sixty at that time. The other two Sir Lewis Cliffords would have likewise been elderly, so one must assume that it was the Garter Knight's son, Lewis, and one is left wondering if the jousting tournament was the cause of his death.

It would appear from his will that Sir Lewis left no male heir, as only his daughter and son-in-law are mentioned. I will return to this will later.[8]

The second Sir Lewis is an altogether more shadowy figure. Froissart, who, although a racy author, is not always an accurate historian, mentions him in 1342 and 1351, and he is mentioned in Rymer's *Foedera* in 1357 as being at the fortress of 'Cruyk' in Normandy, wherever that may be. As already mentioned he was probably a son or cousin of Robert, 1st Baron Clifford (1274-1314). In 1370 he appears to have been received into the Brotherhood of St Albans, which rather suggests that he became a monk.

The third Sir Lewis Clifford, who was dead by 14 August 1410, was the son of Sir Thomas Clifford, third son of Robert, 3rd Baron Clifford and a brother of Hugh. This conclusion was reached by Sir Iain Moncreiffe and Hugh Peskett, who undertook detailed researches in 1982. If they are correct, and the evidence strongly supports them, then this Sir Lewis was also the brother of Bishop Richard Clifford and Robert Clifford, Sheriff of Kent in 1399-1400 (see Chapter Fourteen), which would place him in Generation XII from Pons.

The Appleby Castle MSS tell us that William Clifford of Bobbing, Kent, who died in 1438, and from whom the Lords Clifford of Chudleigh descend, was the grandson of Sir Thomas Clifford, Lord of Thomond, the third son of Robert, 3rd Lord Clifford. It is known that this William Clifford was the son of Hugh, who had a brother called Lewis.[9] It therefore follows that Lewis and Hugh were the sons of Sir Thomas Clifford. This evidence proves that this Lewis has to be distinguished from his senior contemporary, the Garter Knight, who could not possibly have been a son of Sir Thomas. In any case the heraldic evidence supports this view, for the K.G.s arms were an entirely conventional younger son's differencing of those of the Lords Clifford. This point is reinforced by Sir Lewis Clifford, K.G., being called as a witness and then later commissioner to hear the appeal in the Scrope-Grosvenor case mentioned in Chapter Sixteen, which is hardly consonant with his being a man guilty of heraldic impropriety.

In 1379 John de Eccles and Geoffrey de Somerton (Suffolk) granted the reversion of one third of the manor of Hickling called 'La Netherhalle' (Norfolk) then held by William Latymer of Danby, Aubrey de Vere, Richard Story, Lewis de Clifford and

Richard de Ylneye, knights, Hugh Fastolf and Reginald de Eccles for the life of Edward de Berkele (Berkeley), to the prior and convent of Hickling, retaining land in Somerton, Stalham, Walsham and Eccles.[10] In 1391 Lewis Clifford presented a Hugh Clifford to the living of Haddiscoe in Norfolk. A memorandum is recorded in 1420[11] of a deed 14 August 1410 between William Clifford Esquire and Hugh Barton of London regarding certain rents in the manor of Hickling, Norfolk. William states that he holds these as heir of his uncle Sir Lewis Clifford.

In a Chancery suit of 1450 to 1454, *John Fastolf* versus *the Prior of Hickling, re Netherall in Hickling*, it is stated that rents after the death of Sir Lewis Clifford descended to William Clifford as 'cozen and heir', being the son of Hugh, Lewis's brother. William Clifford granted the same to Henry Barton of London and others.

This reconstruction poses a number of questions which further research may succeed in answering. For example: the third Baron Clifford settled lands in Surrey, Dorset and Worcestershire in 1343 on his son Sir Thomas: did Lewis and Hugh (and eventually William) afterwards inherit any of them? Sir Thomas held lands in Thomond, i.e. County Clare: should this Sir Lewis's career be sought in Ireland? The Appleby MSS say that Bishop Richard Clifford had brothers Robert and William who were High Sheriffs of Kent at particular dates. This seems to contradict the theory, unless the MSS confuse Robert's nephew, William, as his brother, or, if not, did Sir Thomas have a sixth son, William, of whom as yet we know nothing?

Apart from the foregoing we have to ask ourselves if it is safe to assume that Robert Clyfford of Wells in Kent (can this be Well Street near Malling?), whose will is dated 18 July 1418, is the Robert Clifford whose father was Sir Thomas?

These pitfalls may be by-passed as follows:

(a) William Clifford succeeded both his father, Hugh, and his uncle, Sir Lewis, by August 1410. Yet (both) Robert Clifford(s) lived until 1418(21).

(b) The (perhaps unrelated) family of Clifford of Ellingham in Northumberland (traceable from about 1214 to 1366) bore forarms 'gold (or silver) three eagles displayed gules'. There is another place called Clifford near Tadcaster in Yorkshire from which they could have taken their name (there was a family of Clifford there) and anyway they were certainly separate from the chequy Cliffords by 1214.

(c) Robert Clyfford of Wells seals with three eagles and refers to goods and chattels in Northumberland.[12]

(d) So this Robert Clyfford may *not* be the Robert who was Sheriff of Kent referred to in the Appleby MSS, but an Ellingham descendant.

(e) But if he is, we must then consider (i) the coincidence that the eagles related not to Clifford of Ellingham but to an Eaglesfield heiress, and (ii) the probability in that case that the other kingdom was *not* Scotland but Ireland, where Sir Thomas Clifford's future lay.

Finally, we must ask ourselves, knowing that Sir Lewis was dead by August 1410, whether William could have been his heir then if Robert the Sheriff and Bishop Richard were still alive. The former was certainly alive, for he survived the bishop who died in 1421. Yet William succeeded at Netherhall in 1410; could this have been a legacy, and was William simply Sir Lewis's heir there?

Before we leave the three Sir Lewises, we must consider which of them might have been a Lollard. The identification is hard to make and is based on references to Clifford, with a number of others by Thomas Walsingham and Henry Knighton in their chronicles, as being sympathetic to Wycliffe in his criticism of the Roman Church, and to the curious wording of the Garter Knight's will. Several other Knights of the King's Chamber are known to have been Lollards and certainly Sir Lewis's connection with them and the similarities in their careers tend to suggest he was involved in the movement. There is no evidence that he had any reputation for heresy before 1392, and when the Duchess of York appointed him one of her executors he was required to arrange her burial in a Franciscan Church, the Order most bitterly opposed to heresy. In 1395 Lollard articles were published at St Paul's, Westminster Abbey and St Albans, which Clifford was supposed to have supported. In 1402 he made what appears to have been a recantation of Lollard beliefs, but K. B. Macfarlane[13] thinks that this may have been a matter of expediency. When Clifford died in 1404, his will was almost identical with those of other well known heretics who had recanted.[14] 'At the begynning', he says, 'I most unworthi and Goddis traytor, recommaunde my wretchid and synfule soule hooly to the grace and to the grete mercy of the blessed Trynytie; and my wrechid carcyne to be beryed in the ferthest corner of the churcheyard in which pariche my wrechid soule departeth fro my body ... '. Furthermore, his executors were chosen from among his close associates who were also believed to be Lollard sympathisers.

W. T. Waugh[15] suggests that Walsingham and Knighton overstated Clifford's association with the Lollard movement, and that he was more probably sympathetic to Wycliffe's early attacks on the papacy, clergy and church property rather than an adherent of the more radical tenets of the faith. Anti-clericalism was common at this period, and there is some evidence that Wycliffe's doctrines commanded support from the nobility. As already mentioned, John of Gaunt was one and Joan of Kent, Princess of Wales, another who was thought to be enthusiastic in support of his views.

But Clifford is unlikely to have held deeply heretical views. The Order of the Passion, which he supported, was founded on ideas wholly contrary to Lollardy, nor was he wealthy enough to risk incurring the displeasure of the king, even though he was now an elderly man. On the other hand it must be said that by 1404 Lollardy was everywhere in decline and its supporters were more secretive, particularly since the passing in 1401 of the Statute de Heretico Comburendo. This would, were he really a heretic, make Lewis Clifford's recantation much more a matter of expediency and might explain why he gave to the Archbishop of Canterbury a list of the most extreme of the Lollard beliefs and betrayed many of its leading protagonists – though it seems unlikely that Archbishop Arundel was altogether unfamiliar with these tenets.

The degree of Clifford's association with the movement must remain, however, a matter for speculation and is unlikely to be proved positively either way.

William Clifford of Bobbing married Elizabeth, the daughter of Sir Arnold Savage, and widow of Sir Reynold Cobham. The date of the marriage is unknown. He died in 1438 and she survived him two years. By her William had five sons and two daughters:

1. LEWIS, who married Anne, daughter of Lord Moleyns, who became the ancestor of the Bobbing branch (see Chapter Sixty-One).

2. THOMAS, living in 1421.

3. WILLIAM, living in 1421.

4. ROGER, living in 1421.

5. JOHN, for whom see Chapter Twenty-Nine.

1. ISABEL, of whom nothing is known.

2. ALIANORA, living in 1436.

Chapter Twenty-Nine

Generation XIV – John Clifford of Iwade (1421-61)

John Clifford, of Iwade in Kent, was the youngest son of William Clifford of Bobbing Court by his wife, Elizabeth Savage. Although the Wars of the Roses broke out during his lifetime – his kinsmen the Lords Clifford in the north playing a prominent part in them, and his own brother-in-law, Sir Thomas St Leger, marrying King Edward IV's sister – the surviving records only tell us about John Clifford's domestic life. Between 1447 and 1454 both he and his nephew, Alexander Clifford, the son of his brother Lewis, of Bobbing Court, brought lawsuits concerning the inheritance of his mother, Elizabeth Savage,[1] who died in 1440.

John Clifford had survived all his elder brothers. Lewis had died in their parents' lifetime and the Savage inheritance at Bobbing had gone to his youthful son, Alexander. So, although his mother had been heiress of several Kentish manors, John had to make his way in the world. However, in Kent the ancient law of gavelkind allowed an equal share to younger sons in cases of intestacy, and some years after his mother's death there was a lawsuit between him and his nephew whose purpose was to secure some of the inheritance for himself.

From this lawsuit it appears that John Clifford had occupied the manor of Bobbing for the last seven years, ever since his mother died, and that he was receiving the profits of the manor of Kemsley 'he knowing that the will of the said Dame Elizabeth was that the said John should have the moiety of all the lands that were holden of the tenure of gavelkind'. Eventually, however, he was allowed to inherit her manor of Iwade, near Bobbing, three miles north of Sittingbourne.

It is unlikely that John Clifford was an adherent of the White Rose, as he was granted the Keepership of Chestonwood in Kent by Edward IV on 11 April 1461, shortly after the great Yorkist victory at Towton in which 'Black-Faced' John Clifford was killed (see Chapter Twenty). The Keepership was renewed in December 1461, but John died soon after making his will in that year.[2] He was dead before 12 August 1462, when the Keepership of Chestonwood,[3] presumably now vacant, was granted to his brother-in-law, Thomas St Leger, then Esquire of the Body to the king.

John Clifford married first Alice Gainsford, daughter of Nicholas Gainsford, and by her, who died in or soon after 1459,[4] he had two sons:

1. WILLIAM of Iwade, who also left two sons, ROBERT (who died childless in about 1510) and NICHOLAS Clifford, who lived at Northfleet, Kent. This Nicholas was sued in connection with the lands of Holmes and Iwade by his uncle, Thomas Clifford (for whom see next chapter), in Chancery between 1504 and 1515.[5] Nevertheless, in his will dated 31 March 1546 at 'Boscome beside Salisbury', Nicholas, whose executrix was his widow, Cicely, appointed his cousin, Harry Clifford of Borscombe (Thomas's grandson and successor), both remainderman and overseer. This will,[6] which was proved in May 1510 includes a legacy 'to young Moris of Grascoes End my sword and buckler. To young Edward of Durford my sword girdle of buff leather and my books of Spanish leather with clasps on the side'. Nicholas Clifford, who died childless, was buried in the parish church at Northfleet for the repair of which he left one cow.

2. JOHN, who died without issue.

John Clifford of Iwade married secondly, by 1461, Florence St Leger, daughter of John St Leger of Uffculme and sister of Sir Thomas St Leger, Knight of the Body to King Edward IV. At the time of making his will, John Clifford's wife was with child, for which he made provision. After his death, his wife gave birth to a posthumous son:

3. THOMAS, for whom see next chapter.

Florence St Leger also had a daughter, Anna, who later married Robert Kemp of Gissing, Norfolk, but whether by John Clifford or a former husband is uncertain. She married secondly, John Brockman of Witham, and died on 18 March 1500/1.[7]

Chapter Thirty

Generation XV – Thomas Clifford of Borscombe, M.P. (1462-1521)

John Clifford's posthumous son, Thomas, was born in 1462. His career is interesting in that, although born into a fairly junior branch of the family settled in Kent, he is next found in Wiltshire married to a landed heiress. According to the late R. Garrett this was mainly due to the powerful influence of his mother's brother, his uncle Sir Thomas St Leger of Guildford.

Sir Thomas had had a meteoric career at the Yorkist Court and is described in the Crowland chronicle as *unus nobilissimus miles*, a most noble knight. First personal Esquire, and then Knight of the Body to King Edward IV, by 1467 he had become the accepted lover of the king's own sister, Anne Plantagenet, Duchess of Exeter, and after she had divorced the duke in 1472, Sir Thomas St Leger married her himself. He was thus now the king's brother-in-law and a very influential uncle for young Thomas Clifford.

In 1463, St Leger had been granted the keeping of large amounts of land in the West Country belonging to the Thorpe family, but which had to be 'kept' because of the 'idiocy' of John Thorpe of Borscombe in Wiltshire and Oldbury in Gloucestershire. In 1479 this 'keeping' was renewed to St Leger on account of the 'idiocy' of John Thorpe's son, William. Borscombe itself is six miles north-east of Salisbury, but the lands were very extensive, including manors in Gloucestershire, Wiltshire, Somerset and Cornwall. In 1482 these lands were regranted by Edward IV to Sir Thomas St Leger and his nephew, Thomas Clifford, now presumably already married to William Thorpe's sister, Thomasina.

But after the deposing of his own wife's little nephew, King Edward V, one of the princes in the Tower, in 1483, Sir Thomas St Leger took part in the Duke of Buckingham's unsuccessful rising against Richard III. As the Lord High Constable was himself the forfeited Buckingham, the dreaded 'Black Knight of Assheton', Lieutenant of the Tower of London, was appointed Vice-Constable of England to try the defeated rebels. The terror he inspired was remembered in the rhyme:

> Sweet Jesus, for thy mercy's sake
> And for thy bitter Passion,
> Save us from the axe of the Tower
> And from Sir Ralph of Assheton.

In spite of Sir Thomas St Leger's being Richard III's brother-in-law, he was condemned to death by the merciless Black Knight and beheaded on 12 November 1483 at Exeter.

Young Thomas Clifford seems to have been implicated with his uncle in the rebellion, but he was lucky enough to receive a pardon on 5 March 1484, as 'Thomas Clifford of Parle, Hampshire, gentleman'. However, this implication evidently benefited him after Richard III's overthrow by Henry Tudor the following year, for Thomas Clifford was one of those exempt from the Act of Parliament in 1487 annulling the grants of the last Yorkist kings, and so he retained the 'keeping' of the Thorpe estates.

In 1491, Thomas Clifford was elected M.P. for Downton. This was the Parliament where Henry VII's Lord Chancellor, John Morton, Archbishop of Canterbury, assembled both Houses and announced the cause of summons in the Chamber of the Cross, taking as his theme, 'We await peace and it is not good, etc.' (Jeremiah xiv), and dealing with the impending war with France. He then ordered the Commons to meet next day in their own House to elect a Speaker. Thomas Clifford's kinsman, the Shepherd Lord, was among the peers. This Parliament ordered all Scots to leave the realm within 40 days in view of imminent hostilities with Scotland, and increased the duty payable on wine imported by Venetian merchants in retaliation for the duty imposed by Venice on wine brought in Candia by English merchants. In 1492, Parliament was dissolved and Thomas Clifford ceased to be an M.P.

Thomasine Thorpe appears to have predeceased her poor 'idiot' brother, William, for at his death in 1509 his heir was her son William Clifford. The Thorpes brought to the Clifford family not only Borscombe in Wiltshire but also Kingsteignton in Devon. The latter remained in the family until the 11th Lord Clifford of Chudleigh sold it after the First World War. The manor had been owned originally by the Burdon family for several centuries before it passed to the Thorpes through the marriage of their heiress, Cecily Burdon to Henry Thorpe in the early 15th century, and the Burdon's name still survives in the farm on the site of the mansion called Ware Barton.

Thomas Clifford of Borscombe died on 10 May 1521. By his first wife, Thomasina, he had a son, WILLIAM, for whom see the next chapter, and a daughter, FLORENCE.

Thomas Clifford married secondly, Jane, whose surname is unknown, and appears to have had no further children. However, between 1533 and 1538 there were lawsuits in Chancery between Jane Clifford and her step-grandson, Henry Clifford of Borscombe, for whom see Chapter Thirty-Two.

Chapter Thirty-One

Generation XVI – William Clifford of Borscombe (1490-1535)

William Clifford, born in 1490, the only son of Thomas and Thomasina, succeeded in 1509 to the estates of his 'idiot' uncle, William Thorpe, in Wiltshire and Devon and also to lands in Gloucestershire, which his father had been administering since 1482. As a result William Clifford did homage to the new sovereign, Henry VIII[1] for the manor of Teyton alias Burdon and for the fishery of the river Teign in Devon, and for his lands in Gloucestershire and Wiltshire.

By a deed of 1515, he made over to his father and stepmother for life the manor of Oldbury, near Doddington in Gloucestershire, which had formed part of his Thorpe inheritance. He appears to have lived quietly during the gathering storm years of the dissolution of the monasteries and the Reformation, and died on 24 June 1535.

William Clifford married Elizabeth Vaux of Odiham, Hampshire, whose parentage has not been ascertained, but according to the College of Arms pedigree of 1672 she was armigerous. Her first husband's name was Chiddisdale or Clydesdall.[2] By her William had one son and two daughters:

1. HENRY, for whom see next chapter.
1. MARY, married Leonard Carrant of Winterbourne in Dorset who, by a deed of 1562, made over his estate at Venn Court in Somerset, now Dorset, to her Clifford nephews for life in return for a sum of money. She was taxed at Wimborne St Giles in 1594 along with her nephew, Henry Clifford, and died in 1599.
2. DOROTHY, perhaps married to a Palmer.[3] William Clifford's widow, Elizabeth made her will in 1537 and was dead by 13 May 1550 when her will was proved.[4] She wished to be buried in Borscombe church.

Chapter Thirty-Two

Generation XVII – Henry Clifford of Borscombe (1515-77)

Henry Clifford, born in 1515, known as Harry (by which name he is called in his cousin Nicholas' will), inherited several estates in three counties. When he was 40, he was also included in the entail of the vast Clifford domains in Westmorland and Cumberland made in 1555 by his kinsman and namesake, Henry, 2nd Earl of Cumberland (see Chapter Twenty-Three). This indicated that the then head of the Clifford family held the view that the Borscombe branch also descended from the 1st Lord Clifford's mother, the Vipont heiress.

In 1562 his sister Mary's husband, Leonard Carrant, made over to Harry Clifford's three sons for life the manor of Venn Court in the parish of Milborne Port for a small consideration. The eldest son was to make a deed[1] only a week before his father, this Henry, made his will, to enable his father to bequeath Venn to his own half brother as he himself was to inherit Borscombe and had no further interest in Venn. He, this eldest son, was also due to inherit Ugbrooke by virtue of his wife, so his interest in Venn was minimal.

By his will[2] dated only a week after the above deed of gift, namely on 17 July 1577, Henry Clifford bequeathed to his wife his house and estate in 'Ambriseburye', plus money to build the church porch at Borscombe and to mend the 'Whitway' upon the West Down of Borscombe. Venn, or Vayne Court, is bequeathed to his second son, with remainder to his third if that should be necessary within the time limit set. Henry obviously died very shortly after writing his will for it was proved on 3 February following. Borscombe went to his eldest son; Venn or Vayne Court to his second son for the term of his life and thence to his third son. His daughters were to receive £200 if they married with the consent of his widow, his sons and overseers.

He was mistakenly thought by the College of Arms in 1740 to have been the ancestor of the Dutch branch (see Chapter Sixty-Two).

He married first, Elizabeth, daughter of Anthony Hungerford of Down Ampney in Gloucestershire, descended from Sir Edmund Hungerford (d. 1484), younger son of Walter, 1st Lord Hungerford, and had by her one son and probably two daughters:

1. ANTHONY, for whom see next chapter.
2. Name unknown who married John Cheke but predeceased her father.
3. BRIDGET, who married ... Rogers and was living in 1577.

Henry/Harry Clifford married secondly on 6 February 1547/8, Elizabeth, daughter of Sir William Caraunte of Tumber in Somerset, by whom he had two more sons and four more daughters. Both these two sons, along with their half brother Anthony, were involved in matters relating to the Venn estate just mentioned, but it was the eldest of these two sons who occupied Venn/Vayne Court for many years, in the parish of Milborne Port, where many births, marriages and deaths are recorded. Dealing with this second family we now have:

2. HENRY, of Venn Court, Somerset, born 1548, married Catherine, daughter of Thomas Hussey of Edmondesham, Dorset, and had issue four sons and six daughters:
   i. MARK Clifford baptised at the nearby parish of Trent, later Under Sheriff of Antrim in Ireland.
   ii. HENRY Clifford, baptised at Milborne Port in 1588, dying there, unmarried in 1634.
   iii. WILLIAM Clifford, who died aged two in 1586.
   iv. THOMAS Clifford, baptised at Milborne Port in 1599. This Thomas Clifford is presently thought to have been the stem of the Perristone Cliffords, for whom see Chapter Sixty-Seven, for it was his great-grandson who bequeathed his property to a Morgan on condition that he assume the name of Clifford.

The six daughters were as follows:
   a. Edith, baptised at Trent in 1578.
   b. Ann, baptised at Milborne Port in 1581, who married Joseph Hussey at Candlepurse.
   c. Mary, baptised at Milborne Port in 1582.
   d. Elizabeth, baptised there in 1586 and married in 1603 Robert Plucknett.
   e. Margery, baptised at Wimborne St Giles in 1595.
   f. Honor, baptised at Milborne Port in 1603, married Thomas Feild in 1631.

3. EDWARD, of Pennington Narvet, living in 1599, married first in 1567 Margaret Hungerford, and secondly Margaret Andrews. In 1589 he was involved in a lengthy law suit[3] in connection with Pennington. Between these two wives he seems to have had very many children if we are to believe the Visitations of Berkshire[4] where a Richard is alleged to have been his twelfth son! Five sons and a daughter have been traced with a degree of certainty and as they have a bearing on events connected with Borscombe they are detailed hereunder:

   i. ANTHONY Clifford (1584-1642), married firstly Susan Braxton by whom he had a daughter Susan who married Sir Edward Grafton. His second wife is of greater interest as she was to be the widow of his first cousin Henry Clifford of Borscombe (1567-1636), the eldest son of Anthony Clifford for whom see next chapter. This cousin Henry's will dated 1636 ties in with his own will dated 1643,[6] and both make interesting reading.
   ii. HENRY Clifford, about whom nothing is known except that he was alive in 1641.
   iii. CUTHBERT Clifford, certainly alive in 1642.
   iv. EDWARD Clifford,[7] alive in 1637. By his wife Elizabeth, who was buried at Milborne Port in 1632, he had two sons: John and Henry, but John died in infancy in 1622. Henry however remains untraced. His daughters were: Ursula, Honor, Mary, Elizabeth and Ann, all baptised at Milborne Port between 1614 and 1625.
   v. RICHARD Clifford, who appears in the Visitations of Berkshire as the twelfth son and is recorded as being aged 65 when the Visitation was completed. He appears to have married Jane Austin of Sherborne but no children are shown in the Visitation of 1644.
   vi. URSULA, his only daughter, married William Norburn of Bremhill by whom she had a son Edward, aged eight in 1623.

   3. DOROTHY, dead by 1580.
   4. FRANCES, living in 1580.
   5. MARGARET, living in 1580.
   6. ANNE, living in 1577, married Francis Richards.

Chapter Thirty-Three

Generation XVIII — Anthony Clifford of Borscombe
(1541-80)

Anthony Clifford was born in 1541, and succeeded his father only three years before his own death. However, although his inheritance included estates from Borscombe in Wiltshire to Kingsteignton in Devon, it was his marriage to the Courtenay heiress of Ugbrooke that settled the family interest firmly in South Devon. He had doubtless made the acquaintance of the Courtenays of Ugbrooke when riding over from Wiltshire.

Anthony Clifford's wife was Anne Courtenay, daughter and heiress of Sir Piers Courtenay of Ugbrooke, who had died in 1553,[1] and so she eventually brought the beautiful Ugbrooke estate into the Clifford family, whose seat it remains to this day. The first house at Ugbrooke, near Chudleigh, had been built before 1280 for the Precentor of Exeter, but after the Reformation and the battle of Fenny Bridge in the Western Rebellion, the Protector Somerset (guardian of the boy king, Edward VI) took Ugbrooke into his own hands for ten years before selling it in 1550 to Sir Piers Courtenay.

The Cliffords could hardly have inherited their position in Devon through a more auspicious ancestry. The Courtenays were the grandest family in medieval Devon. They were descended from the historic Frankish House of Courtenay, whose main line had been established in Devonshire since the 12th century, first as Viscounts and then as Earls. They had given to England an archbishop, several bishops, a Lord Chancellor and other statesmen, a founder knight and three more knights of the Garter, besides ambassadors, admirals and famous peers. On the continent, their kinsmen reigned as Emperors of Constantinople, Counts of Edessa and Peers of France. They traced their descent from Athon, Sire de Courtenay, between Montargis and Sens, about fifty-six miles south of Paris. Athon's grand-daughter, Hodierne de Courtenay, was the wife of Geoffrey II, Comte de Joigny, Sire de Joinville et Vaucouleurs, whose descendants married into the de Lacy family and owned large estates in the Welsh Marches (see Chapter Ten). Her brother, Joscelin went to the Holy Land in 1101 and carved out for himself the County of Edessa. Count Joscelin's eventual heiress, his grand-daughter, Beatrix, wife of Count Otto von Bodenlauben-Henneberg, may have been in the 13th century the legal owner of the Holy Shroud of Turin, before it passed to her French kinsmen of the Charny family. In 1147 Count Joscelin's nephew Renaud, Seigneur de Courtenay, Montargis, Château-Renaud, Champignelles, Tanlay, Charny and Chantecocq followed King Louis VII to the Holy Land on the Second Crusade which was caused by the fall of the Courtenay castle at Tell-Basher. There he quarrelled with the king, who seized his lands on their return to France. The dispossessed Lord Renaud came to England, where he was received with great favour by Henry II. His son, Renaud de Courtenay, became hereditary Sheriff of Devon and Castellan of Exeter by his marriage with

Hawise, Lady of the Honour of Okehampton, co-heiress of her mother, Maud d'Avranches, herself heiress of Baldwin FitzGilbert's baronial family which had held the Honour of Okehampton and Shrievalty of Devon from 1080 to 1142. In the next generation, Robert de Courtenay married a daughter of William de Riviers, 5th Earl of Devon, whose earldom the Courtenays inherited when the Riviers line became extinct in 1335, when Hugh, Lord Courtenay was made Earl of Devon. He became the direct male ancestor of the present earl.

Hugh Courtenay, 2nd Earl of Devon, had eight sons, the sixth of whom, Sir Philip, was Lord Lieutenant of Ireland from 1383 to 1393, and the forefather of Sir William Courtenay of Powderham Castle. By his first wife, Margaret Edgcombe, Sir William was father of George Courtenay, ancestor of the present Earl of Devon, whose seat is still at Powderham, and of Sir Piers Courtenay of Ugbrooke.[2]

It seems clear that after Anthony Clifford's marriage to Sir Piers' daughter, Anne Courtenay, the couple lived much at Ugbrooke with her widowed mother, Elizabeth Courtenay, née Shilston, daughter and heiress of Robert Shilston of Leawood near Bridstow, and on whom the Ugbrooke estate had evidently been settled for life by Sir Piers.

Anthony Clifford made his will on 19 April 1580.[3] He left his stepmother an annuity of £40 a year, settled £200 on each of his sons if they reached the age of 21 and on his daughters if they reached the age of 23 or on their marriage, and his wife £10 a year charged on Kingsteignton until she should come into Lanfords estate in Wiltshire, and the remainder to his eldest son, Henry. He died on 12 September 1580 and is buried in Exeter Cathedral. He was only 39 years old. By Anne Courtenay he had five sons and three daughters:

1. HENRY of Borscombe, born in 1566 (dying 1636), married first, his kinswoman, Mary Clifford, only daughter of James Clifford of Frampton-on-Severn, the estate which had been in the family since Domesday. However, they were subsequently divorced in 1609 *causa frigiditatis*. Perhaps her father had taken umbrage at their rather unsatisfactory marriage settlement, but on the other hand, she remarried John Cage yet died childless, perhaps from the same sad cause (see Chapter Fifty-Six). Having extricated himself from the clutches of the Frampton-on-Severn branch of the Cliffords, Henry married Martha (perhaps Traffles?) by whom he had children and grandchildren but was evidently a broken or disillusioned man by the time he died in 1636. His will,[4] proved in 1636, is of great interest as he cuts out all his own children, bequeathing his manor of Kingsteignton to his wife Martha for life, thence to his brother Simon for the term of his life, and finally to his nephew Simon, his brother Simon's son, and his heirs forever. As Martha seems to have outlived both of these two Simons, Kingsteignton appears to have been taken over by her eldest son at some later date, selling it to Hugh, 2nd Lord Clifford in order to raise money for the marriage settlement on his own daughter detailed below.

Apart from giving Martha Kingsteignton for life he gave her £4,000 which she took with her when she married her late husband's first cousin, as previously stated. It is from this second husband's will[5] that we learn of the following children which she had by Henry:

i. JAMES Clifford (1624-85), was only 11 years and 11 months old when his father died, (see the father's 1636 Inquisition).[6] This only son married Bridget Harwell of Ware by whom he had a son James who died aged 19 in 1681, unmarried. Their only daughter, Mary, married in 1648 Sir Hugh Bampfield of Poltimore from whom descend the Earls of Poltimore.

ii. CHARLES Clifford (1630-42). He was a scholar at Winchester aged 12 but died of smallpox at that age.

The four daughters were:

a. MARTHA, who died unmarried and whose will was proved on 1 June 1668.

b. ANN, alive in 1666 and who married three times: firstly to Middleton, secondly to Swetland and thirdly to Symes.

c. MARGARET, alive in 1666 who married Thomas Brexton.

2. SIMON (1569-1639), was educated at Oxford from 1586 to 1590, becoming a barrister at the Middle Temple in 1594. From his will written on 14 February 1639[7] we find that he has taken over Borscombe from his elder brother as his legacies are to be paid out of 'my lands in Borscombe', and 'my lands in Winterslowe'. By his wife Cecily, daughter of Robert Williamson and widow of John Ingram, he had three sons and seven daughters:

i. SYMON Clifford, of Lockerley (1605-45), who had inherited from his uncle Henry who had cut out all his own children by Martha, did not wait long before disposing of Borscombe. By a deed dated 2 October 1641[8] he accepted £1,140 and the property at Lockerley from George Hunt in exchange for Borscombe which had been in the family since 1504 when it was Thomasine Thorpe's inheritance, thereby upsetting the title 'Cliffords of Borscombe' by which they had been known for some six generations. This Symon married Dorothy Kent by whom he had a son Simon who was killed by the Dutch in 1665; another son Anthony (1638-96) who married a Mary but by whose will there would appear to have been no issue. A further son, Thomas, died aged four in 1645, and finally a son Henry, born 1630, who had an only daughter Mary who married Farmer and was alive in 1695. His own will is dated 1644.[9]

ii. ANTHONY Clifford (1615-85), who, by his wife Thomasine, the daughter of Barnaby Potter, bishop of Carlisle, had a son Nicholas who died before he was nine.

iii. HENRY Clifford (1613-41), about whom nothing is known.

The seven daughters were:

a. Maria, who married John Pinsent of Curlieu, Co. Lincs.

b. Jane, who married Bayles/Bayliss.

c. Anne, alive in 1639 and from whose will appears to have remained unmarried.

d. Elizabeth, born 1608, married Nicholas Hatcher in 1632.

e. Susan, born 1609, married Rutt.

f. Dorothy, alive in 1641.

g. Cecily, alive in 1641 who married Hurst in 1638.

3. THE REV. DR. THOMAS of Ugbrooke, for whom see next chapter.

4. JOHN, baptised 29 July 1577, died aged ten years.

5. HUGH, baptised 6 October 1579. Will proved 1603.

1. JOAN, baptised 10 August 1570, married Henry Gough and had issue.

2. MAGDALEN, baptised 25 July 1575, married first John Ley, alias Kempthorne, of Tonscombe, Cornwall; and secondly Leonard Vasie, of Fenton Vacy.

3. SHILSTON, called after her grandmother's family, baptised 18 June 1576.

Anthony Clifford's widow, Anne, died in January 1604, and her mother, Elizabeth Shilston, 'The Ladye Courtnie' of Ugbrooke died the following November, leaving the reversion of Ugbrooke to her grandson, Thomas Clifford, D.D. The Rev. Robert Woolcombe pronounced the funeral oration, which was published in London, and which was dedicated to her grandson, Thomas Clifford, who erected the monuments in the church to his Courtenay grandparents.

Chapter Thirty-Four

Generation XIX – Rev. Dr. Thomas Clifford of Ugbrooke (1572-1634)

19. Portrait of Rev. Dr. Thomas Clifford by Jansen.

Thomas Clifford was only eight when his father died, and he was evidently brought up by his mother and grandmother at Ugbrooke. He had a varied life. As a young man he joined the army in the Netherlands,[1] studied at Oxford, then attended Robert, Earl of Essex in the naval expedition to Cadiz, and was twice sent by Queen Elizabeth as envoy to German and Italian princes. In Essex's famous naval raid he was, as we have already seen, one of four members of the Clifford family to take part (see Chapter Twenty-Four), his Bobbing Court kinsmen, the brothers Sir Conyers Clifford and Sir Alexander Clifford, being respectively one of Essex's Council of War and the other knighted by Essex on his quarter-deck at Cadiz. Fresh in their memory at that time was Sir Nicholas Clifford, another Bobbing Court cousin, who had been killed earlier that year in the West Indies by the same Spanish cannon-ball that knocked Sir Francis Drake off his stool.

In November 1604 Thomas Clifford inherited Ugbrooke on his grandmother's death, and thus became a Devon landowner. But it was not until he was well into his thirties that Thomas decided to take holy orders. He was made deacon and priest by Bishop William Cotton of Exeter at Silverton on 3 April 1611. The following September he obtained his licence to preach and expound the word of God throughout the diocese of Exeter. The Mayor and Chamber of Exeter appointed him afternoon lecturer at the cathedral in March 1614 at £50 per annum which was later increased by £10 for the rent of a house. In 1619 he was at Exeter College, Oxford taking a degree, and eventually a doctorate of divinity. The Clifford coat of arms in the chapel and in the main quad are said to have been erected as a result of his being Dean of the college.

It is related that when King Charles I visited Sir Richard Reynell at Ford House in September 1625, Dr. Thomas Clifford 'sent a hunted teague, a doe of a year old, for the entertainment'. The same year he was made a Justice of the Peace for Devonshire, and on 29 November Bishop Carey presented him to a prebend in Exeter[2] Cathedral. On 29 April 1626, he was admitted to the rectory of Black Torrington in the Deanery of Holdsworthy.

The remarkable Dr. Clifford is reported to have ended his life in a duck pond, whether by accident or design is not known.[3] He was buried on 3 September 1634 in Chudleigh church and his will[4] was proved on 19 September by his executors, his wife, Amy and his son Hugh.

Dr. Thomas Clifford married Amy Steplehill the daughter of Hugh Steplehill of Bremble, Devon, by his wife Sabine, daughter of William Molford of Cadbury. After being a widow for 20 years Mrs. Steplehill had remarried a substantial yeoman named William Honeywell, who died in November 1614, who had property in Trusham and Ashton, and who kept a journal which is still preserved at Ugbrooke[6] and shows he was a keen businessman. For example, in an account of money due to him in October 1605, Mr. Honeywell records £19 plus interest owed him by Mrs. Steplehill, but shortly afterwards he adds 'All paid by marriage!' In the will of Amy Clifford's brother, John Steplehill, proved in 1605 is a clause which says: 'I devise and give unto my mother Sabyn Steplehill my house called Bremwell (Bremble), with lands thereunto belonging' – leading to this entry in Honeywell's journal the following March 'I enjoy yearly by my wife the house and demesnes of Bremble, valued at £XXIV per annum'.

The Steplehills, whose arms were 'quarterly 1st and 4th argent a chevron sable, 2nd and 3rd gules three fishes naiant argent' were a family of great antiquity in Devon. There is a story that, at Edward I's great defeat of the Scots at Falkirk in 1297, two of the English victors were Steplehill and Prideaux, who found themselves each wearing exactly the same coat of arms. They resolved to settle their claims in a trial by combat, but the king ordered them to cast lots and Prideaux won.

By Amy Steplehill, Dr. Thomas Clifford had two sons and five daughters:

1. HUGH, for whom see next chapter.
2. THOMAS, baptised at Chudleigh, 3 December 1606; married the daughter of John Wood of Taunton and by her had a son, THOMAS, who was killed fighting in the Low Countries in 1666.
1. SABINE, baptised at Chudleigh, 18 May 1604, married Matthew Hale of Efford.
2. SHILSTON, baptised at Chudleigh, 11 October 1605 married James Eastchurch of Lawell in the parish of Chudleigh. Lawell came into the Clifford family later as a dower house, but was then a large separate manor.
3. ELIZABETH, baptised at Chudleigh, 5 July 1608, married John Carew on 30 August 1629.
4. ANNE, baptised at Chudleigh, 23 November 1610, married in October 1629, Thomas Carew of Haccombe, Devon, who died in 1656 two days before her. Their eldest son was Sir Thomas Carew, 1st baronet.
5. AMY, baptised 16 June 1612, was left £300 by her father in 1634, when she was still unmarried.

A portrait of Dr. Thomas Clifford by Cornelius Jansen is in the entrance hall at Ugbrooke. Painted on wood, it is obviously one of the most valuable in the collection. There used to be an inscription:

> Sic cum transieruit mei
> Nullo cum strepitu dies
> Plebeius moriar senes.

Chapter Thirty-Five

Generation XX – Colonel Hugh Clifford of Ugbrooke (1603-39)

Hugh Clifford, Dr. Thomas Clifford's elder son, was baptised at Chudleigh on 27 February 1603. As a good Devon gentleman he was educated at Exeter College, Oxford, where he took the degrees of B.A. and M.A. before being admitted in 1621 to the Middle Temple. After he grew up he lived mainly at Bremble, which he had inherited from his mother's family, as he only succeeded to Ugbrooke some five years before his death. But that he had entered on a military career early in life is indicated by an inventory of his father's effects at Ugbrooke, in which Dr. Thomas refers to 'Captain Clifford's chamber'. According to Anthony Wood he was promoted to the rank of colonel and commanded a regiment of foot against the Scots in their rebellion against Charles I on behalf of the Covenant in 1639. Dugdale also mentions this,[1] adding that he was taken ill on the expedition north and was sent home to die soon afterwards. He was buried in Chudleigh church on 12 February 1639/40.

Colonel Hugh Clifford married Mary Chudleigh, daughter of Sir George Chudleigh, 1st baronet of Ashton, whose estate was up the Teign valley from Chudleigh. The Chudleighs had an impetuous history. 'Love of hard fighting ran in the blood of the men, and the women had the large lustrous eyes, alternately bold and melting, defiant yet alluring, the dark lashes and brows, the exquisite complexion and full red lips of the typical Devon beauty'.[2]

Mary Chudleigh's parents evidently bickered in their married life. We are told that her mother had a sharp tongue and when the Rev. Mr. Sprint had the temerity to preach a sermon on conjugal duty the fiery Lady Chudleigh replied to him with a poem entitled 'The Ladies' Defence'.[3] Mary's father, Sir George, and her brother, Colonel Chudleigh, both fought as gallant cavaliers for King Charles I in the Civil War, and the royalist colonel's daughter, Mary's flighty niece, Elizabeth Chudleigh, was the celebrated Restoration grand courtesan, who as Countess of Bristol was tried for becoming bigamously the Duchess of Kingston.

By Mary Chudleigh, Colonel Hugh Clifford had two sons and a daughter:

   1. THOMAS, 1st Lord Clifford of Chudleigh, for whom see next chapter.
   2. GEORGE, baptised at Chudleigh, 12 August 1632; married Elizabeth, daughter of George Price of Esher, Surrey; died August 1670 leaving a son, GEORGE, and two daughters, ELIZABETH and MARGARET. His elder brother, then a member of the Cabal, obtained for his widow a royal pension of £200 a year.
   3. MARY, baptised at Chudleigh, 5 January 1628, married the Rev. Baldwin Acland, Treasurer of Exeter Cathedral and Rector of St Mary's Tedburne, her brother's old tutor, who was some twenty years her senior. When he died in August 1672, aged 64, he left her all that he possessed and wishing he had more to leave her. Prince[4] described her as being 'one too zealously affected towards Geneva'.

Colonel Hugh's widow, Mary, married secondly in 1644 Gregory Cole of Ashton.

Chapter Thirty-Six

Generation XXI – Thomas, 1st Lord Clifford of Chudleigh (1630-73)

'Out of these divergent elements arose one man of fire and iron', Thomas Clifford, a Restoration Stafford 'heroic, passionate and reckless. Wedded from boyhood to bold measures, rugged and impetuous as the Dartmoor from which is ancient race spring'.[1] So wrote Sir Arthur Bryant in his biography of King Charles II, and he goes on to say[2] of Clifford, 'A hotspur ever ready to pluck bright honour from the pale faced moon, he was the very antithesis of Charles, and therefore perhaps appealed to him more. On this rough hero the mantle of Minette[3] fell. For those things for which she had pleaded he now urged – monarch absolute, the ranks of ordered chivalry riding arrogant over traitors, and the Catholic Church at peace once more in an ancient land'.

Thomas Clifford, afterwards 1st Lord Clifford of Chudleigh, was born at Ugbrooke on 1 August 1630. When his father, Colonel Hugh, died, Thomas was only ten years old. Of his early youth little is known except that when he was about nine the astrologer, John Gadbury, affirmed that he was hit on the head with a spade. The significance of this in regard to his later career is not obvious. When he was 14 his mother remarried to a neighbour of some culture, Gregory Cole of Ashton, who may have encouraged him in his studies. At 16 he matriculated at Exeter College, Oxford, where his tutor, ultimately his brother-in-law, was Baldwin Acland. At Oxford Thomas was an orthodox Anglican, though addicted to the writings of St Cyprian, to Shirley's *Travels* and *The Triumph of Beautie*, to Ben Jonson and Fulk Greville.

Exeter College was notorious for its Royalist sympathies, and it is possible that Clifford and Acland were temporarily expelled as a result of the Parliamentary visitation of 1648, though he remained at Oxford till 1650, when he took his B.A. degree.

The year he came down from Oxford he married his neighbour, Elizabeth Martyn, daughter and eventual heiress of William Martyn of Lindridge, the estate adjoining Ugbrooke. Although newly married, Thomas Clifford became a student at the Middle Temple, and then travelled abroad to widen his knowledge. This did not appear to harm his marriage, for Elizabeth bore him 15 children, of whom only three sons and five daughters survived childhood. Lely's portrait of her turned up at Sydney University in Australia as part of the Nicholson bequest. A copy now completes the Lelys at Ugbrooke and shows her to have been a good-looking woman.

During Cromwell's protectorate the young couple must have lived a quiet life surrounded by their many kinsfolk, most of whom were royalist in sympathy, and some, the Martyns, may have been Catholics. In August 1659 when only 29, Thomas Clifford made his will, which gives some idea of the extent of his estates at that time. In it he made the curious request to be buried at dead of night. His enemies later tried to read into this an intention to commit suicide, but it was his ambition to avoid fuss, and may have been to enable Catholic rites to be used.

Towards the end of the Commonwealth there was much unrest in the county, and Clifford was one of a troop of 120 gentlemen raised by Sir Copplestone Bampfylde and Sir William Courtenay to keep the peace. When General Monck summoned a Parliament in April 1660, Thomas Clifford was one of the two members for Totnes. The king was recalled in May and in August Clifford had an audience of him at which he presented him with 100 pieces of gold from the loyal citizens of Totnes. The following December he was appointed a Gentleman of the Privy Chamber Extraordinary. It was the first rung of the ladder which in 12 years took him to a peerage.

In May 1661, as a major in Sir Copplestone Bampfylde's regiment of Devon Militia, Clifford was presented once more to the king, this time by General Monck, now Duke of Albemarle. He presented an address from the regiment which was racey and aggressive in tone, abhorring republican principles, which attracted the attention of Sir Henry Bennet, later Earl of Arlington. Clifford and Bennet became fast friends, and as Bennet rose in importance he took Thomas Clifford with him.

In the early years of his political life Clifford's chief concern was with local problems, such as the woollen and cloth-making industries of which Chudleigh was an important centre. In view of his later conversion, he was yet a champion of toleration not only for Catholics, but also for non-conformists. In 1662 he supported Bennet and the king when the latter issued the Declaration to Tender Consciences, which the intolerant Anglicans forced him to withdraw. In 1664 he was appointed to

20. Portrait of Thomas, 1st Lord Clifford of Chudleigh, studio of Lely.

21. Elizabeth, 1st Lady Clifford. This painting is a copy by Swann of a portrait by Lely.

22. Portrait of King Charles II by Lely.

23. Portrait of Catherine of Braganza, wife of Charles II, by Heusman.

a committee to improve the nation's trade, which resulted in his lifelong dislike of the Dutch, whose trading methods he saw as a major cause of the English recession. The committee found that losses at the hands of the Dutch amounted to £4m, a factor which led to the outbreak of war, for Charles II was already preparing the navy and negotiating to prevent Louis XIV from siding with the Dutch. For his work on the committee Thomas Clifford was knighted in 1664, the year in which he first made the acquaintance of the diarist Samuel Pepys, who said of him that he 'do speak very well and neatly'.

Sir Thomas now devoted himself to two main causes: the preservation and increase of the king's prerogative and the war with Holland. In November 1664 he was appointed along with Sir William D'Oyly and the diarist, John Evelyn, to a commission for the care of sick and wounded seamen, and the following January he was appointed a Commissioner for Prizes.

When war was declared Sir Thomas put to sea in the *Swiftsure* commanded by Sir William Berkeley. Clifford's letters to his patron, now Lord Arlington, give accounts of encounters at sea and the capture of a Dutch admiral's son. The sea battle off Lowestoft in June ended in an English victory which failed to be followed up, but the Dutch ship *Patriarch Isaac* was captured, and the king issued a warrant for it to be delivered to Sir Thomas at Harwich. He deputed his younger brother George, who was appointed Storekeeper to the Prize Commission.

His reputation as a financier grew apace, and he was appointed to a commission to enquire into the financial affairs of the young Duke of Monmouth. They were in a poor way and their eventual improvement by Sir Thomas may explain the presence at Ugbrooke of the portraits of the Duke and Duchess by Lely given to him in appreciation of his work.

In 1665, England's ambassador to Denmark, then united under the same crown as Norway, was Sir Gilbert Talbot. The Danish chief minister, Count Hannibal Schested, persuaded him that Denmark should connive at an English raid on the Dutch Smyrna and West Indies fleets sheltering in Bergen, and that England and Denmark would share the booty. In 'The True Deduction' composed after the raid, Clifford and Arlington argued that England would never have considered such an action had it not been suggested by King Frederick III of Denmark, but this may have been to justify England's subsequent declaration of war on Denmark.

Thus the fleet, with Clifford aboard, set out for Bergen. The English admiral, Lord Sandwich, lying six miles off the Norwegian coast, sent a squadron of 20 ships to attack the Dutch. With it went Sir Thomas Clifford to help in diplomatic negotiations with the Danes. But the Danish commander prevaricated, though he did not specifically refuse his co-operation. Meanwhile the English squadron, finding its anchorage a difficult one, sailed closer to Bergen. The harbour entrance was narrow, and more than one ship ran aground and two got their rigging intertwined. They omitted in their troubles to salute the castle – a grave error of protocol. The commander intended, so he said, to teach them a lesson and fired a shot across the bows of the leading ship, which broke the leg of a sailor who was in a small boat carrying out the anchor.

The English taunted the Dutch to come out and fight, and it might, perhaps, have been better if they had, but they did not. Edward Montagu, one of Lord Sandwich's sons, was sent to the castle to explain the English position. Negotiations proved long and inconclusive. The Danes demanded the withdrawal of all but six of the English ships, which were to be allowed to blockade the Dutch. Their prime consideration seems to have been to guarantee that the King of Denmark got all the booty. Montagu, puzzled by the Danes' apparent unwillingness to abide by the secret agreement, suggested a compromise proposed by Clifford to share the spoils and cover the safety of the town and hostages.

That night the English tried to improve their position in pouring rain and darkness, and next day further negotiations were re-opened but proved equally fruitless. Suddenly the guns of the forts opened fire on the English ships, which was returned and after a couple of hours the Danes hung out a white flag, but the forts continued firing, probably at the insistence of the Dutch, who had sent sailors ashore to reinforce them. The Danish intervention forced the English to retreat. They lost 112 men killed, including six captains and Edward Montagu. Clifford was struck in the face by a cable and badly cut. Amazingly no ship was actually lost. The Dutch lost 100 dead and wounded and one ship, and the Danes seven killed and 26 wounded.

Sir Thomas thought that the Danes would try to get all the booty for themselves. He offered to go again to the castle, but meanwhile the wind was off-shore, which prevented the possibility of an English attack. During the next three days desultory negotiations between the English and the Danes took place, but meanwhile, Ahlefeldt, the Danish commander, had received a letter from the King of Denmark condemning the English attack, so a secret meeting was arranged between Clifford and Ahlefeldt, but nothing came of it. Since there seemed little point in prolonging matters, Clifford left and the squadron rejoined Sandwich rather than risk being fired on again by the Danes. In any case Lord Sandwich was well out to sea by now and could no longer intercept the expected Dutch fleet.

On their arrival in England, Clifford received the king's congratulations on his personal part in the affair and a command to give Charles a personal account of it. In view of what had taken place, Charles decided to send Clifford as ambassador extraordinary to complain to the Danish king, but officially to settle disputed questions of commerce and navigation. If the Danes were prepared to make amends he was to persuade them to make good the damage and to prepare for another attack on Bergen. If, however, he found the Danish king prepared to treat with the Dutch, he was to do his utmost to dissuade him. King Frederick and his ministers proved evasive, and it later transpired that they were already secretly negotiating with the Dutch. When Clifford asked for an audience to take leave of the king, this set the cat among the pigeons and new overtures were immediately made to Clifford and Sir Gilbert Talbot. On 18 October a treaty was signed to the effect that war was to be made on the Dutch and no separate peace to be made, but it would be void if Sweden did not join. Thereupon Clifford left for Sweden. In spite of general support at the Swedish court for an alliance with England, the lack of Danish enthusiasm convinced Clifford that to achieve an alliance with both Sweden and Denmark would prove impossible, so he handed over the job to the English ambassador in Stockholm, Henry Coventry, and returned home. A little later an alliance between Holland, Denmark and France was announced.

After a few months at Ugbrooke, Clifford returned to London in May 1666, and the following month took part in the four-day inconclusive naval engagement off Harwich, complaining afterwards of the poor state of some of the English ships, the failure to pay the seamen (some had not been paid for 20 months) and the inefficiency of some of the commanders.[4] Mainly due to his efforts, however, the fleet was ready to go to sea again in less than a month. Prince Rupert was so impressed that he recommended the king to appoint Clifford to a position in the fleet.[5]

On 23 July the English fleet was anchored off Orford Ness when a storm broke, causing no little confusion, but on the 25th the English attacked, and, after fighting all day, the Dutch admiral de Ruyter began to withdraw, and soon the Dutch fleet was in full flight. The Royal Navy had won a notable victory. After blockading the Dutch coast for a couple of weeks, the English fleet returned to Sole Bay on 15 August. There was little further naval activity that summer, and on 2 September the Great Fire of London broke out, which helped to persuade the powers that be to call a halt for that year. The next year de Ruyter sailed up the Medway and destroyed most of the English fleet while it lay at anchor in the river. But by this time Louis XIV and Charles II had made peace, the French invaded Holland, so the exhausted Dutch were forced to sign the Treaty of Breda in July. In the meantime, Sir Thomas Clifford had embarked on his meteoric political career.

Finance was Clifford's forte. He now produced a scheme for making the Post Office pay and among other proposals he put to Arlington were the centralisation of the administration, a reduction in the number employed and a small cut in salaries. When his old friend Sir Hugh Pollard died in November 1666, Sir Thomas was appointed Comptroller of the King's Household in his place, which brought him still closer to Charles II. The following month he was made a Privy Councillor; when Lord Treasurer Southampton died early in 1667, the king gave the Treasury over to a Commission under the Duke of Albemarle, Lord Ashley, Sir Thomas Clifford, Sir William Coventry and Sir John Duncombe. In that year Clifford declared that the king had debts of more than two and a half million pounds, half at least owing on the navy. Parliament consistently ignored the king's appeals for assistance, while the Commission struggled to try to make some order out of the chaos in which they found the Treasury.

Arlington, meanwhile, ably assisted by Clifford, was working to get rid of Chancellor Clarendon, and when he fell it is pleasant to record that Clifford took no part in the hounding of the fallen chancellor.

When Lord Fitzhardinge died in June 1668, Clifford was appointed Treasurer of the Household in his place. Though this appointment may also have been due to Arlington, as Evelyn believed, Clifford was now beginning to take a line independent of his former patron. After the announcement of the Triple Alliance between England, France and Holland in 1669, Clifford, whose dislike of the Dutch was fanatical, predicted it would not be long before the English had another war with Holland. He did all he could to keep English enmity towards the Dutch alive, even to the extent of encouraging the East India Company's exorbitant demands against them.

In January 1669 a meeting took place attended by Lords Arlington and Arundell of Wardour and Sir Thomas Clifford with the Duke of York and the king to consider ways and means of 'advancing the Catholic religion in [the king's] dominions'. The Duke of York was, or was about to become, a Catholic: Charles did so on his deathbed; Arlington and Clifford were neither at that time of that persuasion; indeed Lord Arundell was the only one. Clifford had favoured reunion of the major churches ever since his student days at Oxford, and had ever been outspoken for toleration both inside and outside Parliament. However, there was much anti-Catholic feeling in the country and Charles was not the man to flout the mood of the people. At the same time, he had been negotiating with his sister, Henrietta (Minette), Duchess of Orleans, for a Defensive and Offensive Alliance with their cousin, Louis XIV. Charles was prepared to declare himself a Catholic, but would need troops and money to deal with a possible English insurrection. However, no matter what Charles may have said or done, he would do nothing to jeopardise his own position on the throne or English naval supremacy. If Charles could persuade Louis to concentrate his army against Holland, the war at sea could be safely entrusted to the English navy and these primary objectives would be gained. Clifford was the most outspoken in support of the ideal of English naval supremacy. At the same time, he was critical of the slackness he found in the Navy Office – to the obvious discomfort of Pepys at the Admiralty. Sir William Coventry was another antagonist. It was about now that the king's five principal ministers came to be known as the Cabal, from their initials

– Clifford, Arlington, Buckingham, Ashley and Lauderdale. It was a strangely assorted group holding differing views, but having one thing in common – a belief in toleration. Buckingham and Ashley were Protestants; Lauderdale was merely the king's personal adherent; Arlington was thought to be a Catholic, but, through his marriage sympathetic to the Dutch. Clifford, as we have seen, was zealous for religious freedom but supported royal despotism, hated the Dutch and eventually became a Catholic.

While all this was afoot, Cosimo de' Medici, Grand Duke of Tuscany, visited England in June 1669. He became good friends with Clifford, and although the Grand Duke's portrait 'set in diamonds' is no longer at Ugbrooke, many of his other gifts are still in the Clifford family.

Towards the end of June 1669, Louis XIV replied to Charles II's proposals for a Defensive/Offensive Alliance, but was sensible enough to advise him against too early a declaration of his conversion to Catholicism. The need for secrecy in these negotiations was obvious so the normal diplomatic channels were avoided, otherwise Buckingham, Ashley and other Protestant ministers might have become suspicious. Clifford was therefore employed to draw up papers from England and the Abbé Walter Montagu from France, and the reply sent to the Duchess of Orleans in August from her brother, King Charles, was written in Clifford's hand. Clifford recognised that the English and Scots would be strongly opposed to the king declaring himself a Catholic, and he recommended that the Pope make various considerations and 'condiscentions' to make the transition easier. It was advisable, he thought, to wait until old Pope Clement IX died, which could not be long, in the hope of a more amenable successor before broaching that part of the proposed treaty.

But despite their best endeavours to maintain strict secrecy, some people in England were getting suspicious, among them Buckingham, who was becoming increasingly envious of Arlington and Clifford. The latter was kept especially busy drawing up the naval clauses. They were to ensure that when war with Holland started, England must have enough money and supplies to use the full weight of a refurbished fleet. The French ambassador reported that he found Clifford the most obdurate member of the Commission to deal with.

All the while the Duchess of Orleans was the main channel of communication, and Charles and Louis both wanted her to go to England to be present when the Treaty was signed. Minette's odious husband, however, objected, but Louis overruled him. Her main task was to persuade Charles to declare war on Holland first. It was finally agreed that it should be left to Charles to decide when he should declare himself a Catholic, and that Louis should declare war on Holland after England had done so. On her return to France, a week before her tragic death, Minette wrote to Clifford:

> At Paris the 21 Juin.
>
> When I have write the King from Calais i praid him to tel milord Arlington an you what he had promised mi for bothe. his ansers was that hi gave mi againe his word that he did not thing to exequte it now. I tell you this sooner than to milord Arlington becase I know you ar not so hard to satisfie as hee. i should be so my self, if I was not sure that the King would not promise mee a thing to faille in the performance of it. This is the ferste letter I have ever write in Inglis. you will eselay see it bi the stile and ortograf. prae see in the same time that i expose my selfe to be thought a foulle in looking to make you know how much I am your frind.
>
> for Sr Thomas Clifort.

Owing to the necessity to maintain secrecy, the king's promise to make Arlington an earl and Clifford a peer was delayed for two years.

The negotiations leading to the Secret Treaty of Dover were long and tiring, and when completed Clifford went down to recover at Ugbrooke from June till August 1670. As a sequel to the treaty, Clifford put forward a scheme, presumably at the king's request, for the repair and strengthening of the fortifications of important ports and of the navy. It is a long document, in which Clifford envisaged the expenditure of vast sums of money on some seventeen forts, castles and citadels. He also advocated the reform of the Guards, the raising of new regiments by adding companies to those already in garrisons, and a complete review by the king of the appointments of Lords Lieutenant and Deputy Lieutenants. Nor did Clifford overlook education. He recommended the general replacement of heads of colleges in the universities by Catholics, after which liberty of conscience would be declared.

He considered Ireland to be in good hands, but wondered how long in advance the Lord Lieutenant should be allowed into the secret of the king's conversion. Scotland he thought a bigger headache for 'if there should be the least disturbance there the fanatics in England' would take heart from it. Finally he says that the king's conversion should be declared first and war on Holland afterwards; the French wanted it the other way round. While his 'scheme', which is in the Ugbrooke archives today, was being considered, Clifford quarrelled with Sir William Temple, the English ambassador to Holland, who, he thought, was dealing too lightly with the Dutch.

While Charles was not yet ready for a breach with Holland, Louis sent his ambassador, Colbert, to urge him to declare war on the Dutch and leave the declaration of his conversion till later. Charles thought otherwise, and suggested he should await a suitable envoy from the Pope, as he hoped for concessions from that quarter. Louis proposed the Bishop of Laon, but Charles suggested an Englishman, Dr. Leybourn, the head of the English Benedictines at Douai. Clifford was entrusted with the framing of the envoy's instructions, which gave him great pleasure. To the modern Christian interested in ecumenism the document repays careful study. There is no doubt that Clifford was 300 years ahead of his time.

One of the problems facing Arlington, Clifford and the king was how to get those who were not privy to the secret clauses of the Treaty of Dover to co-operate with them. In the end a duplicate treaty with modifications to suit the Protestant ministers was signed on 21 December 1670. In this way the whole Cabal ministry agreed with the French alliance. It was from this cynical dealing that the acronym took on its current sinister meaning.

On Easter Day 1671 Clifford's eldest son, Tom, died in Florence. It was a distressing time for him, but he may have been consoled by the discussions he was having with Father Hugh Cressy on plans to reunite the Churches. Cressy was himself a convert, having been an Anglican parson, a Fellow of Merton College, Oxford, and a candidate for a canonry at Windsor. He refers, in a letter offering Clifford condolences on the death of his son, to the question of the sort of oath of allegiance loyal Catholics could take. To Cressy it seemed that all theoretical differences would fade if the king became a Catholic. On the other hand, it was going to be more than difficult to convince those brought up on Foxe's *Book of Martyrs* that there would be no persecution. That the king's conversion did not take place until he was on his deathbed was due to these harsh political facts, not to any failure of effort by Clifford and Cressy.

In June 1671, Clifford was in Devon where his wife gave birth to another son, Charles, for whom the king stood godfather. That Clifford was still an Anglican at this time is shown by his arranging for Bishop Sparrow of Exeter to dedicate his new chapel at Ugbrooke during this visit. In July 1971 an ecumenical service, attended by the Anglican bishop of Exeter and the Catholic bishop of Plymouth was held to mark the tercentenary of this dedication. One cannot help feeling that Thomas Clifford would have approved. In July 1671 HMS *Centurion*, bearing home the body of 'young Tom', arrived in Plymouth. Escorted by all the military of the garrison it left for Ugbrooke and interment in the new chapel.

As the secret of the French alliance began to leak out, so the solidarity of the Cabal began to weaken. Buckingham and Ashley began to flirt with the pro-Dutch party in the Commons; Clifford and Arlington, now with Lauderdale's support, agreed to inform such people as Prince Rupert and the Duke of Ormonde. Then Louis XIV was persuaded to forego the help of an English land force, which infuriated Buckingham, who was cheated of his promised command. So violent was his abuse of Arlington that the king lost patience and ordered him to co-operate with his colleagues or leave.

On 15 March 1672 the king issued the Declaration of Indulgence, which suspended the penal laws against nonconformists and recusants. In view of what had happened ten years earlier this bold move was warmly welcomed by Clifford but not supported by Arlington, though it was by Buckingham, Ashley and Lauderdale. Doubtless the latter hoped it would win over the dissenters, whereas Clifford's motives were probably deeper than that. This done, everything was ready for war with Holland, the *casus belli* being the Dutch threat to English trade. Charles, having a well-developed sense of humour, did not take this very seriously: not so Louis, who took exception to a cartoon in which his special emblem, the sun, was being outshone by a Dutch cheese.

War being under way, the promised rewards were distributed to the treaty makers. Lauderdale was made a duke, Arlington an earl, Ashley became Earl of Shaftesbury and on 22 April 1672 Clifford became a baron. To distinguish him from the Lords Clifford of the elder branch who had held the earldom of Cumberland, he took the title of Lord Clifford of Chudleigh. As has been seen, Lady Anne Clifford did not die for another four years, nor the last of the elder male line of Borscombe until 1696 (Anthony Clifford of Lambeth), and until they both died the Chudleigh Cliffords bore the cadet branch sign of a crescent on their coat of arms. The senior Bobbing line had also died out through lack of a male heir.

To help Clifford bear the cost of his peerage, the king had granted him in 1671 the reversion in tail male of the Priory of Cannington[6] and Rodway Fitzpain, both in Somerset, and the free chapel of Piddle Wilderton in Dorset. Later that year the patronage of the livings of Ugbrooke and Chudleigh were entailed upon his family by Act of Parliament.

The war with Holland meant Charles could have completed the other part of the Secret Treaty of Dover and declared himself a Catholic. He told Colbert[7] the previous year he was being hard pressed by his conscience to do so; however, he prudently realised that the country would never accept it, so he did nothing.

The Dutch under de Ruyter did well during the war, inflicting immense damage before returning to Holland chased by the Duke of York. The English claimed a victory but the advantage lay with de Ruyter who had preserved his fleet and so frustrated designs for a naval attack on Holland, which would have outflanked the flooded polders by which William of Orange saved his country from Louis' army. This completely upset the Anglo-French plans, and, by merely keeping his fleet in being, de Ruyter changed the course of history.

Meanwhile with the French advancing into Holland, the Dutch tried to make a separate peace with England. Secret negotiations were opened informally by Clifford, Shaftesbury and Arlington. The terms were stringent: an indemnity, Flushing and other islands at the mouth of the Scheldt to be handed over as security, and a share in the East India trade. During these negotiations Arlington went to Holland, leaving Clifford to act as Secretary of State as well as carrying on at the Treasury.

As Clifford came closer to his own conversion to Catholicism so he acted more and more for James, Duke of York. As the Duke was at sea, other affairs also fell into Clifford's hands, mainly the question of whom the duke, now a widower, should marry, and he took part in the abortive scheme for him to marry an Austrian Archduchess. That summer was the worst in memory, and the English fleet blockading the Dutch coast suffered much damage. In August overwork began to tell on Clifford, and he had to go to Bath to take the waters. It is probable that he was already suffering from the gallstones from which he died. The waters seem to have done him some good and he was back in London by the end of the month. There he found the Dutch still obdurate and most of the other ministers somewhat dejected. Clifford was still for invasion and wrote to Lauderdale early in September saying that it was still not too late in the year for the fleet to go to sea.

But what was really holding up the war was lack of money, Louis having refused to advance a further million pounds. Parliament was due to meet at the end of October but it was doubtful if it would vote any more money. Furthermore, members would question the king's issuing of the Declaration of Indulgence. Clifford suggested keeping the fleet at sea all winter so that the sailors need not be paid off – or at all. So the king prorogued Parliament, only allowing time for Thomas to take his seat as Lord Clifford of Chudleigh. In November 1672 he was appointed Lord High Treasurer of England. This appointment clouded Thomas's long friendship with Arlington, who appears to have been jealous of his former protégé, and henceforth they opposed each other.[8]

Clifford was in the post too short a time to do much. There was no money in the Treasury, there was an expensive war on and an appeal to Parliament had to be made. He cut expenditure to the bone and kept a scrupulous account every Saturday morning of monies to be paid. His predecessors had made their fortunes in that office; not so Clifford. He was not only incorruptible himself, but reprimanded and suspended Sir William D'Oyly for buying up orders 'at a great under-valuation'.[9]

As Christmas 1672 approached the king tried to get Clifford and Arundell to persuade his brother, the Duke of York, not to flaunt his Catholicism. But James would not listen. Clifford, though still receiving the sacrament according to the Anglican rite, was already hovering. The firmness and consistency of the Duke of York were qualities he greatly admired and were obviously factors influencing Thomas's final conversion.

When Parliament finally assembled in February 1673, it took a strongly anti-Catholic line, and refused to grant money unless the king gave up his right to suspend the penal laws and to withdraw the Declaration of Indulgence. Under this pressure, and the unwillingness of Louis XIV to give him any more money, the king was forced to give way and the Commons passed the Money Bill. In their triumph they pressed on with their own 'No Popery' Bill. When it came to the Lords, Clifford was the only peer to attack it in its entirety, at the risk of arousing the fury of the Commons against the government.

Arlington, in his new-found hatred of the Lord Treasurer, made a great deal of Clifford's tactlessness and revealed the inner secrets of the king's plan to declare himself a Catholic. Thus Clifford's downfall was engineered.

The Test Act which the Commons passed meant that no Catholic could hold office under the Crown whether in the army, navy, in politics or the Royal Household. The king was forced to accept it, saying he would purge his court of Catholics, except for his barber, as 'he was well accustomed to his hand'.

All the ministers who could take the test or comply with the Act with a clear conscience, did so with alacrity; perhaps there were a few who complied with some pangs of conscience. It started with the first Sunday in April 1673. The second Sunday many more officials took Communion at St Martin's-in-the-Fields. Even the agnostic Duke of Buckingham complied. As the Sundays passed and the Lord Treasurer had not complied, so the rumours multiplied. Was he a papist or was he not? He and his family continued to attend his private chapel at his official residence, Wallingford House. That month his daughter, Elizabeth, married the son and heir of Sir Thomas Carew of Haccombe in this very chapel. Young Henry Carew had known Elizabeth from childhood, as Ugbrooke and Haccombe are but six or seven miles apart. It is reasonable to suppose that he postponed his announcement until after his daughter's wedding.

By the third Sunday in April, the Lord Treasurer was the only one among the great who had not taken the Test. Then it was announced that on 17 May he would see no one, and transact no business, as he was going to prepare for the sacrament in private. He went by coach to Somerset House, left by a side door and then his coach, it was said, overturned in the Strand, depositing him and Father Morgan in the gutter. This added fuel to the rumours which were passed on by many letters at the time.[10] They dwelt on his successor, mainly suggesting Sir Thomas Osborne, Treasurer of the Navy. As the time limit drew near, rumour succeeded rumour. Other reputed Catholics, such as FitzGerald, who had recently been made a Major-General in the expedition being prepared under Prince Rupert to go against Holland, had 'subdued his conscience' to his career.[11] When, on the last Sunday, Clifford did not appear at St Martin's, all knew he was about to resign. He was busy settling the affairs at the Treasury. Applicants crowded his chambers trying to extract from him what they could before he resigned and two letters were delivered there from the king's mistress, the Duchess of Cleveland.[12]

On 18 June, his second daughter, Mary, was married from Wallingford House to Sir Simon Leach of Cadeleigh, Devon. It was now clear that it was for Mary's, not Elizabeth's wedding he had been waiting. The next day he went to attend the king in his bedchamber and, after acknowledging his gratitude to the king, resigned his Lord High Treasurer's staff, which was immediately handed to Sir Thomas Osborne, first Earl of Danby and afterwards Duke of Leeds.

For a few days Lord Clifford shut himself up in Wallingford House, now described as being as 'silent as a convent'. His dignity impressed everyone. But the king and his intimates had known his intention for some time. He did not openly confess his faith till the day of his resignation, and it was only that which made him resign. Those who suggested he was afraid of being impeached by the Commons did not know the man. He delayed his conversion in the hope that his scheme for reunification would succeed. When he saw it would not, he acted. It was a long and slow process.

The king, knowing how Clifford's enemies would react, issued on 3 July a warrant of pardon for anything he might have done before 30 June 1673. It was without precedent. When it seemed the Commons were set on a witch hunt, the other members of the Cabal demanded and were given similar pardons.[13]

At the end of August Clifford went to Ugbrooke to join his wife and family who had returned there immediately after his resignation. All he wanted to do now was to retire to the life of a country gentleman. His friendship with Dryden, for whom he had obtained the position of Poet Laureate and Historiographer Royal in 1670, was one of his consolations on retirement. 'Dryden's Seat' still exists at Ugbrooke, where he is believed to have written his *Hind and the Panther*.

He now set about enlarging his house and planning the park, and arranging his collection of portraits, his Dutch paintings and his Hatton Garden and other tapestries. But his retirement was to be a short one. He fell ill again with a 'fitte of the stone', lost a lot of blood and died on 13 October 1673. This account of his death is amply upheld by contemporary evidence, but it did not prevent the London gossips putting it about that he had 'strangled himself with his cravat upon the bed-tester' (an impossible and futile feat for someone who possessed excellent pistols). In any case, it is quite out of character that so brave and devout a convert to Catholicism could ever have contemplated what the Church so strongly forbids. Let John Evelyn sum up his own view of the late Lord Treasurer's character: 'My lord Clifford was a valiant, uncorrupt gentleman ... ambitious, not covetous, generous, passionate, and a most sincere friend'.

He made his will on 9 October, repeating the wish he had made in his earlier will 14 years before, to be buried at night.[14] His wish was fulfilled on 19 October when he was laid to rest in the vault beneath the chapel at Ugbrooke next his eldest son, Tom.

In a permissive age he was one of the few influential men about whom no scandal was current. The only reference was that of a Dr. Prideaux, who calls the Countess of Falmouth[15] 'an infamous relict of the Lord Clifford'. It is true that one of his last public acts was to arrange a pension for this lady, but there is no other evidence. If Mary Bagot, Countess of Falmouth, had been his mistress, then he at least had taste, for she was one of the great beauties of the age. Clifford was above all loyal to his king and country. James II, in his 'Advice to his son' wrote: 'I never knew but one of the late king my brother's ministers, namely the Lord Clifford, that served him throughout faithfully and without reproach'.

By his wife, Elizabeth Martyn, Thomas, 1st Lord Clifford of Chudleigh had seven sons and eight daughters:

1. THOMAS, died soon after birth.

2. THOMAS, also died in infancy.

3. THOMAS, born 3 December 1652. Unlike his father and grandfather, he was not educated at Exeter College, but at Queen's College, Oxford, where he matriculated on 10 November 1668, aged fifteen. The Provost informed his tutor, Joseph Williamson, that young Tom was so 'constant at his prayers and studies as to be an example to all'. Another tutor[16] reported that with a bit of 'chastisement, the sparkle of intellect' would be awakened in him! After Oxford he was to have gone abroad in the company of his tutor, Henry Smith, but instead he went with Sir Bernard Gascoyne, an international diplomat, a soldier of fortune who had been born Bernado Guasconi in Florence. They sailed in a London ketch to Calais on 18 November 1670, and after a visit to Venice they arrived in Florence in March 1671. Tom was welcomed by Cosimo the Grand Duke and made much of by the Florentine nobility who had been on the official visit to England the previous year. The English resident, Sir John Finch, was very piqued that he could not have a greater say in looking after him. Unfortunately he fell ill after drinking iced wine and beer, developed a fever and died on Easter Day 1671. 'He died', said Sir John in a letter to Arlington, 'with a greate sense of dutie to his father and mother ... Then he desired his body might be embalmed and sent to Plimouth and thence carried to his father's vault ... one last boon of his father ... that before he should be buryed that his father should cause his face to be uncovered and looke upon his sonne once more before he sent him to his grave'. In May the Duke of York gave orders for the release of HMS *Centurion* to sail to Leghorn to collect the coffin. On 19 May covered with a black velvet cloth adorned with the Clifford coat of arms, and drawn by a pair of the Grand Duke's mules, the coffin set out from Florence. Gascoyne and Finch escorted it to England and the vault at Ugbrooke. Dryden's poem 'On the death of a very young gentleman' was written on the occasion of young Tom's death.

4. GEORGE, died in infancy.

5. HUGH, 2nd Lord Clifford of Chudleigh, for whom see next chapter.

6. SIMON, born in 1666 was still alive in 1686, but did not survive his mother.

7. CHARLES, baptised 24 June 1671, died at Ugbrooke 4 July 1691, aged 20, and was buried at Ugbrooke.

1. ELIZABETH died soon after birth.

2. ELIZABETH, born 1655, married 1673 her cousin Sir Henry Carew, 2nd Baronet of Haccombe, but died without issue in 1677, being buried at Ugbrooke.

3. MARY, born in 1658, married 1673, Sir Simon Leach of Cadeleigh, and died 9 October 1715.

4. AMY, born in 1661, married October 1681 John Courtenay of Molland, and had nine children.

5. ANNE, born 1662 died unmarried at the age of sixteen.

6. RHODA, born 1665, died unmarried in 1689.

7. ISABEL, died in infancy.

8. CATHERINE, born in 1670, Queen Catherine of Braganza being her godmother. The queen's christening present, a pair of Portuguese diamond ear-rings, is still among the family heirlooms at Ugbrooke. She died unmarried in 1708.

The first baron's widow, Elizabeth, had a struggle to cope with several small children and a none too wealthy estate. That she did so well financially is to her credit. She even increased the estate by acquiring more land in Kingsteignton and Shaldon. When she died at the advanced age of 79 in 1709, she was buried beside her husband in the vaults at Ugbrooke.

Chapter Thirty-Seven

Generation XXII – Hugh, 2nd Lord Clifford of Chudleigh (1663-1730)

24. Portrait of Hugh, 2nd Lord Clifford of Chudleigh, by an unknown artist.

25. Portrait of Anne, 2nd Lady Clifford.

Hugh, 2nd Lord Clifford of Chudleigh, was baptised at Ugbrooke on 21 December 1663, and succeeded his father when he was not yet quite ten years old. He was educated at both Eton and Winchester, as we learn from his elder brother's deathbed words that he was already at Eton in 1671 and likely to 'prove a pretty schollar'. After his father's death, King Charles II made a grant of £300 in 1677 for his education, which was held in trust for him as he was a Catholic. This did not prevent him completing his education from 1678 to 1679 at Winchester.

Hugh Clifford's upbringing and prospects were limited by the terms of the Test Act, for the army, navy, church and government office were all closed to him as a Roman Catholic. This compelled him, and those in a similar situation, to concentrate upon literature and the arts and the management of his estates. In Hugh Clifford's case his aptitude may be judged by Dryden's dedication of his version of Virgil's Eclogues, where he wrote: 'You have added to your natural endowments, which without flattery are eminent, the superstructure of study and the knowledge of good authors. Courage, probity and humanity are inherent in you. These virtues have ever been habitual to the ancient house of Cumberland, from whence you are descended'.[1]

He was reminded of his kinship with the Cumberland Cliffords when Lady Anne died in 1676. It seems that Hugh Clifford's advisers may have contemplated reclaiming the northern estates, basing their claim on the deed of entail made by the 2nd Earl of Cumberland.[2] But they delayed too long, and finding William of Orange at Brixham and his troops stationed in Chudleigh, they doubtless thought that a Catholic family which supported a deposed king was more likely to lose the estates it had rather than win back its northern one.

In 1684, when he came of age, Hugh had been warmly received at Court, where the Duke of York, soon to become King James II, showed him particular attention because of the close bond which had existed between him and Hugh's father. However, the revolution of 1688 put an end to the brief respite enjoyed by English Catholics, and he returned to Devon when the new administration deprived him of the office of Clerk of the Pipe, which he had been granted by Charles II in 1681. He had accepted the post but had acted as deputy to comply with the Test Act, and was now supplanted by Lord Robert Russell. After this brief excursion into public life, Hugh Clifford remained mostly at Ugbrooke, devoting his time to improving his estate, and he laid out great avenues of trees, some of which survived Capability Brown's later revamping. In December 1695 he bought the manor of Chudleigh,[3] of which Hams Barton remained in the family until just after the Second World War, when it was sold to meet two successive death duties; the Lordship of the Manor of Chudleigh still belongs to the family.

In 1708, Lord and Lady Clifford sheltered a mysterious Sir Charles Clifford, whose relationship to the family has not been traced. He came to Ugbrooke in August and stayed until December, but his presence there seemed to cause Lady Clifford some uneasiness. He left for London just before Christmas, but had the misfortune to lose his clothes and furniture in a fire in the house he was putting up in in the Strand. Like his Devonshire host and hostess, Sir Charles was a Catholic.

During the Jacobite rebellion of 1715, Hugh Clifford, in common with many other influential Catholics, was placed under house arrest, but was released when the rising had been defeated. While the presence of portraits of both the Old and the Young Pretender, and of the Old Pretender's wife, Maria Clementina Sobieska, at Ugbrooke point to where the family's sympathies lay, Hugh cannot have been too outspoken in his opinions, as his arrest seems to have been purely precautionary,[4] and not nearly as severe as that of the Earl of Nithsdale, who had taken part in the Rising, and whose escape is a truly dramatic story. Writing in April 1718 from the Royal Palace in Rome to her sister, Lucy Herbert, Abbess of the English Augustinian nuns at Bruges, Lady Nithsdale told how, on hearing that her husband had been committed to the Tower, he had expressed 'the greatest anxiety' to see her.[5]

'I rode to Newcastle', she continues, 'and from thence took the stage to York. When I arrived there the snow was so deep that the stage could not set out for London. The Season was so severe and the roads so extreamly bad that the post itself was stopt; however I took Horses and rode to London thro the snow which was generally above the Horses Girths, and arrived safe in London without accident.

'On my arrival I went immediately to make what interest I could amongst those who were in Place. No one gave me any hope but they to the contrary assured me that altho some of the Prisoners were to be pardoned, yet my Lord would certainly not be of this number. When I inquired into the reason of this distinction I could obtain no other answer but that they would or not flatter me; but I soon perceived the reasons which they declined alledging to me; A Roman Catholick upon the frontier of Scotland who headed a very considerable party, A Man whose Family had always signalised itself by its Loyalty to the Royal House of Stuart, and who was the only support of the Catholicks against the inveteracy of the Whigs, who were very numerous in that part of Scotland, would become an agreeable sacrifice to the opposite Party.

'They all retained a lively remembrance of his Grandfather who defended his own castle of Calaverok (Caerlaverock) to the last extremity and surrendered it up only by the express command of his Royal Master, now having his Grandson in their Power they were determined not to let him escape from their hands.

'Upon this I formed the Resolution to attempt his escape but opened my intentions to nobody but my Dear Evans. In order to concert measures I strongly sollicited to be permitted to see my Lord which they refused to grant me unless I would remain confined with him in the Tower, this I would not submitt to and alledged for excuse that my health would not permitt me to undergo the confinement.

'The real reason of my refusal was not to put it out of my power to accomplish my designs. However by bribing the Guards I often contrived to see my Lord till the Day on which the Prisoners were condemned after that we were allowed for the last week to see and take our leave of them.

'By the help of Evans I had prepared everything necessary to disguise my Lord but had the utmost difficulty to prevail upon him to make use of them. However I at last succeeded by the help of Almighty God.

'On the 22d of Feb which fell on a Thursday our general Petition was to be presented to the House of Lords, the purport of which was to entreat the Lords to intercede with His Majesty to pardon the Prisoners. We were however disappointed the Day before the Petition was to be presented for the Duke of St Albans who had promised My Lady Derwentwater to present it when it came to the point failed in his word. However as she was the only English Countess concerned it was incumbent on her to have it presented. We had but one day left before the Execution and the Duke still promised to present the petition but for fear he should fail I engaged the Duke of Montrose to secure its being done by one or the other. I then went in company of most of the Ladies of Quality who were then in Town to sollicit the Interest of the Lords as they were going to the House. They all behaved to me with the greatest civility, but particularly My Lord Pembroke who tho he desired my not to speak to him, yet he promised to employ his Interest in our favor, & he honorably kept his word, for he spoke in the House very strongly in our behalf. The subject of the debate was whether the King had power to pardon those who had been condemned by Parliament & it chiefly was owing to Lord Pembroke's speech that it passed in the affirmative. However one of the Lords stood up & said that the House would only intercede for those of the prisoners as should approve themselves worthy of their intercession, but not for all of them indiscriminately. This salvo quite blasted all my hopes, for I was assured that it aimed at the exclusion of those who should refuse to subscribe to the Petition, which I knew was a thing My Lord would never submit to, nor in fact would I wish to preserve his life on those terms.

'As the Motion was passed generally I thought I could draw from it some advantage in favor of my design. Accordingly I immediately left the House of Lords & hastened to the Tower, where affecting an air of joy & satisfaction, I told all the Guards I passed by that I came to bring joyful tidings to the Prisoners. I desired them to lay aside their fears for the Petition had passed in their favor. I then gave them some money to drink to the Lords and his Majesty, tho it was but trifling for I thought that if I were too liberal on the occasion they might suspect my designs & that giving them something would gain their goodwill & service for the next day which was the Eve of Execution.

'The next morning I could not go to the Tower having so many things on my hands to put in readiness, but in the Evening when all was ready I sent for Mrs Mills with whom I lodged and acquainted her with my designs of attempting My Lord's escape, as there was no prospect of his being pardoned & this was the last night before his Execution. I told her I had everything in readiness & that I trusted she would not refuse to accompany me that My Lord might pass for her. I pressed her to come immediately as we had no time to lose. At the same time I sent for a Mrs. Morgan then usually known by the name of Hilton, to whose acquaintance my dear Evans had introduced me, which I look upon as a very singular happiness. I immediately communicated my resolution to her, she was of a very tall & slender make as that I desired her to put under own riding hood one that I had prepared for Mrs. Mills as she was to held hers to my Lord, that in coming out he might be taken for her. Mrs. Mills was then with Child so that she was not only of the same height but also nearly of the same size as My Lord. When we were in the Coach I never ceased talking that they might have no leisure to reflect. Their surprise and astonishment when I first opened my design to them had made them consent without thinking of the consequences.

'On my arrival at the Tower the first I introduced was Mrs. Morgan (for I was only allowed to take in one at a time) she brought in the cloathes that were to serve Mrs. Mills when she left her own behind her. When Mrs. Morgan had taken off what she had brought for my purpose I conducted her back to the staircase and in going I desired her to send me in my maid to dress me, that I was affraid of being too late to present my last Petition that night if she did not come immediately. I dispatched her safe and went partly down stairs to meet Mrs. Mills who had the precaution to hold her handkerchief to her face as was very natural for a woman to do when she was going to bid her last farewell to a friend on the Eve of his Execution. I had indeed desired her to do it that My Lord might go out in the same manner. Her eyebrows were rather inclined to be sandy and My Lord's were dark and very thick. However, I had prepared some paint of the colour of hers to disguise his with. I also brought an artificial head dress of the same colored hair as hers and I painted his face with white and his cheeks with rouge to hide his long beard which he had not time to shave; all this provision I had before left in the Tower. The poor Guards, whom my slight liberality the day before had endeared me to let me go quietly out with my company and were not so strictly on the watch as they usually had been, and the more so, as they were persuaded from what I had told them the day before, that the Prisoners would obtain their Pardon. I made Mrs. Mills take off her own hood and put on that which I had brought for her. I then took her by the Hand & led her out of My Lord's chamber, & in passing through the next room in which there were several people with all the concern immaginable I said, "My dear Mrs. Catharine go in all haste and send my waiting Maid. She certainly cannot reflect how late it is. She forgets I am to present my petition tonight & if I let slip the opportunity I am undone for tomorrow will be too late. Hasten her as much as possible for I shall be on thorns till she comes." Everybody in the room who were chiefly the Guards' wives and daughters seemed to compassionate me exceedingly and the Sentinel officiously opened the door. When I had seen her out I returned back to my Lord and finished dressing him. I had taken care that Mrs. Mills did not go out crying as she came in that My Lord might the better pass for the Lady who came in crying and afflicted and the more so because he had the same dress she wore. When I had almost finished dressing My Lord in all my peticoats excepting one I perceived it was growing dark and was affraid the light of the candles might betray us so I resolved to set off. I went out leading him by the Hand and he held his handkerchief to his eyes. I spoke to him in the most piteous tone of voice bewailing bitterly the negligence of Evans who had ruined me by her delay and then said I, "My dear Mrs. Batty run quickly and bring her with you. You know my lodging and if ever you made dispatch in your life, do it at present; I am almost distracted at this disappointment." The Guards opened the doors & I went down stairs with him still conjuring him to make all possible dispatch as soon as he had cleared the door. I made him walk before me for fear the Sentinel should take notice of his walk, but I still continued to press him to make all the dispatch he possibly could. At the bottom of the stairs I met my dear Evans into whose hands I confided him. I had before engaged Mrs. Mills to be in readiness before the Tower to conduct him to some place of safety in case we succeeded. He looked upon the affair so very improbable to succeed that his astonishment when he saw us threw him into such consternation that he was almost out of himself, which Evans perceiving with the greatest presence of mind without telling him anything lest he should mistrust them, conducted him to some of her own friends on whom she could rely, & so secured him without which we should have been undone. When she conducted him & left him with them she returned to find Mrs. Mills, who by this time had recovered from her astonishment, they went home together and having found a place of security, they conducted him to it.

'In the meantime as I had pretended to have sent the young lady on a message I was obliged to return upstairs and go back to My Lord's room in the same feigned anxiety of being too late, so that everybody seemed sincerely to simpathize in my distress!

'When I was in the Room I talked to him as if he had been really present and answered my own questions in my Lord's voice as nearly as I could imitate it. I walked up and down as if we were conversing together till I thought they had time enough thoroughly to clear themselves of the Guards. I then thought proper to make off also. I opened the door & stood half in it that those in the outward chamber might hear what I said, but held it so close that the(y) could not look in. I bid My Lord a formal farewell for that night & added that something more than usual must have happened to make Evans negligent on this important occasion who had always been so punctual in the smallest trifles, that I saw no remedy than to go in person; that if the Tower was still open when I had finished my business I would return that night, but that he might be assured I would be with him early in the morning as I could gain admittance into the Tower & I flattered myself I should bring him most favorable news. Then before I shut the door, I pulled through the string of the Latch so that it could only be opened on the inside. I then shut it with some degree of force that I might be sure of its being well shut. I said to the servant as I passed by who was ignorant of the whole transaction that he need not carry in candles to his Master till My Lord sent for them as he desired to finish some prayers first.

'I went down stairs and called a coach as there were many on the stand & drove home to my lodgings where poor Mr. Mackenzie had been waiting to carry the Petition in case my attempt failed. I told him there was no need of my Petition as My Lord was safe out of the Tower and out of the Hands of his Enemies as I hoped, but I did not know where.

'I discharged the coach and sent for a Sedan Chair, & went to the Duchess of Buccleuch who expected me about that time. I had begged her to present the Petition for me, having taken my precaution against all events. I asked if she was at home, & they answered me that she expected me and had another Duchess with her. I refused to go upstairs as she had company with her, & I was not in a condition to see any other company with her. I begged to be shewn into a Chamber below stairs, & that they would have the Goodness to send her Grace's maid to me having something to say to her. I discharged the Chair lest I should be persued and watched. When the maid came in I desired her to present my most humble respects to her Grace, who they told me had company with her & to acquaint her that this was my only reason for not coming upstairs. I also charged her with my sincerest thanks for her kind offer to accompany me when I went to present my Petition. I added that she might spare herself any further trouble, as it was judged more advisable to present a general Petition in the name of all, however that I should never be unmindful of my particular obligations to her Grace which I would return very soon to acknowledge in Person.

'I then desired one of the servants to call a Chair, & I went to the Duchess of Montrose who had always borne a part in my distress. When I arrived she left her company to deny herself not being able to see me under the affliction which she judged me to be.

'By mistake, however, I was admitted so there was no remedy. She came to me and as my heart was in an extasy of Joy I expressed it on my countenance. As she entered the Room I ran up to her in the transport of my Joy. She appeared to be extremely shocked and frighted, & has since confessed to me that she apprehended my trouble had thrown me out of myself till I communicated my happiness to her. She then advised me to retire to some place of security, for that the King was highly displeased & even enraged at the Petition I had presented him, & had complained of it severely. I sent for another Chair, for I always discharged them immediately lest I might be persued. Her Grace said she would go to Court to see how the News of my Lord's escape was received. When the News was brought to the King he flew into an excess of passion & said he was betrayed for it could not have been done without some confederacy. He instantly dispatched two persons to the Tower to see that the other Prisoners were well secured lest they should follow the Example. Some threw the blame on one some on another; the Duchess was the only one at Court who knew it.

'When I left the Duchess I went to a house which Evans had found for me & where she promised to inform me where My Lord was. She got hither some four minutes after me & told me that when she had seen him [one word illegible] she went in search of Mr. Mills who by this time had recovered himself from his astonishment, that he had returned to her house when she found him & that he had removed My Lord from the first Place where he had desired him to wait to the house of a poor woman directly opposite to the Guardhouse. She had but one small room up one pair of stairs & a very small bed in it. We threw ourselves on the bed that we might not be heard walking up and down. She left us a bottle of wine and some bread, & Mrs. Mills brought us some more in her pocket next day. We subsisted on this provision from Thursday till Saturday night, when Mrs. Mills came & conducted My Lord to the Venetian Ambassador's. We did not communicate the affair to his Excellency, but one of the servants concealed him in his Room till Wednesday, on which day the Ambassador's coach and six was to go down to Dover to meet his brother. My Lord put on a livery and went down in the Retinue without the least suspicion to Dover where Mr. Mitchell, which was the name of the Ambassador's servant, hired a small vessel and immediately set sail for Calais. The passage was so remarkably short that the Captain threw out this reflection that the wind could not have served better if his passengers had been flying for their Lives, little thinking it to be really the case. Mr. Mitchell might have easily returned without being suspected of having been concerned in My Lord's escape, but My Lord seemed inclined to have him continue with him, which he did, and has at present a good place under our young master.

'This is an exact & as full an account of this affair and of the persons concerned in it as I could possibly give you to the best of my Memory and you may depend on the truth of it ... '.

Lady Nithsdale goes on to tell her sister that finding herself suspected of having contrived her husband's escape, she retired to a house in Drury Lane, but as the King's animosity towards her increased, she made a hazardous journey back to Scotland to settle her son's affairs, and then went abroad.

26.   Weston Hall, Warwickshire, which came to the Clifford family through Anne Preston, wife of the 2nd Lord Clifford.

The second Lord Clifford died at the age of 67 on 12 October 1730 at Cannington in Somerset, and was buried there alongside his favourite son, Thomas. His will, made on 18 October 1726, was proved on 24 May 1731. He had married on or before 1685 Anne Preston, the daughter and heiress of Sir Thomas Preston, 3rd baronet, of Furness in Lancashire, by his wife, Mary Molyneux, daughter of Caryll, 3rd Viscount Molyneux of Maryborough. Lady Clifford died at Ugbrooke in July and was buried on 10 July 1734. She had brought her husband considerable property in Warwickshire, Derbyshire, Lancashire and Westmorland,[6] some of which had belonged to the Preston family since the 12th century. By Anne Preston, Hugh Clifford had nine sons and six daughters:

27. Anne, daughter of Thomas Clifford and Charlotte Maria, Countess of Newburgh. Anne married John Joseph, 2nd Count Mahony.

1. FRANCIS, born in 1686, died in infancy.

2. THOMAS, born in December 1687. In December 1713 he married Charlotte Maria, Countess of Newburgh, Viscountess Kynnaird and Lady Livingston of Flacraig in her own right, all in the peerage of Scotland, only child of Charles Livingston, 2nd Earl of Newburgh. They went to live at Cannington, where Thomas died five years later, and where he was buried on 21 February 1718, aged thirty-two. By the Countess, who went abroad with their younger daughter after his death, Thomas Clifford left two daughters:

i. FRANCES, who lived and died at Ugbrooke and was buried in Chudleigh church on 7 July 1771.

ii. ANNE, who married in Paris, John Joseph (sometimes called James) 2nd Count Mahony on 22 December 1739. Mahony (1699-1757) was a Lieutenant-General in the Spanish service, Governor of St Elmo and Commander of St Januarius, Inspector General of Cavalry in the Neapolitan Army. His father, Daniel O'Mahony, was created a French Count by Louis XIV in 1702 and a Spanish Count by Philip V of Spain in 1710. He had married Cecilia, the daughter of George Weld of Lulworth. Anne Clifford died in Ischia in 1793, leaving an only daughter, Cecilia Carlotta Francesca Anna, Countess Mahony, born in Naples in 1740, who married, in 1757, Benedetto, 5th Prince Giustiniani, and died in 1789. She was the mother of Vincente, 6th Prince Giustiniani, de jure 6th Earl of Newburgh. The present Earl of Newburgh is her descendant, Giulio, 10th Prince Rospigliosi, Duke of Zagarolo.

Thomas Clifford's widow, the Countess of Newburgh, married as her second husband, Charles Radcliffe, later Jacobite titular 5th Earl of Derwentwater (grandson of Charles II by his liaison with Moll Davies). Her impetuous young husband had taken part in the 1715 rebellion, and only escaped execution due to his extreme youth and by escaping from Newgate to join the Stuart family on the Continent. In November 1745 he was captured off the Dogger Bank and brought prisoner to the Tower of London. In November 1746 he was condemned to death under his former sentence and beheaded on Tower Hill on 8 December and buried on 11 December 1746 at St Giles-in-the-Fields, aged fifty-three. His widow died in London in August 1755 and was buried with him.

3. FRANCIS, born on Christmas Day 1690, but died young in Germany.

4. WILLIAM, born 1692, died 1702 and was buried at Ugbrooke.

5. GEORGE, died in infancy.

6. CHARLES, died in infancy.

7. HUGH, third Lord Clifford of Chudleigh, for whom see the next chapter.

8. HENRY, born 1702, travelled abroad as a young man and was invested by Cosimo III de' Medici, Grand Duke of Tuscany, with the Star and Chain of the Order of San Stefano in recognition of the friendship of the two families for more than fifty years. He died on 21 August 1725 and is buried at Cannington.

9. LEWIS, born 1709 and died unmarried in Flanders.

1. ELIZABETH, born 1689, married first William Constable, 4th and last Viscount Dunbar, who died without legal issue 15th August 1718. She married secondly in November 1720, Charles Gregory, 9th and last Viscount Fairfax of Emley of Gilling Castle, Yorkshire, but she died without issue of smallpox in April 1721 and is buried in Bath Abbey.

2. CATHERINE, born 1694, became a nun at the English Benedictine Convent at Ghent.

3. MARY, born 1695 also became a nun at the same convent.

4. PRESTON, born 1707, also became a nun at the same convent in Ghent.

5. ANNE, born 1704, married in 1723 George Cary of Tor Abbey, near Torquay, Devon. He died in 1758 and she died in 1762 and is buried at St Pancras in London.

6. AMY, born 1705, married Cuthbert Constable of Burton Constable, Yorkshire, by whom she had three children. She died aged 26 in 1731 and was buried, like her sister, at St Pancras, where most London Catholics were buried at this time.

Chapter Thirty-Eight

Generation XXIII – Hugh, 3rd Lord Clifford of Chudleigh (1700-32)

28. Portrait of Hugh, 3rd Lord Clifford of Chudleigh, by Hudson.

29. Portrait of Elizabeth, 3rd Lady Clifford.

Hugh was the seventh but only surviving son of the 2nd Lord Clifford of Chudleigh. He was born on 14 April 1700 and succeeded his father at the age of thirty. With his younger brother, Henry, he did the Grand Tour, visited Florence and took a degree of Master of Arts at Montpellier in France. His marriage in 1725 caused his father considerable displeasure, perhaps more because of his assessment of the girl's character than of his feeling that it was a poor match. She was Elizabeth, eldest daughter and co-heiress of Edward Blount of Blagdon, a friend and correspondent of Alexander Pope, the fourth son of Sir George Blount, 2nd Baronet of Sodington, Worcestershire, and his wife, Mary, daughter of Richard Kirkham of Blagdon, Devon.

Elizabeth Blount's mother brought to the Lords Clifford of Chudleigh a renewed and much more recent descent from the senior Cumberland branch of the Clifford family. She was Annabella Guise, the grand-daughter of Lady Annabella Scrope, one of the daughters of Emamuel Scrope, Earl of Sunderland, 11th and last Lord Scrope of Bolton. He was the great-grandson of the 8th Lord Scrope and Lady Catherine Clifford, daughter of the 1st Earl of Cumberland, himself the son of the Shepherd Lord.

Whatever her father-in-law's fears about her background, it has to be admitted that Elizabeth Blount was a poor businesswoman and a spendthrift, which proved disastrous for Ugbrooke and the family during her long widowhood. The 2nd Lord Clifford had shown his displeasure by leaving all his disposable property to his wife, and she had done likewise by disinheriting her son in favour of her daughter, Anne Cary. However, when Hugh predeceased his mother, he prolonged the feud by leaving her '6 pair of white pigeons and 6 bags of vetches'. On his death, Hugh left his wife 'big with her sixth child'.

Hugh, 3rd Lord Clifford of Chudleigh, died, aged 31, on 26 March 1732, at Ugbrooke, and was buried in the concealed crypt beneath the secret chapel disguised as a hall there. His will, dated 12 July 1731, was proved 26 February 1732/3. His widow retired to France, and is the lady referred to in Andrew Lang's *Prince Charles Edward Stuart: the Young Cavalier* (London, 1903), at the time when Bonnie Prince Charlie was at Montmartre in early 1745 'very secretly planning his expedition to Scotland'. Lady Clifford forwarded to the Old Pretender a warning of what was afoot, for neither James nor the French court would have permitted the enterprise had they known about it. However, her warnings went unheeded, and within a few weeks Prince Charles had embarked on the disastrous 1745 rising.

By Elizabeth Blount, who died in Paris 46 years after himself in 1778, Hugh, 3rd Lord Clifford of Chudleigh had four sons and two daughters:

1. HUGH, 4th baron, for whom see next chapter.
2. EDWARD, born 1727, died unmarried 1781.
3. HENRY, died in infancy.
4. THOMAS, born posthumously in 1732, for whom see Part Four, Chapter Fifty-Three.
1. ELIZABETH, died in infancy 1731.
2. MARY, born 1731, married 1766 Sir Edward Smythe, 4th Baronet of Eshe and Acton Burnall, and died 2 November 1784, leaving issue. Sir Edward was a cousin of Marie Anne Smythe (1756-1837), Mrs. Fitzherbert, wife of King George IV.

Chapter Thirty-Nine

Generation XXIV – Hugh, 4th Lord Clifford of Chudleigh (1726-83)

30. Portrait of Hugh, 4th Lord Clifford of Chudleigh.

31. Portrait of Anne, 4th Lady Clifford.

Hugh, 4th Lord Clifford of Chudleigh, succeeded his father at the age of five. His early schooling was at the English Secular College at Douai in France, for it was normal at that time for Catholic families to send their sons abroad to be educated in their faith. At Ugbrooke also, there were from time to time as tutors, priests in disguise, some of whom are buried in a plot near the chapel with no marking on their tombstones. There is still a secret room or priest's hole at Ugbrooke.

It was during Hugh's minority that his mother did so much damage to Ugbrooke and the family fortunes. No scandal attached to her, and her four surviving children were well enough brought up, but she was profligate. Difficult to work with and autocratic, she reduced the trustees, John Chichester and William Paston, to a policy of non-intervention which proved disastrous to her son's property. So, when he came of age, Hugh found himself in debt to the tune of £20,000. Six years later his agent wrote to tell him that he had not enough money to pay the bills. He had other troubles too. Early in 1749 John, 1st Earl of Egmont, who was the owner of Enmore Castle near Cannington, coveted the honour of being Lord of the Hundred of

Cannington. This had been granted to the 1st Lord Clifford by Charles II. Egmont began to insinuate that the young Lord Clifford had less right to the honour than he had, and suggested that he surrender his claim in a neighbourly fashion. Clifford said he would put it to arbitration. At a party in London given by Clifford's aunt, the Duchess of Norfolk, Egmont again tackled young Hugh, who repeated that he would let the matter go to arbitration. Egmont replied that it would be a pity for a young nobleman to start his career with the reputation of being litigious, and threatened him with the Penal Laws. Clifford consulted a K.C., James Booth, and had the case brought before a jury at the next Bridgwater Assizes. During the consultation the evening before the trial he received an anonymous letter warning him that one of his (Clifford's) counsel was brother to Lord Egmont's steward. He handed the letter to his K.C. saying that he had perfect confidence in his honour and integrity. The counsel redoubled his efforts, and Clifford's right was triumphantly established.

Fortunately Clifford shared the ideals and business acumen of his grandfather, and now set himself to the repair and improvement of his house, park and estates. By giving up his town house and economising severely, he was able to complete the rebuilding of Ugbrooke. He consulted several architects, among them John Carr, and some of the suggested plans survive. In 1761 he employed Capability Brown to plan the park. It is possible that James Paine was also involved, though this may be a confusion with Paine's son whose designs for the stables at Ugbrooke are in the British Museum. But it was Robert Adam whom Lord Clifford chose to redesign the house in 1760, and it has been suggested that Ugbrooke's castle style was the first of many executed by the Adam brothers. Though further changes were made at Ugbrooke in the middle of the following century, the chapel and library wing are as Robert Adam left them. The Penal Laws forbade a free-standing chapel for catholics so Adam planned a wing which included both library and chapel with a new facade extending across the whole front of this wing.

Hugh Clifford spent many years in his new house by Robert Adam enjoying his park by Capability Brown, which was described at the time by the following verse:

> Collected here,
> As in a point, all nature's charms appear
> Hills strive with woods, with water woods agree,
> Of Devon's scenes the grand epitome.

Writing 25 years after his death, Dr. Oliver says of Hugh Clifford: 'Kind and benevolent, he considered himself born to do good ... he was an ornament to his country, an honour to the peerage, the delight of his neighbourhood ...   Revered, honoured and beloved, he died peacefully in the arms of his family at Ugbrooke, 1st September 1783, recommending to them with his last breath concord and mutual affection'. His will, dated 18 June, was proved on 31 October 1783.

Hugh Clifford married in London on 17 December 1748, Lady Anne Lee, sister and co-heiress of George, 3rd Earl of Lichfield. Hers was a particularly distinguished ancestry as her paternal grandmother, Lady Charlotte Fitzroy, was the natural daughter of Charles II by Barbara Villiers, Duchess of Cleveland. Through Charles II, Lady Clifford was descended from many of the crowned heads of the two previous

centuries: from Charles I of England, Henri IV of France, Cosimo and Francesco de'
Medici, Grand Dukes of Tuscany, Ferdinand I of Austria, Holy Roman Emperor,
Frederick II of Denmark and, above all, from the tragic Mary, Queen of Scots. As a
child she was educated at the Blue Nuns' School in Paris, and as Dowager Lady
Clifford she went to live at Altona near Hamburg, where she died aged 71 in 1802,
and where she is buried close to her daughter in the Sacristy of the Catholic Church
there, where their monuments survive.

She was a very holy and humble Christian as witness a letter she wrote the year
before her death to the Abbé Menustrier in Paris. She had obviously found it
difficult, being an Englishwoman living on the Continent during the Revolution. She
ends 'Adieu monsieur, je tiens ne sera pas long avant que chanterons ensemble les
cantiques d'adoration et de louanges, que Dieu est bon à ceux que l'aiment!'.

By Anne Lee, the 4th Lord Clifford of Chudleigh had four sons and four daughters:

    1. HUGH, 5th Baron, for whom see next chapter.

    2. CHARLES, 6th Baron, for whom see Chapter Forty-One.

    3. ROBERT EDWARD, born at Ugbrooke in October 1767, who died there unmarried in
February 1817. Prevented by the Penal Laws from becoming a soldier in the English army, he
joined Dillon's Regiment in the French army as an officer with a commission from King Louis
XVI. This famous regiment of Irish Jacobites in the French service, officered by those exiles
known as the 'wild geese', had for Colonel Proprietor from 1690 to 1794 Arthur, Count Dillon and
his sons and grandson. Henry, 11th Viscount Dillon, Arthur's younger son, had married Lady
Charlotte Lee, Lady Clifford's elder sister, so when Robert Clifford joined le Regiment de Dillon,
its then Colonel Proprietor, Lieut.-General Count Arthur Dillon, who was destined to be
guillotined during the Reign of Terror, was his cousin. Robert Clifford served until after the
judicial murder of King Louis, when he deserted and returned to England with maps and plans
of French fortifications. There is a letter from the English general Simcoe saying he had tried to
get Robert Clifford made Adjutant General but failed on religious grounds. As far as can be
gathered, despite the secrecy with which his duties were enshrouded, he was then put in charge
of espionage against the French during the Revolutionary and Napoleonic wars. During this time
he became one of the founders of the Royal Institute, and became interested in education and
science. Among his papers is one of the earlier syllabi for Stonyhurst College. There is a portrait
of him at Ugbrooke by Mather Brown.

    4. THOMAS EDWARD, born in 1774, died at Liege on 2 April 1817. He also served overseas,
and became Chamberlain to the Grand Duke of Mecklenburg-Schwerin. Whilst in Schwerin, he
married on 17 November 1807, Baroness Henrietta Philippina de Lutzow (died 1822), daughter
of Baron Conrad Ignatius, principal Chamberlain and Marshal of the Court there, by whom he
had three daughters:

    i. ELEANORA (LAURA) MARIA (1811-96). She married in 1833 Ambrose Lisle March
Philipps de Lisle, of Garendon Park and Grace Dieu in Leicestershire, who died in 1878, and
whose descendants are still there. Her eldest daughter married Sir Frederic Weld of Chideock,
whose mother was a daughter of the 6th Lord Clifford of Chudleigh.

    ii. MARY CHARLOTTE BERNADINE, who became a nun.

    iii. HENRIETTA MARIA (1815-52) married Henry Whitgreave of Moseley Court in
Staffordshire, by whom she had issue.

    1. FRANCES (1752-1807) died unmarried at Schwerin, buried at Altona.

    2. ANN (1754-90) died unmarried.

    3. MARY ANN ROSAMUND (1755-67) died unmarried.

    4. CHARLOTTE (1773-1800) became a nun.

Chapter Forty

Generation XXV – Hugh, 5th Lord Clifford of Chudleigh (1756-93)

32. Portrait of Hugh, 5th Lord Clifford of Chudleigh, by Opie.

33. Portrait of Apollonia, 5th Lady Clifford, by Opie.

Hugh Edward Henry, 5th Lord Clifford of Chudleigh, was born and baptised on 2 July 1756, and succeeded his father at the age of twenty-seven. Although dogged with ill health, he was according to his contemporary, Dr. Oliver, a man of 'extraordinary beauty of person and fascinating urbanity of manners'. His chaplain, Father Joseph Reeve, the first to whom it was safe to accord an inscription on his tombstone, and who served Ugbrooke for more than fifty years, was given to long and not very good poems. This is what he wrote just after Lord Clifford's death:

> Blithe as the morn, and as Narcissus fair
> In bloom of youth behold the rising heir;
> In converse gay; in sentiment refined;
> In manners courteous; friend to all mankind.
> That sprightly life, which sparkles in his eye,
> That captivating air – soon, soon must die!
> Beside his couch, in vain his consort kneels
> Consoles his pains, and every sorrow feels
> With many an anxious thought and many a sigh

Through all the changes of a foreign sky
By love, by friendship, and by duty led
For him she had from ev'ry comfort fled
For him had sought what titles, honours, wealth
Could ne'er command, the first of blessings, health
Till worn and spent, and lab'ring now for breath
She sees him fainting in the arms of Death.
No help, no friend, no confidant is near,
To soothe her grief, or catch the falling tear.
As a tall poppy, when o'ercharged with rain,
Bends drooping down, and sinks upon the plain,
So sunk the Peer – in life to shine no more,
Consigned to dust on Munich's distant shore,
There, while he sleeps, let hallow'd tapers burn,
And angels watch around his sculptured urn.

Hugh Edward married at Bath on 2 May 1780 Apollonia Langdale, the youngest daughter of Marmaduke, 5th and last Lord Langdale, by his wife Constantia, daughter of Sir John Smythe, 3rd Baronet of Eshe. She was thus already a connection by marriage, as Mary Clifford, the 3rd Lord Clifford's daughter, had married Sir Edward Smythe, the 4th baronet, in 1766.

Three years after Hugh Edward married Apollonia, his father died. Dogged by ill health he wandered the Continent in search of relief and in the hope that Italy would cure him. By Christmas 1790 he and his wife were in Rome. They went north to Florence, and south to Naples, but to no avail. In the autumn of 1792 they went to Germany on their way back to England. Arrived in Munich Lord Clifford fell gravely ill and died on 15 January 1793. He had written his will at Rome in June 1792, six months before his death. It was a moving document which paid tender gratitude to his wife and their servants, Mary, and his man, Nicholas. There were no children of the marriage, and the estates, with the peerage, passed to his brother Charles.

He had left instructions that he should be buried without pomp, wherever he died. The Elector of Bavaria gave permission for him to be buried among the Rococo splendours of the Jesuit Church in Munich. Hermann Kemper wrote the inscription still to be seen on the memorial there, erected by his widow. Apollonia returned alone to England, where she survived her husband by more than twenty years, dying on the last day of 1815 aged sixty. She is buried in St Leonard's church at Hazelwood near Tadcaster, whose owner at that time was her cousin Sir Thomas Vavasour.

The *Annual Register* for 1793 wrote of Lord Clifford: 'His long residence abroad, and the adherence of the family to the Catholic persuasion, whereby they are kept from Parl., have prevented their being much known, but their estates are ample'.

Chapter Forty-One

Generation XXV – Charles, 6th Lord Clifford of Chudleigh (1759-1831)

34. Portrait of Charles, 6th Lord Clifford of Chudleigh, by J. Ramsay.

35. Portrait of Eleanor, 6th Lady Clifford. Before her marriage she was Eleanor Mary Arundell, Countess of the Holy Roman Empire.

Charles, 6th Lord Clifford of Chudleigh, was born in Jermyn Street, London on 28 November 1759 and was educated at the Catholic colleges of Douai, St Omer, Bruges and Liège, frequently under the alias of *Blount*, his grandmother's maiden name, because of the stringency of the Penal Laws. On his return to England, he married at St George's, Hanover Square, in London, on 29 November 1786, Eleanor Mary Arundell, Countess of the Holy Roman Empire, youngest daughter and co-heiress of Henry, 8th Lord Arundell of Wardour, Count of the Holy Roman Empire, by his wife Maria Christina Conquest, daughter of Benedict Conquest of Boughton Conquest in Bedfordshire and of Irnham in Lincolnshire. Through this marriage Irnham came into the Clifford family, and one of the things Charles Clifford did there was to build a chapel. Eleanor Arundell was also co-heiress to the medieval barony of FitzPayne, created by writ in 1299. The first Lord Arundell of Wardour had served as an officer in the imperial forces against the Turks, and, having taken a standard from the Moslem enemy at Gran in Hungary, was created a Count of the Holy Roman Empire by the Emperor Rudolph II in 1595, which title was afterwards recognised by King

36. Sir Thomas Arundell, an officer in the imperial army, taking the standard of the Turks. As a result of his action he was created Count of the Holy Roman Empire.

James I and recorded at the College of Arms in London. It was in the usual form, whereby all his Arundell descendants in the male line were raised to the rank of count or countess, but this did not empower it to pass through heiresses.

After their marriage, Charles and Eleanor went to live at New Park, near Stourhead, which he had rented from his friend Sir Richard Colt Hoare. Here they spent four years, until the death of his brother forced them to return to Devon and become more in the public eye.

Unlike his brother, Charles Clifford enjoyed very good health. Although forbidden by law to be an officer of the forces of the Crown during the French Revolutionary wars, he was so active that before long he was made chairman of the committee for the internal defence of Devon, a post which he held until after Waterloo. He raised the Teignbridge Yeomanry and many volunteer corps, and framed maps of military exercises have been preserved along with other papers at Ugbrooke. For his services, the city of Exeter commissioned a portrait of him in his specially designed unofficial uniform, painted by Allan Ramsay, which was presented to him in 1802. At the same time he was presented with a silver vase and a silver salver in recognition of 'his unremitting attention and indefatigable exertions at a most momentous and alarming crisis'.

As a Catholic he played a leading part in protecting the religious orders fleeing from France and the countries bordering on France which she overran. He installed the Sion Abbey nuns in Chudleigh, and persuaded their reverend mother to write to his friend, the then Duke of Northumberland, owner of the pre-Reformation Sion, explaining the vicissitudes through which they had come, and ending by saying that the sisters still had the original key to Sion Abbey. Northumberland wrote back politely, ending with a P.S.: 'We've changed all the locks'.

After Waterloo the country settled down once more. Various Catholic organisations grew up, led by men like Clifford, with the aim of getting the Penal Laws repealed. There was a small minority who opposed this tooth and nail, but such was the esteem in which Charles Clifford was held that even in the strongly Protestant county of Devon he was admitted to be a very patriotic Englishman. Nevertheless the local press was divided and there were heated debates in the district. Although Clifford was excluded by law from taking his seat in the House of Lords, he never despaired of his country redressing this injustice. He was summoned to attend the coronation of George IV, and George Canning remarked in the House of Commons in April 1822, when moving to introduce a Bill to restore to Catholic peers the right to sit and vote in Parliament, à propos the coronation ceremony: 'Who is it that overtops the barons as they march? The Catholic Lord Clifford ... '.

However, it was to be another seven years before the Duke of Wellington – a personal friend of Clifford's – secured the passage of the Catholic Emancipation Act, which enabled him to take his seat in the House of Lords. By the magistrates of Devon he was received with open arms, being presented with an illuminated address, and on his return from London he was given a great welcome. He was greeted by a deputation of his tenantry and neighbours and a crowd of wellwishers on foot and escorted to Ugbrooke to the strains of 'See the conquering hero comes'. When the cavalcade reached the park gates it was met by 'eight young women, daughters of respectable tradesmen of Chudleigh, in white dresses decorated with head wreaths

37. The passing of the Catholic Emancipation Act in 1829, which enabled the 6th Lord Clifford to take his seat in the House of Lords. To the left of the throne can be seen the Clifford and Arundell of Wardour families, invited by the Duke of Wellington to witness the passing of the Act. The painting, by Jones, now hangs in the Reading Room of the House of Lords.

and garlands, and each carrying a neat basket of flowers, who arranged themselves four on each side of his carriage'. The jollifications ended with the singing of 'God Save the King' and 'Rule Britannia' and the procession returned from the house 'delighted with the manner in which his lordship had expressed himself to be gratified. The number of persons assembled was estimated at about one thousand'.

Charles Clifford was then an old man, but it was certainly a great achievement that he should have been so fêted. His was very much a personal success, for Catholics were still regarded with very great suspicion and, for example, still could not hold a post at Oxford University. For years, while the living of Chudleigh was in the hands of the Wills family (then at Harcombe), the vicar was ordered to preach two anti-Catholic sermons a year. All the letters and information in the archives at Ugbrooke show that Charles spent the whole of his life working for his village, his county and his country. When a serious fire destroyed a great part of Chudleigh, Lord Clifford headed a committee to raise funds for its repair, and his friendship with the banking family of Hoare came in useful. When the town was rebuilt, Mill Lane was renamed Clifford Street. This led to his founding the first fire insurance company in the South West, which later became known as the West of England Fire Insurance Company.

Charles Clifford is said to have been somewhat pompous. It is related that when King George III was returning to London after inspecting the fleet at Plymouth he went for a walk while changing horses at what is now Lower Heightly farm. He saw Lawell House across the valley and asked whose it was. It was, in fact, the dower house, but he was only told that it belonged to Lord Clifford. On meeting Clifford at Court a few months later the king exclaimed 'I saw your lordship's house the other day'. Wondering how this could possibly be as Ugbrooke lay over the hill, Clifford made further enquiries, and then getting enraged that anyone should mistake Lawell for Ugbrooke he summoned his coach and four, left Court, galloped to Devon and ordered that two wings of Lawell be pulled down. What happened to whichever great-aunt was then living there is not recorded.

Charles Clifford was also an artist of no mean ability. His style was very much that of Francis Nicholson, whom, with Francis Towne, he employed to teach his children drawing and painting. During the long period of the Test Act, the family had become very withdrawn, a fact which was no doubt partly responsible for their large output of literary, scientific and artistic achievement. Francis Towne spent much time at Ugbrooke, and there are still a dozen of his sketches and paintings there. Varley, Prout, Bamfylde, Green and many others of that and later periods have works of theirs scattered about the house, all of whom had been patronised by Lord Clifford from the end of the 18th century to the 1830s.

Elizabeth Martyn, the 1st Lord Clifford's wife, had brought the Shaldon estate into the family. The 6th Lord Clifford bought the house there – The Ness (now a hotel), which became the family's summer residence until it was sold by the 11th baron in the 1920s. It seems that the 8th Lord Clifford built a tunnel from the house to the private beach, which is now called the Smugglers' Tunnel, but which is, of course, nothing of the kind.

Charles Clifford kept up a correspondence with many of the leading men of his day, such as Earl Grey, Earl Fortescue, Lord Ebrington and above all the Duke of

38. (*above*) A Regency perspective view of Irnham
Hall, Lincolnshire, drawn by C. Nattes in 1804.

39. (*left*) Charles Thomas Clifford, younger son of the
6th Lord.

Wellington, with whom he worked for many years, and to whom he was especially grateful for the Catholic Emancipation Act of 1829. In the large picture which the present Lord Clifford lent to the House of Lords depicting the passing of the Act, both Clifford and Wellington are included. Wellington especially asked Clifford to witness the Royal Assent, even though he could not have taken his seat in the House at that time.

Charles Clifford died at Ugbrooke on 29 April 1831 at the age of seventy-one. He had been married to Countess Eleanor Mary Arundell for forty-five years. After his death she retired to Spetisbury Convent in Dorset, where she died four years later, on 24 November 1835, at the age of sixty-nine. By her Lord Clifford had seven sons and eight daughters:

1. HUGH CHARLES, 7th Baron, for whom see the next chapter.

2. CHARLES EVERARD, born in 1793 who died in infancy.

3. CHARLES THOMAS, born in 1797, lived at Irnham, where he was High Sheriff of Lincolnshire, and died 11 September 1879. He married in 1822 Theresa Constable Maxwell, daughter of Marmaduke Constable Maxwell of Everingham Park, Yorkshire. They had two sons and four daughters:

i. HENRY WILLIAM, born in 1825 died young.

ii. CHARLES THOMAS, who became a Jesuit and died aged 23 at Preston, Lancashire.

i. MARIA THERESA (1823-95). She married on 26 September 1843, William Bernard, 12th Lord Petre by whom she was the ancestress of the present Lord Petre, the Earl of Granard and the Marquess of Bute.

ii. LOUISA MARY, born in 1826, became a nun.

iii. ELIZA MARY, died in infancy.

iv. AGNES MARY, became a nun.

4. EDWARD CHARLES, born 1798, died in infancy; twin to Apollonia (see below).

5. EDWARD CHARLES, born 5 February 1803, ordained a Benedictine priest at Ampleforth in January 1827. He became a missionary in Africa and Mauritius, which had recently been acquired from the French. The French priests there hated him and accused him of drunkenness and other irregularities. He died at Maheburg on 22 October 1843, and is buried there. When his great-nephew, Sir Bede Clifford, was appointed Governor of Mauritius in 1939, he sought out and found his resting place.

6. WALTER CHARLES, born 26 April 1804, studied at Stonyhurst and Rome and also became a missionary, this time in India. He was drowned in the river Cauvery in May 1844.

7. ROBERT HENRY, born on 31 October 1806, became an officer in the 83rd Regiment as he was enabled at last by the Catholic Emancipation Act to obtain a commission in the British Army. He died unmarried in Limerick in 1833.

1. ANNA MARIA (1788-1805), nun at Newhall in Essex.

2. CHRISTINA MARIA, born at Wardour on 4 February 1789, married 12 February 1811 Humphrey Weld of Chideock, Dorset, where her descendants are to this day. One of her sons was Sir Frederick Weld, Governor of Western Australia, Tasmania and the Malay States, and Prime Minister of New Zealand. Five of her daughters became nuns, and when her husband died, Christina entered St Benedict's Priory at Stafford, where she died on 19 March 1857.

3. MARIA LOUISA (1791-2).

4. ELIZABETH MARY, born 1794, became a Benedictine nun at Cannington Priory at the age of thirty-three.

5. CHARLOTTE MARY, born 1796, married 27 January 1817 Charles Langdale, and died at Ugbrooke on 31 March 1819, leaving two daughters: Mary, who became a nun, and Charlotte who married Vincent Hornyold, Marquis Gandolfi.

6. APOLLONIA MARY, born 14 September 1798, twin with Edward Charles. She became a nun at Taunton Lodge at the age of twenty-two.

7. MARY LUCY, born 22 November 1799, married 1 August 1825 Charles, 19th Lord Stourton, nephew of her sister Charlotte's husband, Charles Langdale. She was the ancestress of the present Lord Mowbray, Segrave and Stourton. Her father divided the Catherine of Braganza diamonds, giving the stomacher to Mary Lucy and retaining the remainder as heirlooms. She died in September 1871 aged 71 and her husband less than three months later.

8. LOUISA MARY, born on 13 May 1801, met a tragic end. According to the Exeter *Flying Post* of 29 September 1857, she committed suicide, after much ill health, in 1842 near Abergavenny, and is buried in the cemetery of Llanfoist. The article says that she was 'abandoned by all her relatives'. The full story will probably never be known.

Chapter Forty-Two

Generation XXVI – Hugh Charles, 7th Lord Clifford of Chudleigh (1790-1858)

40. (*above*) Portrait of Hugh Charles, 7th Lord Clifford of Chudleigh, by J. Ramsay.

41. (*right*) Portrait of Mary, 7th Lady Clifford, by J. Ramsay. Before her marriage she was Mary Lucy Weld.

Hugh Charles Clifford was born at Newpark on 28 May 1790 and educated at the Catholic College of Stonyhurst in Lancashire, where he was a successful student, although his highly intellectual and religious views lacked some of his father's common sense. In later life his uncompromising catholicism alienated many who had been his father's friends. After Stonyhurst, he joined his father in his efforts for the defence of Devon against a possible invasion by Napoleon. Debarred in his youth from applying for a commission, he served as a 'gentleman volunteer' under Wellington in the Peninsular War, and it is said that he was at or near Waterloo at the time of the battle. In 1814 he attended Cardinal Consalvi to the Congress of Vienna when he was only twenty-four.

He succeeded his father when he was 40, and immediately took his seat in the House of Lords, the first of his line to do so since the Disabling Act of 1678. He was a Liberal, voted for the repeal of the Corn Laws, and gave his general support to the ministry of Lord Grey, and afterwards to Lord Melbourne, but seldom took part in debates except on questions connected with Roman Catholicism. However, he was evidently upset by a public affront to the Duke of Wellington as the following letter from the Iron Duke shows:

October 8th, 1831

My Lord,

    I have had the honour of receiving your Lordship's letter of the 5th and return herewith the enclosure.

    I am very glad your Lordship did not make the speach [*sic*] of which you included me the draft. The fact to which you refer on page 1 is not true.

    It is true that a mob came to break the windows of my home three or four days after I had suffered a domestic misfortune. They continued to break them till my servants fired some powder from a blunderbus from the roof of the house. There were no constables there to remonstrate with the mob. If there had been, some persons would probably have been imprisoned for committing this outrage.

    The persons concerned in it ran away as soon as they found that the inmates of the house were prepared, and disposed to defend it.

    The newspapers as usual referred to this transaction in the manner that best suited their purpose. The facts occurred as I have stated to your Lordship: and if the subject had been mentioned in parliament I must have corrected the misrepresentation.

    I have the honour to be, my Lord, your Lordship's most obedient humble servant,

Wellington

The 7th Lord Clifford was the first to assume the title of Count of the Holy Roman Empire in the mistaken belief that he had inherited it from his mother as an Arundell heiress. In fact, such countships were limited to the sons and daughters of the male line of the original grantee, the first Count Arundell, and did not pass through the female line. A similar example of a mistaken claim is that of the (Spencer) Dukes of Marlborough to be Princes of Mindelheim by descent from a co-heiress of the first (Churchill) Duke of Marlborough.

The 7th Lord Clifford spent much of his life writing letters and speeches on religious intolerance, missions and good causes, and he also spent extravagantly on 'lame ducks'. But he was much loved by his children, for he was a very devout and good man. He generously patronised Prior Park College and many charities and gave liberal support to portrait painters. As Dr. Oliver wrote of him: ' ... in many of his undertakings we missed the cool judgment, the practical wisdom of his venerated father; and we regret to add, that with all his pure-minded intentions he involved himself in pecuniary difficulties which impaired his usefulness and weakened the family interest in Devon. After some time he abandoned his native country and submitted to live on a limited income. Repairing to Italy, he passed a sequestered, almost ascetic life, at Albano and Rome. He returned to the latter city on 15th February and died on 28th February 1858 lamented by all who could appreciate his sterling worth'. His wife had died in 1831, and he was buried next to her in the church of San Marcello in Rome.

Hugh Charles had married Mary Lucy Weld, the only daughter of Thomas Weld of Lulworth Castle, Dorset on 8 February 1819. Her mother had been Lord Clifford's own cousin, Lucy Clifford, from Tixall. The Welds were an ancient family descended

(*right*) Portrait of Cardinal Thomas Weld, father
Mary Lucy, by Podesti.

(*below*) Tixall, Staffordshire: the gatehouse.

from William of Weld, Sheriff of London in 1352, and had acquired the manor of Lulworth in 1641. In 1672 William Weld of Lulworth had married Elizabeth, the heiress of Sir Nicholas Sherburne of Stonyhurst in Lancashire. Thomas Weld lost his wife in 1815, and when his only child, Mary Lucy, married Hugh Charles Clifford, he was at liberty to take holy orders, and in due course he became a Cardinal. For a long time he had given proof of his piety and charity by helping many religious communities that had been driven from France during the Revolution, and he concurred with his father in bestowing on the exiled members of the Society of Jesus the mansion of Stonyhurst. Trappist nuns were made welcome at Lulworth.

As a priest he went first to St Mary's in Cadogan Street, which had been built largely by Clifford and Weld contributions for the use of Catholic soldiers in Chelsea Hospital. In 1826, Thomas Weld was consecrated titular bishop of Amycla in the Morea, to be in effect Bishop of Lower Canada as coadjutor to his late wife's kinsman Alexander Macdonell, titular bishop of Regiopolis.

The Duke of Wellington, after the Catholic Emancipation Act was passed in 1829, tried to get Bishop Weld made Catholic bishop of Waterford in place of the Irish bishops' nominee, Dr. Foran. Wellington's championship of 'a fine English gentleman' so impressed the Vatican that they gave him a greater honour by making him a Prince of the Church. He was admitted to the College of Cardinals on 15 March 1830, and he was the first Englishman to sit in Conclave since the pontificate of Clement IX nearly two centuries before.

Cardinal Weld made over Lulworth Castle to his brother, Joseph, the famous yachtsman, who received the exiled Royal Family of France at Lulworth in August 1830 until King Charles X and his suite were able to make arrangements to take up a more permanent residence at the Palace of Holyroodhouse in Edinburgh. But the Cardinal left his principal relics to the Cliffords rather than the Welds because he naturally wanted his personal things to go to his daughter and grandchildren who were Cliffords. This also explains why the Cliffords spent so much time in Rome. There are at Ugbrooke several paintings in which his grandchildren were used as models. One is of the Cardinal with two of them as altar boys and another, by Furse, is entitled 'Christ Blessing the Children' now in the chapel at Ugbrooke.

Having been widowed before entering the Church, Thomas Weld was known as the 'Cardinal of the Seven Sacraments'. His elevation to the Sacred College was received with general satisfaction in England, and his apartments in the Odescalchi Palace were periodically filled by the Roman aristocracy and by large numbers of his fellow-countrymen. Cardinal Wiseman, who delivered his funeral oration, wrote: 'Seldom has a stranger been more deeply and feelingly regretted by the inhabitants of a city than was this holy man by the poor of Rome'. He died in 1837 and was buried beside his daughter and son-in-law Lord Clifford in the Church of San Marcello in Rome.

By Mary Lucy Weld, Hugh Charles, 7th Lord Clifford, had six sons and two daughters:

1. CHARLES HUGH, 8th Baron, for whom see next chapter.
2. THOMAS HUGH (1822-33).
3. WILLIAM, Bishop of Clifton, for whom see Chapter Forty-Four.

4. Sir HENRY, V.C., for whom see Chapter Forty-Five.

5. EDMUND HUGH, who died in infancy.

6. WALTER, born in Rome in 1830, became a Jesuit priest.

1. ELEONORA MARY, born in 1820, became a nun and died in 1871.

2. MARY CONSTANTIA (known as Conny), who married first William Vavasour, third son of Sir Edward Vavasour, by whom she had issue; and secondly, on 7 February 1865, Maurice Denis Kavanagh, by whom she had further issue. She died in March 1898.

It may be observed that at this period it was usual for the old Catholic families to intermarry, so that there are many intermarriages between Cliffords, Smythes, Stourtons, Vaughans, Welds, Petres, Fitzherberts, Stonors, Vavasours and Radcliffes.

Chapter Forty-Three

Generation XXVII – Charles, 8th Lord Clifford of Chudleigh (1819-80)

44. Portrait of Charles, 8th Lord Clifford of Chudleigh, by J. Ramsay.

45. Portrait of Agnes, 8th Lady Clifford.

Charles Hugh, 8th Lord Clifford of Chudleigh, was born in London on 27 July 1819 and educated at Stonyhurst and abroad. During his father's lifetime he lived mainly at Irnham or at Court House, Cannington, as Ugbrooke was at that time largely given over to religious bodies. For example, Dr. Oliver writes that in 1848 there were 13 members of the Society of Jesus, nine of whom were priests, two temporal coadjutors and a rector. In 1852 the house was given over for a spiritual retreat for the clergy of the Plymouth diocese, and two years later it was opened for sessions of the diocesan synod.

Because his eccentric father lived in Rome, Charles became something of a father-figure to his younger brothers and sisters. Thus, as we shall see, the letters of Henry Clifford, V.C., show how important was the firm base provided by Charles and his wife, for Charles had married on 30 September 1845 Agnes Catherine Louisa, daughter of William, 11th Lord Petre by his wife Emma Agnes, daughter of Henry Howard of Corby Castle in Cumberland. Agnes was a descendant of Maud de Clifford, who died in 1282, daughter of the last feudal baron (see Part One, Chapter Eight). The Petres, another old Catholic family, had long been connected with the Cliffords through the intermarriage of cousins, so there can have been no reason for Charles' father to take umbrage at his son's engagement, but he did. Reading between the lines, it would seem that his only reason was that he had not been consulted beforehand.

The year after his father's death, Charles and Agnes came to Ugbrooke in 1859. He was then 40 years old. Luckily, he was one of those members of the family who come along just in the nick of time to save it from going under. We have seen how the 7th Lord Clifford, lacking his father's business sense, had been sent to Rome where it was felt he could do less harm to the estate, but this did not prevent him leaving copious letters of advice to his son. Suffice it to say that the 8th Lord Clifford inherited a near bankrupt estate and yet was able to leave his large family £10,000 each, a very reasonable sum in those days.

Charles Clifford was a Liberal in politics, and attended Parliament fairly regularly, but, after he moved from Cannington to Ugbrooke, he spent most of his time attending to his estates and particularly to the planting of trees. He carried through the work of extending the chapel by adding a Lady Chapel and making additions to the house itself. The scrolls over the windows at Ugbrooke replaced the square Georgian ones, and the conservatory was built over the entrance arch to the courtyard. He died after a long illness on 5 August 1880 at the age of sixty-one. By his wife, Agnes Petre, he had five sons and six daughters:

1. LEWIS HENRY HUGH, 9th Baron, for whom see Chapter Forty-Seven.
2. BEDE WILLIAM HUGH, died in infancy in 1853.
3. EDMUND CHARLES HUGH, died at the age of ten in 1867.
4. WILLIAM HUGH, 10th Baron, for whom see Chapter Forty-Eight.
5. WALTER CHARLES IGNATIUS (twin with his sister EMMA) was born on 14 October 1862 and died unmarried in 1956. He was unhappily born with a club foot which resulted in a limp of which he was very self-conscious, and, after he left Stonyhurst, he decided to emigrate to Canada, where he took up land at Austin, Manitoba. During the economic depression of 1929, Walter Clifford borrowed money from the Clifford trustees and when he died it was thought that he was a very poor man. However, some years later the value of his land increased and there was a surplus after the loan had been repaid, which went to a Harding nephew in Australia.

1. BERTHA MARY AGNES married as his second wife on 4 February 1892 Brodie Manuel de Zulueta, Conde de Torre Diaz in Spain. The Count's first wife had been Bertha's cousin, Constance Petre, who died in 1890. The close family connection with the Zuluetas stems from these marriages, which began when they were Carlist refugees in England. Bertha Clifford, Countess of Torre Diaz, was one of those aunts who keep families in touch with one another. When Charles, later 11th Lord Clifford, arrived in England at the age of 12 it was to this aunt that he went, and, when her great-nephew and great-nieces were very young in Australia, their only link with England were the birthday and Christmas presents which came from the great-aunt they had never seen. Her house in Devonshire Place in London was a centre for the young nephews before and during the First World War, and as a widow, after 1918, she returned to live at Ugbrooke with her widowed nephew Charles. She died on 20 December 1925, leaving many letters which showed how she had spent much of her life 'keeping in touch' and pouring oil on troubled waters.

2. MARY LUCY CONSTANCE, a nun who died in 1912.

3. BEATRICE MARY CATHERINE, who died in 1873 when her dress caught fire after returning from a ball.

4. EDITH TERESA MARY, a nun who died in 1920.

5. CECILIA MARY, who married on 23 September 1884 Rudolph Feilding, 9th Earl of Denbigh and 8th Earl of Desmond, a Lord-in-Waiting to Queen Victoria and King Edward VII, and ADC to King George V. He died in 1939 leaving issue by her. 'Aunt Cissy' was a demon for work and a devotee of her own and her husband's families. During the First World War she turned her home into a hospital and worked herself to death on behalf of the wounded. She died on 8 December 1919.

Agnes Petre, Dowager Lady Clifford of Chudleigh, died aged 65 after a brief illness on 25 May 1891 in London and was buried at Ugbrooke.

Chapter Forty-Four

Generation XXVII – William Clifford, Bishop of Clifton (1823-93)

Bishop William Clifford was born on 24 December 1823, the second surviving son of the 7th Lord Clifford of Chudleigh, and was educated at Hodder and Stonyhurst with his brother, Henry, and his cousin Frederick Weld. When he left Stonyhurst he entered the Collegio Pio in Rome and was ordained priest in August 1850 at Clifton. His contribution to the revival of catholicism in England between 1857, when he was appointed bishop of Clifton, and his death in 1893 is only overshadowed by those of giants like Cardinals Newman and Manning, for he was a man of exceptional ability, whose career developed under a series of unusual circumstances.

In 1851 he was sent back to Rome to study for his doctorate of divinity at the College of Nobles, and returned after a year to the Clifton diocese as parish priest of St Mary's, Stonehouse, and the following year he was chosen as Vicar Capitular of the Plymouth diocese.

The diocese of Clifton in 1857 was in difficulties owing to anxiety over the finances and running of the catholic school at Prior Park near Bath. Clifford's appointment was unusual and controversial: to begin with he was only 32 and was the youngest bishop ever to have been put in charge of a diocese in England. His consecration was likewise unusual, for it took place in the Sistine Chapel and was conducted by Pope Pius IX himself, which showed the pontiff's personal approval of the appointment. Furthermore, Dr. Clifford was the first nobleman's son to have been made a catholic bishop in England since the Reformation. But it is only fair to add that his appointment was based upon his financial and social position as much as upon his personal intellect and brilliance. His episcopacy lasted 36 years, which had a salutory effect upon the affairs of the diocese and he soon became well-known in English catholic circles. His interest in geology led him to intervene in the burning question of the day – the reconciliation of science and the biblical account of the creation.

Soon after his installation as bishop of Clifton he gave £1,000 towards the extinction of the diocesan debt, and soon afterwards was persuaded to re-purchase Prior Park, which had had to be sold, and which was reopened in 1867 as a grammar school once more. It was one of the few mistakes he made, for it led to much opposition and had to be kept going by frequent injections of his own money, for it never paid its way.

Cardinal Wiseman died in 1865 and was succeeded by Manning as Archbishop of Westminster. The appointment was a controversial one, since many believed that Archbishop Errington, the late cardinal's coadjutor, should have been given the post. Bishop Clifford stood by his old friend Errington, and offered him a home at Prior Park and a post as teacher there, both of which were gratefully accepted. In a similar way Clifford stood by Cardinal Newman when he came under attack, and he preached at his funeral in 1890. But Clifford was adept at avoiding squabbles and partisan controversies. He was described as the very soul of chivalry – 'no braver bishop in Rome'.

46. Portrait of William Clifford, Bishop of Clifton, by Podesti.

During the First Vatican Council he warned that the doctrine of papal infallibility, then under discussion, if clumsily defined would lead to many English protestants justifying their belief that the Pope was a despot and a tyrant. After the Council, he intervened in the dispute over the attendance of catholics at Oxford and Cambridge. Then, in 1877, he and Archbishop Ullathorne took active parts in the conflict over regular orders, which can be studied in accounts of the life of Cardinal Vaughan, Bishop Clifford's cousin.

During the last 16 years of his life Prior Park became an increasing worry and burden, which some believe hastened his death in 1893. He was buried in the church cloister at Prior Park near his old friends Archbishop Errington and the college's principal, Mgr. Edward Williams.

Clifton diocese owes him much. He left it flourishing and growing, and he is remembered there as one of the finest English catholic bishops of the last century.

Among the bishop's papers at Ugbrooke is a letter from Louis Napoleon to Colonel Ney in August 1849 justifying the presence of the French Army in Rome. From the family point of view he is remembered for his correspondence with his brothers, mainly about their father, whom they loved dearly, but whose eccentricities caused them much amusement. Besides his interest in geology, the bishop was a keen amateur archaeologist, whose theories concerning the site of the battle of Aethen Dune, which he believed to be on the Cannington estate, have been supported by modern discoveries.

47.   Portrait of Sir Henry Clifford, V.C., by Podesti.

Chapter Forty-Five

Generation XXVII – Sir Henry Clifford, V.C. (1826-83)

Henry Clifford is perhaps best known for having been one of the first soldiers to be awarded the V.C. (1856), for conspicuous gallantry at the battle of Inkerman in 1854. He was a distinguished soldier who had already made a name for himself in South Africa, and who was to serve his country at home and abroad for the rest of his life. His letters reveal not just a courageous and efficient officer, but a man of compassionate and affectionate nature with a stalwart religious faith.[1]

His earliest years were spent at Irnham and Chideock,[2] but at the age of three his family moved to Rome for reasons that have already been explained, and when his mother died he was only five years old. Lord Clifford took his children back to England, where the youngest were left at Ugbrooke in the care of a young widow, Mrs. Catherine Collins, who, having no children of her own, devoted herself to Henry and his young brother and sisters. The result of this upbringing was to produce a very close-knit family of strong personalities, who were devoted to each other, but early able to cope with separations. Despite long years apart such as Henry's two tours of duty in South Africa, Elly's years abroad as a nun, Walter's years abroad as a Jesuit missionary, the children remained close all their lives.

Henry's education began at ten at Prior Park, but was subject to many changes, first in Italy and then at Fribourg in Switzerland,[3] where the difficulties of studying in a foreign language did not make matters easier for a boy who was keener on sports and games than academic pursuits. Nevertheless, he became fluent in French, and wrote it accurately. Lack of physical exercise, however, troubled him and led to a bout of illness during his time at Fribourg, and to his return to the faithful Mrs. Collins at Ugbrooke. After a period of convalescence he returned to Fribourg in 1844 for a final year. By the time he was 16, Henry had already decided to become a soldier. At first he was a trifle anxious lest his father would object on account of the cost of a commission and of the outfit, which in some regiments could be very expensive. Furthermore, a young officer was not expected to live on his pay, but to receive an allowance from his family. But Lord Clifford consented, and after sending him back to Prior Park to improve his mathematics, purchased him a commission in the Rifle Brigade, which delighted Henry very much.

Henry took quickly to army life, and he rapidly learned his duties and impressed his superiors by his efficiency and devotion to duty. But outside his family circle he was shy and found much that was disagreeable and shocking in the social lives of his fellow officers. He was not a prude, but he hated drunkenness, and, as a devout catholic, his religion caused him some difficulties, though his behaviour brought him in the end only respect and trust.

In February 1848 he was sent to join his regiment at the Cape, where he campaigned under Sir Henry Smith against Boer rebels, and saw action in August 1848 at Boomplaats, where his courage gained him the admiration of his fellow officers and men. By contrast his period at Fort Murray was calm and quiet, and enabled him to get to know the natives, whose language he learnt.

His first tour of duty ended in 1850 and was followed by a year at Dover, during which he got leave to visit his father in Rome. Rejoining his regiment in January 1852 he sailed again for South Africa from Plymouth. The next two years were difficult ones for him. During his leave he had met his cousin Francesca Clifford, when staying with his sister, Constantia, at Hazelwood Castle in Yorkshire, and she had gained the impression that he wished to marry her. This was not altogether true, and led to a serious misunderstanding, though Henry was too chivalrous to disabuse her. Nevertheless, he explained his reluctance to marry while he was in the army, which was his true feeling about the matter. He returned to Britain again in 1854 to find the crisis which led to the outbreak of the Crimean War later in the year already in full swing. He was given a new posting, this time as A.D.C. to General Buller under whom he had fought at the Cape. The outbreak of war and his posting to the east effectively led to the breaking off of his 'engagement' to Francesca, rather to his relief.

Henry's vivid letters from the Crimea tell their own story[4] and give an excellent account of the battles in which he took part. Nevertheless, his modesty sometimes veils his own outstanding courage, as in his description of the incident at Inkerman, where, spotting a band of Russian soldiers outflanking the 77th, he led a handful of men in a charge against them and drove the Russians into the hands of the main body of the 77th, who had failed to see the outflanking movement. Only three of the tiny group of men he led were unharmed. When the Victoria Cross was instituted in 1856, Sir George Brown sent in Henry's name, and he received one of the first Victoria Crosses from the hands of the Queen herself in 1857.

His letters reveal a great concern for the overworked and undernourished British soldiers, as well as for the Turks, despised by all his compatriots, and even for the Russians. Though he never complained for himself, he did complain about the treatment meted out to the soldiers, and he was often saddened by the death of friends and comrades, and by British reverses.

During the months before Sebastopol, Henry made many sketches and watercolours of what he saw. Some of these have been published with his letters[5] but the originals have to be seen to appreciate the freshness of the colour and the delicacy of the detail. Many of the subjects are painful and macabre, and it seems almost as if, having avoided describing the horrors in his letters, he used the sketches to exorcise the memory of the ghastly scenes he beheld, which, to one so compassionate as he, must have been particularly painful.

By the end of the campaign Henry had been promoted to Brevet Major, having begun the war as a Lieutenant, and made Deputy Assistant Quartermaster General to the Light Division in the summer of 1855. He returned from the Crimea in the summer of 1856 eager to see his father and to think again about marriage. He spent a few hours in Malta with his brother, Walter, who was teaching there as a member of the Society of Jesus, and not long after he got back to Britain he obtained leave and set out for Rome. His brother William was there and they spent a holiday together visiting Pompeii, Naples, Vesuvius, Sorrento and Capri.

On his return to England, the problem of his marriage once more began to worry him. His father had given him a house, but a livelihood would have to be found for him if he were to leave the army in order to marry. He had been left money by his grandfather, Cardinal Weld but, due to the confusion of his father's affairs, he did not get it until 1858. After initial disapproval, Lord Clifford had come round to the idea of Henry marrying Francesca, but as the wedding grew nearer, Henry's doubts increased, especially as he had met a young English girl, Josephine Anstice, in Rome with whom he had fallen in love. Finally, in October 1856 he broke off his 'engagement' to Francesca, which led to an attempt by her family to destroy his reputation. He appied for long leave on half-pay and made a retreat in Paris under Père Ravignan, from which he emerged determined to stay in the army and to marry Josephine. Lord Clifford did not approve. It was at this point that Henry heard for certain that he was to receive the V.C. and that he would be given the post of Assistant Quartermaster General with a division to leave for China. Anxious not to

48.   Painting of the Battle of Inkerman by Cuneo.

have another lengthy engagement while he was overseas, he obtained a dispensation to be married in Lent, and the marriage was performed by his brother William on 21 March 1857.

Henry disliked China. The Indian Mutiny was taking up British attention and the soldiers in China remained inactive for many months. He was also critical of his commanding officer, whom he regarded as inefficient. With some difficulty he obtained permission to return home in October 1858 and to his house at Cannington. The following July his first daughter was born, but she died when she was two years old. Soon after he acquired an appointment at the Horse Guards where he was in charge of sending overseas soldiers' wives and families. In 1860 he was posted to Aldershot, where he remained for several years. By now he was a colonel and A.Q.M.G. At the end of 1868 he was promoted D.Q.M.G. and not long afterwards he was appointed A.D.C. to the Commander-in-Chief, the Duke of Cambridge, for three years and then Adjutant-General. He received the C.B. in 1869, a pension of £100 in 1874 and was gazetted Major-General in 1877. After the British defeat at Isandlhwana in January 1879, Henry was sent out to South Africa once more with reinforcements and was put in charge of lines of supply, and later became commander-in-chief Transvaal, returning home in 1880. He had been knighted and awarded the K.C.M.G. in December 1879, and his brother Charles paid the dues for him, but he died before Henry returned home.

Sir Henry's next appointment was commander-in-chief Eastern Division at Colchester, but he did not hold the post for long as he fell ill with cancer and he died on 12 April 1883 at Ugbrooke, which his nephew Lewis, Lord Clifford, had offered him as a home during his own absence in New Zealand.

By his wife, Josephine Anstice, Sir Henry Clifford had five daughters and three sons:

1. Sir HUGH CHARLES, for whom see next chapter.
2. Brigadier-General HENRY FREDERICK HUGH, born 13 August 1867; served in the Boer War from 1900 to 1902, being awarded the Queen's medal with three clasps and the King's medal with two clasps; and also in the First World War as Lieutenant-Colonel and Brevet Colonel in the Suffolk Regiment, being wounded, mentioned in despatches, awarded a brevet, the D.S.O., and the 3rd Class Order of St Stanislas of Russia. Promoted Brigadier-General in command of a brigade of the B.E.F., he was killed in action on the Western Front on 11 September 1916.
3. The Rev. EVERARD LOUIS HUGH, born 2 June 1871; served in the Boer War in 1900; became a Benedictine monk and died 16 December 1935.
1. MAY (1859-61).
2. EMILY JOSEPHINE, born 23 July 1860, married 22 April 1885, Major Hubert George Howard Galton, Royal Field Artillery, of Hadzos House, Droitwich; and died 28 December 1923 leaving issue. He died 21 September 1928.
3. BLANCHE WINIFRED MARY, born 3 November 1861 married 1 July 1885, as his second wife, William Joseph FitzHerbert Brockholes, C.B.E., of Claughton Hall, Lancashire, and died 1 October 1918 leaving issue. He died 21 January 1924.
4. ALICE MARY, born 26 November 1862; married 7 November 1882 Sir Walter Hamilton-Dalrymple, 8th baronet of North Berwick, and died 8 April 1927 leaving issue. Sir Walter died in 1920.
5. SIBYL MARY, born 12 October 1864, died unmarried in 1948.

Josephine Anstice, Lady Clifford, died on 15 January 1913.

Chapter Forty-Six

Generation XXVIII – Sir Hugh Clifford, G.C.M.G.; G.B.E. (1866-1941)

Sir Hugh Clifford was the eldest son of Major-General Sir Henry Clifford, V.C. His career in the British colonial service was unusually distinguished, and, had he not suffered a stroke in 1929, it is possible that he might have been Viceroy of India, which would have brought a second peerage to the Clifford family. After his death *The Times* described him as 'one of the most celebrated administrators of his time, and the article about him in the *Dictionary of National Biography* tells us that 'Clifford's charming, forceful, but never dictatorial personality won him the respect and confidence of all races'. He was also highly regarded as a writer of short stories, topical articles and several novels, most of which stemmed from his experiences in Malaya where he began his colonial career at the age of 17 in 1883.

Once in the Malay States he acquired a mastery of the language and wrote the first English-Malay dictionary. At the tender age of 21 he concluded a treaty with the Sultan of Pahang, thereby adding some 15,000 square miles to the British Empire. In 1900 he had a short-lived period as governor of Borneo and then rejoined the Malay service before returning home in 1901 for a leave which lasted nearly two years due to a severe illness he had contracted while in the East.

From 1903 to 1907 he was in Trinidad, first as Colonial Secretary to the Governor, and briefly as acting governor. Promoted in 1907 to the prestigious position of Colonial Secretary of Ceylon, Hugh Clifford served the Governor in a colony where Buddhist Sinhalese and Hindu Tamils, not to mention a strong Dutch trading community, called for tactful handling. In the course of the next five years he had regular periods as acting governor and was probably best remembered for the legislative reforms he introduced to protect the indigenous people from the colony's better educated opportunists. For these public services he had been appointed C.M.G. in 1900, was knighted and promoted to K.C.M.G. in 1909, later becoming G.C.M.G. in 1921 and G.B.E. as well in 1925.

In 1925 he was appointed governor of the Gold Coast (Ghana), a post he held till 1919. During this period he supervised with the French the conquest of the German colony of Togoland, which was shared between the British Gold Coast and the French Dahomé (Benin). He had created a more representative legislative council, provided the foundations for numerous other schemes not possible to implement in wartime, and left his successor with a surplus of more than one and a half million pounds.

In 1919 he was promoted to be Governor of Nigeria where he succeeded Sir Frederick Lugard (later Lord Lugard) in what was then the jewel in Britain's African crown. The period was significant for a reappraisal of Lugard's handling of the Abeokuta uprising and the policies the latter had promoted for the peoples in the

49.   Sir Hugh Clifford in Malaya, June 1927.

east whose disaffections Clifford repaired. The colony's legislative council was reconstructed along with the courts and a more liberal view was taken of native taxation policies.

Sir Hugh returned to Ceylon in 1925 as Governor and then went on to the Malay States again in 1927 after an absence of 27 years. In Ceylon he described the constitution he inherited as a 'perennial joke' but a subsequent Royal Commission which reported after he had left came out in support of every major criticism he had levelled. Towards the beginning of 1929 his health began to fail and he had to retire to enter a nursing home where he remained until he died on 18 December 1941.

Sir Hugh's first wife had died in a road accident in 1907. She was Minna, daughter of Gilbert à Beckett, and they were married on 15 April 1896. By her he had a son and two daughters:

50. Minna, first wife of Sir Hugh Clifford, who died in Trinidad in 1907.

1. HUGH GILBERT FRANCIS, born 20 January 1897; Lieutenant Lincolnshire Regiment, killed in action on July 1 1916, the first day of the Battle of the Somme.
1. MARY AGNES PHILIPPA, born 2 April 1898; married 19 June 1920, Major-General Sir Noel Holmes, K.B.E., C.B., M.C., who died on 21 December 1982, leaving issue by her.[1] Lady Holmes died on 17 April 1978.
2. MONICA ELIZABETH MARY, born 4 May 1903; married first 9 June 1925, Major Cecil Edward Trafford, M.C., who died 15 December 1948. She married secondly, 10 October 1952, Major Richard Désiré Girouard, only son of Major-General Sir Edward Girouard, K.C.M.G., D.S.O., and died on 11 January 1965.

Sir Hugh married secondly, on 24 September 1910, Elizabeth Lydia Rosabelle, widow of Henry Philip Ducarel de la Pasture, and daughter of Edward Bonham of Bramling, Kent, but had no further issue. Lady Clifford was awarded the C.B.E. in 1918 for her work in the Gold Coast. She died 30 October 1945. Lady Clifford's daughter by her first husband was the celebrated novelist E. M. Delafield. At this time Hugh Clifford had become known as a writer of adventure stories. He wrote regularly for *Blackwood's Magazine* and published a history of the Gold Coast Regiment and another on the German colonies in Africa. He became a friend of Rudyard Kipling, Edmund Gosse, Thomas Hardy and Joseph Conrad. Of these his greatest friend was undoubtedly Conrad, whom he helped to publish his first book *Chance*, which was dedicated to him, and which established Conrad's literary fame. Hugh Clifford was a great man in every respect, not only in his career but in all he attempted. Physically large he was an active sportsman and in the van of all that was new, be it motor cars or aeroplanes as driver and pilot. For Lady Clifford it was particularly tragic that this once dynamic, clever and successful man should have ended his life as an invalid without the opportunity to profit himself and his country by engaging in other pursuits for which there had never been time during his career.

Ironically his death in December 1941 coincided with the Japanese invasion of Malaya. It was as well that he never knew, for it would have broken his heart.

Chapter Forty-Seven

Generation XXVIII – Lewis, 9th Lord Clifford of Chudleigh (1851-1916)

51. Portrait of Lewis, 9th Lord Clifford of
Chudleigh, by H. Thaddeus.

52. Portrait of Mabel, 9th Lady Clifford, by
H. Thaddeus.

Lewis Henry Hugh, 9th Lord Clifford of Chudleigh, was born at the Villa de Cinque
at Albano near Rome on 24 August 1851. He was a bright scholar at Stonyhurst and
passed into London University, where he took his B.A. in 1872, becoming a barrister
of the Inner Temple in 1882. At this time Catholics were still barred from both
Oxford and Cambridge.

From his school days he was, to judge by the letters he wrote to his parents, a
dutiful son, and as he was a great traveller his letters are full of interest. For example
he gives a full description of a special visit he made in 1872 to what was then the last
word in modern sea transport, the steamship *Great Eastern*.

His father had been to Munich University with an American, Thomas G. Reynolds, who, after graduating as a lawyer, was elected in 1860 to be Lieutenant-Governor of Missouri and Governor two years later. In 1873 Lewis Clifford was sent on a tour of North America under the 'protection' of Thomas Reynolds, though the word 'protection' is not strictly accurate, since he had an extremely adventurous time in the United States not unmixed with danger. During this visit young Lewis made the acquaintance of General Custer, and, together with his travelling companion, Lewis Molesworth, a son of Sir William Molesworth, he joined Custer's expedition against the Indians and took part in the battles of the Yellowstone River against the Indian chief Sitting Bull.

The expedition, which set out in June from Fort Rice on the upper Missouri (North Dakota), was ostensibly to survey the Yellowstone River. It consisted of a party of surveyors and scientists with a military escort of 1,700 men under the command of General Stanley, who invited Clifford and Molesworth to come along for the 'very decent hunting' they anticipated en route. Their guide was half Indian, half French, but 'at present' Clifford wrote to his father on 6 June 1873 'he is too drunk to do much'.

By August the expedition had reached Helena, Montana, by way of the Yellowstone and Powder river valleys. On the 4th Lewis joined the main column under Custer having stayed with the engineers, which he found in a state of excitement due to the discovery of the bodies of the cavalry sutler and vet pierced with arrows and bullets 'though unscalped'. They heard that the Indians had attacked Custer, who was ahead of them with 80 cavalrymen, and following the skirmish 'all night we heard the Indians howling over their dead on the opposite bluffs'.

On the evening of the 9th at about ten o'clock at night Custer started in pursuit without about five hundred mounted men, 25 Indian scouts and a few volunteers including Clifford and Molesworth. It was bright moonlight as the troop of horse rode across the plain.

About five in the morning we halted in a hollow where there was grass for our horses, regaled ourselves on a repast of coffee, hard tack and raw ham, and put in what sleep we could until eight when we started again and travelled till after midday. We then halted till six and just before we started were allowed to make small fires to cook something to eat with. We then marched till nine when we found the Indians had crossed the river. The river was deep and rapid, which necessitated a halt on our part for though the Indians, accustomed from infancy to cross rivers, could swim their ponies over with ease, and provided with boats made of hide on which to carry children and goods, found no difficulty in crossing, to us it was a serious difficulty. That night we slept soundly beneath the cotton woods on the bank of the river, the crossing of the river to be attempted the first thing at daybreak. At daybreak we prepared to cross, and when one or two good swimmers had swum across, and one or two men on good swimming horses had with difficulty crossed the streams, the heart of many a man in that command sank within him as if a bad or indifferent swimmer he contemplated swimming his heavily laden horse across that rapid current. That such men should swim their horses across was not Custer's intention but he hoped to get a line of picket-ropes across and drag a raft with the men and arms on it.

With some difficulty they managed to get the line across but such was the force of the current that the very weight of the rope smashed it. A detachment or two were sent to see if they could discover a ford further down, but the passage of the stream was virtually given up much to the delight of a great many. It was amusing to hear the remarks made whilst we were waiting to see the issue of the attempts made at crossing. No one seemed to know how to swim and every now and then you would hear some man offering two or three months pay to be back in South Carolina. Fortunately the Indians were not aware of our presence, as from the woods on the other side they might have opened a distructive [*sic*] fire on the whole command, which, for some time, was stationed on a sandbank in the river, and nothing could have saved the first men who had crossed over to the other side of course without arms of any kind. That evening however, a little before sunset an Indian was seen to ride over the hills on the other side, and on seeing the cavalry vedettes, reined up his horse and turned back. We had then little doubt that having removed their women and children they were coming back to fight us. From their subsequent conduct I believe they were under the impression there were only the eighty men they had attacked the day before, and that they could capture the whole force.

Next morning the bugle sounded and was answered by a shot from the other side. One of our party, which consisted of two of Stanley's aides and the *Tribune* reporter besides ourselves, remarked that the shot came from the other side; a volley which followed about five minutes after, left no doubt of the matter, and effectually woke us up, which the first shot had decidedly failed to do. Still, the shooting at first was not accurate, though the range was only about five or six hundred yards, and we proceeded to cook our breakfast and pack up our blankets. Whilst some of us moved down to the river bank about twenty yards off to see if the enemy were strong, and to get a shot at them, when the order should be given, as Custer had stopped the promiscuous fire with which we had answered their first volley. He expected by this means to get them to expose themselves more openly. As I was packing up my blanket a bullet struck the tree about a foot over my head followed by several among the branches warning me to move my horse and belongings away from the bank. The reporter who was standing near was much startled by this little demonstration on the part of the Indians.

When I had finished moving our horses I was unable to find my breakfast, so returned to the river and got behind a tree to watch the skirmishing. For two hours the fighting across the river continued with only, however, two casualties on our side. Custer's orderly was shot through the head and another man shot in the arm. During this time the Indians were reported crossing the river above and below, and advancing on the plateau on the bluffs near the river. We immediately advanced up the hill in skirmishing order, and were met by a heavy fire from the Indians as we ascended. A lieutenant was badly shot through the thigh. I rode up the hill with Custer with his guidon flying and his band playing. This of course attracted a pretty lively fire from some Indians in a ravine. Custer and one of his aides lost their horses but otherwise the fire had no dangerous effect. The command was given to charge, and away went the Indians with the Cavalry in pursuit. The whole time the band (was) playing (and as the firing ceased, playing in something of time) the scattered band of Indians and the troops of cavalry charging at full speed looked quite theatrical. At this point the main Command came up and shelled the Indians out of the woods on the other side of the river.

After that we saw no more Indians from thence to the Musselshell, with the exception of half a dozen who shot at some people fishing, amongst whom was one of the Scientific Corps ... Near the Musselshell we struck buffalo for the first time.

They then made for Fort Benton on the upper Missouri, 'and in crossing the river we missed the ford and had to swim across and arrived in Benton with no luggage but our rifles and blankets and wet through up to the middle'. Lewis describes Benton as a 'hard little trading town where every inhabitant lives by trading whisky to the Indians and some few of them combining it with the duties of U.S. Officers and molesting those of the inhabitants in their illegal commerce who did not bribe them to be quiet'.

From Fort Benton he went to Helena, Montana, and then on to Salt Lake City and back to St Louis, where his journey had begun, and which he reached in October. In December he was in Chicago, from where he went to Toronto by way of the Niagara

Falls. On his return to England he went back to London University to read law, and as already mentioned, he was called to the bar in 1882.

There is a tradition in the family that when Lewis returned from soldiering in America he wanted to join the army and to follow his uncle Henry into the Rifle Brigade. However, his father thought otherwise, and decided that it would be better for the estate if he qualified as a lawyer. He did, however, join the 10th Rifle Volunteer Battalion of the Devonshire Regiment in which he served as a captain between 1877 and 1879.

In 1876 he visited Ceylon and Japan, and four years later, in 1880 on his father's death, he succeeded to the family honours and estates. The latter comprised at that time 4,416 acres in Devonshire, 1,562 acres in Warwickshire, 896 in Somerset, 858 in Buckinghamshire, and 128 in Cornwall, a total of 7,860 acres worth £9,109 a year.[1] Still unmarried, he continued to travel a great deal, which enabled him to lend Ugbrooke to his uncle, Major-General Sir Henry Clifford, V.C., as explained earlier.

At this time there was a reorganisation of the Volunteers and Major the Lord Clifford became Lieutenant-Colonel in 1881, and in 1885 the government finally recognised the Volunteers as a permanent part of the armed forces. Lewis applied for the old name dating from the Napoleonic wars, and formed the corps into the 5th (Haytor) Volunteer Battalion of the Devonshire Regiment. In 1901 he was appointed Volunteer A.D.C. to King Edward VII, and became the first Brigade Commander of the South-West Brigade when the Territorial Army was formed in 1908.

In 1877, Lewis's young brother, William, had been sent to New Zealand to cousins there, and in 1882 Lewis decided to visit him. He sailed from Plymouth in July, arriving at the Cape early in August, where he went overland to Port Elizabeth and back to join another vessel (a sailing ship) on 22 August. His observations on South African life make interesting reading a century later. 'The mistrust of the native and Dutch population', he wrote, 'appears to have a depressing effect on the English settlers, and the fact that a great part of the manual labour is done by blacks rather seems to make the English farmer think that labour on his farm is unbefitting his position as a white man'.

He landed at Melbourne on 10 September and two days later took ship for New Zealand, where he arrived five days later. He went ashore at Invercargill, but rejoined the ship two days later and sailed for Dunedin and Wellington, which he reached on the 22nd. After travelling round the south part of North Island, Lewis Clifford returned to Blenheim in South Island, where he spent a month with his brother at his farm, which he had called Ugbrooke. In January he sailed for Australia, where he spent several months, returning to England by way of the Dutch East Indies and Singapore.

On his return home he took his seat in the House of Lords as a Liberal, and continued to travel extensively until 1890, when at the age of 39 he married Mabel Towneley, the youngest daughter of John Towneley of Towneley in Lancashire by his wife Lucy Ellen, daughter of Sir Henry Joseph Tichborne, 8th Baronet. Mabel was a large, somewhat overpowering woman with a passion for entertaining and amateur dramatics. She made her husband build her a theatre at Ugbrooke and organised house parties six months ahead so that her guests could take part in her productions. The theatre was later sold and re-erected as a village hall at Kingskerswell.

An ancient Catholic family, the Towneleys owned large estates in Lancashire, Yorkshire and County Durham, and had lived at Towneley Hall, near Burnley, since the 12th century.

The house became a recusant centre during the reigns of Elizabeth I and James I, and later became a focal point for the study of natural sciences, members of the family contributing to the newly-formed Royal Society. The family were involved in both the 1715 and 1745 Risings. Francis Towneley, captured at Carlisle while commanding the Manchester Regiment during the retreat of Prince Charles' forces, was tried and executed in London on 30 July 1746. The Roman classical statuary collected by Charles Towneley was bought at his death in 1805 by the nation and is housed in the Towneley Collection in the British Museum.

Lord Clifford's contributions to House of Lords debates were many and varied. They included subjects as different as the marriage of deceased wives' sisters, lunacy, workmen's compensation, education, fertilisers, Torquay tramways and many other eqally disconnected subjects. He joined the Liberal Unionists over the Irish question and continued to play an active part in national and local politics up to 1906, but his greatest interest lay in the volunteer forces and their welfare and development. He devoted much time to the management of his estates, farming the Home Farm himself, where he built up a good herd of South Devon cows. He was twice President of the Devon Agricultural Association, and a keen supporter of agricultural innovations of all kinds.

He was chairman of the committee which supervised the plan to restore Buckfast Abbey, and was one of the community's most generous benefactors. The Clifford arms are quartered with those of the abbey in accordance with medieval custom, and Lady Clifford was later granted the privilege of entrance to the enclosure of the monastery by the Holy See. In 1885 he paid for the erection of the South Cloister and later of the East Cloister as well. His nephew, the 11th Lord Clifford, paid for the North Cloister. Lewis Clifford has been described by the historian of Buckfast Abbey, Dom Adam Hamilton, as the 'quasi-founder of the restored abbey'.[2]

When the railway reached Chudleigh he had the drive diverted so that it led directly to the station for the convenience of his guests who could be met off the train and driven direct to Ugbrooke. At the same time the old main entrance on the Exeter-Newton Abbot road was closed. A hundred years later when the railway was closed under Lord Beeching, the position was reversed.

Lewis, 9th Lord Clifford of Chudleigh, died on 19 July 1916, and, since there were no children of his marriage to Mabel Towneley, he was succeeded by his brother, William. Lady Clifford died on 24 January 1921.

Chapter Forty-Eight

Generation XXVIII – William, 10th Lord Clifford of Chudleigh (1858-1943)

53. Portrait of William, 10th Lord Clifford of Chudleigh, by Perry.

William, 10th Lord Clifford of Chudleigh, was known to his family as 'Silly Willie'. This is, perhaps, an unfair nickname, for though he took after his grandfather in matters to do with money, he was anything but silly in other ways. When he died in 1943, *The Times* wrote: 'Lord Clifford of Chudleigh, died at the Hall, Headcorn, Kent on July 5 ... He was educated at Beaumont and left England for New Zealand in 1876 where he was employed for two years on a farm. In 1882 he bought a station near Blenheim in Marlborough Province and remained there for eight years. A breakdown in health compelled him to leave New Zealand in 1890 for Tasmania, where he engaged in farming, and became connected with various business enterprises in Hobart ... Lord Clifford was an authority on radiology, discovering in 1922 the "Clifford Colour Rays". He made visible the colours of ultra-violet and infra-red rays. His publications inclu-ded *Light Rays: What they are and how they cure*, and articles in journals on radiology. He also wrote *The Portal of Evolution* (1922), *The Evolution of Civilisation and Society* and *The Theology of Creation*. He was a Fellow of the Geographical and Zoological Societies.'

William had never got on with his father, though he was said to have been his mother's favourite. At Beaumont his prowess at cricket compensated for his intellectual eccentricities. At the age of 18, therefore, he was exported to New Zealand to the many Clifford, Vavasour, Petre and Weld cousins there, and soon ran through all the money with which he had been provided by his father. His brother, Lewis, took a slightly censorious view of him, saying that he was incapable of sticking at anything long enough to make a success of it, which was hardly fair coming from a man who spent so many years travelling from one part of the world to another. Nevertheless, William built with his own hands the house he called Ugbrooke, near Blenheim, which stands to this day, and which is now owned by some of his Vavasour cousins. His building experience was to stand him in good stead later.

When Lewis Clifford returned to England in 1883, he left William enough capital to re-establish himself. But two years later letters from New Zealand began to arrive at Ugbrooke telling how 'lovesick' Willie had fallen for the beautiful 16-year-old daughter of a small local farmer, named Richard Bassett, who had emigrated from north Devon. By all accounts he was a successful farmer, but the cousins disapproved of him strongly as not being quite out of the top drawer, and they disapproved even more strongly when William married Catherine Bassett, prophesying that the marriage would be a disaster. It was. The reason he left New Zealand is not as printed in *The Times* obituary; his son, the 11th Lord Clifford, told a very different story. Seeing so many rabbits on his property which no self-respecting Australian or New Zealander would think of eating, he decided that he could make his fortune by canning them and exporting them to Europe. In 1887 not much was known about canning, and by Silly Willie nothing at all. After he had killed half a dozen people with ptomaine poisoning, the cousins, by then eminently respectable pillars of society, suggested it was time that he moved on. So it was next stop Tasmania, where he settled at Brown Mountain outside Hobart, and where he separated from his wife. According to his sister, Bertha, Countess de Torre Diaz, the marriage broke up because of his wife's mental instability brought on by the birth of their son, Lewis, who was an abnormally large child. She took to the bottle and William Clifford sued for a legal separation and sent her back to her parents in New Zealand. At least that is what he thought he had done, but it seems that 18 months after she left Tasmania she gave birth to a son whom she registered as Leopold Clifford. All the family and legal correspondence from this event have been carefully preserved just in case of claims to the title and estates in the future. The warnings of the Tichborne case were taken to heart by the Cliffords.

From that time onward, William became an object of shame or amusement to his sons. Charles, the eldest, was sent to school in England at the age of eleven. By then it was clear that Lewis and Mabel Clifford were not going to have any children, and that William, and ultimately, Charles, were heirs to the title and estates. William was making no money from his farming enterprise so he set up as a builder. It is related than when his brother died he had to be called down from the roof of a chicken house he was building for a neighbour to be told he had become a peer. By this time two of his sons were in the war, and Lewis, who had broken his hip, which had been wrongly set, was in business in Hobart. It was Lewis who paid for his father's passage back to England, no doubt to his great relief. That William was an embarrassment to his sons is only too clearly revealed in a letter one of them wrote to his brother: 'Father turned up at – 's reception in a dirty jacket bringing his latest housekeeper, a filthy looking harridan'.

William took ship from Hobart to Sydney with his belongings in a sack on his back – 'Humping his bluey' as the Australians call it. On arrival in Sydney he went at once to Government House where a family connection, Sir John Strickland, was Governor. He went up to the door looking like a tramp, but when a young footman tried to send him away he was greeted with a tirade about his not being at the front. The footman was so cowed that he let William in; he stayed with the Stricklands until a boat was found on which he could sail for England.

Lewis Clifford had such a poor opinion of William's financial acumen that he had left all he could of the estate to his nephew, Charles, William's eldest son, who, to his credit, made arrangements for his father's financial support for the rest of his life.

It was after his return to England in 1917 that William's second life began. It lasted until he died in 1943, and he became increasingly immersed in the theories and experiments of which *The Times* obituary spoke. He lived for many years at 67 Maddeley Road in Ealing and in the middle thirties he bought the Hall, Headcorn, in Kent where he died. The present Lord Clifford remembers being dragged off to see his grandfather William's 'Light Ray' clinics. It seems that he had made some cures, but his family remained for ever dubious about them. In an article in the *Evening Standard* in the 1920s he is reported to have been found in morning dress, covered in wood shavings, in his workshop holding his latest invention, which he described as 'this little device which will save half a ton of coal per year per grate'. He founded a Mystic Evolution Society and described the creation of the world in terms 'of an electrical textbook'. His theory stated that from A.D. 4000 to A.D. 14,000 would be the Period of Prevention of War, that the Age of Charity would endure until A.D. 18,000, and the Age of Perfect Government until A.D. 20,000. The society never had more than eighty members.

His theories on evolution led to his having some peculiar ideas about his own role in the order of things, and, as his sons put it, he imagined himself a Messiah. About this time he had an operation on his throat, which meant that he could only talk in a loud whisper. He was trying to make a speech in the House of Lords when a fellow peer moved a motion, which was carried *nem. con.* that 'As the noble Lord cannot be heard, he be no longer heard'.

William, 10th Lord Clifford, died on 5 July 1943, gaunt, bearded, odd, and probably more than half mad. Silly Willie was certainly eccentric, but the former Sir John, later Lord, Strickland once said that he thought him 'just off a genius'. He had married in 1886 Catherine Mary, daughter of Richard Bassett, who died in Wellington, New Zealand in 1943. Even in old age she was renowned for her beauty, and was reputed to have been, as a young girl, the most beautiful woman in New Zealand. By her William had three sons:

    1. CHARLES OSWALD HUGH, 11th Baron, for whom see next chapter.
    2. LEWIS JOSEPH HUGH, 12th Baron, for whom see Chapter Fifty.
    3. Sir BEDE EDMUND HUGH, G.C.M.G., Governor of the Bahamas, Mauritius, Trinidad and Tobago, for whom see Chapter Fifty-One.

William Clifford, as a widower of two months, married secondly on 29 May 1943, Grace Muriel, daughter of W. St Clair Munro. It was less than two months before his own death. She died childless on 18 February 1963.

Chapter Forty-Nine

Generation XXIX – Charles, 11th Lord Clifford of Chudleigh (1887-1962)

Charles Oswald Hugh, 11th Lord Clifford of Chudleigh, was born in New Zealand on 27 April 1887. At the age of 11 he left Tasmania to be brought up in England. As mentioned in the last chapter, he went to his aunt, the Countess de Torre Diaz, in London. His Aunt Bertha became *in loco parentis* until he was sent to a preparatory school in Belgium in 1899. To send an 11-year-old Tasmanian to a French-speaking school, at a time when the Continent was going through an anti-British spell due to the Boer War, was not a kindly act. But Charles survived for three years until he was sent to Downside at the age of fourteen. If he had any home at all it was with his Aunt Bertha, for his Aunt Mabel, Lady Clifford, was so envious of him, having no son of her own, that he was only allowed to visit his uncle at Ugbrooke when she was away.

Charles's great ambition was to join the Navy. Though he passed the examination with credit in the top ten of his year, he was turned down because he was deaf in his right ear as the result of an attack of measles when he was a child. He then

54. Portrait of Charles, 11th Lord Clifford of Chudleigh, by Anne Norwich.

tried to get into the Navy 'by the back door', that is to say through the Merchant Navy. His uncle, Lewis, arranged for him to join the training ship *Illawarra*, one of the last sailing vessels, in which he went round the world. In his somewhat earthy description of how the cadets knew when to change their socks, he tells us that it was time if the socks stuck to the cabin roof when they were thrown at it. Within three years Charles had obtained his first mate's certificate and had twice visited his father and brothers in Tasmania. They rather scorned his inability to be proficient in outback activities, and showed him scant sympathy when he nearly cut off his leg with an axe, a wound, which in later life, caused him much pain.

On his next visit to Australia he found his younger brother, Bede, surveying in Western Australia, so he signed him on at Fremantle as assistant purser, and brought him back to England with him, where they had six months leave together visiting their many cousins, taking part in the London season, and seeing the last of the old privileged pre-war world. At the outbreak of the 1914 War he joined, as a Sub-Lieutenant, Royal Naval Volunteer Reserve, the Naval Division which was rushed to Antwerp and which got cut off in Holland, where he was interned for the rest of the war. There he was helped with clothes and food parcels by Baroness van Clifford of the Dutch branch of the family at the Hague. (Towards the end of the Second World War the debt was repaid, to a lesser degree, by Major Jack Wolff, husband of Charles's niece, Mary Clifford, taking the Baroness food parcels on the liberation of the Netherlands.)

Later in the First World War, the Naval Division internees in Holland were paroled, and Charles worked in the British Legation there, being allowed to visit England twice, once to settle estate affairs on his father's succession to the title, and the other to get married. While he was in England on the first occasion he became engaged to Dorothy Hornyold, of an old Catholic family. They married in November 1917 on his second parole leave. Dorothy came to Holland before the end of the war but returned to England to have their expected baby there the following year. The daughter, Agnes, was born in November 1918 and her mother then fell ill with 'Spanish' influenza and died on 3 December 1918. It was a sad homecoming for Charles, who went down to Devon, to Lawell, the dower house, and began negotiating to run the entailed part of the estate for his father. His uncle Lewis had considered William totally incompetent to deal with the running of affairs, so left what he could to Charles. It was finally agreed that William should receive an annual income of £2,000 free of tax in return for handing over the entailed estate. He hoped that by doing this that the death duties he had had to find on his uncle's death would not have to be repeated on William's. Owing to incompetent legal advice, however, that was not to be, and 20 years later he had to pay death duties all over again on his father's death. Though a better businessman than his father, Charles sold off more of the estates than he need. The Cornish, Warwickshire and Buckinghamshire properties went as well as more than half the Somerset and practically all of the Kingsteignton estate. The latter had been in the family the longest time; and the Creslow estate in Buckinghamshire was the most important from an historical point of view, for it contained what had once been the headquarters of the Knights Templar.

Charles also dismissed the last of the Knight family, who were practically hereditary agents to the Cliffords, and replaced him by Sir George Hammick, an ex-internee friend from Holland. When his Aunt Mabel died in 1922, he left Lawell and went to live at Ugbrooke with his Aunt Bertha, then herself a widow.

George Hammick, the agent, lived at Ugbrooke at first, as he too had been widowed, and in the twenties he and Charles spent much time hunting and shooting together. Then George Hammick got married again and moved into a house on the estate. Aunt Bertha died soon afterwards, and in 1925 Charles's youngest brother, Bede, married in the United States and the following year his brother Lewis's wife, Amy, died in Australia, leaving him with three young children. Charles arranged for the eldest, Hugh, then aged 11, to be sent to England in January 1928, and his two sisters followed three years later. This enabled them to have Ugbrooke as a home during their holidays from school until 1936, when he left Ugbrooke to live again at Lawell, where he spent the rest of his life.

Charles married again on 3 January 1940, Clare, widow of Charles Ogilvie, daughter of Captain Jasper Graham Mayne, C.B.E., and maternal grand-daughter of Sir Frederick Weld of Chideock (see Chapter Fifty-Four). Although Charles Clifford inherited the title in 1943, he did not take his seat in the House of Lords until after the War, during which he became the Home Guard Intelligence Officer for the area with the rank of Lieutenant-Colonel, having previously served in the local Territorials as a captain in the 5th Battalion the Devon Regiment.

During the War he let Ugbrooke rent free to an evacuated school from London, turning down £2,000 a year from an insurance company. As the masters from the school were called up, discipline was left to nuns who let things get out of hand. Several of the pictures were badly holed by being used for archery practice by the young evacuees. After the War the house was taken over by the Ministry of Pensions at a rental of £10 a year, as a hostel for disabled Poles from General Anders' army. They left in 1952, when Lord Clifford used the downstairs Adam rooms as a grain store. This likewise did the pictures still on the walls no good. In 1957 he left the house to his nephew, the present Lord Clifford, who set about repairing the damage. Charles Clifford died on 2 February 1962, when the entailed estate passed to his nephew, and the title to his brother Lewis. By his first wife Dorothy Hornyold, daughter of Alfred Hornyold of 97 Eaton Place, London, he had an only daughter:

AGNES MARY, born 25 November 1918; married 22 April 1944, Robert Weathered Stallybrass, Lieutenant, R.N.V.R., and has issue, a son Hugh and two daughters Helen and Emma.

By his second wife, Clare Mary, who survived him, the 11th Baron had no further issue.

Chapter Fifty

Generation XXIX – Lewis, 12th Lord Clifford of Chudleigh (1889-1964)

55. Portrait of Lewis, 12th Lord Clifford of Chudleigh.

Lewis Joseph Hugh, 12th Lord Clifford of Chudleigh, was born in New Zealand on 7 February 1889, just before the family moved to Tasmania. He was educated at his uncle Lewis's expense at Zavier College in Melbourne, where he excelled as an athlete. When he left school he went farming outside Hobart, Tasmania, in the Brown Mountain area until he had a serious accident while jumping his pony over a wire fence. His hip was broken and badly set, causing him much pain and some disablement in later life. While in hospital following this mishap he met the daughter of the chief doctor in Hobart, Amy Beaumont Webster. By the time he came out of hospital – the treatment paid for by money he borrowed from his uncle Lewis – he was already unofficially engaged to her.

When he left hospital, limping badly, Lewis Clifford had to start a new life. His first job was in the daytime as a butcher's accountant; he went on to night school to get mining and accountancy degrees; as if that were not enough, for one day he followed it by being reader on the Hobart daily paper. Once he had qualified as an accountant, however, he set up an office in the Stock Exchange Building in Hobart, where so many of his clients asked for advice on investments that he became a stockbroker as well. His mining degree obtained him a place on the board of the Mount Farrel Tin Mines, where he was the youngest director. Unlike his father, he was good with money, and one of his proudest moments came when he was able to repay his uncle the money he had borrowed to pay his hospital bill. According to his son he was a purist and a puritan where money was concerned, never having received any from his father or anyone else other than what he had borrowed and repaid. He went on to become a company promoter and the director of 32 companies in Australia.

When the 1914 War broke out he tried to join up, but the injury to his hip prevented him. He collapsed when trying to run round a table as part of the medical test and had to return to hospital. When he came out he renewed his acquaintance with the Webster family and married Amy. Meanwhile Dr. Webster, who had emigrated to Australia from Lancashire, tried to join the Australian Medical Corps, but was rejected because he was too old, so he went back to England where the age limit for the R.A.M.C. was higher. He and his son, John, who joined the Royal Flying Corps, were both killed, the latter on the last day of the War against the Turks.

Lewis Clifford's disability did not prevent him indulging his passion for motorbikes. He twice won the Launceston to Hobart race on a big Indian machine, but his increasing business interests prevented him indulging this hobby to excess. In 1922 he floated what was to be his biggest success, the Hume Pipe Company, with a capital of some £22,000. It is now a multi-million pound enterprise. Two years later he moved to Melbourne which he made his business base for the rest of his life. But in January 1926 tragedy struck, and he lost his wife, leaving him with three children. His son, Hugh, was sent to school in England in 1928 and his daughters, Mary and Rosamund, followed three years later.

As his business interests expanded, Lewis Clifford travelled extensively, setting up branches in Singapore, Kuala Lumpur, Hong Kong, India and South Africa. He arranged for local companies in America and Europe to develop his inventions under licence, and was one of the first foreign representatives to visit the Lake Baikal region of Siberia, where he was consulted by the Soviet Industrial Committee on water supply (Lake Baikal is the deepest fresh water sea in the world).

On 14 December 1934, Lewis Clifford married again, Mary Elizabeth Knox, daughter of Sir Adrian Knox, Chief Justice of Australia. During the War he bought a property in Victoria called Yarra Brae, where he founded a herd of pedigree Friesian cattle.

One of Lewis's great interests was Shakespeare. He could recite whole plays, and while a widower, whenever he visited in England, he paid lengthy visits to Stratford-on-Avon. In the 1920s he had run a theatre in Australia, though this, inevitably, had been a loss-making enterprise. He was also keenly interested in the Boy Scout movement, and had two Far East Pacific jamborees and one World Rover moot on his property.

As he grew older the trouble with his hip grew worse, and he was already partially bed-ridden when his elder brother died in 1962 and he succeeded as 12th Baron. Most of the last two years of his life were spent at San Roque in Spain, and he died in the King George V Hospital in Gibraltar on 27 August 1964.

By his first wife, Amy Beaumont Webster, daughter of Dr. John Arthur Webster, M.D., he had one son and two daughters:

1. LEWIS HUGH, 13th Baron, for whom see Chapter Fifty-Two.
1. MARY, born 2 April 1919; married on 17 August 1943 Major Jack Philip Albert Galvin Clifford Wolff, M.B.E., late Intelligence Corps, of Barkham Manor, Berkshire, and has issue.
2. ROSAMUND ANN, born 22 May 1924; married first, on 21 July 1945, Geoffrey Forrester Fairbairn, son of James Valentine Fairbairn, of Mount Elephant, Derrinallum, Victoria, Australia, the wartime Minister of Air in the Australian government, and has issue. The marriage was dissolved by divorce in 1965, and she married secondly in 1970, as his second wife, John Vavasseur Fisher, 3rd Lord Fisher, DSC, brother of the present Lady Clifford.

The 12th baron was survived, but had no further issue, by his second wife, Mary Elizabeth Knox, who died at San Roque in July 1984.

Chapter Fifty-One

Generation XXIX – Sir Bede Clifford, G.C.M.G., C.B., M.V.O. (1890-1969)

56. Portrait of Sir Bede Clifford, by Anne Norwich.

Bede Edmund Hugh Clifford, G.C.M.G., C.B., M.V.O., Knight of St John of Jerusalem, Governor and Commander-in-Chief of the Bahamas, Mauritius, Trinidad and Tobago, was born at Hobart, Tasmania, in 1890, the third son of the eccentric future 10th Lord Clifford of Chudleigh. At the age of five he remembered being taken to see his eldest brother, Charles, off to England, and later, his father falling ill, he and his brother Lewis being looked after by friends. At 10 and 11 they were sent to Zavier College in Melbourne, and, though Bede did not even know the alphabet when he arrived there, he subsequently won the first prize in every form. Because of the distance and the fact that their mother had been sent back to New Zealand, Bede and Lewis only went home to Tasmania during the long summer vacations, spending their other vacations at school.

When he left Zavier, Bede joined the Australian Intelligence Corps which was then responsible for compiling the ordnance survey maps of the continent, where he learnt the rudiments of surveying. After a brief spell at Melbourne University he went to Western Australia as a surveyor, but there joined his brother Charles on the *Mottisfont* and went back with him to England. There he joined in the social life of the county at Ugbrooke, but on the outbreak of war he joined up as a private, but was later commissioned in the Royal Fusiliers. As already mentioned, his brother Charles was interned in Holland during the war, and many of Bede's letters to him from the front have survived, as also has his war diary. Regrettably it is not possible to quote more than short passages from these letters and diary, but these brief extracts reveal much of Bede's character and attitude to life.

The first letter is dated February 1916 from the front.

Dear old Charles,

  Sorry not to have answered your letter before, but I've been in the trenches since February 2nd and have just come back for a rest. The weather has been ghastly. Tramped up and down the trench for three hours in a blissard [*sic*]. Snow flakes as big as your hand. Veritably frozen alive.

Don't think I've thawed yet for that matter. Added to this every kind of frightfulness is in vogue. The thing that causes most excitement is the Minnie' [minenwerfer = trench mortar, literally mine-thrower]. 'It consists of a metal case about the size and shape of a large maul with the handle removed and contains 60 lbs of H.E. They can be seen coming & give you about 1 second's grace to get out of the way. This fact coupled with the terrific upheaval when they go off is the reason·why they are feared so much. It is quite impossible to dodge a shell, you just trust to luck & stay where you are. But a Minnie gives you time to think about it with the result that you spend that time in getting *into* a terrible funk as well as *out of* the way. After they have been coming over for about an hour your nerves get into such a state that you become nearly insane. The trying part is judging where the damn thing is going to fall. This is not so easy as it would seem because they come over at a great height and seem to come down nearly perpendicular. If you don't judge accurately you run into the damn thing ...

Talking about the end of the war, I don't think I can do anything to help you but would suggest you join our Divisional 'Peace At Any Price' league. By the way did you ever get the Bairnsfather pictures I sent you? Cheerio old thing. We're all downhearted here. So is the Hun.

Yr affect Bro

Bede.

Four months later, Bede was writing from 'This bloody hole still' and 'The Ditch'. On June 12, he wrote:

Dear Old Charles

We are back in the trenches for the last three or four days; things have been extraordinarily quiet. I think everybody got fed up with the awful strafe of May 21st to June 2nd that the reaction has set in now. There are quite a decent lot of Huns opposite us. I was up in the sap-head at one of the craters & I suppose I made a bit of a noise because one of the Huns opposite threw a lump of chalk over & hit one of our chaps in the back. Then a mutual bombardment began between the Hun and our fellows both sides throwing chalk at one another. Isn't this a funny war? One day you're going for one another like mad dogs & the next day all is peace. It just shows how little one is personally affected by the destinies of nations. The private soldier fights on on both sides & really bears no malice to the chap opposite & doesn't really know what all the row's about ...

The following extract from Bede's war diary begins on 25 July 1916, nearly a month after the launch of the Battle of the Somme. His unit had come into the front line on 19 July where they bivouacked close to the old German front line. He noted how all their dugouts were supplied with electric light and now much more comfortable the enemy was than our men. He noted the long racks in which to fasten their rifles in order to fire the deadly rifle grenade, and how the trench mortars were fired by electricity from a dugout. In the German support trench he saw a veritable munitions factory with lathes, dynamos and implements for making bombs, mortars and rifle grenades.

On the 25th we reached the support and from now onwards lived in hell with the lid off. Everywhere one sees dead men, dead horses, and smashed up guns and vehicles. Our gunners are really splendid. The roar and din of guns going off & shells exploding is terrific. Our trench, if you could call it a trench, runs between the guns of a 4.5 in. howitzer battery. Batteries have been pushed right forward for enfilade purposes. There was a major and three subalterns in charge & today the major and one of them was hit. The major carried on with his battery long after he was wounded. Our brigade is now in the front line & hold a portion of L – and the edge of the wood adjoining. The shelling here is very intense. The night of the 26th was worse than Vimy. Tear shells fell in thousands, but the feature of the bombardment was the new German gas shell. It makes a buzzing noise as it passes through the air but the explosion is hardly noticeable, and apart from the gas, is quite harmless unless one gets a direct hit. One instance of this was poor

Barham who got hit in the legs. He had to have them amputated above the knee & died of shock. But the gas, though not as poisonous as the ordinary chlorine gas, is very troublesome, and leads to vomiting and debility, as well as making it nearly impossible to see. A combined gas and 'heavy' bombardment is terrifying and demoralising. We were used as carrying party all night to and fro from the dump to the front line, taking up stores for the brigade attack in the morning. The roads and tracks – there are few trenches now – were crammed with men, the night was of an inky blackness, the air was heavy with gas, everybody's eyes were running, some men's noses were bleeding, no one could move either back or foward owing to the congestion, the German heavies began to fall and all was Chaos. The crowding of men under fire invariably leads to big casualties & what is much worse demoralization & panic.

Finally, after much tribulation they got away with their loads & reached the wood. Then they made the trip again. At about 4 a.m. the steady artillery barrage gave way to a gigantic bombardment. At 7.10 our brigade began the attack. The effect on the Hun was electrical. Some ran forward with their hands up, others fired a few shots and fled for their lives only to be mostly mopped up by the artillery barrage behind them. We took all the wood, most of the village and prisoners, three officers and 166 men. During the afternoon the Hun counter-attacked twice but was beaten off.

In these battles no real fighting takes place. By the time it reaches that stage one side or the other takes to flight. Our brigade greatly distinguished themselves. They accomplished a task in which another famous Div. had failed three times.

The home newspapers make me sick. They really ought to be stopped, and Beach Thomas should be slain. They speak of this push as though we were already in Germany. The *Daily Mail* (Beach Thomas) gives a glorious but quite legendary account of the above battle, which he probably viewed from 10 miles back, & relied on the drivers of ambulances for his information. There was nothing glorious about the whole business. It was better than 'glorious'. Very few glorious deeds are done here, and what are done can easily be ascribed to neglect of duty. No, this battle was won by grim & resolute courage not by dash. By pluck & endurance, not by heroics. The side that sit there and be shelled, see it through & still remain more or less alive & sane wins the day. Stunts like the charge of the Light Brigade are things of the past. This the greatest of all battles won't lend itself to epic poetry. The most glowing account must needs be very sordid – that is if it makes any attempt at being truthful. On all sides the sickly stench of dead men and beasts assails the nostrils. Everywhere the cries of wounded men pleading in vain to be evacuated; everywhere the poisonous fumes & crashing din of shells, everywhere columns of smoke and dust, everywhere ceaseless demands for water. Strings of walking wounded wander out with their tunics cut open & covered with blood and bandages. Many are suffering with shell shock. They are in a stupified condition, smeared with dirt and mud and sweat; they stare at you with blood-shot eyes which gleam uncannily behind haggard, filthy faces. There are woods where every tree is blasted, villages where every house has become a heap of stones, fields where every yard has it shell hole. As you get further back mangled heaps of transport, horses, guns, waggons and motors are added to the limitless mass of destruction. The whole countryside is a shambles.

One cannot help wondering how men can attack at all or for that matter, defend a position, which has been shelled to the same extent as L – and the wood. But attack it they did, and with immense success. Opposed to them were some of the fatherland's best troops, to wit the Brandenburg Grenadiers of the 5th Guards Division. The Kaiser in his address referred to them as the flower of his army, coming as they do from that province which was the cradle of Prussia. Well the new army can manage them. But the Hun is a brave and skilful fighter nevertheless.

Sept 15th (1916). A great day. At last we are seeing the reward of all our past sufferings. True, other divisions are reaping the reward of our toil, but as long as someone does, I suppose it won't matter much who. But it is worth while remembering that during all those dull days a change was reported in the situation that countless regiments were doggedly fighting away wearing down the Hun, and losing their lives, and what is more, making way for the success of their followers.

The tanks have caused huge excitement. Though they have not been as useful as might be supposed, they have nevertheless caused high excitement among the men & cheered them on no end. One telegram humerously [sic] reports 'Tank seen walking down High St. St Flers surrounded by infantry cheering wildly'. A German battalion commander whom we took prisoner reported that one got 'astride' of his trench and totally enfiladed it, killing so many that the balance readily surrendered. It is reported that they are armed with two light Q.F. guns and four machine guns, and will stop anything in the way of missiles from a field gun downwards. Some of them got upturned. A house is no obstacle to their progress. That is to say the ordinary French cottage is not. It is very refreshing to see we are not afraid to try this type of experiment, and I hope we are not too quick in giving it up.

March 2nd (1917). Had a row with the general about the question of overworking one's men. Generals don't always know what a man can do, and when he'll absolutely refuse to go on much further. Perhaps I was a little impertinent over this, but anyhow he gave me a hell of a dressing-down, which, as one only has to be bad enough at one's job, or disliked enough by one's superiors to get a good fat job, I listened to with a vacant smile. This annoyed him more, so he reported me to the colonel. Unfortunately for my new job the Col. and Brig. Major took my point of view and the matter dropped. Some people have all the bad luck.

March 5th & 6th (1917) ... We left our huts on the side of the wooded hill a little after 6 pm and marched through the wood along an old trolley line. Of course it has been snowing and thawing since early February, and the slush is too awful for words, and there are great mud holes between the sleepers ... A heavy snow storm is in progress and everyone is tired, wet and wretched. And now comes the worst trial of all. The German trench is only 200 yards away and our destination some 300 yards to the right. It took over an hour to do that 300 yards. The mud on top is very heavy. A leg gets stuck up to the knee. One tries to free it & succeeds after a herculean struggle only to find that in doing so the other leg has become hopelessly fast. Despite the snow and intense cold one breaks into a heavy perspiration – the perspiration of sheer exhaustion. The Germans hear us and a flare goes up. They see us. The artillery open on us. We lie down in shell craters for protection. These are half full of snow slush. The splinters all round. Two men are hit close by. Many have lost their gumboots and socks in the wet mud. Their bare feet are lacerated with barbed wire: their loads have become unendurable; many cast them away. Above the screeching of the shells can be heard the curses and blasphemy of the men. It is meaningless blasphemy, terrible as it is. One is taught by religion to offer a prayer under such circumstances and one reads in books that this is what people actually do. That in moments of despair the worst men turn to God. They don't. But they thank Him when it's all over. Nice feelings vanish. Almost all are egoists. In this general *sauve qui peut* the officer's turn comes. You could have seen and heard us that night helping and exhorting the men. Cursing them for making a noise & drawing fire, but always giving them a helping hand. They are not a bit grateful. There is a charming corporal in No. 1 by name Hector Munro, a travelled and educated man, who has written several very fine books. He was stuck fast. I helped him out of the mud, and in endeavouring to get his balance he struck me in the chest with his arm, knocking me backwards into a shell hole. Though ordinarily of a generous nature, he left me there and went on without so much as an apology. We reach our post exhausted and covered in mud. The scene soon changes to one of cheerful optimism as soon as one's pack is off and the trouble over. The affair was treated as a huge joke. Such is the soldier's philosophy – 'Sufficient unto the day ... '. He has no thought but of the present. The attitude of the soldier out here is not depicted at all correctly in the leading articles of the daily press. A fat gentleman smoking a fatter cigar in an easychair writes: 'There is no compromise possible in war. It must be a fight to the end. The Allies are determined that this war will finish only with the complete overthrow of Prussian militarism. This attitude is shared by every soldier in the trenches.' It isn't. What does the editor know about the soldier in the trenches? and you can't believe what a man says when he comes home on leave. He forgets his feelings in momentary enjoyment. As a matter of fact if he thinks about the war at all he regards it as more or less endless. He has a hope that some day long hence it will finish, but he doesn't know, and he doesn't much care. He merely looks forward to comfort which he thinks will once more be his. This comfort is magnified by his present discomfort. But alas he is doomed to disappointment. If he survives the war, it will be only in order to struggle against taxation and starvation. No, the best index to the soldier's attitude towards the war is the soldiers' song. He sings:

> When this bloody war is over
> Then how happy I shall be
> When this bloody war is over
> No more soldiering for me.

But he does himself an injustice: if another war broke out a few years hence, he would forget the past and think only of his duty with the Colours. Distance lends enchantment.

Soon after he wrote those prophetic words, Bede Clifford was gassed and invalided home. As soon as he was fit enough he returned to Australia, where he was appointed A.D.C. to Sir Ronald Munro Ferguson, the Governor General, a post he held when the war ended. His friendship with the Munro Fergusons helped him to the next step in his career. Lady Helen Munro Ferguson was a daughter of the Marquess of Dufferin and Ava, and through her he obtained the post of Political Secretary to the Governor General of South Africa, Prince Arthur of Connaught, but, before he left Australia, Bede joined Lord Jellicoe in 1919 on a surveying cruise of the Solomon Islands and Guadalcanal. The usefulness of this expedition was proved years later, for Jellicoe had been convinced, even as early as 1919, that the next war would be against the Japanese, so this visit to the Coral Sea dependencies and New Guinea was important.

In 1920 the Prince of Wales visited Australia during his famous world tour, and Bede Clifford got to know him and members of his staff since he was responsible for many of the arrangements, for which he was awarded the M.V.O. At the end of the royal tour, Bede returned to England by way of Canada and America, where he visited his uncle Walter and made the acquaintance of Franklin Roosevelt, with whom he became friendly and remained on friendly terms for the rest of Roosevelt's life.

As already mentioned, his next posting was to South Africa, and, when Prince Arthur of Connaught left, he was succeeded by the Earl of Athlone, and Bede was promoted official secretary and later Imperial Secretary. In 1925 the Prince of Wales made an official tour of South Africa, and Bede was once more responsible for some of the arrangements, and in particular for showing him the protected territories. Later that year, at the age of 35, Bede married; his bride was Alice Gundry from Cleveland, Ohio, and they were married on 21 October 1925.

He returned to South Africa, where in 1928 he took part in an expedition to cross the Kalahari desert from the south to the Victoria Falls. Much of the success of this enterprise, which Livingstone had twice attempted unsuccessfully, was due to Bede's surveying experience in Australia. He followed the crossing of the Kalahari by surveying the great Makgadkgadi salt lake in Botswana, to the east of Bulawayo. On this expedition Bede nearly lost his arm from blood poisoning, but happily recovered, and in 1931 he returned to lead a third expedition to define the borders of Bechuanaland (Botswana).

When the Statute of Westminster was passed in 1926, Bede became the U.K. representative in South Africa, a post equivalent to that of ambassador. Not long afterwards he had the difficult task of persuading King George V to be civil to General Hertzog, the South African Prime Minister, whom he greatly disliked, at the Commonwealth Prime Ministers' Conference. He managed this by suggesting that

Hertzog, as the longest serving prime minister, should be invited to take the chair, which meant that all the others were heard first, which gave Hertzog's nationalistic views time to mellow. About the same time Bede Clifford laid the foundations for the Imperial Airways, later B.O.A.C., route to South Africa.

After ten years' service in Africa, Bede was awarded the C.M.G., and posted to the Bahamas, where he was the youngest governor in the Colonial Service, and where he was knighted as K.C.M.G. His arrival in the Bahamas in 1931 coincided with a visit by Winston Churchill, who was recovering from being knocked down by a New York taxi. Bede's main achievement was the establishment of the Bahamas as a tourist resort. This was to replace the islands' almost total financial dependence on taxes from rum runners, which had declined since the repeal of prohibition in the United States. To this end he persuaded well-known people – royalty, the titled, film stars and others – to spend holidays in the islands and to publicise them. The Duke and Duchess of Kent spent part of their honeymoon as his guest at Government House. He also had a golf course and a race course laid out, and arranged direct air and telephonic communications with New York and Washington so that wealthy Americans could keep in touch with their businesses back home.

While Governor of the Bahamas, Bede and Alice Clifford paid many visits to America, where they often stayed with the Roosevelts at the White House. His old friendship with the President stood him and the country in good stead when, towards the end of the war, he was appointed Governor of Trinidad.

In 1937, Sir Bede was transferred to Mauritius. He was not the first Clifford to have served there, for as we have already seen Edward Clifford, O.S.B., the son of the 6th Lord Clifford of Chudleigh, had died there in 1843, having been a missionary for many years in the island. While in Mauritius, Sir Bede developed the island's hydro-electric resources, and successfully maintained the export of the sugar crop during a period of industrial unrest, which earned him the displeasure of the leftist press in England and the congratulations of his superiors. He was the first governor to appoint Indians to his Council.

Soon after the outbreak of war in 1939, Bede returned to England hoping for some employment closer to the centre of things, but this was not to be, and he was sent back to Mauritius, where he became host to two unwilling guests, the quisling Yugoslav minister, Stoyadinovitch, and the Shah of Persia. In 1942 he was transferred to the governorship of Trinidad, where he played an important part in helping to settle differences, which arose in the Caribbean after America's entry into the war, among British generals and admirals who did not take kindly to playing second fiddle to their American opposite numbers, and much of his time was spent in smoothing down ruffled feathers. Bede also had to deal with industrial unrest in the Trinidad oilfields, which he did successfully, though once more he suffered much abuse from the left-wing press in Britain. There is some suggestion that his decision to retire in 1946 may have been influenced by these attacks, for he was still some years short of retirement age.

But retire he did, and in his retirement he wrote his autobiography, which he published under the title *Proconsul*, and ghost-wrote for his old friend Princess Alice, Countess of Athlone, her memoir *For my Grandchildren*. He also began this history of the Clifford family, which he was unable to finish. He died in 1969. Not an unsuccessful life for, as he put it, 'the boy who had herded cattle, built log fences, fought bush fires and nursed his chilblains on remote Australian farms, had never enjoyed such ordinary advantages as a mother's care and affection ... '. Yet both he and his brother, Lewis, had imbibed much of their family's pride and history. Bede and his American wife were the strongest supporters of his nephew, the present Lord Clifford, in the latter's effort to restore the family place, Ugbrooke. In 1972 the present Lord Clifford recognised this debt by erecting a memorial to his grandfather, father and two uncles in St Cyprian's, Ugbrooke. All are now buried in its crypt, and, as the memorial has it, 'So they came home'.

Sir Bede Clifford married on 21 October 1925, Alice Devin Gundry, daughter of John Murton Gundry, of Cleveland, Ohio. By her he had three daughters:

1. ANNE FRANCES MAY, born 5 January 1929, who married on 5 August 1952, John Julius Cooper, 2nd Viscount Norwich, the author and broadcaster.

2. PATRICIA DAVID PANDORA, known as Pandora, but christened David after her godfather, the Prince of Wales, afterwards King Edward VIII and Duke of Windsor. She was born 29 January 1930 and married first, on 23 January 1948, Timothy Angus Jones, eldest son of Sir Roderick Jones, K.B.E., and his wife Enid Bagnold the playwright. Their marriage was dissolved by divorce in 1960, and she remarried secondly, on 12 July 1961, Michael Langhorne Astor, M.P., third son of Waldorf, 2nd Viscount Astor, but this marriage was also dissolved in 1968.

3. ALICE DEVIN ATALANTA, known as Atalanta, but christened Alice after her godmother, Princess Alice, Countess of Athlone. She was born on 10 May 1932, and married, first, on 10 September 1955, Richard Fairey, elder son of Sir Charles Fairey, head of the well-known aviation company. Richard Fairey lost both his legs in the Second World War and died on 27 July 1960. She married secondly, on 31 October 1963, Wing-Commander Timothy Ashmean Vigors, D.F.C., whom she divorced; and thirdly, in 1972, Michael Henry Dennis Madden, of Higher Tregawne, in Cornwall.

Sir Bede Clifford died in 1969 and is buried in the crypt of St Cyprian's church at Ugbrooke.

Chapter Fifty-Two

Generation XXX – Hugh, 13th Lord Clifford of Chudleigh (born 1916)

Lewis Hugh, 13th Lord Clifford of Chudleigh, was born in Tasmania on 13 April 1916, the only son of Lewis, later 12th Lord Clifford, and Amy Beaumont Webster. Moving to Victoria, Australia in 1923 he was educated first at the Junior House of Melbourne Grammar and then, after his mother died, at the Junior House of Geelong Grammar School. In 1928 he was sent to England to be brought up by his uncle, Charles, later 11th Lord Clifford. He was sent to Beaumont College and afterwards to Hertford College, Oxford, where he gained a B.A. Honours degree in jurisprudence. Commissioned into the Devonshire Regiment in January 1936, he served first at Dover with the 2nd Battalion and then in India with the 1st.

In March 1940 he returned to England and spent a year instructing at Sandhurst. In May 1941 he joined 50 Division Reconnaissance Regiment (ex 4th Battalion The Royal Northumberland Fusiliers) and immediately went to the Middle East, where he served in Cyprus, Syria and the Western Desert. He was wounded and taken prisoner on 6 June 1942 at the Battle of Devil's Cauldron, and sent to Prison Camp 29 in northern Italy. In September 1943 he escaped and joined the Italian Partisans in the Apennines, winning the Italian Partisan Medal, Provincia de Parma.

At the end of 1944 he returned to England and joined the 1st Airborne Division and was one of the first into Oslo when Norway was liberated. When the 1st Airborne was disbanded he served for three months at 16th Holding Battalion, Plymouth, before going to the Staff College at Haifa in Palestine. At the end of 1946 he went as second in command of the 1st Devons to Singapore. He spent most of 1947 with his regiment in Hong Kong, returning to Singapore and Malaya during the 1948 emergency, and was posted back to England towards the end of 1949. He was appointed second-in-command and Training Major of the 5th Battalion The Devonshire Regiment (T.A.).

In mid-1950 he resigned his regular commission and went to Australia. While farming in Victoria he joined the Australian Intelligence Corps (C.M.F.). Seven years later he came back to England and was asked to command the T.A. battalion, which he did until 1960 becoming Deputy Brigade Commander 130 Brigade. At that time he was appointed A.D.C. (T.A.) to the Queen and awarded the O.B.E. in 1962. On his retirement he became honorary colonel of the T.A.V.R. 3 which in 1970 became the Royal Devon Yeomanry Squadron of the Royal Wessex Yeomanry. He continued to hold that position until he went to live in Guernsey in 1983.

In addition to his military appointments, Lord Clifford was President of the Devon branch of the Country Landowners Association from 1973 to 1975, of the Devon branch of the Royal British Legion from 1969 to 1980, and of the Devon County Agricultural Association from 1973 to 1974. In 1964 he had been appointed Deputy Lieutenant of Devonshire and the same year he took his seat in the House of Lords

57. Hugh, 13th Lord Clifford of Chudleigh, with his wife Katharine and their family. The painting is by Edwards.

58. Collyer Quay and Clifford Pier, Singapore.

where he sits on the cross benches. He was founder honorary secretary of the All-Party Defence Study Group under Lord Shinwell, and has taken a keen interest in local government, Commonwealth and agricultural affairs.

Lord Clifford married on 29 January 1945 Katharine, daughter of the 2nd Baron Fisher of Kilverstone, and has two sons and two daughters:

1. THOMAS HUGH, born 17 March 1948, Coldstream Guards (1967-1977), who married Suzanne Austin in 1980 and has issue:
    i. ALEXANDER THOMAS HUGH, born 25 September 1985.
    i. GEORGINA APPOLLONIA, born 20 June 1983.
2. ROLLO HUGH, born 15 March 1954, who married Fiona, daughter of Richard Todd, in 1976 and has issue:
    i. CHRISTOPHER ROLLO, born 4 December 1982.
    ii. ALISDAIR ROLLO, born 23 June 1986.
    i. ELIZABETH ALICE, born 4 February 1981.
1. CECILIA ALICE, born 15 November 1945, married in 1968 Commander Nicholas Breakspear Kirby and has issue one son and three daughters.
2. SARAH AMY, born 22 June 1956, married Robert Richardson in 1981 and has issue one daughter.

PART FOUR

*THE CLIFFORDS OF TIXALL, STAFFORDSHIRE, AND
FLAXBOURNE, NEW ZEALAND*

Chapter Fifty-Three

Generation XXIV – Thomas Clifford of Tixall (1732-87)

Thomas Clifford, the posthumous son of Hugh, 3rd Lord Clifford of Chudleigh, was born in London on 22 August 1732. As a young man he lived adventurously, serving in the French army in Louis XV's regiment of musketeers into which those of noble birth were recruited. When war broke out in mid-century he returned to England, where he married Barbara Aston, daughter and co-heiress of James, 5th Lord Aston of Forfar in Scotland.[1] Her mother, Lady Barbara Talbot, was a daughter of George, 14th Earl of Shrewsbury and Lady Mary Howard, sister of Thomas and Edward, Dukes of Norfolk.

Following the death of Lord Aston in 1751 at the age of 28, his daughter inherited the ancient Aston family seat of Tixall in Staffordshire, and after her marriage to Thomas Clifford they built there a new house since the old one was in a state of ruin. Barbara's sister and co-heiress, Mary, married Sir Walter Blount, Baronet of Sodington and Mawley, Worcestershire;[2] she took the Bellamore estate on her father's death.

At this point we must revert to the marriages of the two daughters of Hugh, 2nd Lord Clifford of Chudleigh, to members of the Constable family in order to explain why the eldest son of Thomas Clifford of Tixall assumed a different surname. When William Constable, 4th and last Viscount Dunbar, who had married Elizabeth Clifford, died without heirs, his estates went to his nephew, Cuthbert Tunstall-Constable, who was himself married to Elizabeth's sister, Amy. Their son, William Tunstall-Constable, settled the estates on two nephews and, in default of their issue, on the sons of Thomas Clifford and Barbara Aston. The latter's eldest son, Thomas, married Mary Macdonald Chichester of Arlington, Devon, and was created a baronet on 27 December 1814, at the express wish of Louis XVIII of France. He succeeded eventually to the Constable estates of Burton Constable and Wycliffe in Yorkshire, and in 1821 took the name and arms of Constable instead of Clifford. Thus another of the many Clifford baronetcies became divorced from the name Clifford.

Sir Thomas's son and heir, now Constable, married a Chichester of Calverleigh Court, Devon. His son, the 3rd and last baronet, was Major Sir Frederick Constable, who died without issue. Sir Thomas (Clifford) Constable died at Ghent on 25 February 1823 and his monument was in Ghent cemetery beyond the Antwerp gate.

> Hic sepultus est nobilissimus dominus,
> Dominus Thomas Hugo Clifford de Constable,
> Baronetus Anglus, qui obiit die XXV Februarii
> AD MDCCCXXIII, aetus suae LX. R.I.P.
> Beati Mortui qui in Domino moriuntur
> opera enim illorum sequuntur illos.

Thomas Clifford of Tixall had nine sons and six daughters:

1. THOMAS HUGH (1762-1823) who assumed the surname of Constable.

2. EDWARD, born 1766, died young.

3. HENRY (1768-1813), married Ann, daughter of Edward Ferrers, but died without issue.

4. Rev. WALTER (1773-1806), died at Palermo, Sicily.

5. EDWARD J (1774-living 1817).

6. JAMES FRANCIS (1775-1855), who became a civil servant in the Navy Pay Office in Plymouth, died without issue.

7. ARTHUR (1778-1830), married in 1809 Eliza Matilda daughter of Captain Donald McDonald of Berwick-on-Tweed, by whom he had a daughter Rosamund who married J. S. Charlton of the 63rd Regiment. He published *Cliffordiana* and *Collectanea Cliffordiana*.

8. LEWIS (1778-1806), twin to Arthur, died without issue.

9. GEORGE LAMBERT, born in 1779; married in 1812 Mary Coyney of Foxearth, Staffordshire, daughter of Walter Hill Coyney, by whom he had six sons and several daughters. Three of his sons, Edward, George and Walter became priests; Alphonso (1830-93) married and had three daughters. Three of his six daughters were Mary Lucy (d. 1868), Constancia (d. 1894), and Francesca, who was for some time engaged to marry Major-General Sir Henry Clifford, V.C. (See Chapter Forty-Five).

For George Lambert's eldest son, CHARLES, see next chapter.

59. Portrait of Thomas Clifford, 2nd son of the 3rd Lord Clifford of Chudleigh, and his family. The painting was executed at Liège in Belgium in 1778-9. The child on the table in his mother's arms is George Lambert, youngest son, and the two boys in brown coats are dressed in the costume of the students of the Jesuit College in Liège.

Chapter Fifty-Four

Generation XXVI – Sir Charles Clifford of Flaxbourne (1813-93)

Charles Clifford's life has been described by Douglas Cresswell in his *Early New Zealand Families*; by Lady Lovat in her *Life of Sir Frederick Weld*, and perhaps in the greatest detail by R. Gaudin in his thesis submitted for an Honours B.A. in History at the University of New Zealand, in November 1950, entitled *Clifford of Stonyhurst*. This chapter is based on Mr. Gaudin's thesis.

Charles Clifford, the eldest son of George Lambert Clifford, was born at Mount Vernon, Liverpool in 1813. After being educated at Stonyhurst, he became a builder of railways and canals in partnership with a Joseph Binns. This venture did not flourish. His father, who was then winding up the estate of Cardinal Weld in Rome, tried to get Charles the job of agent at Ugbrooke, but the Knight family had an almost hereditary right to the post, so he was not successful.[2]

It was probably through his Petre relations that Charles became interested in New Zealand, as Henry Petre had been to Wellington in 1840 in the *Oriental* and had enthused about it. Then a Vavasour cousin, Sir Edward, approached Charles and suggested that he take his son, William, to New Zealand as a partner. An agreement was drawn up in June 1842 and the firm of Clifford and Vavasour was founded as engineers, surveyors, farmers and commission agents.

They sailed in the *George Fyfe* in June and arrived at Wellington in October 1842. During the voyage they ran out of fresh food and water, and Charles Clifford, on behalf of the passengers, made the captain put in at Cape Town. A list of passengers' grievances against the victualler was sent home to Lord Petre who had arranged the journey. On arriving at Wellington, Clifford and Vavasour made their first clearing, erected a tent and had a party for their friends from the *Fyfe* who were going on to Nelson. They got their 'town section' at Thorndon Flat, but there was some delay before they obtained their country blocks, so Charles set up in business as a commission agent, but the market was depressed owing to the non-settlement of land claims. He took Henry Petre into the partnership, but this did not work and Petre was bought out in 1844. The year 1843 was one of recession, which compelled Charles Clifford to turn his mind to other ventures, but he showed great foresight in prophesying a good future for sheep farming, as a letter to Sir Edward Vavasour, which he wrote in October 1843, shows. He therefore tried to arrange a lease of suitable land in the Wairarapa district and led a party there in May 1843. From this party Vavasour got separated and had to be brought back to Wellington by the Maoris. Two young chiefs later visited Wellington and encouraged Clifford to settle in the district. He returned with them and took up about twenty-five thousand acres to the east of Ruamahanga River. Thus the first New Zealand station devoted entirely to sheep stocked from Australia was established. He bought 500 ewes in Sydney, but had it not been for Sir Edward Vavasour's gift of over £3,000 they would have been hard put to it to pay for them.

60. (*left*) Sir Charles Clifford, first speaker of the New Zealand House of Representatives.

61. (*below*) Land clearance for Sir Charles Clifford's first cattle and sheep station in New Zealand.

Another relation, Frederick Weld, had meanwhile arrived in New Zealand. He was then 20, and went on to become a colonial governor and to be knighted. He helped Clifford drive his sheep to Wharekaka in May 1844. Life on the early sheep stations was tough, and Vavasour decided to go back to England in 1845. There he married Constantia, a daughter of the 7th Lord Clifford, and their descendants are in New Zealand to this day.

Charles Clifford had now lost two partners, who were, in effect, remittance men who idled away their time in the billiards room of *Barrett's Inn*, so he invited Frederick Weld to join him. But things went badly until they got an expert manager, Tom Caverhill, to join them. He so increased the flock that they had to expand and thus acquired Flaxbourne. Meanwhile, Clifford had gone to Australia for more supplies and for rams, which he bought in September 1845 from the Macarthur sheep station, reputed to be Australia's best. Clifford's merinos did much better in the hills of their new station at Flaxbourne and Stonyhurst than on the plains of Wairarapa. During this period of the partnership, Clifford had been living in Wellington and Weld at Flaxbourne, but, when Caverhill died in 1848, it became necessary for them to combine to live somewhere where the new manager could be supervised. Increasing native unrest persuaded them to give up Wairarapa and concentrate on Flaxbourne and Stonyhurst. This property had been bought in 1846. He had found the land to his liking and had agreed with the native owner to lease 'all the land from the Blind River to the East Coast round Cape Campbell to Kekerengu for £12 per annum'. This was between two and three hundred thousand acres, and obviously too big to handle, so in 1849 it was decreased considerably. The 'Nelson Government' in that year granted 66,000 acres freehold and 12,000 acres leasehold. In 1847 Clifford bought more stock for the new station from Australia.

By now Charles Clifford saw his future assured and sent to England for his fiancée. She was Marianne, daughter of John Hercy of Critchfield House in Berkshire. She brought with her a dowry of £8,000, an annuity and other property. Their son, George, was born on 10 October 1847.

In 1850 Charles Clifford returned to England, where he raised more money for the enterprise, which had suffered from a drop in wool prices after the Wellington earthquake. Though reduced in size Flaxbourne was still very large, and a lot of surveying had to be done. There was also a need for constant vigilance to prevent it being reduced in size further. After his return to New Zealand, Charles applied for the Stonyhurst run at the end of 1850, and the following year his partner, Frederick Weld, took his turn and sailed for England. On his return he brought his younger brother, Alphonso Weld, with him. Alphonso had brought £1,000 to set himself up, but, while he was with his brother and Clifford, he missed his way when rounding up sheep and lost 730 of them. Charles blamed Weld's map for this disaster, and in future, whenever it was necessary to move sheep long distances, they were driven to the coast and taken by ship.

There was another setback in 1853 when the new manager sent a cargo of greasy, unwashed wool to England, which naturally fetched a very low price. Further disasters occurred in 1855 following the Wellington earthquake. Charles's mother and father died within a short time of each other, and his family contracted scarlet fever, from which his three-year-old son, Aston, died. By this time Clifford was

62. Stonyhurst, New Zealand.

63. Portrait of Sir Frederick Weld, by
Venables.

64. Sir George Clifford with the Prince of
Wales at the races in New Zealand, 1920.

Speaker of the House of Representatives, and was therefore unable to return to England to settle his father's affairs. But the Weld-Clifford partnership continued to expand and to flourish, and in 1860 Charles decided to return to England and Weld entered the Colonial Service to become Governor of Western Australia in 1869. By this time, Charles wanted his son, George, to join the partnership, but Weld's wife opposed the idea so Clifford, as the senior partner, offered to buy Weld out. Weld asked a quarter of a million pounds, which was an enormously high price, but eventually the partnership was extended for a further ten years at the end of which Clifford was able to buy Weld out at valuation. Meanwhile George Clifford took over the running of Flaxbourne and Stonyhurst, which flourished. But the time came when the demand for land for small farmers threatened to break up the big sheep runs and in 1905 the Government took possession of Flaxbourne and 45,000 acres of it were sold and 12,500 acres of Stonyhurst were also sold to avoid graduated land tax.

Charles Clifford took a great interest in the political life of his adopted country, and when New Zealand was granted a constitution in 1852 he stood for Parliament and was elected M.P. for Wellington. He proposed himself for the office of Speaker, and was duly elected. It was a difficult post calling for great firmness and tact at a time when New Zealand politics and politicians were rough and tough. Clifford was elected Speaker again in 1857 and offered a knighthood. Beyond his Speaker's duties he took an interest in the local affairs of Wellington, and also in national education. In 1860 his active participation in politics came to an end, and he retired to live in England, but his links with the New Zealand Parliament remained, for he designed robes for the Speaker and Clerk of the House, and on a visit to New Zealand in 1871 he presented his portrait to the House. During the 1870s there was conflict with the Maoris over land rights, during which Clifford was called upon to act as an unofficial mediator between the New Zealand and British governments. In 1887 he was created a baronet in recognition of his services to New Zealand. He died on 27 February 1893, at the age of seventy-eight.

His partner, Frederick Weld, also had a distinguished career after leaving New Zealand, of which he was briefly prime minister.[3] He returned to England in 1871 at the age of 44, but soon returned to the antipodes as Governor of Western Australia, and later of Tasmania, where he was knighted. After leaving Tasmania in 1880 he undertook a prolonged tour of Malaya, which led to his appointment as Governor of the British Protectorates there. He died in England in July 1891. Together Sir Charles Clifford and Sir Frederick Weld helped to lay the foundations of New Zealand government. While Governor of Malaya, Sir Frederick recruited Hugh Clifford into the Colonial Service, to become one of its most distinguished governors. In his turn, Sir Hugh Clifford recruited Bede Clifford, yet another distinguished colonial administrator.

Chapter Fifty-Five

The New Zealand Cliffords after Sir Charles Clifford,
1st Baronet of Flaxbourne

We have seen in the last chapter that Sir Charles Clifford retired to England, sending his son, George, to New Zealand to run the estates. Sir Charles had five sons and a daughter by his wife Mary Hercy. George, the eldest, succeeded him as 2nd Baronet. He married three times; by his first wife, Mary, daughter of Sir James Lawson, he had no children; by his second, Janet Burnell of New Zealand, he had one son, Charles Lewis, 3rd Baronet, who died unmarried in 1938; and by his third wife, Helen Dennis, he had three daughters – Beatrice, born in 1892, married George Macdonald and had four sons and a daughter; Mary, who married Henry Douglas, to whose eldest son, John, the main New Zealand property, Stonyhurst, was left, and who added the name Clifford to his own; and Helen, who married Count J. Sapio and has issue.

When the third baronet died without issue in 1938 he was succeeded by his uncle Walter who had married Katherine Ball, by whom he had three daughters.

The first baronet's daughter Lucy Mary married Arthur Moore of Mooresfort, Co. Tipperary. They had a son, Charles, who served in the Irish Guards and became manager of the Queen's horses and lived at Hampton Court. He married Lady Dorothy Fielding, daughter of the Earl of Denbigh and his wife, Cecilia, daughter of the 8th Lord Clifford of Chudleigh. Their son, Arthur, the present owner of Mooresfoot, married a great-grand-daughter of Sir Henry Clifford V.C. Sir Charles Clifford's next son, Charles William, remained in England and lived at Market Drayton. By his first wife, Mary Chichester, he had a son who died in infancy, and by his second, Cecily, daughter of Sir Humphrey de Trafford, he had three sons and two daughters. The eldest son, Gilbert, who married Alice Calder, was killed in action in 1940. His second son, Lewis, was a Jesuit priest, a wartime army chaplain and later headmaster of Beaumont College. He succeeded as 5th Baronet on the death of his uncle Walter in 1944 and died himself in 1971. He was succeeded by his younger brother, Roger, as 6th Baronet. Sir Roger had gone to New Zealand in the late 1930s and served in the New Zealand Army during the war. He lived at Waikenai outside Wellington and married Henrietta Kiver by whom he had twin sons and a daughter. When he died, he was succeeded by his son Roger as 7th Baronet. Charles Clifford of Market Drayton's younger daughter, Rosamund, born in 1904, was a Senior Commander in the A.T.S. during the war, and Agnes, born in 1899, married Francis, later 6th Viscount Southwell, and died in 1981.

PART FIVE

OTHER BRANCHES OF THE CLIFFORDS

INTRODUCTION

This book would be incomplete without reference to other branches of the Clifford family, of which we shall consider no fewer than fourteen. It would, of course, be impossible to go into greater detail, but we shall attempt to give some idea of the origin and history of each of them. All the branches descend from Pons and subsequently from Walter Clifford of Clifford Castle (see Chapter Four), and each sub-branch has been taken back to an ancestor from the main line. Some of these branches died out through lack of male heirs; one, the Frampton branch, continues in the female line to the present day; another assumed the name of Clifford but died out; others have not been traced back far enough to establish a definitive starting point, but continue to the present day, and finally, there are other branches which have either no unequivocal beginning or end, such as the Northumberland and early Devon branches.

In order to summarise what follows the branches described in this part are shown below with the dates during which they are known to have flourished.

1. Frampton-on-Severn, through the male line 1200-1747
2. Frampton-on-Severn, through the female line 1684-
3. The Devon branch (unconnected with Chudleigh) 1215-1439
4. The Northumberland branch (unconnected with Westmorland) 1215-1396
5. The Brackenborough branch (a cadet line of Westmorland) 1437-1687
6. The Bobbing branch (connected with the Chudleigh line) 1438-1677
7. The Dutch branch (connected perhaps with Frampton) 1542-
8. The Sligo branch (connected perhaps with Westmorland) 1581-1713
9. The Stow-on-the-Wold branch 1598-
10. The Swindon (Gloucestershire) branch 1600-
11. The Annesley, Wexford and other Irish branches 1650-
12. The Perristone Cliffords 1760-1860
13. The Chestal Cliffords 1913-
14. Other Overseas Cliffords . . . . Various dates

Where final dates are given above, this means that research to date has been unable to trace further descendants with any degree of certainty.

Chapter Fifty-Six

The Cliffords of Frampton-on-Severn 1200-1747

Frampton-on-Severn was one of the Clifford holdings as early as the middle of the 12th century, and it came to Richard de Clifford, the son of Walter I, Baron of Clifford (1127-1187) in 1191. Richard, who died in 1213, married Leticia de Berkeley by whom he had three sons, Hugh, Richard and Henry. Frampton descended in the senior male line for another century, but around 1303, through lack of male heirs, it passed to John de Clifford, the great grandson of Henry, Richard's youngest son. In about 1360 Fretherne, the neighbouring manor, was added to Frampton, only to be sold, re-acquired and re-sold in later years.

It is not hard to trace the male line of descent from John, who was living in 1400, to Henry III, who died in 1558 (see the accompanying table), leaving four sons, James IV, George, John and William. By 1500 the Cliffords of Frampton also held the manor of Swindon, near Cheltenham, the manor of Woodmancote, and properties in Dursley, Fretherne, Saul, Arlingham and Framilode, all in the Severn Vale of Gloucestershire. The skeletal pedigree shows the line of descent to the middle of the 16th century, after which the family properties began to descend between the four families sired by Henry III. As none of the Cliffords from John, who was born in 1337, down to Henry III, who was born in 1516, were people of any importance there is little that can be said about them. They seem to have severed all connection with their ancestral home in Herefordshire and with their powerful northern kinsmen. Nor do they seem to have fallen into or out of favour with the dozen or so kings of England during this 220-year period. In fact so little is known about them as individuals that it is only when we begin to consider the families descending from James IV, George, John and William (families A, B, C and D respectively) that there is anything worthy of note to record.

James IV Clifford took over all the Frampton properties when he was a man of 24 in 1558. He was wealthy enough to seek a place at Court and he married well, in 1564, Dorothy, the daughter of Sir Charles Fox, by whom he had only one surviving child, a daughter, Mary, born about 1582. His appointment as one of Queen Elizabeth's Council of the March of Wales, besides becoming a Gentleman of the Privy Chamber, appears to have gone to his head, for he is known to have lived well beyond his means, so much so that by the time he died he was in debt to the tune of £20,000 and more. He built a large mansion at Fretherne in the hope that Queen Elizabeth would pay him a visit. She never did, but from all accounts he entertained the queen's favourite, Dudley, there on more than one occasion.

In an effort to retrieve the situation now that he was getting on in years and was so much in debt, he arranged for his only daughter, Mary, to marry Henry Clifford of Borscombe (see Chapter Thirty-Three). Although the marriage appears to have taken place, there was much rancour between Henry Clifford and his father-in-law

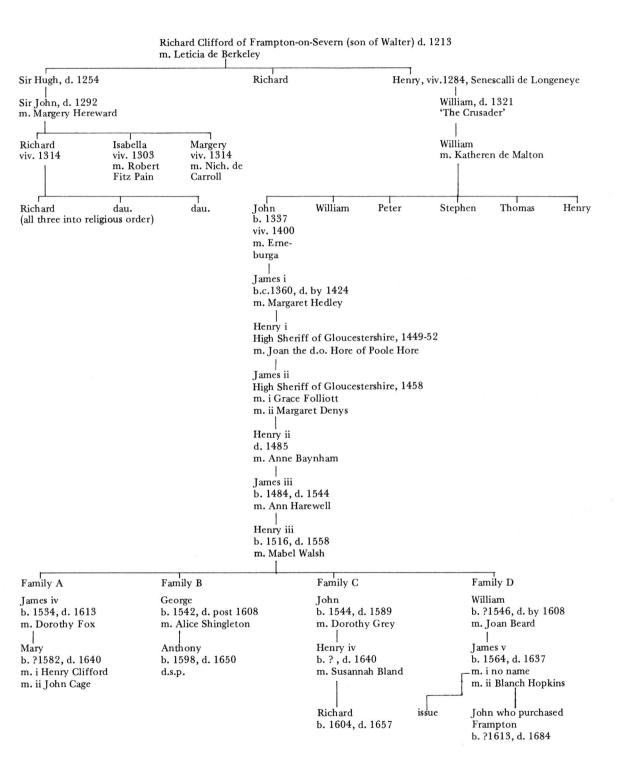

Richard Clifford of Frampton-on-Severn (son of Walter) d. 1213
m. Leticia de Berkeley

Sir Hugh, d. 1254   Richard   Henry, viv.1284, Senescalli de Longeneye

Sir John, d. 1292   William, d. 1321
m. Margery Hereward   'The Crusader'

Richard   Isabella   Margery   William
viv. 1314   viv. 1303   viv. 1314   m. Katheren de Malton
                 m. Robert   m. Nich. de
                 Fitz Pain   Carroll

Richard   dau.   dau.
(all three into religious order)

John   William   Peter   Stephen   Thomas   Henry
b. 1337
viv. 1400
m. Erne-
burga

James i
b.c.1360, d. by 1424
m. Margaret Hedley

Henry i
High Sheriff of Gloucestershire, 1449-52
m. Joan the d.o. Hore of Poole Hore

James ii
High Sheriff of Gloucestershire, 1458
m. i Grace Folliott
m. ii Margaret Denys

Henry ii
d. 1485
m. Anne Baynham

James iii
b. 1484, d. 1544
m. Ann Harewell

Henry iii
b. 1516, d. 1558
m. Mabel Walsh

Family A   Family B   Family C   Family D

James iv   George   John   William
b. 1534, d. 1613   b. 1542, d. post 1608 b. 1544, d. 1589   b. ?1546, d. by 1608
m. Dorothy Fox   m. Alice Shingleton   m. Dorothy Grey   m. Joan Beard

Mary   Anthony   Henry iv   James v
b. ?1582, d. 1640   b. 1598, d. 1650   b. ? , d. 1640   b. 1564, d. 1637
m. i Henry Clifford   d.s.p.   m. Susannah Bland   m. i no name
m. ii John Cage   m. ii Blanch Hopkins

                                              Richard   issue   John who purchased
                                              b. 1604, d. 1657   Frampton
                                                                            b. ?1613, d. 1684

The Cliffords of Frampton-on-Severn, Gloucestershire

to do with the marriage settlement, which led to the annulment of the marriage in the Ecclesiastical Court in 1609. The reason put forward was *causa frigiditatis*.

As James IV was still living when the marriage was annulled, he was clearly still concerned about the future of his estates, so he married Mary to John Cage, the son of a well-to-do London grocer, from whom he hoped for a large financial subvention, but it never materialised. Since Mary was unable to give her new husband any children, James left his estates to her for life with remainder to the surviving males of families B and C. James IV died on 10 June 1613, heavily in debt and mortgaged up to the hilt, which led to lengthy litigation. As Mary did not die until 1640 the property did not pass to the other Cliffords until after that date, when it came to Anthony Clifford of family B, but he died without issue in 1650, during which time he did what he could to pay off his uncle's debts and redeem the mortgages.

On the death of Anthony Clifford in 1650, what was left of the estate came to Richard of family C. But Richard Clifford's estates were in Northamptonshire so he arranged to sell Frampton to John Clifford of family D. John, however, died in 1684 without male issue, and, having purchased Frampton, the entail had been broken, which allowed him to bequeath it to one of his daughters. It is through his bequest to her son that the property descends to the present-day owners, although through the female line and two changes of surname since 1684, as is explained in the next chapter.

Although John Clifford was the last of the male line to occupy Frampton, this family continued through his half-brothers. James V, John's father, married twice. By his first wife he had two sons and three daughters; John was the only son of his second wife, Blanch Hopkins. The male Clifford line can be traced to 1730 from the two elder sons, after which research has so far failed to reveal further descendants. Similarly, Richard, of family C, had male issue to 1706, with cousins living in 1733.

Chapter Fifty-Seven

The Later Cliffords of Frampton-on-Severn (1684-)

The John Clifford of family D who bought Frampton in 1650 was a lawyer. His father, James V Clifford, was Rector of Swindon, Gloucestershire, and an executor of the will of his uncle James IV, a task the other two executors declined to take on in view of the difficulties they foresaw arising from the huge debts with which the estates were encumbered. John Clifford was therefore well aware of the situation, since his father had been involved in litigation in Chancery in connection with these tangled affairs. Who better, then, than John to purchase the estate? It is not known how much he paid, but it is safe to assume that the deal was a shrewd one. By purchasing the property, he not only helped to clear some of the debts but by this means broke the entail, so that it would not be necessary to leave it to a male heir of the Frampton line, of which, as we have already seen, there were several then living. By 1650, the date of the purchase, John Clifford had four daughters by his first wife, who died soon after, aged thirty-one. His second and third marriages were both childless, though he had an illegitimate son, 'Jackson', to whom he left a small legacy.

By the time John Clifford died in 1684, his eldest daughter, Mary, who had married Nathaniel Clutterbuck, had provided him with no fewer than 13 grandchildren, but as she had predeceased her father, he settled the estate on his grandson, William Clutterbuck, who can to all intents be regarded as the stem of the present-day Cliffords of Frampton.

William Clutterbuck was but a young boy when his grandfather died, besides which he had been orphaned only a few weeks before, as his own father had died in the same month as his grandfather, his mother having died in 1680. The Clutterbuck grandparents thereupon took the orphans and the estate under their wing until William came of age.

The accompanying skeletal pedigree shows the line of succession through nine generations to the present day, with two changes of surname in 1801 and 1943. The property passed through the female line in 1729, 1757 and 1917.

Before we leave John Clifford, it is worth noting that this branch of the Cliffords threw in their lot with Cromwell during the Civil War. John's half-brothers, both of whom were nonconformist ministers, seem to have taken an active part in ecclesiastical affairs during the Interregnum, and were later ejected from their parishes after the Restoration, and John Clifford himself was a puritan sympathiser. His will is also worthy of mention, for it reflects his sadness at having no male heir. He writes:

> And whereas providence hath so ordered it that after so many generations of our family at Frampton I am like to be the last of our name there (Kingdoms and Families have their periods) I leave it to the discretion of my executor and two daughters if they think fit to erect some decent monument thereof on the wall near my grave, the charges thereof not to exceed ten pounds.

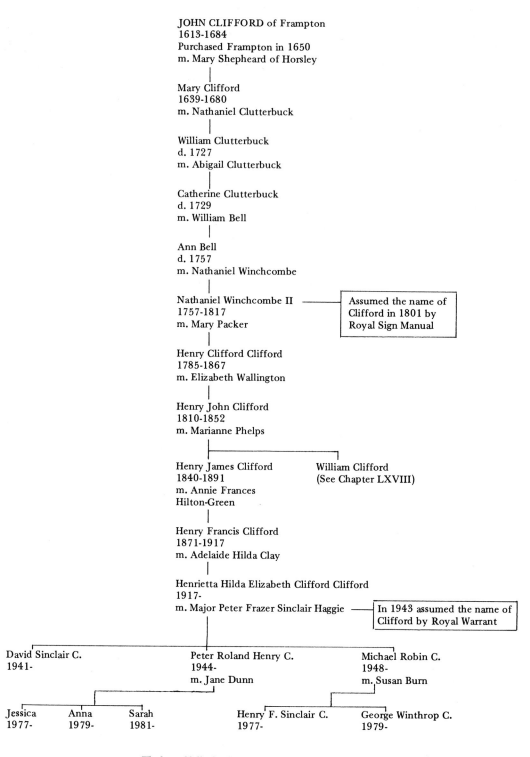

JOHN CLIFFORD of Frampton
1613-1684
Purchased Frampton in 1650
m. Mary Shepheard of Horsley

Mary Clifford
1639-1680
m. Nathaniel Clutterbuck

William Clutterbuck
d. 1727
m. Abigail Clutterbuck

Catherine Clutterbuck
d. 1729
m. William Bell

Ann Bell
d. 1757
m. Nathaniel Winchcombe

Nathaniel Winchcombe II ——— | Assumed the name of
1757-1817 | Clifford in 1801 by
m. Mary Packer | Royal Sign Manual

Henry Clifford Clifford
1785-1867
m. Elizabeth Wallington

Henry John Clifford
1810-1852
m. Marianne Phelps

Henry James Clifford   William Clifford
1840-1891   (See Chapter LXVIII)
m. Annie Frances
Hilton-Green

Henry Francis Clifford
1871-1917
m. Adelaide Hilda Clay

Henrietta Hilda Elizabeth Clifford Clifford
1917-
m. Major Peter Frazer Sinclair Haggie ——— | In 1943 assumed the name of
                                            | Clifford by Royal Warrant

David Sinclair C.   Peter Roland Henry C.   Michael Robin C.
1941-   1944-   1948-
                           m. Jane Dunn   m. Susan Burn

Jessica   Anna   Sarah   Henry F. Sinclair C.   George Winthrop C.
1977-   1979-   1981-   1977-   1979-

The later Cliffords of Frampton-on-Severn, Gloucestershire

It will be seen from the pedigree that the estates descended from 1684 through William Clutterbuck's daughter and granddaughter to Nathaniel Winchcombe II, who assumed the name of Clifford by Royal Sign Manual in 1801. A second change of surname became necessary after Henry Francis Clifford (1871-1917) was killed in Palestine whilst on active service soon after his marriage to Adelaide Hilda Clay. His only and posthumous daughter was christened Henrietta Hilda Elizabeth Clifford Clifford, and, shortly after her marriage to Major Peter Frazer Sinclair Haggie of the 14th/20th King's Hussars, he obtained permission, by Royal Warrant in 1943, to assume the surname of Clifford. In 1957 permission was also granted to him to use the Clifford arms, checky or and azure with a bend gules, with three lioncels rampant of the first.

Another branch of this Frampton Clifford line, subsequent to the 1801 assumption of the surname, lives in Canada. The Chestal Cliffords, another cadet branch of this Frampton line, is described in Chapter Sixty-Eight.

Chapter Fifty-Eight

The Cliffords of Devonshire (1215-1439)

The Devonshire branch of the Clifford family – namely the branch which did not own Ugbrooke – descends from Sir Giles Clifford, the fifth and youngest son of Walter, 2nd Baron of Clifford (d. 1221) (see Chapter Six), and his wife, Agnes de Condet (Cundy), who was probably born about 1215. He is known to have married Eva, the daughter and heiress of Reginald Alba Monasterio (Whiteabbey), and the widow of William de Champernoun, by whom she had a daughter, Joan. By Eva, Sir Giles de Clifford had a son, Reginald, named after his father-in-law. After Eva's death in 1255 Sir Giles married Alice, the widow of Wymond de Ralegh, who had himself died the same year. By her Giles had another son, Giles, who took holy orders and became the vicar of Stoke-in-Teignhead. Some documents suggest that Sir Giles's first wife was called Juliana, but nothing is known of her, or whether she was identical to, or previous to Eva. It is also thought that Sir Giles may have had three other sons, Richard, William and John, all of whom were alive in 1274, with John a Canon of Exeter from 1277 to 1281.

Besides his estates in Devonshire, Sir Giles held lands in Lincolnshire, Northamptonshire, Berkshire and Wiltshire. His Devonshire properties included the manors of Columbjohn, Everleigh, Combe-in-Teignhead and Godford. His eldest son, Sir Reginald, was probably born about 1257 and was living in 1317. His appointment as Overlord in Devon in 1293 is recorded in *The Knights of Edward I*. His wife's name is unknown, but he had no less than five sons and three daughters by her. Walter, his youngest son, was a cleric and so, probably, was his third, Reginald, who was parson of Combe-in-Teignhead. Peter, his second, and Nicholas, his third son, inherited Rocombe and Godford, near Honiton, respectively. His eldest son, Sir John de Clifford, had two sons who died in childhood, so his estates passed to his daughter, Elizabeth, and through her to the Prideaux family. His second son, Peter, married Isabel de Brenta, heir to Netherton, near Newton Abbot, by whom he had a son, likewise named Peter (II). After Isabel's death, Peter the elder married Joan, the daughter of Sir William Bigbury, shortly before he died, when Joan remarried Roger de Prideaux, the son of Elizabeth Clifford, Sir John's daughter, her former husband's niece.

Nicholas Clifford, Sir Reginald's fourth son, does not appear to have left any male heirs, so this Devonshire branch was continued by Peter the younger, who inherited Godford from his uncle and Netherton from his mother.

Peter the younger was succeeded by another Peter (III) who was an esquire in the Earl of Devon's household in 1384. He may have had two other sons, Richard and Thomas, both alive in 1418, but this is not certain. Peter III died in 1386 and was succeeded by his son, John, who was then under age, but little more than this is known about him. There were several other Cliffords in Devonshire about this time

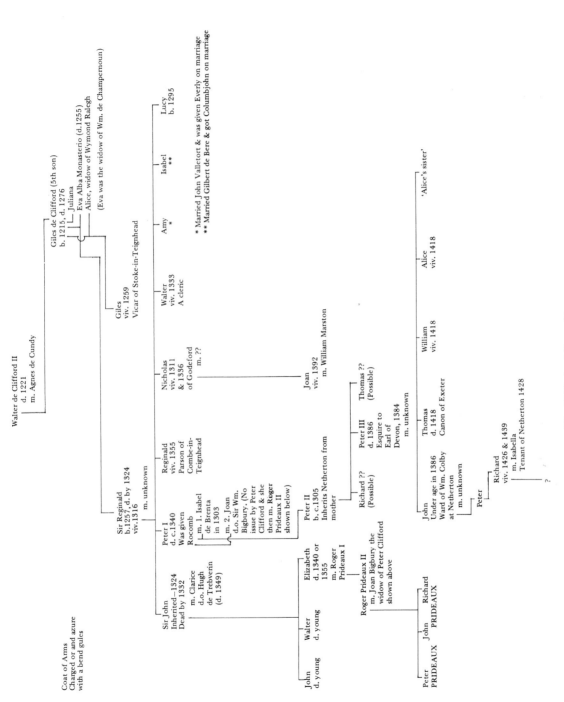

The Cliffords of Devonshire

who may have been related to Peter III. They are Thomas, a Canon of Exeter, William, Alice and a sister married to a Lennoy, all of whom are mentioned in the Canon's will made in 1418. John, who succeeded Peter III, is presumed to have had a son, Peter IV, and a grandson, Richard, who was a tenant at Netherton in 1428. Richard is known to have married a wife called Isabella, but it has not been possible to continue this line of descent any further.

The Prideaux family inherited the bulk of Sir Giles de Clifford's estates, and as the remaining Cliffords had little or no property to hand on to their heirs, there are no Inquisitions post Mortem relating to them, from which to reconstruct a pedigree.

There was a Nicholas Clifford who was Deputy Admiral of the West in 1380 and King's Admiral of the West in 1392, who might just possibly be Sir Reginald's fourth son, but, since that Nicholas was aged 21 in 1332, he would have been over eighty in 1392, so the admiral may have been his son or nephew.[1]

Clifford and Clifford Bridge on the edge of Dartmoor are named after this branch of the family.

Chapter Fifty-Nine

The Cliffords of Ellingham, Northumberland (1208-1396)

The origin of this branch of the Cliffords is not known. A Robert de Clifford obtained land from the brothers Adam and Alexander de Horde (Ord) by a deed sealed between 1197 and 1208. This Robert was appointed Sheriff of Norham in 1214 and held that office until 1226, in which year he became Sheriff of Northumberland, and was styled Robert de Clifford of Murton, near Ord in Islandshire (near Berwick-upon-Tweed). He is known to have married Mabel, the daughter of Ralph de Gaugy the younger, Baron of Ellingham, and it is by virtue of this that these Cliffords came to be styled as 'of Ellingham'.

Murton is in the old shire of Islandshire just south of Berwick, and the barony of Ellingham originally consisted of lands in Ellingham, Doxford, Osberwick (now known as Newstead), Cramlington, Heaton, Hartley, Jesmond and Whitelaws. Whether or not this branch descends from the Cliffords of Clifford Castle is impossible to establish with certainty, but, if Robert of Murton was of full age in 1214, he must have been born in the 1190s at the latest, which could make him a son or grandson of Walter Clifford I (1116-90). The fact that they sealed their deeds in 1296 and 1344 with 'three eagles displayed', as is evident from those in the archives at Durham, and did not use the chequy or and azure with either a bend or fesse, makes it even more difficult to ascertain their correct lineage. The effigy on the tomb of Robert Clifford of Kent, the brother of Bishop Richard Clifford as shown in Chapter Fourteen, shows Robert bearing arms with three eagles displayed alongside the chequy arms, which makes it appear there was a connection between the Ellingham Cliffords and the family of Robert, 3rd Lord Clifford (1305-44) at any rate. As the Eaglesfield and Strother families also bore three eagles displayed during the 13th and 14th centuries one has to ask oneself if there is not a link between these Cliffords and either of those two families which prompted the use of such similar arms.

The Ellingham Cliffords can be traced through five generations, as the accompanying pedigree shows, from Robert of Murton to Robert V, John and Thomas. So can the descent of the barony of Ellingham, which originally belonged to the Grenvilles up to 1162, then to the de Gaugy family and afterwards to the Cliffords until 1366. In that year the lands were forfeited after John de Clifford murdered John de Coupland in December 1363, when all the lands were given to Joan de Coupland as compensation.[1] John had no male issue, but as these lands had been forfeited there were no Inquisitions post Mortem when he and his younger brother, Thomas, died, so there is no record of the next heir or heiress.

The more northerly the estate the more prone it was to the depredations of the Scots, and for much of the time those portions in Clifford hands were said to be of little or no value. John de Clifford made good use of the border as is shown by the following account of the Coupland murder.

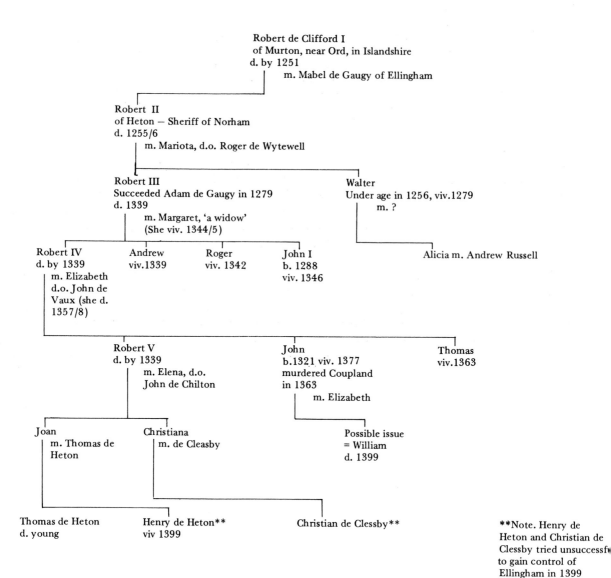

Robert de Clifford I
of Murton, near Ord, in Islandshire
d. by 1251

m. Mabel de Gaugy of Ellingham

Robert II
of Heton — Sheriff of Norham
d. 1255/6

m. Mariota, d.o. Roger de Wytewell

Robert III
Succeeded Adam de Gaugy in 1279
d. 1339

m. Margaret, 'a widow'
(She viv. 1344/5)

Walter
Under age in 1256, viv.1279
m. ?

Robert IV
d. by 1339
m. Elizabeth
d.o. John de
Vaux (she d.
1357/8)

Andrew
viv.1339

Roger
viv. 1342

John I
b. 1288
viv. 1346

Alicia m. Andrew Russell

Robert V
d. by 1339

m. Elena, d.o.
John de Chilton

John
b.1321 viv. 1377
murdered Coupland
in 1363

m. Elizabeth

Thomas
viv.1363

Joan
m. Thomas de
Heton

Christiana
m. de Cleasby

Possible issue
= William
d. 1399

Thomas de Heton
d. young

Henry de Heton**
viv 1399

Christian de Clessby**

**Note. Henry de
Heton and Christian de
Clessby tried unsuccessfu
to gain control of
Ellingham in 1399

This family of Cliffords used 'Three Eagles Displayed' as their coat of arms and seal in 1296 and 1344.
A Richard de Clifford sealed a deed concerning Northallerton in 1328 with these three eagles but with
a fesse.

The Cliffords of Ellingham, Northumberland

On Wednesday the vigil of St Thomas the apostle, John de Clifford, knight, Thomas his brother, Thomas Forster, his servant, Robert Huchounson, William de Vaus, Alan de Fenwick a Scot, John Prestesson and others (named) with five pages, nine being armed with lances and 11 being archers, lay in wait at Bolton Moor for the arrival of John de Coupland from the south, and feloniously killed him and Nicholas Bagot of Newcastle-on-Tyne by a premeditated assault. So far as the jurors know, no person was procurer hereof; nor did anybody receive the felons thereafter, because they at once fled to Scotland.

Later John de Clifford was pardoned when Richard II came to the throne in 1377, but by then his forfeited lands had been sold by Joan de Coupland, so he does not seem to have been fully reinstated, which makes tracing his descendants difficult. There is evidence, however, which suggests that in 1399 descendants of his elder brother, Robert V de Clifford, through the female line tried unsuccessfully to regain the manor of Ellingham, but the exact reason for this claim has not been ascertained.

Although there is a gap in the story of these lands, another Robert de Clifford, as yet unplaced in the pedigrees, married a Jacoba de Emeldon before 1380, who, as part of her own inheritance, held Jesmond, part of the barony of Ellingham. How Jacoba came to be in possession of these lands does not concern us here, but there is some slight evidence to support the thesis that this Robert Clifford was none other than Robert the Sheriff of Kent, whose tomb, since destroyed, in Canterbury carried the eight coats of arms as described in Chapter Fourteen.

Chapter Sixty

The Brackenborough Cliffords (1437-1687)

This branch of the family was a cadet branch of the main Westmorland Cliffords, stemming from Robert Clifford, the younger brother of John Clifford, The Butcher, who was killed at Towton in 1461 (see Chapter Nineteen). Robert's parents were Thomas, 8th Lord Clifford (1414-55), and Joan Dacre and he was born about 1440 and was their third son. His career and those of his descendants have already been described in Chapter Nineteen. This branch died out in 1687 through lack of male heirs with the death in that year of Ursula Clifford, a recusant.

It will be remembered that Henry Clifford, 2nd Earl of Cumberland, drew up an entail in 1555 (see Chapter Twenty-Three) in which Thomas and George Clifford, the sons of Sir Thomas and Helen Clifford, are given as possible successors to his estates should there not be sufficient male heirs. As it turned out neither had male heirs in 1642, when Henry, 5th Earl of Cumberland died, suitable to inherit. The word 'suitable' is important, for, as the accompanying pedigree shows, there was a male heir living at that date, William, who did not die until 1670. Technically he might have claimed the earldom and the estates, but he was a priest living in Paris. In 1643 he was already approaching fifty, and obviously had no ambitions to take on such heavy responsibilities; the fact that he lived another 26 years is beside the point. As a Catholic priest there was no prospect of an heir. The letter he wrote to Lady Anne Clifford in 1664, quoted in Chapter Nineteen, is clearly replying to her offer to take on the mantle which he respectfully appears to decline.

It is perhaps worth speculating at this point about the Catholic tradition in the family. Thomas Clifford, 1st Lord Clifford of Chudleigh, did not convert to Rome until 1673 (see Chapter Thirty-Six) yet his Brackenborough kinsmen had clearly adhered to the old faith as William and his niece, Ursula, bear witness.

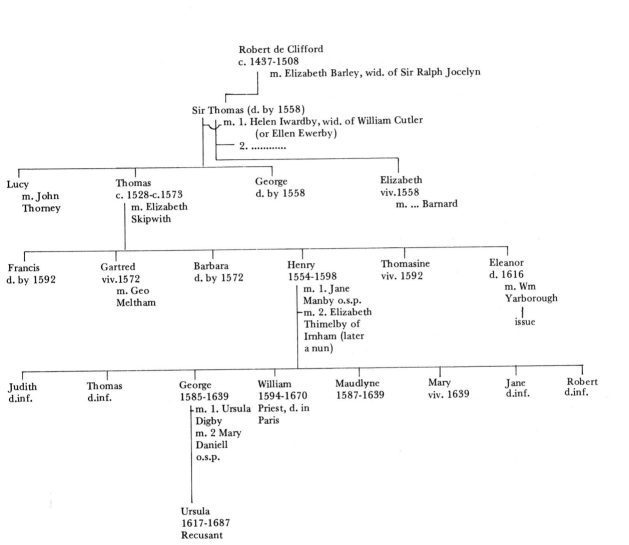

Robert de Clifford
c. 1437-1508
m. Elizabeth Barley, wid. of Sir Ralph Jocelyn

Sir Thomas (d. by 1558)
m. 1. Helen Iwardby, wid. of William Cutler
(or Ellen Ewerby)
2. ....

Lucy
m. John
Thorney

Thomas
c. 1528-c.1573
m. Elizabeth
Skipwith

George
d. by 1558

Elizabeth
viv.1558
m. ... Barnard

Francis
d. by 1592

Gartred
viv.1572
m. Geo
Meltham

Barbara
d. by 1572

Henry
1554-1598
m. 1. Jane
Manby o.s.p.
m. 2. Elizabeth
Thimelby of
Irnham (later
a nun)

Thomasine
viv. 1592

Eleanor
d. 1616
m. Wm
Yarborough

issue

Judith
d.inf.

Thomas
d.inf.

George
1585-1639
m. 1. Ursula
Digby
m. 2 Mary
Daniell
o.s.p.

William
1594-1670
Priest, d. in
Paris

Maudlyne
1587-1639

Mary
viv. 1639

Jane
d.inf.

Robert
d.inf.

Ursula
1617-1687
Recusant

The Cliffords of Brackenborough, Linclonshire

Chapter Sixty-One

The Cliffords of Bobbing, Kent (1438-1677)

The Cliffords of Bobbing, near Sittingbourne in Kent, were close kin to the Cliffords of Borscombe, from whom the Cliffords of Chudleigh descend. They were, in fact, senior to the Chudleigh line for they stemmed from Lewis, the eldest son of William Clifford (see Chapter Twenty-Eight), the grandson of Thomas Clifford, Lord of Thomond, while the Borscombe-Chudleigh Cliffords descend from his youngest brother, John. They were not particularly distinguished during the century and a half which followed Lewis, who died some time before 1438, and it was only during the reign of Elizabeth I that some of them achieved knighthood for services to the Crown. The branch appears to have died out with Martin Clifford in 1677, but it has to be said that the descendants of his great-uncle, Henry Clifford, who died in 1599, and who had three sons, have not been traced, and may, perhaps, survive.

The Bobbing branch is said to have borne arms chequy or and sable, a fesse and bordure gules and on the fesse a crescent argent quartered with the arms of Savage. This presents us, if accurate, with a puzzle, and one wonders if, indeed, it can be correct, for all the other Cliffords bore chequy or and azure. The addition of the crescent is of interest, for it indicates descent from a second son. This is possible if the line is taken back beyond the William at the head of the attached pedigree, for he was the son of Hugh, who was a younger son of Thomas Clifford of Thomond, third son of Robert, 3rd Baron Clifford (1305-44) (see Chapters Fourteen and Twenty-Eight). Thus the Bobbing line can be said to descend from a younger son, though we cannot be absolutely certain that Hugh was Thomas's second son and thus senior to Lewis, Robert and Bishop Richard.

The attached pedigree does not at first sight indicate the importance of this branch of the family until one examines more closely the wives, who all came from leading county families. For instance, Ann Molyns was the daughter of Lord Molyns and the marriage established kinship with the Earl of Arundel and the Earl of Huntingdon. The Culpepers and Bournes were landed gentry similar to the Cliffords; Mary Harpur was the daughter of Sir George Harpur; Ann Stafford was the daughter of Henry Lord Stafford, Earl of Wiltshire. Sir Conyers Clifford's wife, Mary Southwell of Wymondham Hall in Norfolk, was the widow of Thomas Sidney of Wiken, and after Sir Conyers' death she married Sir Anthony St Leger, a prominent Kentish man.

Turning now to some of the above it will be seen that Nicholas Clifford, who married Mary Harpur, had no male issue, so that Bobbing reverted to his brother, Richard and his heirs, and ultimately to the descendants of his elder son, George. Of Richard's three grandsons to receive knighthoods, Sir Alexander, Sir Conyers and Sir Nicholas, the date of birth of the first is not known. Alexander was the second son of his father's 11 children, and was knighted at Cadiz in 1596 (see Chapter Twenty-Four) and appears to have been a vice-admiral in command of the

Dreadnought during that encounter. We next find him commanding a unit of infantry during the Munster war in 1601, and he seems to have stayed in Ireland till 1603 for he received an allowance of £2 for entertainment[1] and was listed among the captains and officers lately discharged. Since his aunt was Anne Devereux, we may suppose that his appointment in Ireland at this time had something to do with Robert Devereux, Earl of Essex, the queen's favourite, soon to be executed for treason. Sir Alexander Clifford died in 1621 and was survived by his wife but his son had predeceased him, apparently without issue.

Sir Conyers Clifford was born in 1563 and knighted in 1591 after distinguishing himself at the siege of Rouen. He also served at Cadiz with his brother, Alexander, in the capacity of sergeant-major of troops in 1596. In 1597 he was appointed president of the province of Connaught in Ireland, where he was to be killed by the rebels under the command of O'Rourke when he and his troops were ambushed in the Carlow mountains in December 1599. In 1593 he was elected M.P. for Pembroke and two years later was made an honorary Master of Arts of Cambridge University. By his wife, Mary Southwell he left two sons, and as she was to marry again and have another son, Anthony St Leger, the Bobbing property was left to all three boys. This division of the estate resulted in much of it being sold, and as his sons were very young when their father was killed, they did not inherit for many years, by which time the disintegration of the estate was far advanced.

Sir Nicholas Clifford, cousin of Alexander and Conyers, had a somewhat checkered history, for he was a prisoner in the Tower in 1594, though for what reason has not been discovered. His only real claim to fame is that he was killed by the same cannon ball which knocked Sir Francis Drake off his stool in 1596 in the West Indies. To perpetuate his memory it would appear that a ship was launched and named after him some years later. The only clue to his imprisonment in the Tower comes from the Irish State Papers.[2] In 1592 Captain Nicholas Clifford was commanding a unit which was found to contain spies who were reporting back fo the Prince of Parma and Sir William Stanley. Nicholas was in the Tower in the custody of Sir Michael Blount in April 1594, and this may have been the reason.

The apparently last member of this line, Martin Clifford, had a distinguished and adventurous career. He was born in 1624 and named after his grandfather Bishop Martin Fotherby, Bishop of Salisbury, Fellow of Trinity College, Cambridge and author of a theological work entitled *Atheomastix*, published in 1622 and not much read these days. Martin Clifford was educated at Westminster School and Cambridge, where he obtained his B.A. in 1643. After this not much is known about him for certain, but 'after the Restoration he hung about town, mainly supported by the dissolute noblemen of the court, among whom his licentious tastes and powers of buffoonery were especially acceptable'.[3]

A Martin Clifford appears as a headright supporting the claim for a grant of land in Virginia in November 1654 by Francis Hamon (or Hamond). In early Virginia emigrants were entitled to 50 acres of land each time they crossed the Atlantic, but if their passage was paid for by someone else, that person was entitled to it instead. Since the more wealthy planters tended to wait until they had a fair number of such headrights, and since all the emigrants did not come out together, it is not uncommon to find that grants, supported by lists of headrights, were made anything

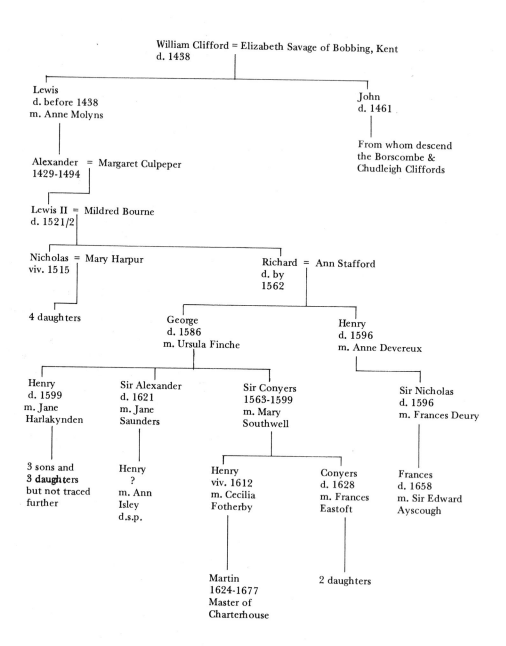

William Clifford = Elizabeth Savage of Bobbing, Kent
d. 1438

Lewis
d. before 1438
m. Anne Molyns

John
d. 1461

From whom descend
the Borscombe &
Chudleigh Cliffords

Alexander = Margaret Culpeper
1429-1494

Lewis II = Mildred Bourne
d. 1521/2

Nicholas = Mary Harpur
viv. 1515

Richard = Ann Stafford
d. by
1562

4 daughters

George
d. 1586
m. Ursula Finche

Henry
d. 1596
m. Anne Devereux

Henry
d. 1599
m. Jane
Harlakynden

Sir Alexander
d. 1621
m. Jane
Saunders

Sir Conyers
1563-1599
m. Mary
Southwell

Sir Nicholas
d. 1596
m. Frances Deury

3 sons and
3 daughters
but not traced
further

Henry
?
m. Ann
Isley
d.s.p.

Henry
viv. 1612
m. Cecilia
Fotherby

Conyers
d. 1628
m. Frances
Eastoft

Frances
d. 1658
m. Sir Edward
Ayscough

Martin
1624-1677
Master of
Charterhouse

2 daughters

The Cliffords of Bobbing, Kent

up to ten years after the emigrant or emigrants listed had come over to the colony, usually, but not always, as indentured servants. Francis Hamond's claim was for 2,000 acres in York County, and is dated 1 November 1654. It was situated on the south bank of the Mattaponi river in what is now King William County, and was close to the plantation of Edward Digges. Francis Hamond, a Kentish man, had married Frances Digges, the daughter of Sir Dudley Digges of Chilham, in 1633, and sister of Edward Digges, who was appointed Governor of Virginia during the Commonwealth, and served from 1655 to 1658. It is known that Digges recruited his settlers in Kent, and Hamond seems to have done the same. We cannot be certain that the Martin Clifford who appears as Hamond's headright is identical with Martin Clifford of the Bobbing branch, but it is significant that he is not recorded as having taken out a patent for land of his own, so he may only have spent a short time in Virginia, and have gone there in his youth after he left Cambridge.

That Martin Clifford must have been a favourite of Charles II is clear, and his friendship with the Duke of Buckingham resulted in his election as Master of Charterhouse, or Sutton Hospital as it was then also called. He died on 12 December 1677, while still holding this appointment, and was buried in the chancel of St Margaret's, Westminster. One is left wondering how he got on with his distant cousin, Thomas, 1st Lord Clifford of Chudleigh, whom he must certainly have known at Court. Unfortunately it has not yet been possible to discover whether he married and had issue, but maybe a reader of this book has been able to trace his ancestry back to him. We would like to know. There is no evidence to support the view that other Cliffords in early Virginia, of which there were a Henry, John and Oliver, who were headrights of planters in Northumberland County in 1664, New Kent County in 1658 and Elizabeth City, York County, in 1640 respectively. Of these, John's master, Edward Lockey, was a neighbour of Edward Digges and Francis Hamond, so it is possible that he was a close kinsman of Martin. A Robert Clifford had a grant of 320 acres in partnership with John Easterly in New Kent County in 1683, and his land was adjacent to that of Edward Lockey. The land had originally been granted to John Maddison in 1664 and sold to Isaac Collier who deserted it. This Robert, too, may be connected with John and Martin or one of them. Further research in Virginia might reveal whether either of them left descendants.

The Calendar of State Papers (Domestic) for the years 1655-6 contains a letter from Thomas Ross or Roe to Sir Edward Nicholas, Charles II's secretary. It is in cipher and contains the cryptic sentence '... Albert might find a way by Mart Clifford or some other to feel his (Sir George Aysane's) pulse'. This is most interesting, for Charles II was in Middelburg and Bruges at this time, and Sir Edward Nicholas was with him. The letter also refers to the 'King's pleasure', all of which suggests that the Mart Clifford in question was closely connected with the exiled English court.

If this is the same as the Martin Clifford who was a headright in Virginia in 1654 (and there is evidence from contemporary passenger lists that a Martin Clifford went to Virginia that year), then it is clear that his stay in America was a brief one. Virginia remained throughout the Civil War and afterwards staunchly Royalist, and from these scraps, and the fact that Martin Clifford was known to be a favourite of the king and a friend of the Duke of Buckingham, it is possible to suggest that he may have played a part in ensuring the colony's loyalty to the Crown.

Chapter Sixty-Two

The Dutch Cliffords (1542-)

In 1740, George Clifford of the Dutch branch of the family approached the College of Arms for a pedigree and grant of arms, and in due course he was told that he descended from Henry Clifford, Rector of Landbeach, Cambridgeshire, which he may already have known, and that his ancestor had been born at Aylsham in Norfolk in 1542. But the College genealogist was in some doubt about Henry's origins, for in his certificate he merely suggested that the Rector might have been the second son of Henry Clifford of Borscombe, by his second wife, Elizabeth Carrant (see Chapter Thirty-Two). This has now been disproved on two grounds: first, the Henry Clifford/Elizabeth Carrant marriage took place in 1547, five years after the Rector's known year of birth, and their son Henry was not born until 1548. The Rector's year of birth is proved by his marriage in 1569 and his matriculation at Cambridge University in 1559. Secondly, Henry Clifford of Borscombe has been traced in a deed of 1562 to Ven House in the parish of Milborne Port in Somerset, where many of his children were baptised, none of whom correspond with those of the Rector of Landbeach. A third discovery, which points in the true direction of the Rector's origins, is the memorial to his son, Philip Clifford (1589-1638), Rector of Fordingbridge, Hampshire, on which are engraved the arms of the Cliffords of Frampton-on-Severn, which are quite different from those of the Cliffords of Borscombe. This means that the Dutch branch almost certainly descends from the Frampton branch, though it does not tell us whose son the Rector of Landbeach may have been. Datewise he might have been the twin brother of George of Family B (see Chapter Fifty-Six), who was also born in 1542, the son of Henry III. It is, perhaps, worth pointing out in support of this guess that the names Henry, John and George are found in the Rector's family as well as in Families B and C of the Frampton branch.

The attached skeletal pedigree brings the Dutch line down to the present day. It will be noted that the baronial line has now died out for lack of male heirs, but there still remain many other Dutch Cliffords living today.

The coat of arms issued by the College of Arms in 1740 shows chequy or and azure with a fesse gules. This is natural in view of the (erroneous) belief that the family descended from the Cliffords of Borscombe. In fact it should have been chequy or and azure with a bend gules, the arms of the Frampton branch. On the fesse the College placed a crescent in the belief that the Rector was a second son, but on either side of the crescent they put a six-pointed star or estoile for difference. They gave as supporters a wyvern and a chained monkey, the former being an ancient Clifford supporter and the latter a reference to the family's connection with the Dutch East Indies.

Up to at least 1639 this branch continued in East Anglia, and it was the Rector's grandson, George (1623-80), who went to Holland some time between 1634 and 1640, where he died. Could it be that the Dutch connection had something to do with the presence of so many Dutchmen in and around Landbeach at this time, when the great level of the fens was being drained by men like Andrew Bocard, John Corsellis, Lukas van Valckenberg, Samuel van Peenen, Jacob Cats, Pieter Cruypenninck, Joachim Liens, Edward van Dussen, Jan von Goch and above all Cornelius Vermuyden? Perhaps a closer examination of the records of these enterprises might provide an answer. At all events, George, the migrant's grandson and namesake, had qualified as a lawyer at Leiden University and was a member of a banking firm, George Clifford & Son. It was he who applied to the College for a grant of arms, and it was he who established the famous horticultural gardens of his country estate at Hartekamp, importing rare and exotic plants by virtue of his contacts with the United East India Company in which his son, Pieter (1712-88), was an Administrator. The gardens were placed under the supervision of Linnaeus, who wrote up the collection in his *Hortus Cliffortianus*, and these gardens are an attraction to the present day. Other members of the family held high office in Holland, and in 1874 Hendrik Maurits was created Baron Clifford. His wife, Anna Fredericka, Countess of Limburg-Stirum, was a member of one of the most distinguished families in Holland.

The custom in Holland of incorporating the mother's name, where one branch of a family needs to be differenced from another, means that the Dutch Cliffords are now known as Oetgens van Waveren Pancras Clifford. A study of the attached pedigrees will explain how this has come about.[1]

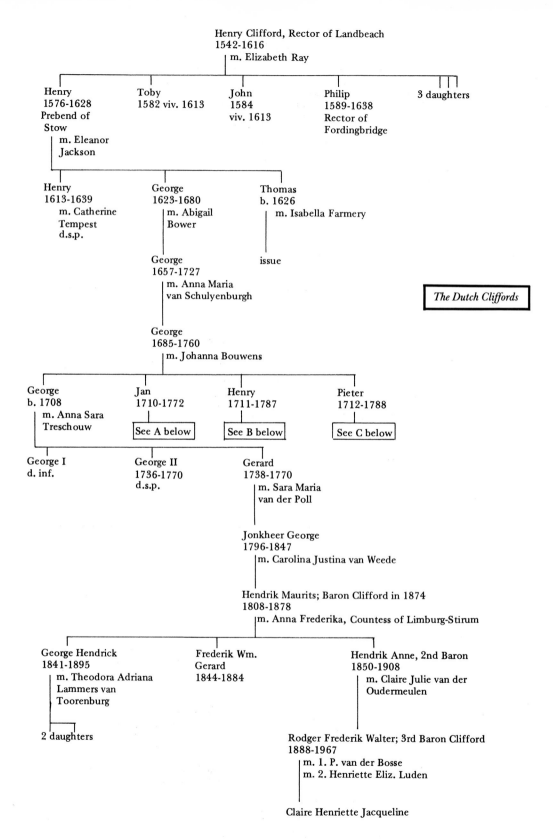

Henry Clifford, Rector of Landbeach
1542-1616
m. Elizabeth Ray

Henry
1576-1628
Prebend of
Stow
m. Eleanor
Jackson

Toby
1582 viv. 1613

John
1584
viv. 1613

Philip
1589-1638
Rector of
Fordingbridge

3 daughters

Henry
1613-1639
m. Catherine
Tempest
d.s.p.

George
1623-1680
m. Abigail
Bower

Thomas
b. 1626
m. Isabella Farmery

George
1657-1727
m. Anna Maria
van Schulyenburgh

issue

The Dutch Cliffords

George
1685-1760
m. Johanna Bouwens

George
b. 1708
m. Anna Sara
Treschouw

Jan
1710-1772

See A below

Henry
1711-1787

See B below

Pieter
1712-1788

See C below

George I
d. inf.

George II
1736-1770
d.s.p.

Gerard
1738-1770
m. Sara Maria
van der Poll

Jonkheer George
1796-1847
m. Carolina Justina van Weede

Hendrik Maurits; Baron Clifford in 1874
1808-1878
m. Anna Frederika, Countess of Limburg-Stirum

George Hendrick
1841-1895
m. Theodora Adriana
Lammers van
Toorenburg

Frederik Wm.
Gerard
1844-1884

Hendrik Anne, 2nd Baron
1850-1908
m. Claire Julie van der
Oudermeulen

2 daughters

Rodger Frederik Walter; 3rd Baron Clifford
1888-1967
m. 1. P. van der Bosse
m. 2. Henriette Eliz. Luden

Claire Henriette Jacqueline

Note 1: The Baronial Line dies out for want of male heir in 1967, as shown above
Note 2: Families of Jan, Henry and Pieter, as in A, B and C above, follow

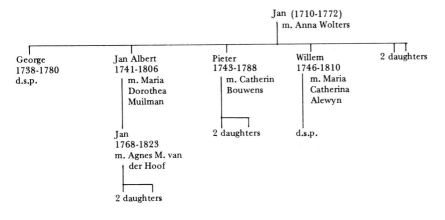

Jan (1710-1772)
m. Anna Wolters

George
1738-1780
d.s.p.

Jan Albert
1741-1806
m. Maria
Dorothea
Muilman

Pieter
1743-1788
m. Catherin
Bouwens

Willem
1746-1810
m. Maria
Catherina
Alewyn

2 daughters

Jan
1768-1823
m. Agnes M. van
der Hoof

2 daughters

d.s.p.

2 daughters

Note: For lack of male heir this line has died out

B

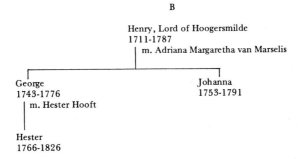

Henry, Lord of Hoogersmilde
1711-1787
m. Adriana Margaretha van Marselis

George
1743-1776
m. Hester Hooft

Johanna
1753-1791

Hester
1766-1826

Note: For lack of male heir this line has died out

C

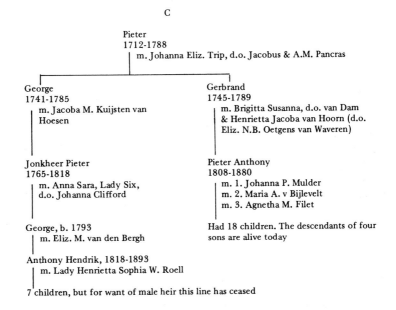

Pieter
1712-1788
m. Johanna Eliz. Trip, d.o. Jacobus & A.M. Pancras

George
1741-1785
m. Jacoba M. Kuijsten van
Hoesen

Gerbrand
1745-1789
m. Brigitta Susanna, d.o. van Dam
& Henrietta Jacoba van Hoorn (d.o.
Eliz. N.B. Oetgens van Waveren)

Jonkheer Pieter
1765-1818
m. Anna Sara, Lady Six,
d.o. Johanna Clifford

Pieter Anthony
1808-1880
m. 1. Johanna P. Mulder
m. 2. Maria A. v Bijlevelt
m. 3. Agnetha M. Filet

George, b. 1793
m. Eliz. M. van den Bergh

Had 18 children. The descendants of four
sons are alive today

Anthony Hendrik, 1818-1893
m. Lady Henrietta Sophia W. Roell

7 children, but for want of male heir this line has ceased

Chapter Sixty-Three

The Cliffords of Sligo, Ireland (1581-1713)

To bring in at this point an account of the Sligo branch of the family, covering as it does less than a century and a half, might be confusing, but, having listed the various branches in chronological order, this seems the place to fit it in. Although it has not been possible yet to trace this branch beyond 1713, it is hoped that the publication what is known may lead to the discovery of connections with either the Westmorland branch or with other branches living today.

The two Cliffords at the start of this account and at its end are William Clifford, the Sheriff, and Robert Clifford, the Brigadier. The descendants of the former leading to the latter have been traced through Irish land records.

William Clifford is first recorded as an under-sheriff of Sligo in the 'Annals of Loch Ce' in 1581. Four years later he was working alongside Sir Conyers Clifford (see Chapter Sixty-One) and both are mentioned in a document as receiving a 'pardon'. A 'pardon' in those days was not so much concerned with any crime committed as a dispensation for conduct which was, perhaps, reprehensible but committed in the course of official duty. In this case we find 'Pardon to William Clifford of the Carrick, late Sheriff of Sligo, for any offence committed in execution of martial law, treating with the rebels and taking victuals for the Queen's service'. It is possible to trace his career from such entries as this in the Irish State Papers; but it was not a long one, for, during his service in Connaught and Thomond under Sir Richard Bingham, he lost his life in 1593 in a skirmish with the rebels when some of Bingham's troops were ambushed.

William Clifford is known to have married Elizabeth, the daughter of Captain Robert Mostain and grand-daughter of Phelim O'Melaghin, the King of Meath. After William's death, his widow married John Crofton, taking with her his three children, the eldest of whom, Francis, was eight years old. Francis Clifford became the ward of Crofton, his step-father, and is later found to convey to the Croftons parcels of land which he had inherited from his father. Margaret, William's only daughter, married William O'Molloy, whose descendants are still living, and represented by the MacDermot family in Ireland, among others. His second son, George Clifford, is known to have married Shily, daughter of Meloghlin O'Donelane by his wife Mary McSweeny. George had sons and daughters, and it is from one of these sons that we come to the more renowned Brigadier Robert Clifford.

Francis Clifford, born about 1586, married a wife named Joan, who was living in 1635, and by her had a son, Henry, and a daughter, Elizabeth. Henry married Elizabeth Roche, and by her had a son and a daughter, John and Joan. Joan is known to have married Richard Waller, and, although the name of John's wife is unknown, his son, John, later figures in Exchequer Bills of 1692 in respect of a dispute concerning lands originally held by his great-grandfather. Elizabeth, Francis' only daughter, married a man named Irwin, or Kirowen, and she too is mentioned in Exchequer Bills in 1686 and 1692 in relation to these same lands.

Robert Clifford, the grandson of George, was born about 1650. He was a soldier of fortune, who fought in the Duke of Monmouth's Regiment in the service of Louis XIV between 1673 and 1678 as a captain. He served in the Royal Dragoons under James II, when he prevented the desertion of troops under his command to the army of William of Orange in 1688 near Salisbury, where many officers and men defected. Although promoted for his loyalty he lost his command when James II fled to France. He seems to have followed James in exile (was he, too, a Catholic convert?) and commanded a regiment of Clifford's Dragoons at the Battle of Limerick in 1691. In this battle he found himself confronting his old regiment, the Royal Dragoons, and was consequently reluctant to do battle with them when they crossed the Boyne, and so was directly responsible for King James's final defeat. His court-martial for his apparently treacherous conduct was only averted by the signing of the treaty of Limerick, when he reverted to civilian life as Robert Clifford, Esquire, of Dublin. The Orangemen included him, along with a multitude of others, as traitors, and although many were pardoned his name does not appear amongst those who were lucky enough to be forgiven.

Robert Clifford married Alethea Clayton of Lea Hall in Shropshire, probably in about 1687 when his regiment, the Royal Dragoons, was stationed in Shrewsbury. Alethea is mentioned in the Domestic State Papers during the time he was in the service of James II, but in 1705 or thereabouts he was imprisoned in the Marshalsea for reasons which are not apparent, unless they stemmed from his service in the Jacobite army. When he made his will in 1713 he cut his wife off with a shilling 'by reason of her unkindness and bad usage to me during my being a prisoner in the Queens Bench and Marshalsea in Southwark these eight years past and upwards'. He appears to have had no children as none are mentioned in his will, but it is possible that others of this line of descent from William the Sheriff of Sligo can be traced. Proof of Robert's descent from the Sheriff is to be found in a poem by Peadar O'Mulconry, an Irish Bard, written shortly before James II's final defeat in 1691. The original manuscript still survives and translations clearly show intermarriages and descendants. The poem is entitled 'A Welcome to Colonel Robert Clifford'. In verse 23 the poet describes Robert as 'this champion of the Earl's descendant', so the question remains; which earl? Neither the first nor second Earl of Cumberland had a legitimate son named William.

Chapter Sixty-Four

The Cliffords of Stow-on-the-Wold, Gloucestershire (1598-)

Walter de Clifford, who first bore the family name, was among those who helped to shape the future of Stow-on-the-Wold. This ancient hilltop market town is situated where seven roads meet. The settlement was developed by Evesham Abbey to take commercial advantage of this location. Others then built just outside the town boundary to exploit the benefits. Late in the 12th century Walter de Clifford was persuaded to demolish these houses in order to secure the interests of the Abbey. This land once held by Walter is now included within the borders of the town. In this period the Cliffords possessed part of the manor of Swell one mile from Stow, and in 1265 Roger Clifford, great-grandson of Walter, held the manor of Westcote close to the opposite side of Stow Hill.

During past centuries many of the name have lived in this part of Gloucestershire. Scarcity of records is a hindrance to research in the medieval period but matters improve from the 16th century. The first entry in Stow parish register is of Harry Clifford who was baptised in 1583. One whose line continues to the present day was William Clifford, a master mason. He is mentioned in a deed of 1632 which gives details of his family and residence. Master masons were once responsible for the construction of every major edifice combining the duties of architect and builder. John Clifford, whose birthplace is unknown, was a master of the Masons' Mystery and chief mason of London Bridge in 1388. At Stow one descent from William continued this occupation for six generations until the end of the 18th century. During this period the family prospered and divided into several branches. Some, who are recorded as gentry, owned land and property throughout the area. Others moved to Bourton-on-the-Water, Moreton-in-Marsh, and surrounding villages.

In the time under review most local references to the name are at Stow. Several hundred persons are recorded and much of individual interest is to be found. The Cotswolds thrived on wool and Cliffords are commemorated by a wool merchant's tomb in Stow churchyard. The *Dictionary of British Sculptors* mentions Richard Clifford, some of whose work is in the church. In 1683 Captain John Clifford of Frampton assisted the fund which enabled this fine building to be restored.

At Stow in the election of 1776 four Cliffords voted among a total of 47 other freeholders. John Clifford, who is listed as a voter, endeavoured to benefit the community. In about 1800 he used a wind driven pump and hollow logs to bring a water supply to Stow from Lower Swell. Members of various branches of the family were yeoman farmers. Among them were some who farmed near Leach, 12 miles from Stow, which was another manor held by Walter de Clifford in 1144.

Of those who moved to Bourton-on-the-Water in the 18th century, some continued as master masons. These included William Clifford who built Daylesford Church for Warren Hastings in 1816. Harry Clifford was the author of works on subjects of local interest including the *History of Bourton-on-the-Water* which was published at Stow in 1916. Reference to one whose interests were close to our subject may be a fitting point at which to conclude this account of a North Cotswold branch of the family.

Chapter Sixty-Five

The Cliffords of Swindon, Gloucestershire (c. 1600-)

The village of Swindon, now part of Cheltenham, has been connected with the Frampton-upon-Severn branch since the Middle Ages but did not come under their direct control until the Dissolution of the Monasteries in 1539. Up to that time the village had formed part of the Church property.

In 1712 Sir Robert Atkins described Swindon thus: 'It is a small parish, five miles in compass and consists mostly of rich pasture. There are 24 houses and 90 inhabitants of whom 6 are freeholders'.

James Clifford of Frampton was Lord of the Manor in 1608 and he died seized of it in 1613. The advowson of the parish was retained in their hands, and as mentioned in Chapter Fifty-Seven, his nephew James Clifford also of Frampton was appointed the incumbent of St Lawrence church there in 1627 and remained until his death in 1638.

The present-day descendants of the Cliffords of Swindon do not trace their ancestry to either of these James but they could descend from Thomas Clifford of Swindon who died in 1541/2 or William Clifford of Swindon who died at a great age in 1563, both of whom were farmers. Precisely how they were related to each other, and how in turn they relate to the main Frampton branch, has not been established. Perhaps further research will do so one day.

The earliest reference in parish records is of Ann Clifford who was baptised there in 1575, the daughter of William Clifford, whilst her brother James was baptised in 1577. Wills and other points of reference confirm that the family remained a long time in Swindon, marrying into families in nearby villages including Tirley, Elmstone Hardwick and Boddington.

One line of descent can be traced to Bath in 1754 where young William Clifford, a stonemason, found employment during the Regency building period and married there. Descendants moved to Shepton Mallet where they married into local families and settled on the land. Children of this particular branch were being baptised there as late as 1839 and there are descendants of this family still living thereabouts. After the mid-1800s this branch dispersed far and wide.

Another line threads its way out of Swindon in 1725, through the market town of Leonard Stanley to the City of London. William Clifford left Leonard Stanley in 1760 at the age of 22 and set up his own business in the City in the mid-1770s as a warehouseman and factor. He prospered and became a Freeman of the City. Descendants have continued to live and work in London ever since but one emigrated with his family in 1889 to Australia, where there is now another thriving branch of the Cliffords of Swindon.

Chapter Sixty-Six

The Cliffords of Annesley, Wexford and Other Irish Branches (1650-)

As the Annesley and Wexford branches of the Clifford family both stem from Robert Clifford of Dublin in 1650 (not to be confused with the Robert Clifford of Sligo mentioned in Chapter Sixty-Three) it is best to deal with them together. Both branches have for many generations borne a crest consisting of a dexter hand holding a fleur-de-lis in one form or another, and present research tends strongly in the direction of kinship with the Frampton-on-Severn branch. Until proof is forthcoming, and Robert's exact position in the pedigree is established they must be treated as a separate branch.

The line of descent from Dublin in 1650 to the present time is not difficult to establish since a pedigree is included in the 1846 edition of Burke's *Landed Gentry* and in *Miscellanea Genealogica et Heraldica*, Fifth Series, Volume V (pp. 313-25). The latter claims that Robert of Dublin was the son of John Clifford, fifth son of James Clifford V of Swindon (Family D in Chapter Fifty-Six), but this is uncertain. It is known that Robert Clifford of Dublin married Anne Knight, the sister and co-heir of Colonel William Knight of Cromwell's army, by whose will made in 1670 we learn of his nephews and nieces, his sister's children. Colonel Knight was given land for his services to Cromwell, but it is not known precisely where, nor when his sister married Robert Clifford. It can be calculated that the marriage took place between 1650 and 1655. Both the Annesley and Wexford Cliffords descend from this marriage, and traces of the family can be found in Wexford church records down to the early 1800s. After this the family began to split up to seek their fortunes elsewhere, but some retained links with the county. Some became soldiers, others sought service in the East India Company, and, after the Company's interests were taken over by the Crown, the tradition was continued by service in the Indian Army and the Indian Civil Service. The Indian Mutiny claimed the lives of two serving officers, and it was during that period that one of them wrote home to say that among his possessions which had been lost in a fire was a letter written by Cromwell to his ancestor. That letter might have thrown light on the origins of Robert Clifford.

A twelve-generation pedigree of the Annesley and Wexford Cliffords is available for consultation extending the one printed in *Miscellanea Genealogica et Heraldica*.

There are certainly two other Irish branches, but much less is known about them. One has its origin in Cork where a certain Walter Clifford alias Yelverton from Devon was settled during the Commonwealth period. From his will of 1685 he is known to have had property in Rathmore, Rathbeg, Killevallig and elsewhere, but lack of research alone prevents further details of this branch being known. A second branch descends from a John Clifford who was given land in Sligo during the Cromwellian period, but is unrelated to the branch described in Chapter

Sixty-Three. This branch can be traced to 1851, when land originally granted to John at Cloonelarge was sold.

It would be wrong to think that these are all the Irish branches there are. The loss of so many valuable records in 1922 makes research in Ireland particularly difficult, but it can be expected that further information is yet to be found.

Chapter Sixty-Seven

The Perristone Cliffords (1760-1860)

This branch flourished for barely a century, and details can be seen in Burke's *Landed Gentry*. It traces its descent from Sir William Morgan, knight, of Tredegar, whose descendants retained the name Morgan for three generations down to a Richard Morgan who married Abigail Phelps. Their young son, William Morgan, assumed the surname Clifford in 1760. The circumstances under which this was done are as follows: Thomas Clifford of Newport, Monmouthshire, died childless bequeathing his estate to William Morgan on condition he changed his name to Clifford. The will was proved in 1756. Part of the bequest consisted of £3,635 1s. 2d. in Old and New South Sea Annuities, the South Sea Bubble having burst some thirty-five years before. This Thomas Clifford had himself descended through four generations of Thomas Cliffords, all of whom had been only sons, which meant that he had no near relations, cousins or nephews to whom he could leave his fortune. His own mother had been Elizabeth, sister of Henry Probert, and his nearest relative was Eleanor Probert, Henry's daughter, who was William Morgan's grandmother. Since much of his wealth had come to Thomas Clifford from the Proberts this bequest becomes more intelligible.

This line of descent is clearly traceable for another three generations of Morgan Cliffords, and died out for lack of male heirs when Henry Somers Morgan Clifford died in February 1856, unmarried and aged only twenty.

Although not fully researched, it appears that the last named Clifford's sister, Marion, persuaded her husband, James FitzWalter Butler, eldest son of Lord Dunboyne, to assume the name of Clifford by Royal Licence in 1860. There may be descendants of this family still living. The Morgan Cliffords bore the Morgan coat of arms quartered with that of Clifford with the fesse and motto 'Semper Paratus' with the wyvern as crest, so it would seem that they claimed descent from the Chudleigh Cliffords, but this has not yet been proved.

Chapter Sixty-Eight

The Chestal Cliffords (1913-)

Details of this branch of the Cliffords can be found in more up-to-date editions of Burke's *Landed Gentry*, and although they assumed the name as recently as 1913 by Royal Licence, they can trace their ancestry back to Pons through the female line alongside the Cliffords of Frampton-on-Severn. In Chapter Fifty-Seven it was pointed out how Nathaniel Winchcombe changed his name to Clifford in 1801, and how subsequent generations continued the name to the present day. From the pedigree it will be noted that Henry John Clifford (1810-52) married Marianne Phelps and that their son Henry James continued the line. The second son, William, was the ancestor of the Chestal Cliffords.

William and his other brothers and sisters were very young when their father died in 1852, and they were looked after by the Phelps family, their mother's parents. Their uncle, William John Phelps, died without issue in 1891, making his nephew William Clifford his heir. As William had already been christened William Phelps Clifford and was now to succeed his uncle, he obtained permission to drop the surname Clifford by Royal Licence in November 1891, and sanction to use the Phelps' coat of arms. He was 46 when he assumed the surname Phelps, but his children had all been born Clifford, and his eldest son, Arthur William, who was born in May 1878, before the assumption of the name, did not continue to use the Phelps name after 1913, when he was empowered to continue the name under which he had been born, though he still continued to use the Phelps coat of arms assumed by his father, quartered with those of Clifford.

This somewhat complicated matter explains how the Chestal Cliffords descend from Nathaniel Winchcombe. The youngest male descendants of this branch are the sons of the late Arthur John Clifford, who was unfortunately murdered in Hong Kong in August 1956, shortly after their birth in the colony.

Chapter Sixty-Nine

Other Overseas Cliffords

It would be incorrect to think that there are no Cliffords other than those described in this book, for the formation of the Clifford Association is bringing to light many who bear the name, and who have, or hope to trace, direct links with one or other of the branches described above. The name occurs widely in the United States, and there are many Cliffords in Australia, whose links with the family have not yet been established.

The Cliffords of Tixall continue as a cadet branch of the Chudleigh line in New Zealand following the emigration of Charles Clifford (1813-93), whose career was described in Part Four. In Canada there is a branch stemming from Edward Arthur Clifford, a younger brother of the stem of the Chestal Cliffords, who emigrated in 1868. With five male members of this line living today it seems set to continue.

Martin Clifford, who emigrated temporarily to Virginia in the 17th century (see Chapter Sixty-One), was not the only Clifford to go to that first English colony in America. A John Clifford was exporting indentured servants from Bristol to Virginia in July 1672. It is possible that he was the John mentioned in Chapter Sixty-One who appears as a headright of Edward Lockey of New Kent County in 1658. A Benedict Clifford was sentenced in October 1718 to transportation at the Middlesex Sessions of Gaol Delivery but to which colony is not stated. A later American branch stems from a Henry Clifford who emigrated in 1871. This is a cadet branch of the Frampton Cliffords. It is not yet known whether there are any living members of this branch. The publication of this book may discover many other overseas Cliffords.

PART SIX

MISCELLANEA

Chapter Seventy

The Name 'Pons' in Pre-Conquest Normandy

The personal Christian name Pons, sometimes spelt Poinz, was very rare in Normandy, though not so in other parts of France. It is, of course, originally derived from the Latin Pontius (as in Pontius Pilate) by way of Saint Pons[1] who was martyred at Cimiez, near Nice in Provence, in about A.D. 259. The name was included in the calendar of saints in Languedoc and the whole of the south of France, and St Pons came to be venerated also in Burgundy, where we find many children baptised with this name in the 11th and 12th centuries. St Pons' feast day was 14 May, and it was gradually celebrated throughout the whole of the Romance-speaking world. The best known bearer of the name in the 11th century was Pons, born in 992, whose mother was a daughter of the Count of Provence, and who himself was Count of Toulouse from 1037 to 1061. Other magnates in the South by the early 11th century bearing this personal name were Pons de Rians, near Marseilles, about 971, ancestor of the famous House of Les Baux; Pons, Count of Marseilles, his son and successor, who died in 1034; Pons de Mont-Saint-Jean, seigneur de Charny in Burgundy, ancestor of Geoffrey de Charny, sometime owner of the Shroud of Turin, who lived in the early 13th century; and Pons, Count of Tripoli, in the early 12th century.

Pons was, however, a very unusual Christian name in Languedoeil, the north of France, where Normandy is situated. (In southern France the word for 'yes' was *oc*: hence Languedoc, the language of oc, in northern France, 'yes' was *oeil* (now *oui*): Languedoeil, the language of oeil). The collected acts of the dukes of Normandy between 911 and 1066 contain only three references to the name Pons during this entire period,[2] and the first and last mentioned may well have been the same seigneur: the other was a monk who could have been his nephew.

There is no doubt that the last Pons mentioned in the ducal acts, namely the one who witnessed Duke William's charter to the church at Fécamp in 1066, anticipating his victory across the Channel, was the same Pons to whom William granted lands in England after the Conquest, and who was the undoubted ancestor of the House of Clifford. And since he died before 1086, and perhaps some years earlier than that, it is quite likely he was the first Pons to be mentioned. This Pons witnessed a charter to the abbey of Fécamp[3] by William's grandfather, Duke Richard the Good, in 1025. This document is indeed remarkable for the number of its important witnesses, a list which includes two of the duke's sons, two archbishops, four bishops, 12 vicomtes and 100 other distinguished witnesses. Pons comes thirty-ninth among the 107 after the vicomtes.

It may possibly be significant that the fifteenth and sixteenth witnesses' names below Pons are 'Ernis' and 'Rodulphus frater ejus'. These are identified by Dr Lucien Musset[4] in his index as Erneis Taisson, seigneur of Fontenay, and his brother Ralf

Taisson. The only other mention of a Pons in the ducal acts[5] is Pons fitz Erneys (Pons son of Erneis), who was a monk at St Wandrille in Normandy sometime between 1049 and 1066. He is mentioned in a charter whereby William the Bastard (later the Conqueror) confirms a grant made to the monastery of St Wandrille by the monk Pons' brother, Robert fitz Erneys, identified by Musset as the son of Erneis Taisson.[6] Since the earlier Pons and Erneis are not placed next each other in the earlier (1025) charter, it is clear that they were not brothers. But in view of the rarity of both names, they may well have been related, perhaps by marriage.

In this connection it is, perhaps, worth noting, in view of the close association between Ralf de Toeni and Pons' family, that, at the time of the Domesday Survey in 1086, Ralf de Toeni and Dru (Drogo) fitz Pons held between them (with one single exception belonging to William of Eu) *all* the estates in England – in Gloucestershire, Worcestershire and Essex, and including Dru's manor of Frampton – that had been held under Edward the Confessor in 1066 by a certain Ernesi. Now, Ernesi, like Pons, is a unique name in Domesday Book, and although it should represent the old English Earnsige (latinised as Ernsius), there were a number of foreigners settled in England under Edward the Confessor, so it could perhaps represent the old French Erneis (latinised Ernesius), and indicate some link not only between the Clifford ancestor Pons with the family of Erneis Taisson in Normandy, but also some pre-Conquest English connection of the Taisson family before Pons' family took over Frampton from 'Ernesi'.

Chapter Seventy-One

The Traditional Viking and Norman Descent of the Clifford Family

Tacitus mentions the Fenni, or Finns, as the least-known people in Europe, and it is to the semi-mythical King Fornjöt of Finland that the Dukes of Normandy traced their ancestry. As Sir Bede Clifford put it, when gathering his notes for this family history, the descent from the King of the Finns appeared to him a somewhat fishy story! Be that as it may, early Norse genealogies purporting to take pedigrees back to the fifth and sixth centuries were perpetuated in the Sagas and not written down until the ninth or tenth. Some time around 875, Rolf, or Rollo, the Ganger, son of Rognwald, a Norse chieftain with lands in Norway, was banished from his native country. Three years earlier Rognwald had helped King Harold to defeat a rebellion from Telemark, Holdaland and other parts of northern Scandinavia at the battle of Harfmersfiord near Stavanger, which established Harold as king of all Norway. Many of the rebels fled to the Orkneys, Shetland, Faroes and as far away as the Isle of Man, from where they carried out periodic raids on the mainland of Norway. Harold retaliated by capturing Shetland and Orkney, which he offered to Rognwald as a reward for his loyalty.

Rognwald is known as the most powerful chief in northern Norway as well as Earl of Orkney and Shetland, but he had many wives, concubines and children, one of whom colonised Iceland, and another, Rollo, born about 850, was the famous Viking who founded kingdoms stretching from the rugged cliffs of Norway to the Mediterranean and from Normandy to Vinland, in what is now New England in North America.

There is no space to go into the reasons for Rollo's banishment in 875, but before we look more closely at this young man's career, a word should be said about Viking marriage and inheritance customs. Polygamy continued well into Christian times and, though opinions differ, it seems that the children of mistresses enjoyed equal rights with legitimate offspring. This custom was known as Udal or Danish Marriage, and, not surprisingly, was gravely frowned upon by the Church. Nevertheless all the dukes of Normandy from the ninth to the 11th centuries with the exception of Duke Richard III and his brother, Duke Robert II, nicknamed 'the Devil' and 'the Magnificent', were sons of Danish marriages, as, of course, was William the Conqueror himself. The custom in Norway led to what would nowadays be termed a population explosion, which proved to be a hefty impetus towards the piratical and colonising activities of the Vikings, leading to the establishment of Norse colonists not only in the islands of the North Atlantic but also in Normandy, England and Sicily.

The sea-girt lands of northern Europe were a constant temptation to the Norse pirates. After the collapse of the Roman Empire, Europe lapsed into disorder until Charlemagne established a strong government in the ninth century. But because the system of primogeniture was not the established rule of succession, Charlemagne's empire was divided amongst his sons, and soon fell apart after his death. Suffice it to say that his grandson, Charles the Bald, was unable to control the lands he had inherited in what is now France, and when he died in 877 further divisions followed. Charles, his elder son, became King of Aquitania, which stretched from the Loire to the Mediterranean west of the Rhone, and Louis the Stammerer, his younger son, became King of Neustria, otherwise known as the Kingdom of the West Franks, which took in the whole of northern France, excluding Brittany, and most of modern Belgium. When Louis died in 879, his cousin, Charles the Fat, tried to seize his lands, and there followed a period in which large areas of northern France were up for grabs. Rollo was one of the grabbers. He was, as we have seen, banished from Norway in 875, and after several years in the Hebrides, and perhaps Brittany, he is next recorded in 886 as sailing up the Seine, and probably took part in the siege of Paris in 887, which was being invested by Hugh of Lorraine. The records are meagre and confusing, but it seems certain that Rollo captured the Cherbourg peninsula (the Cotentin) about 890, and had occupied the cities of St Lo and Bayeux by then. At the latter place Count Berenger de Senlis was killed, and his daughter, Poppa, taken in Danish marriage by Rollo. From this union was born William Longsword, the second Duke of Normandy.

There followed ten years of confusion in which little is heard of Rollo, until in 911 he attacked Chartres. It is after this that the treaty of St Clare-sur-Epte recognised him as Duke of Normandy, though what the boundaries of his duchy were then is far from clear. One of his bands of marauders established itself between Chartres and Blois, on the Loire; another, the chief body, made Rouen its headquarters and dominated Evreux and Bayeux, holding both banks of the Seine. The native Celtic and Gallo-Roman population was Christian, and looked upon the heathen invaders with dismay. On the other hand the Norsemen led them to peace and prosperity, and Rollo's rule came to be seen as a boon to all who came under it. When the archbishop of Rouen approached Rollo with the proposal that he should become a Christian, the pill was sugared with the offer of the hand of Gisella, the daughter of King Charles the Simple, provided Rollo acknowledged the king as his overlord and promised to live in peace within the kingdom. Rollo, who had learnt to admire the grandeur of Alfred the Great while he was in the British Isles, was ambitious to found a well-ordered state, so the bargain was closed and he swore fealty to the king and was baptised with the name Robert after the Duke of France, and his men, following his example, likewise became Christians. The story of Rollo's act of fealty has its humorous aspect. The Viking chieftain was too proud to bend down and kiss his overlord's foot, so he got one of his men to do it for him. The clumsy soldier strode up to the king, seized his foot and lifted it to his lips, causing the king, who was very much overweight, to fall over backwards off his throne.

The Normans, already quite familiar with the French after a century of contact with them, soon adopted the manners and speech of their subjects. In 20 years' time Normandy was far in advance of the rest of France, and Norman-French became the idiom of the language. But Rollo proceeded to populate his duchy with his own kind and their descendants, among them the Danes from England, who were encouraged to go to Normandy by King Alfred's daughter, Aethelflaeda of Mercia, and his grandchildren and their children frequently intermarried with the reigning house of England, which was then of Viking origin like themselves.

The Viking duke gave Normandy a code of law which enabled his successors to control their barons better than other feudal monarchs. The legacy he left still survives in the Channel Islands, where the 'clameur de Haro' – the appeal to Rollo – still exists.

In 920 the Duke of Paris, Robert, rebelled against King Charles the Simple, who was defeated and the duke was proclaimed king in his stead. But Duke Rollo of Normandy remained loyal to his oath of fealty, and in 923 helped defeat King Robert at Soissons. Rollo, or Duke Robert I, as we should call him since his conversion, was by now an old man, and he died in about 927 and was buried in the cathedral. He was succeeded by his son, William, who was the child of his 'Danish' wife, Poppa.

William Longsword, second Duke of Normandy, was an entirely different character from his father. Born in Rouen of a French mother, his education was French rather than Norse, and he was, of course, the first of his line to be born a Christian, yet his chief advisers were all of Viking origin, the most important of whom was known as Bernard the Dane. In foreign affairs he continued his father's policy of support for the King of France, Charles the Simple, then in the hands of the ambitious Count Herbert of Vermandois. Between 930 and 936 William was chiefly engaged in consolidating his duchy against the heathen Norsemen in Brittany and around Bayeux, and in cementing his relationship with the French king against the Count of Flanders. His career, however, reveals a vacillating man whose loyalties wavered between France and Scandinavia, and who twice threatened to abdicate when the opposition to him became too tough. In the end he was perhaps unwise not to do so, for he was assassinated in 943. He is buried in Rouen cathedral, and was succeeded by his ten-year-old son, Richard.

The duchy at Richard's accession was divided into three factions – the heathens, the Christians who supported Hugh of Paris and the Christians who supported Louis, Charles the Simple's son. Louis inveigled young Richard into his power intending to have him killed as his father had been killed, but the aged and wily Bernard the Dane played the French off one against the other with the aim of saving Richard's life and of preventing the Normans being sent back to Scandinavia.

At the age of 14, Richard was firmly established as Duke of Normandy, and soon after he contracted a 'Danish marriage' with a girl called Gunnor. This was no hindrance to a proper marriage for diplomatic reasons, and Bernard the Dane suggested an alliance with Emma, the only daughter of Hugh, Duke of Burgundy, Count of Paris and Duke of France, but since she was then too young, the couple were merely betrothed.

Though attributed to Duke Richard, the establishment of the feudal system in Normandy can properly be ascribed to Bernard. Through his son, Torf, and grandson, Thorold, he is said to be the ancestor of many noble families in England, notably those of Harcourt and Beaumont. Richard eventually married Emma in 960, but she died eight years later without issue. He then decided to marry his mistress, Gunnor, who died in 1031, and so assure the legitimacy of his children in the eyes of the Church.

The years between 960 and 983, when Richard was 50, saw the thorough establishment of the Norman dynasty. Other continental states had tried for years to banish the pirates back to Scandinavia, but the Normans were now recognised as a permanent, strong power. Through the foresight of Bernard, feudalism had been introduced and firmly established, and Normandy became, in effect, the model for the rest of Europe. Richard encouraged monasticism and founded many abbeys, and his reign saw the establishment of a more modern army as well as a new system of land tenure based on military dues and service. Although primogeniture was not fully established in his day, Richard nominated his eldest son and namesake as his successor, but he made sure that his other children, not all of whom were by Gunnor, inherited substantial patrimonies. Apart from Richard, the first of the Norman dukes to be recognised as French rather than Scandinavian, he had Robert, whom he appointed Archbishop of Rouen; Mauger, who was created Count of Mortain and Corbeil; William, Count of Hiesme and later Count of Eu; Geoffrey, at first Count of Eu and Brionne, who was assassinated; Maud, Countess of Blois; Emma, afterwards Queen of King Ethelred the Unready of England; and Avice, who married the Duke of Brittany. There were doubtless others, but they played no part in the politics of their time.

At the beginning of Richard's reign the peasants revolted, resentful of baronial jurisdiction. The rebellion was put down, but was soon followed by a more serious insurrection led by Richard's brother, William of Eu, who was almost certainly the ancestor of the Cliffords. William had been created Count of Hiesme by his brother, the duke, but he sought further lands and prestige, so with a number of other barons he made more demands on Richard. When he failed to get what he wanted, he rebelled. Richard's forces defeated him and he was taken and imprisoned in Rouen for five years. During this time he had a love affair with the daughter of his gaoler, Alice, who smuggled a rope to him, by means of which he made his escape. For some time William led an outlaw's life in the forest of Vernon, but eventually made his peace with his brother and was pardoned and given the County of Eu, which had reverted to the duke on the death of their brother Geoffrey. After his rehabilitation, William married Alice, the daughter of his gaoler, the Count of Turquetil, a grandson of Bernard the Dane, by whom he had four sons, Robert, Count of Eu, Hugh, Bishop of Liseux, William, Count of Soissons and Pons, or Pontius (for whom see Chapter One).

Richard II died in 1026 and was succeeded by his son, Richard III who only reigned for two years, dying in mysterious circumstances to be succeeded in turn by his brother, Robert, leaving his son, Nicholas, to be content with the post of Abbot of St Ouen. Robert began his reign by quarrelling with his uncle, the Archbishop of Rouen, who was also Count of Evreux. He forced this not very reverend gentleman to flee to France (roughly coterminous with the modern Ile de France), whence he hurled anathemas at his nephew and the whole duchy. The quarrel was at length patched up by the French king, and the archbishop returned to continue building his cathedral.

Owing to the dubious circumstances under which Robert had come to the ducal throne, he earned the nickname of the Devil. His reputation was not enhanced when he took as his mistress, or 'Danish' wife, a tanner's daughter from Falaise named

Arlette, but he appears to have remained comparatively faithful to her, though she only bore him one son who survived, later to become the conqueror of England. The tanners plied an unpopular, and certainly a very non-aristocratic trade, and Fulbut, Arlette's father, no less than most of them; added to which he was also a brewer. Duke Robert's affair with Arlette caused such a scandal that her name, according to some authorities, passed into the English language as harlot to indicate a low-born woman of loose morals. In fact, a rebellion which broke out soon after this misalliance is said to have been caused by the Norman aristocracy's fear of having a bastard foisted on them as their duke, but this seems an unlikely story in view of the generally accepted habit of entering upon 'Danish' marriages.

Duke Robert, whose aunt had been Queen of England, and whose cousin, King Edmund Ironside, was fighting to preserve the independence of his kingdom against Canute, whose father, King Sweyn of Denmark, claimed it by right of conquest, made several attempts to interfere in English affairs, especially after Edmund died in 1016 and was succeeded by Canute. But since Canute was king not only of England but of an empire which stretched from Russia to the north of Scandinavia, Robert did not get very far, although his actions almost certainly inspired his son to follow his example 50 years later. Robert prepared a fleet to help the sons of Edmund Ironside, known as the Athelings, against Canute by invading England, but contrary winds prevented it ever sailing.

The fear that the world would end as the year 1000 approached died away when that year was safely past, but it revived as the thousandth anniversary of the crucifixion approached in 1032. Coincidentally the years 1030 to 1032 were appalling ones for Europe. Contemporary records tell of the incredible miseries endured in France, and how the seasons seemed to have wandered from their courses. There was such cold, rain and wind as had never been experienced before, and famine ruled the continent from Greece to Britain. Thousands died, the poor ate roots and grass, then after three years of suffering came a sudden plenty and mankind revived. In 1035 Robert le Diable summoned his vassals, told them he was going to Jerusalem to give thanks for the deliverance from the famine, and presented his only son, William, to them, praying them to accept him as their overlord should he die overseas. The barons took the ten-year-old boy and swore fealty to him as their lord, more out of fear of Robert than anything else. Before departing on his pilgrimage, Robert appointed his kinsman, Alan of Brittany, as regent, and then set out, never to return, dying in mysterious circumstances at Nicaea on the return journey, whereupon William became Duke of Normandy.

Meanwhile Robert, Count of Eu, and his brother Pons were also growing up, which made William's lot a difficult one. All his life the fact that he was illegitimate was held against him, and his position was not made any easier when in 1040 Alan of Brittany was poisoned and Geoffrey de Brionne, his great-uncle, the fifth son of Duke Richard I, was murdered. By the time he was 16 in 1041, William was already toughened by events, which may have prepared him for the future. In 1042 and again five years later he had to put down rebellions designed to deprive him of the ducal throne and he was obliged to seek refuge with the King of France when half his duchy went over to the rebels, though the counties of Eu and Rouen still continued to support him. At the battle of Val-es-Dunes William finally defeated his enemies and

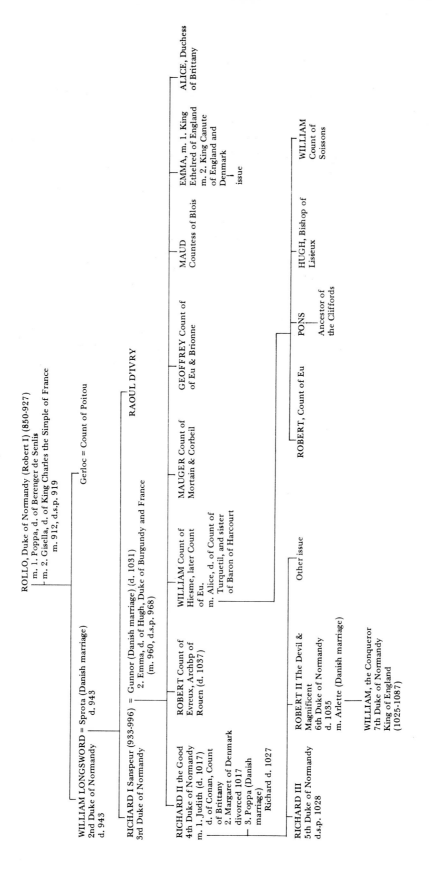

The Norman descent of the House of Clifford

consolidated his hold on the duchy, and in 1048 he captured Alençon from Geoffrey of Anjou.

In 1053 William married Matilda, daughter of Count Baldwin of Flanders, at Eu. It was an important diplomatic alliance for Baldwin became Regent of France during the minority of King Philip I, who ascended the throne in 1060. In 1054 and 1058 France again attacked Normandy, but on both occasions was held at bay by William. After the death of King Henry I of France and Philip's accession, William's father-in-law became regent, and, with no threat to his rear, William was now able to plan his invasion of England. His cousin, Robert, Count of Eu, and his brother, Pons, were men of high standing in Normandy, and both took part in the invasion. This is not the occasion to go into the political events leading up to the expedition of 1066, but it is enough to say that William, having gained the Pope's support for the enterprise, set sail on 29 September, taking with him among others the Count of Eu and Pons, his brother; Robert and Ives de Vassy, ancestor of the English Vesci family who were rewarded with lands in the north near Alnwick; William d'Aubigny, ancestor of the Earls of Arundel and Sussex; and Robert de Vieux-Pont (Vipont in English), all of whom in the course of time became ancestors of the Cliffords. As Sir Iain Moncreiffe told the present Lady Clifford, this is one of the most interesting families in the history of these islands: he did not exaggerate.

Chapter Seventy-Two

Ugbrooke Park

Despite its elegant 18th-century appearance, Ugbrooke Park has a very long history. Its name derives from the Saxon 'Wogbroga' meaning an ugly or winding brook, and within its boundaries are the remains of an Iron Age fort. Early archaeologists thought it was Roman, and others that it was Danish, for it is now called Danish Camp, and it presides over the surrounding countryside to remind people of the great antiquity of the place. The first documented records date from 1080, when nearby Chudleigh, together with more distant Paignton, were made the sites of new rural palaces for the bishops of Exeter. Two hundred years later the Manor of Chudleigh was annexed to the precentorship of Exeter Cathedral, and from then until the mid-16th century Ugbrooke House and the manor remained ecclesiastical property.[1]

In 1547 Lord Protector Somerset divided it among a number of owners, and three years later it became the property of Sir Piers Courtenay. When, later in the century, his daughter Anne married Anthony Clifford of Borscombe (see Chapter Thirty-Three), it passed into the ownership of the Cliffords, with whom it has remained ever since.

Ugbrooke House has been described as a 'square, battlemented box with towers at each corner, a Victorian castle, or better, a rather heavy attempt at one'.[2] Strange composition-stone mouldings rim all the windows, unrelentingly grim, and positively ungainly at the top of each tower. The park, too, has the distinct air of 'nature improved' in the taste of the 18th century, and even when one inspects the house more closely, it has the appearance of an 18th-century building 'improved' in the nineteenth. Indeed, such is the case, since park and house owe much of their present appearance to Hugh, 4th Lord Clifford of Chudleigh, who devoted much energy to them in the 1760s (see Chapter Thirty-Four).

When Thomas, 1st Lord Clifford, inherited Ugbrooke it was not very large, for there is no mention of it in Sir William Pole's 'Collections towards a description of the County of Devon' compiled before 1635. But as Thomas's career progressed, and he grew richer and more important, so did his house. We have already seen in Chapter Thirty-Six how the family chapel of St Cyprian was consecrated in 1671; two years later it was being surrounded by more building. Some plans drawn up about 1740 show the chapel in the middle of a rambling system of rooms, which appear to have grown up bit by bit, and it is hard to distinguish Thomas Clifford's additions from what was there before. Perhaps they were the two north-west wings which were retained to form the nucleus of the new 18th-century house. These must have been in better shape than the rest of the old house, and may, therefore, have been more recent.

The remodelling was entrusted to Robert Adam, who removed almost every trace of the earlier house. The chapel was left standing in an isolated, bow-fronted wing to the south-east of the main square block, though inside it and all the main rooms were modernised.

Much the same as was done to the house was done to the park, where the formal avenues and pieces of water that once existed have all gone, save for a few lines of trees here and there.

It is only among the contents of the house that visible reminders of Thomas Clifford of the Cabal and his forebears survive. These comprise two tapestries – *Romulus and Remus* and *The Rape of the Sabines* – given to Thomas by Cosimo de' Medici, Grand Duke of Tuscany, the Jansen's portrait of Thomas Clifford of Ugbrooke, and a rich collection of Restoration portraits – Charles II, Catherine of Braganza, the Duke and Duchess of York, and Lely's portrait of Sir Thomas Clifford, as he then was. Perhaps the most sumptuous reminders of this epoch are Charles II's gifts to his godson, Charles Clifford – a silver-gilt ewer and dish by Johann Jaeger of Augsburg.

Hugh, 4th Lord Clifford of Chudleigh, is one of the most interesting of the many aristocratic patrons of architecture who flourished in the 18th century. He is unexpected in several ways, not only as a character (see Chapter Forty-Nine) but as a patron of architecture because of the style he chose, and also for the fact that he rebuilt the house at all. His native caution, in contrast to his mother's profligacy, would make him unlikely to indulge in newfangled styles, and yet we find him in the early 1760s embarking on an embattled, castle-like house. Why? The answer seems to be thrift. He had inherited such huge debts he would not contemplate extravagances of his own. His portrait by Downman shows him against a background of the hills and trees of Ugbrooke, a simple, kindly man, whose general pose is relaxed, but whose face looks intent, as if he were going over something difficult in his mind. It is his business sense which most impressed his contemporaries, so it is natural that such a man should go into the rebuilding of his house with such great care, making estimates of whether the new convenience and lack of maintenance to be gained from it would warrant the initial expense. And so it was only after 'mature reflection whether he was able to complete the building without injury to his fortune and family' that he began by demolishing part of the older house.[3] To get the best out of the old place, Hugh Clifford consulted several architects, whose plans are still preserved at Ugbrooke. Some, very crude and local in character, are hard to relate to the present house, but one set of designs, probably by John Carr, shows a plan for a rectangular house in front of the chapel, with a long entrance facade to the south with Gothick bay-windows at either end similar to his Yorkshire houses at Methley Park and Kirkleatham Hall.

About the same time, Capability Brown, who later landscaped the grounds, submitted a plan, now, alas, lost, and tradition also links the architect James Paine with Ugbrooke. This may only be a confusion with his son, whose unexecuted designs for a grandiose stable block are in the British Museum, but there is also one classical scheme at the house that might be attributed to Paine's office.

Despite these various schemes, by far the greatest number of drawings at Ugbrooke came from Robert Adam's office, and it is obvious why Lord Clifford's choice fell on him. The design he finally chose was the simplest and therefore the least expensive: but his prudence has had fortunate results for architectural history.

In the 1760s building in a castle style was a new departure for the Adam brothers. As this style was to reach a high level of sophistication, drawings which record their early ideas are important. The first Ugbrooke design has many similarities with Luton Castle, which Robert Adam built for Lord Bute. It is a heavy, ponderous affair, and a good thing it was never built. The next design is more elegant, recalling parts of Diocletian's Palace at Split, a source from which Adam was wont to borrow for his castle, as well as his classical schemes. Attractive as it is, it is a shame that Lord Clifford insisted on something even plainer, for in the end the design was whittled down to its present form – a four-square, two-storey block, eleven windows by ten, with towers at each corner, and the chapel in a wing by itself. Alterations made a hundred years later have changed the character of the house – not for the better, alas – though the general effect remains as Adam envisaged it. The chapel and library wing escaped this remodelling and remain completely authentic. The same rigorous economy controlled the interior design. A less elaborate staircase was built than the one originally proposed, and the hall and library have an elegant simplicity about them, though this may have caused Adam disappointment as the house was never finished to the standard he had intended. The working drawings show finer and more elaborate detailing than was carried out, and it is typical of country builders that the overdoors intended for the drawing-room were put up in the hall.

The work proceeded steadily, if slowly, from 1763 to 1768, Lord Clifford continuing to live in the old house while the new one was building. Except for the chapel and vaults, most of the old house was now demolished. Contemporary legislation forbade free-standing Catholic churches, so Adam had to plan three rooms to extend in a new facade across the front of the chapel. This became the library wing containing a long, narrow anteroom, the library itself with a generous bow to the west, and a small study at the end of the suite. The end was now in sight, and it is almost as if Lord Clifford wished to leave a monument to Adam's taste for the library was built without regard to expense and all Adam's details were followed to the letter.

About 1835, Hugh, 7th Lord Clifford (see Chapter Forty-Two), began to alter the chapel at Ugbrooke, enriching the apse with marbles and adding an organ loft on the south side; but it was his son, Charles, who really carried through this work, himself preparing further plans for the building in 1841. He did not confine himself to the chapel. After he came into the estate after his father's death in 1858, he seems to have considered turning the house into a gawky French château with high Mansard roofs and prickly wrought-iron cresting. Luckily it proved too expensive, so he contented himself with a series of piecemeal 'improvements' carried out over a period of years. In these he was his own architect, and the effect of all this was to Victorianise the house's appearance. Gargantuan tube-like mouldings were added to the red stone arch forming a back entrance to the house in 1858, and this odd style provided the model for the rest of the building – the other doors, the tower windows and the battlements all (as Alistair Rowan so aptly puts it) Brobdingnagianised in 1874. In general, it has to be said, the 8th Lord Clifford would have done better to leave well alone.

In the chapel, however, Charles Clifford's alterations were altogether more effective. To complement the opening of the organ loft, he created a loggia turning the plan of the chapel into a Greek cross with a cupola surmounting the crossing. In 1866 he added a baptistry and a Lady Chapel completing the transformation from family chapel to public church. The tall, narrow Lady Chapel is very dramatic, reminiscent of a reliquary chapel in some Italian cathedral. The name of the architect of this small masterpiece is unknown, but it is too grandiose for the design of a noble amateur, and is probably the work of some Italian brought from Rome by a member of the family. Since the 8th Lord Clifford's death in 1880, the house has undergone no further major changes. From the end of the Second World War to 1957 it began to fall into decay, but with the advent of the present Lord Clifford it has been restored and brought once more back to life.

When Robert Adam had finished rebuilding the house about 1768 Ugbrooke Park dominated a wide, shallow valley with a bank of lawn falling down north-west from its front to a slow-flowing stream. Looking to the left from the house, the ground rises to a small hillock known as Dryden's Seat, and beyond is a more dramatic valley thick with woods and confined by steep hills. To the north rolling country extends to the Iron-Age fort, misnamed Danish Camp.

It is not known precisely when Capability Brown carried out his many improvements which consisted in the planting of judiciously placed clumps of trees, the damming of the stream to create a string of lakes and a modest cascade, but it was in the 1770s, for about that time Lord Clifford got permission to divert the road

65.   A hand-coloured print of Ugbrooke, Devonshire, by T. Allom, c.1830.

from Biddlecombe Cross to Winstow Farm out of sight of the house. The three thatched cottages that serve as lodges may be by Brown, but it is more likely that they were designed by a local man, William Spring, or by Joseph Rowe, who designed the stables in 1793. This is an unpompous park – there are no temples or obelisks, just the simple delights of natural beauty. Father Joseph Reeve's poem *Ugbrooke Park*, published in 1776, sums up the ideals of the Georgian 'improvers' and evokes for us the clear light of 18th-century sensibility.

> 'Tis yours, my lord, with unaffected ease,
> To draw from Nature's stores and make them please:
> With taste refined to dress the rural seat,
> And add new honours to your own retreat:
> To shade the hill, to scoop or swell the green
> To break with wild diversities the scene,
> To model with the Genius of the place
> Each artless feature, each spontaneous grace.
> For, as you work, the Genius still presides,
> Directs each stroke and each improvement guides.
> Hence thro' the whole irregularly great,
> Nature and Art the won'drous work complete:
> In all so true, so unperceived the skill,
> That Nature modified is Nature still.

66.   A modern view of Ugbrooke.

What contemporaries experienced at Ugbrooke was Nature taken at leisure and perceived in detail, with a precision that is rarely granted to the busy visitor of today. Here at Ugbrooke we find that sense of excitement and change in the peaceful groves and placid lakes which are the delight of every landscaped park.

> Here limes and masterful beech, with nodding pride,
> O'er a wild tribe of vulgar trees preside.
> Now bowing greens their woven shades unite,
> And dimly shade the quivering gleams of light:
> Now op'ning glades disclose the pathless way,
> And in full brightness pour the rushing day.

George Oliver, D.D. (1781-1861)

In his preface to his *History of Exeter*, Dr. George Oliver wrote of a previous history of the city by the antiquarian Alexander Jenkins: 'Of Mr. Jenkins' late compilation, which he is pleased to entitle *The History and Description of the City of Exeter*, the writer of the present work could wish to say as little as possible. Mr. Jenkins deserves praise for endeavouring to collect information: but he should not suppose that what may satisfy his mind will content a discerning public'.

We do not need to be so waspish about Dr. Oliver's history of the Clifford family, but the cap he places on the unhappy Mr. Jenkins' head certainly fits his own. Dr. Oliver wrote his history of the Cliffords at a time when access to many essential records, now conveniently accessible in Public and County Record Offices, was difficult, if not impossible without a great deal of travelling and effort. It is only natural, therefore, that 19th-century family historians such as he should make mistakes and leave omissions, which we are now fortunate enough to be able to rectify.

Dr. Oliver is justly remembered for his masterpiece – his great *Monasticon Dioecesis Exoniensis* – published in 1846. W. G. Hoskins describes it as 'the greatest work of medieval scholarship ever published about South-Western England'. It surveys all the monastic houses in Devon and Cornwall, the collegiate churches, hospitals and friaries. To compile this great work, Dr. Oliver was among the first to be able to make use of the Public Record Office, for in 1853, the year before the *Monasticon* appeared, was published the *Handbook to the Public Records* as a rough guide to what amounts to possibly three-quarters of the national archives.

Throughout his long incumbency of the Roman Catholic parish in Exeter, he was helped and patronised by the Lords Clifford of Chudleigh, and it was to them that Dr. Oliver dedicated his histories of Exeter and of the south-western monasteries.

The authors of the present work on the Clifford family owe Dr. Oliver a debt, even when they find that they have to disagree with some of what he wrote. Without his work, this one would have been much more difficult to compile.

Will of Roger de Clifford the Elder, 1284

Ref. Register of Bishop Godfrey
GIFFARD., p. 283
of *Worcester*

Under heading 1286.

Will of *Roger de Clifford the elder* dated Thursday before the feast of *All Saints 1284*. He leaves his body to be buried in the church of *Dore*, and with his body *his war-horse trappings (dextrarium meum co-opertorium)* or 30 marks. To ten chaplains celebrating divine service for three years for his soul 100 li. For the honourable burial of his body and to be distributed to the poor 40 li. In aid of the religious houses in the counties of *Worcester* and *Hereford*, according to the disposition of his Executors, 10 marks. To the nuns of the house of *Westwood*, 10 li. In aid of the church of *Temedebiry* [Tenbury] 10s. To the nuns of *Accornebur'*, 40s. In aid of the church of *Stok'* 10s. In aid of the church of *Monnmue* [Monmouth] 10s. To the church of *Brug'*, 10s. To the church of *Erdesl* [Erdisley] 10s. *To Alice, his daughter*, 40 marks. To a certain man going to the Holy Land, 50 marks. *To his wife*, all his silver utensils and other things. *To Stephen Pech'*, 20 marks. *To Reginald*, the clerk 20 li. The residue of his goods to be expended as his executors shall deem expedient for the benefit of his soul. He appoints as his executors the *abbot of Dore*, the *abbot of Persore, Andrew, vicar of Stok*, and *Roger, vicar of Temedebyr'*. And he directs that *his wife may* have her chamber free, and all her jewels, and all things which pertained to her of his goods

> NOTE: The above is found in the detailed register on page 283 but there follows another entry, under the same year which is 1286, on page 293, as under:

Fol. 257d. Writ to distrain *Andrew, vicar of Severestok'* [Severnstoke], and *Roger, vicar of Temedebur* [Tenbury], executors of the will of *R. de Clifford*, the elder, to appear and answer *William Barach', chamberlain of London*, and *Eymer de Ponte*, his fellow merchants, together with the abbot of *Dour* [Dore] and the abbot of *Persore*, the co-executors of the same will, concerning 12 marks which the deceased owed, as they say. Dated 3rd July, 14 Edward 1. ... (1286).

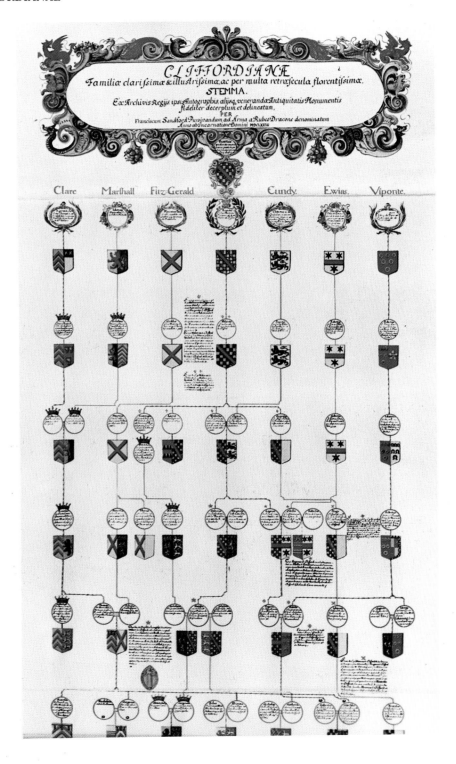

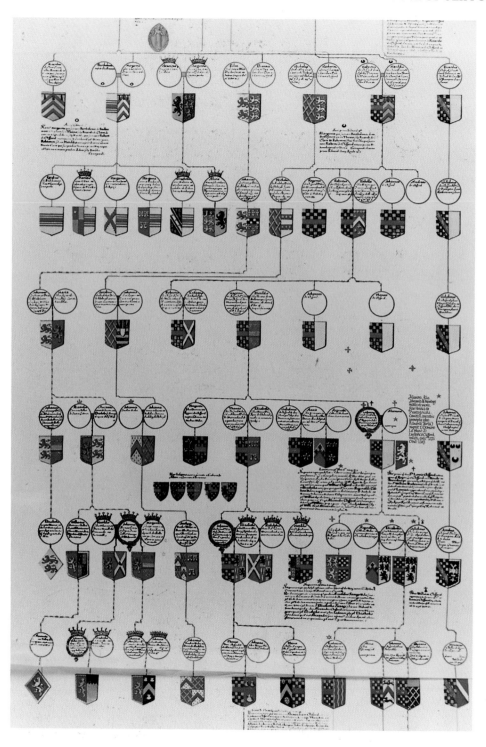

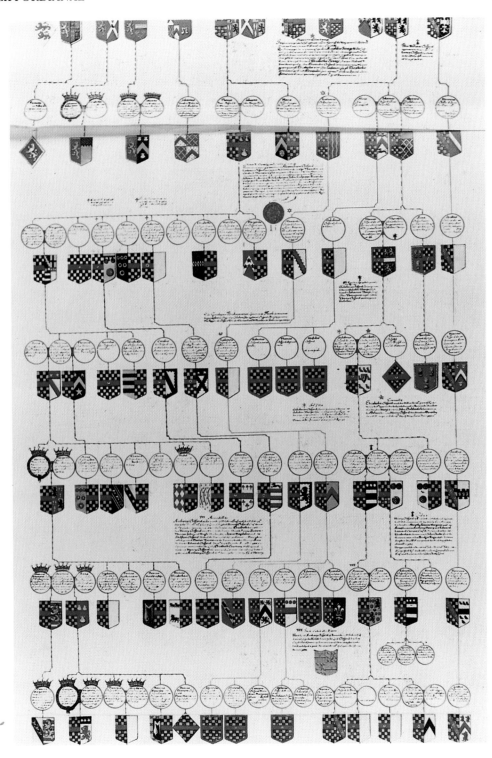

The Armorial Bearings and Pedigree of
Colonel The Right Honourable LEWIS HUGH, 15th BARON CLIFFORD OF CHUDLEIGH, OBE, ADC, DL.

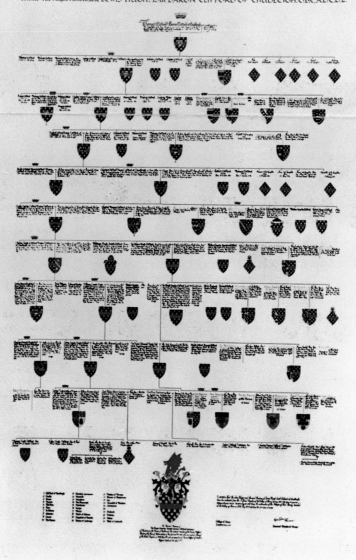

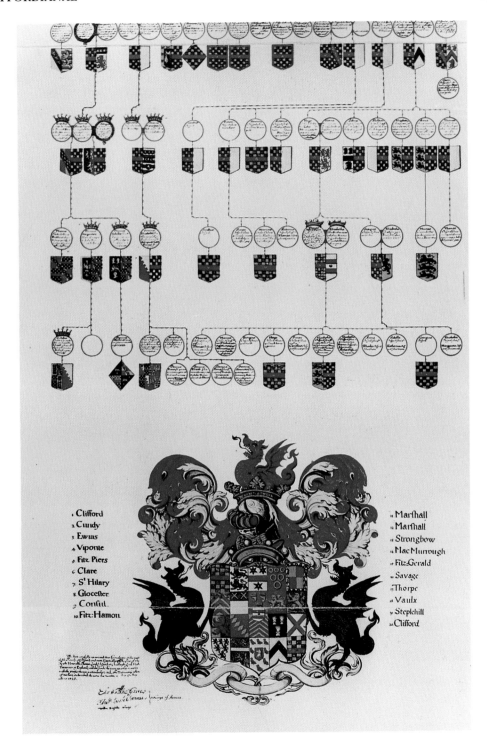

1. Clifford
2. Cundy
3. Ewias
4. Viponte
5. Fitz Piers
6. Clare
7. St Hilary
8. Glocester
9. Consul.
10. Fitz-Hamon

11. Marshall
12. Marshall
13. Strongbow
14. MacMurrough
15. Fitz-Gerald
16. Savage
17. Thorpe
18. Vaulx
19. Steplehill
20. Clifford

Notes

Chapter One

1. Davis, H. W. C., and Whitwell, R. J., *Regesta Regum Anglo-Normanorum, 1066-1154*, vol. 1, no. 1. Oxford 1913.
2. White, Geoffrey H., revised ed., *GEC's Complete Peerage*, vol. 12, part 1. London 1953. Appendix 50, pp. 47-8, 'Companions of the Conqueror' lists the names of only twenty whose presence at Hastings can be proved with certainty.
3. For the House of Clare, see the revised *GEC*, vol. 3, *sub* Clare.
4. See Chapter Seventy-One.
5. For the twenty names of those known to have fought at Hastings see note 2 above.
6. Fauroux, Marie, *Recueil des actes des ducs de Normandie de 911 à 1066* with index by Musset, Lucien (Société des Antiquaires de Normandie, tome 36, Caen 1961), no. 35, pp. 131-5. See also Appendix A.
7. *Victoria County History of Hereford* (London 1908); also revised *GEC*, vol. 12, part 1, pp. 754-64 *sub* Tony; and Musset, Lucien, *Aux Origines d'une classe dirigeante: Les Tosny, grands barons normands due Xe au XIIe siècles* (Soc. Ant. de Normandie). But note that *GEC* styles him Ralph de Toeni III, while Musset calls him Raoul II de Tosny.
8. See Clifford, Arthur, *Collectania Cliffordiana*, reprinted by Skipton Castle Ltd., Skipton, Yorkshire, 1980. It should be noted that Walter II de Clifford in the 13th century had a daughter, Basilia.
9. Round, J. H., *Ancient Charters*, part 1 (London 1888), p. 24.
10. See revised *GEC*, vol. 10, *sub* Poyntz.
11. See Maclean, Sir John, *Historical and Genealogical Memoir of the Family of Poyntz*, Exeter 1886.
12. *ibid.*, pp. 222-5. The curse was on the Brownes, Viscounts Montagu of whom Colonel Poyntz's wife was the heiress.
13. Dugdale's *Monasticon*.
14. *Victoria County History of Berkshire*, vol. 4, p. 59.

Chapter Two

1. Morgan, Philip, introduction to *Domesday Book: Berkshire* (Phillimore 1979) citing Robert Losinge, Bishop of Hereford 1079-95 (*English Historical Review* 22, 1907, 44), and *Dialogues de Scaccaria*, 1, 16.
2. The 'Drogo' who appears in Domesday Book as holding 73 manors in Devon of the Bishop of Coutances was NOT Dru Fitzpons (as often stated in error) but Dru FitzMaulger.
3. See, *inter alia*, Sanders, I. J., *Feudal Military Service in England* (O.U.P. 1956).
4. It has been shown by Round, Hoskins and Cohen that the *servitia debita* in England, Normandy and southern Italy were based on units of five and ten knights' fees (the Normans conquered Sicily about the same time as they conquered England).
5. A virgate was a quarter of a hide, but both were usually arable units assessed for tax rather than fixed areas of land. We are much indebted to Professor John Dodgson and Dr. F. R. Thorn for advice about Dru Fitzpons' Domesday holdings.
6. See Chapter Seventy.
7. Lloyd, Sir John, *History of Wales* (1911), vol. 2, p. 375.
8. Clifford Castle passed to the Clifford family in the 12th century.
9. Ewyas Harold Castle was acquired by Sir Lewis Clifford, K.G., in the 14th century.
10. Nelson, Lynn H., *The Normans in South Wales, 1070-1171* (University of Texas Press, Austin, and London, 1967), p. 71.
11. *ibid.*, p. 72.
12. *Victoria County History of Herefordshire.*, ed. W. Page, vol. 1 (London 1908), pp. 277-8.
13. Round, J. H., *Feudal England*, pp. 241-5: 'The Worcestershire Relief'.

Chapter Three

1. Lloyd, Sir John, *History of Wales*, vol. 2, pp. 393-4.
2. Nelson, Lynn H., *op. cit.*, pp. 87 *et seq.*
3. Nelson calls Richard Fitzpons 'lord of Clifford' here, but although the Fitzpons family were among the barons who held lands within the 'castlery' of Clifford at this time, it was not until the next generation that the actual lordship of Clifford passed by marriage into the family.
4. For Bronllys Castle, see Clark, G. T., 'Bronllys Castle' in *Archaeologia Cambrensis*, vol. 8, 3rd series, no. 30 (April 1862), pp. 81-92; also illus. and plan; *Archaeologia Cambrensis*, vol. 4, 6th series (1904), pp. 158-60; Cathcart King, D. J. 'The Castles of Breconshire' in *Brycheiniog*, vol. 7 (1961) ed. D. J. Davies; and *Cambrian Archaeological Association* (August 1974).
5. The position of these conquistador Marcher lords has been analysed by Edwards, J. G., F.B.A., in *The Normans and the Welsh March*.
6. *Proc. British Academy*, XLII (1956), pp. 155-77.
7. Dugdale's *Monasticon*, 3, p. 448.
8. *Lib. Land* 37; and Rot. Pip., 31 Henry I.
9. Round, J. H., *Ancient Charters, Royal and Private, prior to 1200*, part 1 Pipe Roll Soc., London 1888; nos. 6 (pp. 8-10), 12 and 13 (pp. 20-5).
10. See revised *GEC*, vol. 6 (1926), *sub* Hereford.
11. *Dictionary of National Biography*, vol. 7 (1908), *sub* Gloucester, Miles de. At the dawn of heraldry Miles of Gloucester, Earl of Hereford, bore for arms 'Gules two bends the upper gold the lower silver': see 'The Arms of the Constable and the Marshal', chap. 14 of *Heraldry and the Heralds* by Rodney Dennys, Arundel Herald, London (1981).
12. Eyton, Rev. R. W., *Antiquities of Shropshire* (London 1857), vol. 5.
13. See note 9 above.
14. See note 9 above.

Chapter Four

1. Nelson, Lynn H., *op. cit.*, p. 153 *et seq.*
2. Williams, Mary, *Life in Wales in Medieval times* (Soc. of Cymmrodorion 1914-15), pp. 136-94.
3. Eyton, Rev. R. W., *Antiquities of Shropshire*, vol. 5 (London 1857), p. 148; also *Monasticon*, vol. 1, p. 551.
4. Margaret is usually said to have been the daughter of Ralph II de Toeni, the Domesday lord of Clifford, but the dates rule this out absolutely. Ralph's daughter, Godeheut, who died in 1097, married Baldwin de Boulogne, afterwards king of Jerusalem. Nevertheless there is no reason to doubt that Margaret was Ralph IV's daughter. He married in 1103; she is not known to have married before the 1130s.
5. Maclean, Sir John, *Memoir of the Family of Poyntz* (Exeter, 1886), p. 6 citing *Cart. Monas S. Petri. Glouc.* vol. 1, pp. 311 *et seq.*
6. For Adelaide, natural daughter of Duke Robert the Devil of Normandy by a different mistress from the Conqueror's mother, see the revised *GEC*, vol. 12, part 1, App. K.
7. Lloyd, Sir John, *op. cit.*, vol. 2, p. 469 *et seq.*
8. *ibid.*
9. See Chapter Five below.
10. Boon, Geo. C., 'Treasure Trove from Angevin Wales' in Seaby's *Coin and Medal Bulletin*, July 1981, pp. 195 *et seq.*
11. *Brut.* 118; *Annales Cambriae*, p. 48.
12. Lloyd, Sir John, *op. cit.*, p. 505 *et seq.*
13. *Archaeologia Cambrensis*, vol. 4, 6th series (London 1904), pp. 158-60.
14. Eyton, R. W., *op. cit.*, vol. 5, pp. 162. 162.
15. *ibid.*, 5, p. 197.
16. *ibid.*, 4, p. 306.
17. *ibid.*, 5, p. 150.
18. *ibid.*, 5, pp. 151-4.
19. *ibid.*, 4, p. 302 *et seq.*
20. *ibid.*, 5, p. 308. For Lucy Clifford's second marriage see same page.

Chapter Five

1. Pernoud, *Eleanor of Aquitaine*, p. 199.
2. *Encyclopaedia Britannica* (14th ed.).
3. *Walter Map: De Nugis Curialium*, ed. Wright (Camden Soc.).
4. Hearne, ed., *Leland's Itinerary 1678-1735*.
5. *ibid.*

Chapter Six

1. Eyton, *op. cit., passim*.
2. Foster, Canon C. W. in *Reg. Antiq.* (Lincs. Rec. Soc.), vol. 1, pp. 282-95.
3. *Trans. Woolhope Nat. Field Club* (Herefordshire, vol. for 1936-8), pp. 140-8.
4. Nelson, Lynn H., *op. cit.*, pp. 137-8.
5. Williams, Dr. Mary, *op. cit.*, pp. 169-70.
6. Round, J. H., *Geoffrey de Mandeville*, pp. 392-6. To this group – Mandeville, Say, Fitzjohn, Beauchamp of Bedford, Clavering and de Vere, Earls of Oxford – should be added Sackville of Buckhurst.
7. Sir Iain Moncreiffe of that Ilk, Albany Herald, considered that the gold and blue chequy coat of Vermandois was an example of double coats (a shield with a device and a banner with a geometrical pattern of the same colours later inherited by separate branches of the same family), in this case based on the royal azure semée de lys, or of France. For the subject, see his 'Double Coats at the Dawn of Northumbrian and Scottish Heraldry', published in *The Armorial*, vol. 6, no. 1 (Edinburgh, 1970), pp. 19-31.
8. In the revised *GEC*, vol. 12, part 1, at App. J. To this group should obviously be added the Cliffords and almost certainly the Stewarts, afterwards kings of Scots and then of Great Britain: but it is not clear yet how they came to belong to it.
9. Their contemporaries did not call them Beaumont, but historians find the later surname convenient.
10. Revised *GEC*, vol. 10, pp. 780 and 803n.
11. Foster, Joseph, *Some Feudal Coats of Arms* (London 1902).
12. See Chesney in L. C. Lloyd's *The Origins of some Anglo-Norman Families*, ed. C. Clay and D. Douglas, Harleian Soc., vol. 103, pp. 27-8.

Chapter Seven

1. Lloyd, Sir John, *op. cit.*, vol. 2, p. 643 and p. 678 *et seq.*
2. Eyton, *op. cit.*, vol. 5, pp. 155-6.
3. Eyton, *op. cit.*, vol. 5, p. 158.
4. Sanders, I. J., *English Baronies: A Study of their Origin and Descent, 1086-1327.* Oxford 1960.
5. *ibid.*, 35-6.
6. *Dict. Nat. Biog.*, vol. 21, p. 369; *sub* William de Fors.
7. Rymer's *Foedera*.
8. Patent Rolls, 2, 184.
9. *Cambrian Arch. Assoc. Proc.*, 1974.
10. *Brycheiniog*, vol. 7, ed. D. J. Davis (1961), p. 76.
11. Eyton, *op. cit.*, vol. 5, pp. 197-8.
12. William Addams Reitwiesner, 'The children of Joan, Princess of Wales', *The Genealogist* (New York, 1980), vol. 1, no. 1, p. 83.
13. *Ency. Brit.*, 11th ed. (1911), *sub*. Wales.
14. Lloyd, Sir John, *op. cit.*, vol. 2, p. 678.
15. Eyton, *op. cit.*, vol. 5, pp. 158-9.
16. Delaborde, M., *Jean de Joinville et les sieurs de Joinville*, Paris 1886.

Chapter Eight

1. Paris, Matthew, vol. 5, pp. 557, 609.
2. Revised *GEC Complete Peerage*, vol. 5, p. 642, *sub*. Giffard citing Patent Roll, 55 Hen. III, m. 19. See

also *ibid.*, vol. 11, p. 284, *sub.* Salisbury.
3. *ibid.*, vol. 5, p. 642n (h) and the references therein cited.

Chapter Nine

1. Sanders, I. J., *op. cit.*, pp. 7, 43, 57; Pipe Roll, 14 John, p. 137.
2. Marshall, G., 'The Norman Occupation of the Lands in the Golden Valley, Ewyas and Clifford'. (*Trans. Woolhope Nat. Field Club 1936-8*, pp. 322-5); Bannister, A., 'History of Ewias Harold' (1902), *Burkes Peerage*, 1970 ed. *sub.* Sudeley.
3. *Dict. Nat. Biog.*, vol. 16, p. 653 *sub* Ralph the Timid, Earl of Hereford; also revised *GEC Complete Peerage*, vol. 6 (1926), pp. 446-7, *sub.* Hereford; Harmer, F. E., *Anglo-Saxon Writs*, part 4, Biographical notes *sub* Ralph Earl of Hereford.
4. Wagner, Sir Anthony, in *Burke's Peerage*, 1970, *sub.* Sudeley, citing Professor David Kelley.
5. Sanders, I. J., *Feudal Military Service in England* (London 1956), p. 109, note 4.
6. Lloyd, Sir John, *op. cit.*, vol. 2, pp. 667-9.
7. Sanders, *ibid.*, pp. 121, 128.
8. See pp. 33-5 above, Chapter Seven.
9. See above, Chapter Seven, note 15.

Chapter Ten

1. *Complete Peerage*, vol. 12, part 2 (1959), *sub.* Tregoz.
2. Ex information Lord Sudeley, citing Bannister, A., 'History of Ewias Harold' (1902).
3. *Complete Peerage*, *ibid.*, p. 19, note (a), excerpted *Rot. Fines*, 1, p. 219; Sanders, I. J., *op. cit.*, p. 68; Cal. Patent Rolls, 14 Hen. III.
4. Ex information Sanders, I. J., *Documents of the Baronial Movement of Reform and Rebellion, 1259-1327* (Oxford 1973).
5. Lloyd, Sir John, *op. cit.*, vol. 2, pp. 731-2.
6. Coplestone-Crow, B., *The Baskervilles of Herefordshire*, Woolhope Nat. Hist. Soc. 43, part 1, 1979.
7. Clifford, A., *Collectanea Cliffordiana* (Paris 1817, republished Skipton Castle Ltd. 1980), pp. 187, 329.
8. *Complete Peerage*, vol. 7, p. 631, *sub.* Leyburn.
9. See note 7 above, also *DNB*, vol. 4, p. 529.
10. Salmon, Mary, *A Source-book of Welsh History* (London 1927), p. 166.
11. *Annales Mon.* (Rolls Series), vol. 3; also *Cal. Docs. Ireland 1252-1284.* (Camden Soc.).
12. Eyton, *op. cit.*, vol. 5, p. 183.
13. *Ypodigma Neustriae* (Rolls Series), p. 158; Hemingburgh, vol. 1, p. 320, *Cal. Docs. Ireland, 1258-1266.*
14. Eyton, *op. cit.*, vol. 4, p. 183.
15. *ibid.*, vol. 4, p. 182, note, 3.
16. Runciman, Sir Steven, *A History of the Crusades*, vol. 3, pp. 335-8, 348.
17. *DNB*, vol. 4, p. 529 and sources cited therein.
18. *ibid.*, also *Cliffordiana*, p. 190.
19. *ibid.*
20. Dugdale's *Baronage. Cliffordiana* has it as 'Lorraine', which is clearly incorrect.
21. Hemingburgh, vol. 1, pp. 337-40.
22. *DNB, ibid.*
23. Rishanger, William, *Chronicle* (Camden Soc.).
24. As translated by Mary Salmon; *op. cit.*, p. 176.
25. *DNB, ibid.*
26. Clay, J. W., 'The Clifford Family' in *Yorkshire Archaeological Journal*, vol. 18 (1905), pp. 355-6, citing *Cal. of Close RollsPS and PSCal. of Patent Rolls*. See also revised *GEC Complete Peerage, sub.* Clifford.
27. Clay, *ibid.*
28. See Appendix B.

Chapter Eleven

1. Clay, J. W., *The Clifford Family*, p. 356.
2. Revised *Complete Peerage*, vol. 5, p. 437, *sub* Fitzjohn. He is sometimes mistakenly said to have been killed on the baronial side at Evesham.
3. *Cliffordiana*, p. 180.
4. Sanders, I. J., *op. cit.*, pp. 103-4, 133, 147.
5. *Complete Peerage, ibid.* See note 2 above.
6. *DNB*, vol. 4, p. 529.
7. Salmon, Mary, *op. cit.*, pp. 176-7. See also Sir John Lloyd, *op. cit.*, vol. 2, p. 762; *DNB, ibid.*; and *Complete Peerage, ibid.*
8. *ibid.* (translation).
9. *Inq. Post Mortem* series, vol. 2, no. 478.
10. Clay, *op. cit.*, and Sir Bede Clifford's MS.

Chapter Twelve

1. Sanders, I. J., *op. cit.*, pp. 104, 133.
2. *ibid.*, pp. 84, 104.
3. *ibid.*, p. 142; Clay, J. W., *op. cit.*, p. 357.
4. Barrow, G. W. S., *Robert Bruce* (London 1965), p. 119.
5. *DNB*, citing Rishanger, 183. Barrow, *op. cit.*, p. 135 citing *Chron. Guisb.*, 307-98. Also *Roll of Caerlaverock*, p. 11n.
6. *Roll of Caerlaverock*, ed. with translation and notes by Thomas Wright (London 1864).
7. Clifford's seal in 1301 is illustrated by Joseph Foster in *Some Feudal Coats of Arms* (Oxford and London 1902), p. 17.
8. Barrow, *op. cit.*, pp. 179, 201.
9. *DNB*, citing *Reg. Pal. Dun.*, iii, 58, 59; iv, 261.
10. Barrow, *op. cit.*, pp. 243-4.
11. *ibid.*, p. 247n.
12. *DNB*, Clay and *Complete Peerage, op. cit.*
13. *Scots Peerage*, ed. Balfour Paul, 3, p. 143; Barrow, *op. cit.*, p. 247n.
14. *Complete Peerage* and *DNB*.
15. *Parl. Writs*, 617-8.
16. Foster, *op. cit.*, p. 18.
17. Sanders, *op. cit.*, p. 84.
18. *DNB*, and authorities therein cited. Clay, *op. cit.*, p. 357n.
19. *DNB*.
20. *Cal. Pat. Rolls* (1312), pp. 498, 500; (1313), pp. 21, 22. The pardon also included a John de Clifford, possibly Robert's Ellingham cousin, Sir John.
21. *DNB*, citing *Parl. Writs*, 688; *Chron. Edw. II*, 201.
22. Barrow, *op. cit.*, p. 313 *et seq.*, and authorities cited therein.
23. *Ency. Brit.*, 11th ed. (1911), *sub.* Clare; also revised *Complete Peerage, sub.* Gloucester.
24. He is also said to have had a son JOHN, but this may have been the John who was a younger son of his contemporary Robert Clifford, baron of Ellingham in Northumberland, with whom Robert, Lord Clifford is often confused (see W. Percy Hedley, *Northumberland Families*, vol. 2, Soc. Antiq. Newcastle-upon-Tyne, 1970). Dodsworth indicates that this Robert Clifford married as his first wife the daughter of Humphrey Bohun by whom he had two daughters, Idoine already mentioned, and Margaret. This Margaret married according to Dodsworth again, firstly Peter de Mauley of Iwardby who died in 1355, and secondly Giles de Badlesmere.

Chapter Thirteen

1. Clay, J. W., *op. cit.*, p. 359n, citing Patent Rolls (1317-21), p. 55.
2. Clay, *op. cit.*, citing *ibid.*, p. 433.
3. Clay, *op. cit.*, citing Cal. Close Rolls (1318-23), p. 513.

4. *Leland's Collectanea*, ed. Thomas Hearne (1774), pp. 463-5.
5. *ibid.*
6. Harleian MSS 6177, p. 22.
7. Williamson, Dr. George, *Lady Anne Clifford* (1967), p. 8.
8. *The Baildons*, vol. 1, pp. 65-9, citing Assize Roll 1117, m.5d.
9. Hothfield MSS: Kendall Record Office.
10. Curwen, John F., *Kirkbie Kendal* (Kendal 1900).

Chapter Fourteen

1. Williamson, G., *op. cit.*, pp. 9-11.
2. Cal. Patent Rolls (1381-5), p. 99; *ibid.* (1385-9), pp. 288, 443.
3. Richard Clifford, Bishop of London, is variously described as his son or grandson, but as Sir Thomas could not have been born before 1334, and the bishop was already a canon in 1385, there hardly seems room for an intermediate generation. Moreover, there is a reference for 1388 in Rolls Series vol. 28, to Sir Thomas Clifford of Thomond being banished from Court when his son Richard was imprisoned. There is however another possibility. The Clifford barons of Ellingham in Northumberland are known to have also borne either or or agent three eagles displayed gules as appear on their seals of deeds in the Durham archives. It would be chronologically possible for Sir Thomas to have had a sister who married an Ellingham Clifford and was mother of Bishop Richard and Sheriff Robert. He may have two more, Lewis and Hugh (see Chapter Twenty-Eight).
4. McFarlane, K. B., *Lancastrian Kings and Lollard Knights* (Oxford 1972), p. 82.
5. *ibid.*
6. *DNB.*
7. *ibid.*
8. Blackham, R. J., *The Story of the Temple, Gray's and Lincoln's Inn* (London 1930), pp. 130-31. See also Mitchell, M., *History of the British Optical Association 1895-1978* (London 1982), p. 172; and *British Optical Association Yearbook 1930*, pp. 295-301.

Chapter Sixteen

1. Williamson, G., *Lady Anne Clifford* (1967), p. 11.

Chapter Seventeen

1. Reese, M. M., *Master of the Horse*, pp. 64-5.
2. But see Chapter Fourteen, note 3.
3. *Scots Peerage*, ed. Balfour Paul, vol. 3 (1906), pp. 463-4.
4. *Test. Ebor.*, vol. 2, p. 18.

Chapter Eighteen

1. *Cliffordiana*, III.
2. Hothfield MS at Kendal Record Office.

Chapter Nineteen

1. Seward, Desmond, *Richard III: England's Black Legend* (London 1983), p. 164; see also Clay, *op. cit.*, p. 369.
2. *Plumpton Correspondence* (Camden Soc.), p. 64.
3. *Yorks. Arch. J.*, vol. 4, p. 225, also *Visit. Essex*, p. 124.
4. Whitaker's *Richmondshire*.
5. *Test. Ebor.*, vol. 3; *Genealogist*, no. 3, p. 380.
6. Waterton Family History.
7. Hothfield MS, Kendal Record Office.

Chapter Twenty

1. Yorks. Arch. Soc., vol. 9, p. 117, 'Yorkshire Deeds'.
2. Cal. PR, 15 H, 7, part 2: 25 July 1500 states: 'Licence of entry without proof of age for Henry Clifford Kt, alias Lord of Clifford, Westmorland and Vesci, son and heir of Margaret, formerly wife of John Clifford Kt and brother and heir of Richard Clifford Esq., deceased, on all lands of the said Margaret and Richard ... From the above it appears that he died by this date, and that he had no legitimate children. It is possible that this Richard went to Aylsham, Norfolk, where he had issue who could have been ancestors of the Dutch Branch (see Chapter 62).'
3. Dodsworth, *op. cit.* vol. 83, f. 76.

Chapter Twenty-One

1. See also Chapter Twenty, note 2, and Chapter Sixty-Two.

Chapter Twenty-Two

1. Calendar Letters etc., Hen. VIII, vol. 17, p. 158.
2. *DNB.*
3. Listed by Clay, *op. cit.*,p. 375n.
4. Cumberland's will, like those of a number of other Cliffords, is printed in full by Clay, *op. cit.*

Chapter Twenty-Three

1. *DNB* and *Complete Peerage.*
2. *DNB*, citing Cal. of State Papers, Venetian, ed. Rawdon Brown, p. 1707.
3. Clay, *op. cit.*, pp. 386-7.
4. Hill MSS/Machelle, p. 567; and Whitaker's *Craven*, 2nd ed., p. 198.

Chapter Twenty-Four

1. Sackville-West, V., *The Diary of Lady Anne Clifford, with an Introductory Note* (London 1923).
2. Collins *Peerage*, 3 January 1569/70, vol. 1, p. 262.
3. *Alum. Cantab.* 2, p. 416.
4. Dowland, John, *A Musical Banquet, furnished with variety of delicious airs collected out of the best authors in English, French, Spanish and Italian.*
5. Holborne, Anthony, *Pavans, Galliards, Almains and other short Airs both grave and light, for violins or other musical wind instruments.*
6. Whitaker's *History of Craven.*
7. Cecil MSS, iii, 347.
8. Wright's *Original Letters*, 2, p. 401.
9. *DBN.*
10. The 3rd earl had a collection of the most impressive tilting armour, which the Cliffords of Chudleigh tried to buy when his female line descendant, Lord Hothfield, sold it from Appleby Castle in the 20th century, but in the event it went to America.
11. Monson's *Naval Tracts*, vol. 1.
12. Lord Thomas Howard, afterwards Lord Howard de Walden and Earl of Suffolk, K.G., second son of Thomas, 4th Duke of Norfolk, K.G.
13. Tennyson's epic ballad *The Revenge.*
14. The letter is quoted in full in Dr. Williamson's *George, Third Earl of Cumberland* (Cambridge 1920) at pp. 76-8.
15. Younger son of 4th Lord Burgh, he was afterwards killed in a duel with Raleigh's relation, John Gilbert.
16. Williamson, *op. cit.*, pp. 108-9.
17. Williamson, *op. cit.*, p. 116.
18. Williamson, *op. cit.*, pp. 126 *et seq.*

19. Or *Malescourge*.
20. Cumberland to Cecil, 15 August 1595.
21. Afterwards Sir Francis Slingsby. He read the story of these voyages to Lady Anne Clifford, who mentions it in her diary of 24 November 1619.
22. The present Lord Clifford of Chudleigh's father (later 12th Lord Clifford of Chudleigh) was able to acquire a copy of the earl's portrait for the (East) India Club of New York where he was introduced, incorrectly, by Charles M. Schwab, head of Bethlehem Steel, as the descendant of the first Company President.
23. Drake's *Eboracum*, 131-2, and app. 50 and 51 and the York Records; cited by Williamson, pp. 259-60.
24. Williamson, *op. cit.*, p. 260, citing Sir R. Winwood, *Memorials of Affairs of State* (1723), 2, p. 44.
25. Hailstone, E., *Skipton Castle, its History and the Owners*.
26. Spence, R. T., Thesis on the Earls of Cumberland.

Chapter Twenty-Seven
1. PRO class C 22/214/43; SP 23/79.
2. Whitaker's *Craven*.
3. Holmes, Martin, *Proud Northern Lady*, Phillimore, 1975, 1984.

Chapter Twenty-Eight
1. Cottonian MS. Julius C. IV (296).
2. *Test. Vetusta*.
3. *Complete Peerage, sub*. Mowbray.
4. Patent Rolls.
5. *ibid*.
6. Feet of Fines 2255.
7. Kettridge, G. T., 'Lewis Chaucer or Lewis Clifford?' *Modern Philology*, xiv, no. 9.
8. PCC 4 Marche.
9. Wriothesley's *Pedigrees from the Plea Rolls*, p. 390; De Banco Mich., 25 Hen. VI, Norfolk.
10. *Inq. ad Quod Damnum*.
11. Close Rolls, Hen. V, vol. 2, pp. 62-3.
12. See Hedley, W. Percy, *Northumberland Families*, vol. 2, Soc. Antiq. Newcastle-upon-Tyne, 1970, pp. 2-3.
13. Macfarlane, K. B., 'The Lollard Knights'.
14. PCC 4 Marche.
15. Waugh, W. T., 'The Lollard Knights', *Scottish Hist. Review*, vol. 9 (1913), pp. 58-63, 88-92.

Chapter Twenty-Nine
1. PRO, C1/19/142 and C1/22/142.
2. Walter Langley was his trustee.
3. For Chestonwood see Patent Rolls 1461-7, pp. 16, 77, 213.
4. Alice, wife of John Clifford, was mentioned in the will of Joan Knowght in 1459. Canterbury Archdeaconry Will A1/30.
5. C1/125/47.
6. PCC 13 Coode.
7. Burke's *Landed Gentry*.

Chapter Thirty-One
1. Rot. 93, 1 Hen. VIII.
2. Her will refers to her son, John Chiddisdale.
3. See her mother's will, but also Visitation of Dorset, Wiltshire and Somerset, folio 60.

General Note: The spelling of the Thorpe family's estate in Wiltshire varies between Boscombe and Borscombe. Even today it varies in this way, but we have settled on Borscombe in order to prevent confusion with the better-known Boscombe near Bournemouth.

Chapter Thirty-Two

1. The Deed is mentioned in Henry Clifford's will. PROB.11/60.
2. *ibid.*
3. Chancery Proceedings, C2 Eliz. C20/31.
4. Harleian Visitations for Berkshire, Clifford of Kintbury Eaton.
5. PROB 11/171 and PROB 10/641. The latter will is an original to which is attached the seal, depicting a Wyvern.
6. *ibid.*
7. This Edward is sometimes mistaken for a different Edward, Vicar of Blackawton, who married an Anne (d. 16 October 1578) and himself died in 1585 (will proved 26 October 1585, Exeter C.C.).

Chapter Thirty-Three

1. Sir Piers Courtenay's will was proved before Bishop Miles Coverdale on 19 September 1553.
2. See Burke's *Peerage, sub* Devon, for genealogical history of the Courtenay family.
3. Anthony's will. Written and proved 1580. PROB.11/62.
4. Henry's will. Written 1635, proved 1636. PROB.11/171.
5. Anthony II's will. Written 1642, proved 1644. PROB.10/641.
6. Henry's Inquisition of 1637. PROB. Ward 7/27/8.
7. Simon I's will. Written and proved 1639. PROB.11/182.
8. Simon II's deed re Borscombe/Lockerlie. Chancery C/3/451/30.
9. Simon II's will. Written 1644, proved 1645. Winchester R.O.

Chapter Thirty-Four

1. MS additions to Dugdale's *Baronage*, Nicols *Collectanea*, vol. 2.
2. Void by the death of the Rev. Richard Bowding.
3. Mentioned in Samuel Somaster's MS volume in the British Library, finished in 1694, and in Hartman's *Clifford of the Cabal.*
4. Proved 19 September 1634.
5. 'An account of some noble families in Devon etc. in the year 1640'.
6. A copy of the Honeywell journal is now in the Devonshire County Record Office.

Chapter Thirty-Five

1. In his addition to his *Baronage*, vol. 2, Nicols *Coll.*, p. 348.
2. Pearce, Charles E., *The Amazing Duchess, Elizabeth Chudleigh, Countess of Bristol*, vol. 1 (London 1914). For Chudleighs see *GEC's Complete Baronetage.*
3. Pearce, *ibid.*
4. Prince, *Worthies of Devon.*

Chapter Thirty-Six

1. Bryant, Arthur, *King Charles II* (Longman 1931).
2. *ibid.* p. 218. On the occasion of the tercentenary of the Cabal administration, Sir Arthur Bryant gave a speech at a dinner given by the present Lord Clifford at the House of Lords. He said on that occasion that the best reference work on Thomas, 1st Lord Clifford, was C. H. Hartman's *Clifford of the Cabal* (Heinemann, 1937).
3. Minette was Charles II's sister, Henrietta Anne, Duchess of Orleans.
4. Cal. State Papers, Domestic. 1665.

5. Prince Rupert to the king, 1 July 1666. CSPD 1665/66, p. 486.
6. Cannington Priory was granted at the dissolution to Edward Rogers.
7. July 1671.
8. See Clarke's *Life of James II*, vol. 1, p. 481.
9. Treasury Books, 1673, p. 47.
10. Letters to Williamson: Ball, 18 and 23 May; Yard, 23 May, 1673.
11. Earl of Ossory to Lord Conway, 2 June 1673.
12. Now in the Clifford MSS.
13. Pardons to the former Cabal: Clifford, 3 July; Lauderdale, 3 October; Shaftesbury, 7 November; and Buckingham, 9 November 1673.
14. In 1631 Francis, 9th Earl of Erroll, a devout convert to Catholicism was buried at midnight by his own wish, eschewing the usual state funeral which would have been according to the rites of the Established Church. It was a not uncommon practice at the time, for there are many other instances of it.
15. Hist. MSS Comm. 5th Report: MSS of J. R. Pine Coffin of Portledge, N. Devon, p. 375.
16. Rev. Henry Smith.

Chapter Thirty-Seven

1. Fol. ed. 1697, London, printed for Jacob Tonson.
2. Hartmann, C. H., *Clifford of the Cabal*, pp. 223-4.
3. He paid £253 7s. 0d. for it. Thomas Hunt had paid 400 marks for it a century before, on 17 November 1598.
4. See the *Protestant Mercury of the Exeter Post Boy* of Friday, 16 December 1715, printed by Joseph Bliss at his new printing house near the London Inn 'without Eastgate'.
5. The original of this letter is at Ugbrooke.
6. For the Prestons of Furness, see *The Complete Baronetage* by *GEC*, vol. 2.

Chapter Forty-Five

1. The contents of this chapter was contributed by Dr. P. B. Grout, Ph.D. Except where otherwise stated, all quotations come from unpublished letters and material in the possession of Lord Clifford of Chudleigh, Mr. Cuthbert Fitzherbert or Mr. Nicholas Fitzherbert, to all of whom we are indebted.
2. The family party included Thomas Weld and his sister-in-law Constantia Clifford, but excluded the two oldest Clifford children, Charles and Eleanora, who had been left behind at school in the care of their Clifford grandparents.
3. This kind of confused planning was typical of Hugh, Lord Clifford, and Henry was not the only one of his children to suffer from it.
4. Henry Clifford's letters from the Crimea have been published by his grandson, Mr. Cuthbert Fitzherbert in *Henry Clifford VC, His Letters and Sketches from the Crimea* (London, 1956).
5. See above, note 4.

Chapter Forty-Six

1. The material for this chapter was supplied by Hugo Clifford Holmes, who gives the following bibliography of his grandfather:
Clifford, Sir Henry: *Henry Clifford, His Letters and Sketches from the Crimea* (Michael Joseph, London, 1956).
Gailey, H. A.: *Clifford: Imperial Proconsul* (Rex Collings, London 1982).
Stockwell, A. J.: 'The early Career of Sir Hugh Clifford', *Journal of the Malayan Branch of the Royal Asian Soc.*, 49.
– 'Hugh Clifford in Trinidad, 1903-1907', *Caribbean Quarterly*, 24 (1978).
Cookey, S. J. S.: 'Sir Hugh Clifford as Governor of Nigeria', *African Affairs, Journal of the Royal African Soc.*, vol. 79, no. 317, October 1980.
Clifford Papers – being a score of Sir Hugh's scrapbooks containing newspaper cuttings and letters of an

official, semi-official and personal nature, covering the years 1890-1929 in the custody of his grandson, Hugo Clifford Holmes of Woking, Surrey.

Chapter Forty-Seven

1. *GEC Complete Peerage*, vol. 3, p. 307. Actually this land census was taken in 1883, but the position had not changed.
2. *History of Buckfast Abbey*, p. 297.

Chapter Fifty-Three

1. The Astons were Knights of the Shire from the reign of Henry III till the time of Charles I, when Sir Walter Aston of Tixall, Ambassador, was made Baron Aston of Forfar.
2. See Chapter Fourteen for the marriage of the 3rd Lord Clifford of Chudleigh to a Blount.

Chapter Fifty-Four

1. Pegasus Press, Christchurch, 1952.
2. The last Knight living at Axminster was dismissed in 1919, after the family had been agents at Ugbrooke for more than two hundred years.
3. *The Life of Sir Frederick Weld, GCMG, A Pioneer of Empire*, by Alice, Lady Lovat. (John Murray, 1914.)

Chapter Fifty-Eight

1. The information given in this chapter was supplied by the late R. E. F. Garrett and by Hugh Peskett.

Chapter Fifty-Nine

1. Calendar of Patent Rolls, 10 February 1366.

Chapter Sixty-One

1. Calendar of State Papers (Ireland).
2. *ibid.*
3. *Dictionary of National Biography*.

Chapter Sixty-Two

1. Our thanks are due to Mr. A. A. Bouvy, a direct descendant of this branch through his mother, Eleanora Clifford (d. 1966), for his kind help in compiling this chapter.

Chapter Sixty-Four

1. This chapter was contributed by David Clifford of Paignton, Devon.

Chapter Seventy

1. Ex information Philip E. Bennett, Dept. of French, Edinburgh Univ., and Professor Dominica Legge of Oxford.
2. Marie Fauroux, 'Recueil des actes des ducs de Normandie de 911 a 1066' (*Soc. Antiq. de Normandie*, tome 36, Caen, 1961).
3. *ibid.*, no. 35, pp. 131-5.
4. *ibid.*, p. 496.
5. *ibid.*, no. 190, pp. 372-3.
6. *ibid.*, p. 528.

Chapter Seventy-Two

1. We are grateful to *Country Life* and Alistair Rowan for permission to quote from his four articles on Ugbrooke in July and August 1967.
2. *ibid.*
3. *ibid.*

Index

Compiled by Noel Currer-Briggs

Clifford: persons

For reasons of space, the compiler has only included in this index those Cliffords who lived to maturity or married. He has omitted the numerous children who died in infancy. The names in brackets after female Cliffords are their married names. Those persons who changed their name from Constable to Clifford are distinguished by *. Individuals are identified by geographical location, shown as an abbreviation in **bold** type after their name (e.g. **F**), according to the following list:

Annesley & Wexford: **A & W**; Aspenden: **AS**; Berkshire: **BE**; Berwick: **BW**; Bobbing: **BO**; Bolton: **BO**; Borscombe: **BC**; Brackenborough: **BK**; Chestal: **C**; Chudleigh: **CL**; Craswall: **CR**; Cumberland: **CU**; Devonshire: **D**; Dublin: **DB**; Dutch: **DU**; Ellingham: **E**; Flaxbourne: **F**; Fordingbridge: **FO**; Frampton: **FP**; Iwade: **I**; Landbeach: **LA**; Lambeth: **LM**; Lanesborough: **L**; Lockerley: **LK**; London: **LO**; Market Drayton: **MD**; Newport: **N**; Norburn: **NO**; Pennington Narva: **PN**; Perristone: **P**; Sligo, Ireland: **S**; Stow-on-the-Wold: **ST**; Swindon: **SW**; Tenbury: **TE**; Thomond: **TH**; Tixall: **T**; Ugbrooke: **U**; Venn Court: **VC**; Virginia: **V**.

General Index

Before surnames became hereditary men and women were known either by a patronymic (Fitz) or by the name of their estate or abode. Hence some of the earlier names in this index have been listed under first names, e.g. William de Beauchamp, Walter, 1st Baron of Clifford, etc.; all later names are listed surname first.

List of Subscribers

P. B. E. Acland
Charles Armitage
Robert Armitage
Mrs. Portia Clifford Bailey
Beverley Barrat (née Clifford)
Ruth Bell
A. A. Bouvy, Esq.
H. J. Bouvy, Esq.
Mrs. John Bradley
Jean Bridger (née Clifford)
Mrs. Elizabeth Buckley-Sharp
Ruth Bunting
Thomas W. Clark
A. E. Clifford
Mr. A. J. Clifford
A. R. E. Clifford, M.A., A.C.A.
Ann Clifford
Anne Clifford
Anne Caroline Clifford
Andrew John Clifford
Barbara I. Clifford
Bruce Clifford
Christopher Beneway Clifford
D. J. H. Clifford, Esq.
David Clifford, R.D.
Mr. David Harrison Clifford
Denis and Eileen Clifford
Eduarda A. Clifford
Edward Lambert Clifford
Mr. Gary D. Clifford
Geoffrey J. Clifford
Graham D. Clifford
Mrs. H. D. Clifford
H. E. J. (Theo) Clifford
H. J. F. Oetgens van Waveren
    Pancras Clifford
Mrs. H. L. Clifford
Mr. Henry Purnell Clifford
Joan Candace Clifford
John A. Clifford
Mr. & Mrs. Joseph F. Clifford
June Dorothy (Betty) Clifford
Mr. Leonard Clifford
Michael C. S. Clifford
Norman P. Clifford
R. H. R. Clifford
R. J. Clifford, M.R.C.V.S.
R. N. Clifford
Richard L. P. T. Clifford
Robert A. Clifford

Robert Laning Clifford
Stanley Cedric Clifford
Mr. & Mrs. Sydney Clifford
Timothy John Clifford
Mrs. Barbara J. Clifford-Keller
The Hon. Mrs. Clifford-Wolff
Lt. Col. W. H. R. Clifford, O.B.E.
William Franklin Clifford
William Henry Morton Clifford,
    C.B., C.B.E.
Major & Mrs. John Court
Grover and Jane Cronin
Sheila Dack
T. R. Darvall
R. G. Douglas
J. B. Douglas-Clifford
J. C. Douglas-Clifford
P. G. Douglas-Clifford
T. J. Douglas-Clifford
V. A. M. Douglas-Clifford
Geneva M. Downes
Shirley Duncan
Joseph Fattorini
Wilfred Fattorini
Richard and Angela Fort
Anthony George and Margot
    Garcia
Helen Blake Taft Gardiner
Brendan Garry
Major-General P. Gleadell
Robert Goldblatt
Elizabeth Mary Jane Goodson
Dermott Griffith
Major Peter Hamilton
Maisie Clifford Hastilow
Dr. W. J. Heely
Major J. A. Hibbert
Admiral of the Fleet Lord Hill-
    Norton, G.C.B.
Geoffrey Hitchcock
Hugo Clifford Holmes
Mrs. Loretta Clifford Holmes
Mrs. Prunella Howard
F. Clifford Johnston
Anne Clifford Kazlouskas
The Honourable Mrs. C. A.
    Kirby
E. R. B. Kirby
Mrs. Portia B. Kirkpatrick

Ann Argyle Lewis-Taylor
Erick Fellowes Lukis
C. A. MacDonald
C. W. MacDonald
I. A. MacDonald
J. R. MacDonald
Muriel McGivern
Mrs. W. W. McGregor
Atalanta Madden (née Clifford)
James Marr
Captain Michael Mellish
Mr. T. Guy de J. Michelmore
Tom Mitchell
Jurat L. A. Moss
The Lord Mowbray & Stourton,
    C.B.E.
Bruce V. Nathan
Anne Norwich
Catherine O'Dwyer
Damien O'Dwyer
Joseph and Joan O'Dwyer
Michael O'Dwyer
Paul O'Dwyer
Major J. L. Parker
Antoinette Parkes
Mrs. Charles G. Parkinson
Dr. H. Stuart Patterson
The Viscount Portman
Mrs. A. C. M. Rowe
Hon. Giles St. Aubyn, L.V.O.
Sarah Clifford Sheehan
Mrs. Cornelia Clifford Smith
Mrs. M. L. Smith
Sir Robert Southey, C.M.G.
Dr. Richard T. Spence
Captain P. H. W. Studholme
Henry Tempest
Mrs. Jean Thompson
Simon Towneley
Hugh Gerald Vavasour
D. C. H. Waddy
M. I. Waddy
J. H. Walbeoffe-Wilson
Ann Walkinton
Rosamund Wallinger
Mrs. Pamela Kay Wrighton (née
    Clifford)
Charles P. T. Wrinch
Philip de Zulueta